AF228452

DISTINCTIVE MARKS
OF SAVING FAITH

Alexander Comrie

DISTINCTIVE MARKS OF SAVING FAITH

Alexander Comrie

Translated by Bartel Elshout
Edited by Joel R. Beeke

Reformation Heritage Books
Grand Rapids, Michigan

Reformation Heritage Books
3070 29th St. SE
Grand Rapids, MI 49512
616-977-0889
orders@heritagebooks.org
www.heritagebooks.org

Scripture taken from the King James Version. In the public domain.

Printed in the United States of America
24 25 26 27 28 29/10 9 8 7 6 5 4 3 2 1

Library of Congress Cataloging-in-Publication Data

Names: Comrie, Alexander, 1706-1774, author. | Elshout, Bartel, 1949- translator. | Beeke, Joel R., 1952- editor.
Title: Distinctive marks of saving faith / Alexander Comrie ; translated by Bartel Elshout ; edited by Joel R. Beeke.
Other titles: Verhandeling van eenige eigenschappen des zaligmakenden geloofs. English
Description: Grand Rapids, Michigan : Reformation Heritage Books, [2024] | Translation of: Verhandeling van eenige eigenschappen des zaligmakenden geloofs. | Includes bibliographical references and indexes.
Identifiers: LCCN 2024005108 (print) | LCCN 2024005109 (ebook) | ISBN 9798886861099 (hardcover) | ISBN 9798886861105 (epub)
Subjects: LCSH: Faith (Christianity)—Early works to 1800. | Fruit of the Spirit—Early works to 1800. | Salvation—Christiantiy—Early works to 1800. | Bible—Criticism, interpretation, etc.—Early works to 1800. | Reformed Church—Doctrines—Early works to 1800.
Classification: LCC BV4637 .C582513 2024 (print) | LCC BV4637 (ebook) | DDC 234/.23—dc23/eng/20240326
LC record available at https://lccn.loc.gov/2024005108
LC ebook record available at https://lccn.loc.gov/2024005109

Contents

Introduction

The scholarly recognition of the intimate link between English Puritanism and the Dutch Further Reformation (*Nadere Reformatie*), two distinguished components of European Reformed piety, continues to expand. The interconnectedness and congruity between the two movements are such that the designation "North Sea Piety" has been coined to highlight their intimate experiential relationship. The recent translation and publication of works by authors representing the Dutch Further Reformation have opened the door for English-speaking scholars to explore the evident kinship between the two. This kinship is such that one can justifiably refer to many of the godly men of the Dutch Further Reformation as Dutch puritans with a small *p* even though both movements have their own distinctive features. Most notable among these recent translations are the major works of Wilhelmus à Brakel (*The Christian's Reasonable Service*) and Theodore VanderGroe (*The Christian's Only Comfort*).[1]

We are delighted, therefore, that we may now present the translated magnum opus of another significant representative of the Dutch Further Reformation, Alexander Comrie. By publishing this work, we continue to redress the imbalance there has been for centuries between Dutch translations of English Puritans and English translations of Dutch puritans. To date, the former still by far outnumber the latter!

As is true for Brakel's *The Christian's Reasonable Service*, Comrie's work serves as a unique bridge between the two flanks of North Sea Piety. That

---

1. Wilhelmus à Brakel, *The Christian's Reasonable Service*, ed. Joel R. Beeke, trans. Bartel Elshout, 4 vols. (Grand Rapids: Reformation Heritage Books, 2011); Theodore VanderGroe, *The Christian's Only Comfort in Life and Death: An Exposition of the Heidelberg Catechism*, ed. Joel R. Beeke, trans. Bartel Elshout, 2 vols. (Grand Rapids: Reformation Heritage Books, 2016).

bridge function is in no small part due to Comrie being a Scot by birth. (For additional biographical details, see Dr. Leen Van Valen's introduction.) Comrie was spiritually nurtured and educated by the famous Scottish Puritans Ebenezer and Ralph Erskine and also sat under the preaching of Thomas Boston. God richly blessed their Christ-saturated and experiential ministry to the heart of the young Comrie.

Thus, when Comrie became an ordained minister of the gospel in the Netherlands, he was a Scottish theologian and pastor engaged within the context of the Dutch Further Reformation. Though Dutch was not his native tongue, this Dutch Scotsman became one of the venerated champions of Dutch Reformed orthodoxy. He was not only a competent theologian and Christ-centered exegete but was also a gifted pastor who knew how to connect the objective truths of the gospel to the subjective experiences and daily lives of his flock. His ministry exemplifies "intelligent piety" that fits the Puritan mold.

With English being his native tongue, Comrie was also instrumental in translating into Dutch many Puritan works. One of his most notable translation efforts was the publication of the Dutch version of Edward Fisher's *The Marrow of the Gospel*. Comrie wholeheartedly embraced the contents of this remarkable and controversial book. Along with Boston, the Erskines, and all the so-called Marrow Men, he endorsed Fisher's presentation and defense of the gospel as well as Boston's copious annotations!

Comrie was unapologetically a "Marrow Man," and this "marrow" theology, therefore, constitutes the warp and woof of this work about the distinctive marks of saving faith. A beautiful and moving illustration of this can be found in chapter 3 of this work. Here Comrie, with pastoral warmth and wisdom, sets before us a dialogue between faith and a struggling soul:

> *The soul…asks*: "How can I come [to Jesus] when I have neither the disposition nor a broken, contrite, and humble heart which must characterize the one who comes?"

> *Faith responds*: "Do you first wish to help yourself and then come to be helped? Do you want to bring some sort of payment with you to the market of free grace? That is not the way! Your tenderness does not render the blood of Jesus more effectual. Whether you are hard or tender, the blood of Jesus is equally effectual. Where else can a diamond be melted except in this blood? You will not mourn until you look and come unto Him whom you have pierced."

The soul replies: "I desire to do so, but I am groping for it as a blind man gropes for the wall."

Faith answers: "Oh, do but open your eyes! The fountain is not so far away and distant that you would have to say, 'Who will ascend into heaven to bring it down, or who will descend into the depths to bring it up?' (Rom. 10:6–7). No, it is near at hand. Behold, it has been opened wide. 'Whosoever will, let him take the water of life freely'" (Rev. 22:17).[2]

Here we are listening to a pastor-theologian who sat at the feet of the Erskine brothers and who, like them, passionately directed sinners to Christ and Him crucified!

You will find this work to be the ripe and mature expression of Comrie's warm, Christ-centered, and experiential ministry. In these fourteen treatises, he gives us a multifaceted scriptural exposition of saving faith and its various exercises—a work in which he consistently exhorts struggling and established believers, by faith, to embrace Christ and all His benefits. His overarching desire was—as he would so often put it—to unite an infinitely rich and precious Christ and a bankrupt sinner. And thus, he writes in his preface, "To bring about the union between Jesus and your immortal soul was so important to us that, while sighing, we have cast forth the net on this and then again on that side."[3] How fitting that the title of the first treatise of this work is "Faith, a Grace That Unites the Soul Most Intimately to Christ"!

May that indeed be your experience as you read these pages. May the Holy Spirit use the work of His servant, Alexander Comrie, to lead sinners to Jesus Christ, the able and willing Savior of sinners, and cause believers to grow in the grace and knowledge of this altogether lovely Christ who is "white and ruddy, the chiefest among ten thousand" (Song 5:10).

—Joel R. Beeke and Bartel Elshout

---

2. See p. 71.
3. See p. 4.

Translator's Preface

As I grew up, I heard my late and greatly beloved father, Arie Elshout, often speak about the works of Brakel, VanderGroe, and Comrie. Increasingly I recognized that these "old writers" were highly esteemed and venerated by the church community to which I belonged. All three of these godly servants of Christ preached an unfettered gospel in which they warmly and fervently offered Christ to the vilest of sinners. But they were also Spirit-taught physicians of souls who knew how to connect experientially with struggling and doubting believers and direct them to the only resting place for their souls, Jesus Christ and Him crucified.

However, my father was especially fond of Comrie. In his sermons, he would often quote from a work greatly loved by God's children, *The ABC of Faith*[1]—a work in which Comrie addresses in alphabetical order the varied descriptions of faith in Scripture. My father's fondness for Comrie dated back to his seminary days when one of his teachers repeatedly urged him to read Comrie. He followed that advice and became an avid reader and student of Comrie, including this magisterial work about the distinctive marks of faith. God used the reading of Comrie's works to teach him the fundamentals of the gospel—especially the free and unconditional offer of Christ in the gospel.

Never could I have imagined as a young man that God would sovereignly direct me to translate the major works of the men whom my father held in such high esteem. And thus, according to God's determinate counsel, I have had the privilege of translating not only Wilhelmus à Brakel's *The Christian's Reasonable Service* and Theodore VanderGroe's *The Christian's Only Comfort* but now also Alexander Comrie's magnum opus.

---

1. Alexander Comrie, *The ABC of Faith*, trans. J. Marcus Banfield (West Yorkshire, UK: Zoar Publications, 1978).

Translating this work proved to be a challenging task for several reasons. As is true for other "old writers," Comrie's sentences are often very long and complex, sometimes covering an entire page. Furthermore, Comrie was not a native Dutch speaker. His Dutch, therefore, is often not very fluent and can even be awkward, making it rather difficult at times to grasp exactly what he is saying. Consequently, as I have done in my other translations, I have made a conscious effort to break up the long and complex sentences into shorter and more readable ones.

However, this task would have been even more difficult had a beloved friend not provided me with an updated version of Comrie's *Distinctive Marks*. In this version, the original work of Comrie has been recast or retranslated into modern-day Dutch. This work is the accomplishment of the highly respected and qualified Dutch linguist C. Bregman.[2] Consulting this updated Dutch version alongside Comrie's original has been immensely helpful in deciphering and analyzing complicated and challenging passages.

In addition to expressing my indebtedness to Bregman's work, I also wish to acknowledge the following individuals for their valuable assistance: Ralph VanZweden, as my faithful and highly competent initial proofreader; Cornelis Vogelaar, for always giving me his reliable counsel when called upon; Gary and Linda den Hollander, who have been my valued and faithful friends for so many years and whose typesetting expertise is second to none; and again, my beloved friend and brother (for more than half a century), Dr. Joel Beeke, as the highly qualified final editor of this translation.

A hearty thanks is also in order to Leen J. van Valen for his able preface on Comrie with a focus on his experiential piety. Furthermore, I wish to express my hearty thanks to the Dutch Further Reformation scholar Frans Huisman from the Netherlands. Mr. Huisman was prepared to help once more when called upon—this time by providing us with a picture of Alexander Comrie and a crisp copy of the original title page and Comrie's signature. He also directed me to pictures of Comrie's church and pulpit.

I am also grateful to Reformation Heritage Books, to Jay Collier for his astute and helpful observations, and to Paul Smalley for assisting with the complex sub-point system that at times went to eleven levels! Finally, I am very grateful to my loyal and supportive wife, Clarice, for her quiet and consistent encouragement throughout the entire translation project.

---

2. Alexander Comrie, *Verhandeling van enige eigenschappen van het zaligmakend geloof*, trans. C. Bregman [retranslated by C. Bregman] (Apeldoorn: De Banier, 2012).

Although all editorial input has contributed significantly to the final quality of this translation, I remain fully responsible for the final wording—and thus for any remaining improprieties and deficiencies in the translation.

Finally, and most importantly, I wish to express my humble gratitude to my gracious God and Father in Christ for having enabled me also to complete this translation task. May He be pleased to use this English rendition—in Comrie's native tongue—to the instruction and edification of many. Above all, may the Spirit of Christ enable us to embrace, by faith, the Christ Comrie so passionately preached, and may we thus experience that faith is indeed a grace that intimately unites us to Christ.

—Bartel Elshout

Alexander Comrie:
Advocate of Experiential Piety

Leen J. van Valen

Lodesteijn expresses it so well: he who has no more than the letter is but a heretic.[1] O my beloved friends, if you seek to inquire whether the morning star of this true knowledge of the way of redemption has ever arisen in your hearts, you will, according to God's Word, know experientially that God Himself has revealed it to you.

—ALEXANDER COMRIE

Biography

Alexander Comrie (1706–1774) was born in Perth, Scotland, on December 17, 1706. He was the son of Patrick Comrie and Rachel Vaus. Rachel was a daughter of John Vaus and Rachel Gray, and Rachel Gray's father was Andrew Gray, the well-known young pastor of Glasgow (1633–1656). Gray was thus Comrie's maternal great-grandfather, and Gray's widow was married again to George Hutcheson. Gray and Hutcheson were authors of pietistic writings, some of which were translated into Dutch. A great-uncle, James Fraser of Brea, who was married to a sister of Gray, was a prominent pastor who, among other things, left as his legacy a pietistic diary. Thus, Comrie was related both spiritually and genealogically to well-known Scottish pastors.

Comrie grew up in a pietistic environment. Though Comrie says very little about his childhood and parental home, he speaks of his religious training in the church of Perth and of the sermons of well-known pastors, the brothers Ebenezer and Ralph Erskine. He heard them preach in his youth, most likely in Perth and the surrounding area. Their warm-hearted and experiential preaching made a deep impression on him.

---

1. The Dutch rhymes: "Die niet heeft als de letter is maar een ketter." Our translation renders this as literally as possible. The thrust of Lodensteijn's adage is that the person who possesses no more than an intellectual knowledge of the truth is a deluded and deceived soul.

About 1727 Comrie left his homeland to settle permanently in the United Provinces of the Netherlands. The reason for his migration is unclear. In any case, after graduating from grammar school in Perth, he did not register at any of the Scottish universities. After he arrived in the Republic, he found employment in the office of a merchant in Rotterdam, probably Adriaan van der Willigen. In 1729 he registered as a student of theology at the University of Groningen. In 1733 he left for Leiden University to continue his studies in theology and philosophy. This university awarded him the degree of Doctor of Philosophy. In October 1734 he defended his dissertation, *De moralitatis fundamento et natura virtutis* (The foundation of morality and the nature of virtue), in which he critically examined the ethical views of the philosopher René Descartes. Willem Jacob's Gravesande functioned as his promoter.

After completing his education and being admitted to the ministry, Comrie accepted a ministerial call from the congregation of Woubrugge, where he was installed on May 1, 1735, by Nicolaas Holtius, the pastor at Koudekerk aan de Rijn. In 1737 he married Johanna de Heyde. He lost his wife a year later after she had given birth to a daughter. Comrie remarried twice. He served the congregation of Woubrugge until his retirement in 1773. He then pastored in Gouda during the short period preceding his death in 1774. When he passed away, he was buried in the Grote of St. Janskerk of this city.[2]

Spiritual Guidance

The foundation for Comrie's spiritual life was laid in Scotland in his youth. In St. John's Church in Perth, he not only heard the preaching of the famous pastors Ebenezer and Ralph Erskine but also received catechetical instruction from them. He later referred to Ralph Erskine as "my faithful old friend whom God has used for my spiritual guidance." Both Ralph and Ebenezer had made a deep impression on him: "As I received my instruction from the two brothers, the great Erskines, the Word of God was implanted in my heart, and there I learned the essentials of the faith."[3]

During his student days in the Netherlands, Comrie came into contact with like-minded godly people who could speak of their spiritual experiences

---

2. Leen J. van Valen, "Comrie, Alexander (1706–1774)," in *Encyclopedie Nadere Reformatie* [Encyclopedia of the Dutch Further Reformation] (Utrecht: De Groot Goudriaan, 2015), 1:183–84a.

3. J. Schipper, *Alexander Comrie, zijn leven en werk* [Alexander Comrie, his life and work] (Apeldoorn: De Banier, 2015), 8–12.

The church in Woubrugge

and God's leading in their lives. He makes mention of his fellow student Ewaldus Hollebeek, who later became a professor in Groningen and then in Leiden. Comrie writes about their encounters in Zeeland and Brouwershaven: "When I would speak to him about the necessity of heart-renewing grace and the experiential ministry of the Holy Spirit, I perceived that he had a tender heart."[4]

In Groningen, Comrie studied theology under Cornelius Van Velzen and Anthonius Driessen, and he had a high regard for both. In his sermons on the Heidelberg Catechism, Comrie reminisced about an encounter that greatly affected him at Professor Driessen's home. He writes, "I witnessed this clearly in a professor under whom I studied. Once, when I visited him, he had

___

4. Alexander Comrie, *Berigt nopens de waarschuwinge van de heer J. J. Schultens, professor en regent van het Staten Collegie te Leiden; tegen de catechismus-verklaringe van den heer Alex. Comrie, gegeven door een brief* [Declaration regarding the warnings of Mr. J. J. Schultens, professor and regent of the State College of Leiden, and his denunciation of the exposition of the catechism, by Mr. Alex. Comrie] (Amsterdam: N. Byl, 1755), 63–64.

such terrible anguish of soul that he already seemed to be in the depths of hell while he was still on earth. He crawled like a worm on the floor, exclaiming, 'O God! If there is still a way of escape, make it known to me!'"[5] Driessen had struggled with depression during his entire lifetime. By using this anecdote, Comrie wished to illustrate that one's intellectual knowledge will be of no avail when a person is in spiritual distress.

Van Velzen was also an experiential theologian and lectured in practical theology. He was particularly interested in Scottish and English devotional writings and wrote a preface to the Dutch edition of *The Fourfold State* by Thomas Boston, published in 1742.[6]

The Spiritual Shepherd of Woubrugge

Following his ordination as the pastor of Woubrugge in 1735, Comrie became acquainted with children of God who testified of a living hope in Christ and His righteousness. In the polder land of Rijnland, where the village was located, godly people would convene in conventicles to speak about the experiential life of faith. Among them were those who had experienced a spiritual breakthrough under the ministry of Comrie's predecessor, Rev. Carolus Blom (1671–1734).[7]

Reverend Blom had been the pastor of Woubrugge from 1702 to 1734. Comrie commented later that for years there had been nothing more in this village than an outward form of religion. Comrie remarks, "People were outwardly civil and religious and believed that Christ was their Savior with a historical faith. The sorrows of death had never compassed them. They remained unmoved by the essential truths of religion and had no concern for the salvation of their immortal souls. They lived a life of carnal tranquility as if there were neither hell nor a final judgment."[8]

Tradition has it that a young farmer and subsequent elder Claes Janszoon Poldervaart was the means in God's hand to bring about a change in Woubrugge for the better. As a peat farmer from Benthuizen, he and other

---

5. A. G. Honig, *Alexander Comrie* (diss., Utrecht: H. Honig, 1892; repr., Leiden: J. J. Groen en Zoon, 1991), 40.

6. Schipper, *Alexander Comrie*, 21–27.

7. Schipper, *Alexander Comrie*, 34–37.

8. Alexander Comrie, *Samuel in zyn leven zeer gelieft, in zyn doodt betreurt en hooggeëert ofte lykreden over 1 Sam. XXV. vs. 1* [Samuel greatly beloved during his life and mourned over and highly honored in his death, or a funeral sermon about 1 Sam. 25:1] (Leiden: J. Hasebroek; Amsterdam: N. Bijl, 1749), 25.

men were compelled to come to Woubrugge in 1706 to continue to ply their temporal trade. Comrie describes him as "a man of utmost simplicity, and yet most edifying, godly, and loving in his walk."[9] Poldervaart was a leader among the religious conventicles. He used all available means to awaken people from their spiritual slumber of death, urging young and old to renounce their fictitious confidence. He never failed to bring the souls surrounding him before the throne of grace in his prayers. He did this for eight years, but it was without effect.

Comrie said about this, "Yes, after eight consecutive years—that is, until the year 1714—and after much prayer and being burdened about the blindness of the people, he finally decided to invite some of the people to his home to read some excerpts from Brakel and VanderKemp. He deemed himself incapable of speaking about these truths extemporaneously."[10] Comrie is here referring to *The Christian's Reasonable Service* of Wilhelmus à Brakel and Johannes VanderKemp's exposition of the Heidelberg Catechism that had just been published.

It was not long before the first stirrings of the Lord's saving work became evident. "God did not permit the labor of this 'father' to be unfruitful…. Around the year 1716, some people were truly stricken and convicted of their sin, after which they came to Christ."[11] The news of this blessing, according to Comrie, spread throughout the entire country. "Thus, spiritually seasoned men from all parts of the country came to hammer on the same anvil and, like Aquila and Priscilla, expound to them 'the way of God more perfectly'" (Acts 18:26).[12]

Reverend Blom initially did not know how to deal with this revival in his congregation. He even suspected that "some seeds of heresy were sown,"[13] which caused him to oppose this revival. "However," Comrie wrote, "at the height of his zeal in opposing it, God, by His Holy Spirit, touched his heart."[14] Reverend Blom experienced a spiritual crisis in 1716 and came to saving faith himself. He spoke of this in the pulpit when he preached about the Philippian jailer, doing so, according to Comrie, "to the astonishment of many of

---

9. Comrie, *Samuel in zyn leven zeer gelieft*, 25–26.
10. Comrie, *Samuel in zyn leven zeer gelieft*, 26.
11. Comrie, *Samuel in zyn leven zeer gelieft*, 26.
12. Comrie, *Samuel in zyn leven zeer gelieft*, 26.
13. Comrie, *Samuel in zyn leven zeer gelieft*, 26.
14. Comrie, *Samuel in zyn leven zeer gelieft*, 26.

[them], and many still speak about it with the greatest delight."[15] Reverend Blom's preaching soon changed, which resulted in many conversions. Both Reverend Blom and Elder Poldervaart became spiritual counselors for souls who had been awakened and were crying out for mercy. The work of the Lord was so noteworthy and remarkable that many came every Lord's Day from different localities in the region to witness this outpouring of spiritual blessing. Comrie even mentions that two hundred families were blessed, but he probably meant that two hundred persons had been converted.[16]

The news of the revival of Woubrugge also reached Scotland. For example, an assistant of the historian Robert Wodrow attests that the blessing upon Rev. Blom's ministry was such that the revival that occurred encompassed almost the entire village. Occasional revivals also occurred in other localities in the republic, especially in the northern part of the nation. These were forerunners of the great revival that commenced in 1749 in Nijkerk and elsewhere.[17]

Thus, a time of abundant spiritual harvest had arrived for Woubrugge and the surrounding region. Later Comrie spoke of his predecessor's ministry with great respect: "Since old times, the Lord has established a congregation here and sent you many eminent men. As you know, during that time, the work of powerful conversions broke forth remarkably among you through the ministerial labors of your deceased and beloved pastor, the honorable, learned, and now blessed Rev. Carolus Blom, my esteemed predecessor in the work of the Lord among you."[18] And what characterized this spiritual revival? Comrie describes it as follows: "The Lord's work in our village was such that for all who were truly converted and sealed by the Spirit, Christ was the continual and common focal point of their spiritual lives, and thus, they cast aside everything except the Surety Himself."[19] Such was the encouraging foundation upon which Comrie was permitted to assume the role of his predecessor as the shepherd of this village.

---

15. Comrie, *Samuel in zyn leven zeer gelieft*, 26.

16. Schipper, *Comrie*, 37–41; Comrie, *Samuel in zyn leven zeer gelieft*, 25–27.

17. F. A. van Lieburg, "De Libanon blijft ruisen: Opwekkingen in Nederland in de gereformeerde traditie" [Lebanon continues to shake: Revivals in the Netherlands in the Reformed tradition], in *Een golf van beroering: De omstreden religieuze opwekking in Nederland in het midden van de achttiende eeuw* [A wave of emotion: The controversial religious revival in the Netherlands in the midst of the eighteenth century], ed. J. Spaans (Hilversum: Verloren, 2001), 27.

18. Schipper, *Comrie*, 37, 39.

19. Schipper, *Comrie*, 41.

An Example of Experiential Piety

Besides Poldervaart, Cornelis van Schellingerhout (his cousin by marriage) and Arnoldus de Sterke also greatly supported Comrie. Van Schellingerhout was the master craftsman and bailiff of Esselickerwoude and 's Heer Jacobswoude, the jurisdiction to which Woubrugge belonged. He lived in the estate "Huis ter Aar" in Woubrugge. His brother Pieter was the sheriff and clerk of Oudshoorn, a village near Alphen aan de Rijn, near Woubrugge.

Comrie had probably become acquainted with this family as an employee of the merchant Van der Willigen. Because of the excellent spirit that dwelt in these men (Dan. 6:3), bonds of friendship and spiritual ties were established, promoting unity in the entire congregation.

Cornelis van Schellingerhout had been converted during the revival under Rev. Blom. Comrie spoke of this at the funeral of the deceased bailiff, delivered on July 27, 1749: "At last, in the year 1717 or 1718, it pleased God to reveal to him with such light and clarity the matters of which he had often heard with his ears and had seen with his eyes, that he realized that he was utterly lost in himself. This happened one afternoon when he was resting from his work. In this quiet solitude, he experienced that he was lost in himself and that his exemplary conduct and historical faith could not save him. He often said that he perceived this as in a moment and with intense conviction. He realized that he was still without God and Christ."[20]

His conviction of his lost state was not accompanied by fear and terror as others would experience. However, a spiritual breakthrough soon followed: "Now the person of Christ was revealed to him, not only as to His necessity and suitability but also as to His complete willingness to save not only others but also him. I and others with me have heard him say how heartily and how willingly he then surrendered himself to Christ! Moreover, not only had he surrendered himself unconditionally, but in so doing, he perceived that his soul had become one with Christ and that he was most intimately united to Him. Thus, a peace and serenity entered his heart, and he was privileged to experience this most wonderfully. Though he later learned that it is not easy to exercise faith, when God had so revealed Himself to him, his own perception was that it was so easy to believe. To believe is to say, 'Amen,' and to receive the gift that God Himself gives."[21] Almost simultaneously with Cornelis, his "brothers and sisters were also wrought upon effectually by the

---

20. Comrie, *Samuel in zyn leven zeer gelieft*, 27.
21. Comrie, *Samuel in zyn leven zeer gelieft*, 27.

Spirit of God, without the one knowing it of the other or having the courage to speak to each other about it."[22]

Van Schellingerhout was a Christian who was assured "that the triune God was his and that God loved him. He did not know of the many doubts that many struggle with. He usually experienced much peace in his heart when he thought of God. He often said, 'Christ is mine, all is mine, and oh, what a rich Father I have! And therefore, everything is mine.' How content he was with his spiritual state, even in trying circumstances! He would customarily say, 'I have nothing but the Lord, and His glory is my salvation.' There is a text in which he greatly delighted because God had enabled him to be thus disposed: 'Therefore we are always confident, knowing that, whilst we are at home in the body, we are absent from the Lord: (for we walk by faith, not by sight)' (2 Cor. 5:6–7)."[23]

Comrie writes of van Schellingerhout's life of sanctification in striking language:

> What an intense desire he had for evangelical holiness! He knew that when one's worship and obedience are merely a matter of routine and are performed in one's own strength and carnally—and thus, apart from a believing in and relying upon Jesus—it cannot please God. He knew experientially that his transgressions caused a separation between God and his soul. They greatly burdened his conscience, being dead works that rendered him incapable of serving the living God suitably. They would be as a thorn in his flesh that prevented him from daily going boldly to the throne of grace to "obtain mercy, and find grace to help in time of need" (Heb. 4:16). And therefore, though he knew that "once a child of God, always a child of God, and once justified, always justified" (without that state ever being altered), he continually came before the throne of grace to confess his daily transgressions and to make use of Jesus Christ unto justification. To a greater or lesser degree, he had to truly feel that his conscience was being cleansed again of dead works and that God caused him to experience in his soul a renewed sense of his acquittal by speaking peace to his soul. And therefore, how determined he was to "follow holiness" (Heb. 12:14), and to that end, he made use of Christ by faith, leaned upon Him, and let the Holy Spirit work in him.[24]

---

22. Comrie, *Samuel in zyn leven zeer gelieft*, 27.

23. Comrie, *Samuel in zyn leven zeer gelieft*, 29.

24. Comrie, *Samuel in zyn leven zeer gelieft*, 27–31.

Preacher of Law and Gospel

Comrie preached in accordance with the order of salvation as articulated in the Heidelberg Catechism—including what must be known of our sin and misery, deliverance in Christ, and gratitude to God.

He preached the necessity of knowing one's misery before embracing Christ by faith. However, he did not preach this as a condition. He insisted that salvation is offered to all hearers. All are invited to flee to Christ. Thus, he observes, "Although the elect are saved, the offer of grace is made to all who hear the gospel. We wish that this offer would be proclaimed in every sermon. Sermons would then be more efficacious for poor and convicted souls! What a pity it is that this is done only intermittently, in a restricted way, and with the addition of duties and conditions! Some ministers make it so complicated that, instead of poor sinners coming as they are in response to the call of the gospel, they must remain where they are until they have certain stipulated experiences. Oh, how often the waters of the sanctuary are troubled! How few there are who exalt the gospel highway and proclaim to a poor and wretched people, 'Take of the waters of life freely.'"[25]

Inside the church at Woubrugge

25. Quoted in T. van Es, *Nieuw licht: De strijd om en de prediking van het aanbod van genade in de periode 1750–1800* [New light: The battle for and the preaching of the offer of grace during the period 1750–1800] (Kampen: De Groot Goudriaan, 2005), 155–56.

In Comrie's *ABC of Faith*, we read, "It is Jesus who makes this offer: Today Christ comes among us in the gospel as if entering a prison, and He carries with Him an all-encompassing pardon for the greatest of rebels. He says, 'Men and women, old and young, bond and free, rich and poor, however great your guilt may be, here is a pardon. Are you willing to receive it? I sincerely and wholeheartedly offer it to you. You need not do anything but receive it.' Oh, son of man! Now the prison door is opened. Woe to him that will not accept this pardon."[26]

Comrie earnestly urged his hearers to flee to Christ, the true City of Refuge:

> I must tell you: Shall such a man say, "I do not understand this way"? Instead, I will tell you what I shall do! I will go to Jesus and exclaim, "O divine Savior, I see that I am unable to pay. But I come to Thee; I have no money to pay. Wouldst Thou be pleased to lend me something? I will endeavor to turn one talent into two talents by an earnest and diligent use of them. I will do as much as I can to pay by making good use of the strength Thou art granting me—of the money Thou art lending me. That will enable me, such a poor creature as I am, to make an honest payment toward my incurred debt and not to fall into ruin again." Such is a cunning construct of Pelagianism! Did you ever understand this? Moreover, as attractive as it may seem, you must understand that this will not contribute one iota toward your acquittal, nor will it culminate in your gracious acceptance.[27]

Comrie goes on to say:

> My beloved, we may stoop so low and cast ourselves at the feet of the Surety that with spontaneous sincerity we will exclaim, "O Divine Surety, I have nothing to pay, not even a farthing. Oh, for God's sake and out of free grace, give me funds to pay—funds that will be and remain Thine—and I will say and acknowledge that I received it from Thee in my desperate plight. I desire nothing more than to pay with the funds Thou art providing. Though these are Thy funds, if only I may but present them. And if the acceptance of Thy funds may be counted as my deed, I shall be content."[28]

He does not gloss over what awaits the unconverted if they ignore the gospel. In his exposition of the Heidelberg Catechism, he exclaims,

---

26. Quoted in van Es, *Nieuw licht*, 157.
27. Quoted in van Es, *Nieuw licht*, 178–79.
28. Quoted in van Es, *Nieuw licht*, 179.

The doctrine of eternal punishment has been set before us. However, to what extent do you believe it? And what effect does it have on our hearts and minds to stir us up to flee God's wrath and the fierceness of His divine anger? In what measure are we stirred inwardly by the doctrine of eternal punishment? Though the joints of Belshazzar were loosed, many of you remain as hard and insensible as the tombstones that cover the graves. Oh, how stunning this is! All other things may inwardly stir you, but you will hear the doctrine of eternal punishment expounded as if it did not pertain to you—as if you had nothing to fear from it, though the fearfulness and certainty thereof be irrefutably set before you. Even if there may be a few who have some concern, it will merely be like a morning cloud and an early dew![29]

Comrie then concludes:

O my friends, consider seriously the magnitude of the punishment you will be subjected to after this life in both soul and body. You will forever be deprived of beholding God's countenance, and you will forever be banished from His fellowship. Presently, not beholding God's countenance is a matter of joy to you since you find all your delight only in sin, but then the absence of God's favor will be a foremost aspect of your damnation. You will then feel and acknowledge that absence, and your weeping and wailing will never admit you into God's fellowship and favor. Now there is still hope for you. However, once God's woe has been pronounced upon you—"Depart from me, ye cursed" (Matt. 25:41)—it will forever be impossible.[30]

His Writings

Comrie, a prolific author of pietistic writings, also wrote several polemical works—some with his friend and colleague Nicolaas Holtius.[31] He also translated English and Scottish Puritan works.

His first publication—a translation of an English booklet about a converted Jew—is not referenced in the primary scholarly assessments of Comrie. The Dutch title is *Een verstandige, en zeer christelijke belydenis van meester Salomo, een Jood in de vergaderinge van meester Humphry te London*

---

29. Alexander Comrie, *Stellige en praktikale verklaaringe van de Heidelbergschen Catechismus volgens de leere en gronden dere Reformatie* [...] [Doctrinal and practical exposition of the Heidelberg Catechism, according to the doctrine and foundational principles of the Reformation] (Leiden: J. Hasebroek; Amsterdam: N.Byl, 1753), 243–44.

30. Comrie, *Catechismus*, 244–45.

31. Van Valen, *Encyclopedie Nadere Reformatie*, 1:184a–86a.

gedaan (A sound and very Christian confession of master Solomon, a Jew, made at the assembly of master Humphry in London) (1731).

His second work was *Het ABC. des geloofs, of verhandeling van de bena-amingen des saligmaakenden geloofs* (The ABC of faith, or A treatise of the descriptions of saving faith) (1739), which expounds biblical descriptions of true faith in alphabetical order. It is very pastoral in tone and focuses not only on the exercises of faith but also on the object of faith—God in Christ. Knowing Him is of crucial importance in this work. The soul is passive in her experience of the foundational truths of the Holy Scriptures. However, there is also an active aspect in addition to this passive aspect. This includes the exercises of faith that focus on Christ Himself as well as on His promises and offer of grace. The description of the spiritual exercises of the heart is an invitation to experience them.

Comrie's third book was *Verhandeling van eenige eigenschappen des zaligmakenden geloofs* (*Distinctive Marks of Saving Faith*) (1744). The author discusses in detail how the Holy Spirit works faith in the soul and what its fruits are. Comrie also addresses temporary faith. The little ones in the faith are pastorally encouraged to seek after the assurance and strengthening of their faith.

In the two-volume work *Verzameling van leerredenen, waarin vertoont wordt uit verscheide teksten de afgezakte kranke en kwynende staat der geloov-igen* (Collection of sermons in which the declining, ailing, and languishing condition of believers is addressed in various texts) (1749–1750), Comrie places more emphasis on the negative spiritual frames of the faithful, such as spiritual barrenness, lack of divine comfort, and a sense of misery. He coun-ters this by pastorally setting forth the way to healing.

During the year when the first volume of *Verzameling van leerredenen* was published, Comrie also published *Samuel in zyn leven zeer gelieft, in zyn doodt betreurt en hoog-geëert ofte lyk-reden over 1 Sam. XXV. vs. 1* (Samuel greatly beloved during his life and mourned over and highly honored in his death—or a funeral sermon about 1 Sam. 25:1) (1749). In this sermon, deliv-ered at the funeral of Cornelis van Schellingerhout, some events of Comrie's own life are also discussed. His description of his own spiritual life is brief and to the point.

Comrie's personal theological emphases are especially apparent in his *Stellige en praktikale verklaaringe van den Heidelbergschen Catechismus, vol-gens de leere en gronden der Reformatie* (Doctrinal and practical exposition of the Heidelberg Catechism in conformity to the doctrine and fundamentals of the Reformation) (1753). These catechism sermons deal only with the first seven Lord's Days.

During a period of six years, ten volumes of a theological and polemical work were published anonymously. Comrie and his friend Nicolaas Holtius were the authors of this work, titled *Examen van het ontwerp van tolerantie, om de leere in de Dordrechtse Synode anno 1619: Vastgesteld met de veroordeelde leere der remonstranten te verenigen* (Examination of the proposed tolerance regarding the doctrine of the Synod of Dordt in the year 1619: Proposed to harmonize this with the condemned doctrine of the Remonstrants) (1753–1759). The theological accents of the above-mentioned devotional literature are also evident in this series, which aimed at combatting the emerging Enlightenment thinking. The authors wished to call attention to a growing departure from the confessions in favor of Arminianism. They wished to defend the doctrine of the Synod of Dordt held in 1618–1619, and they sharply condemned the spirit of tolerance they detected in Enlightenment theologians.

To defend his view regarding the doctrine of justification against the criticisms of some opponents, Comrie wrote two works: *Missive, wegens de regtvaardigmakinge des zondaars* (Formal declaration regarding the justification of the sinner) (1757) and *Brief over de rechtvaerdigmakinge des zondaars, door de onmiddelyke toereekening der borggerechtigheit van Christus* (Letter about the justification of the sinner by the immediate imputation of the mediatorial righteousness of Christ) (1761).

Comrie also stimulated an increased interest in Scottish Pietist writers. He did so by translating Thomas Boston, *Eene beschouwing van het verbondt der genade* (A consideration of the covenant of grace) (1741). This translation includes Comrie's introduction regarding the covenant of works. He also wrote a preface for *Sakelyke en prackticale verklaringe van de twaalf kleine propheten* (A doctrinal and practical exposition of the twelve minor prophets) (1748) by the Scottish author George Hutcheson.

But the Dutch Scot was also interested in English Puritan writings. He facilitated several translations: Walter Marshall, *The Mystery of Evangelical Sanctification* (1739); Thomas Shepard, *The Parable of the Ten Virgins Expounded and Applied* (1743); and Isaac Chauncy, *The Doctrine of Truth Which Is after Godliness* (1757). The last work is an exposition in question-and-answer format of the Westminster Shorter Catechism.

Comrie also translated the English Puritan work that had given rise, in his father's day, to the so-called Scottish "Marrow Controversy," entitled *Mergh des euangeliums, ofte kort sommier van de leere van Godts verbonden* (Marrow of the gospel, or a brief summary of the doctrine of God's covenants) (1757). Although the extensive preface of this work is sometimes attributed to Comrie, it was, in reality, extracted from a work by the Scottish theologian James Hog, who prepared the Scottish edition of this book for printing.

Comrie also wrote a preface for Stephen Charnock's work *Godt verzoend, de wet in haren tweederleyen eisch verheerlykt en van haren vloek ontwapent* (God reconciled, the law magnified as to its twofold demand and disarmed from its curse) (1757) and for John Owen, *De inwonende zonde in de gelovigen* (Indwelling sin in the believer) (1760).

Theological Emphases

Comrie was a Reformed pietist.[32] He is best known for three devotional works: *The ABC of Faith*, *Distinctive Marks of Saving Faith*, and *A Collection of Sermons*.

A characteristic feature of these works is his focus on the varied spiritual frames of the heart. He addresses, therefore, various marks by which true faith can be identified. The inner experience resulting from the application of salvation comes more to the foreground in these books than does his exposition of the salvation merited by Christ. His books fit into the tradition of the eighteenth-century piety of the Dutch Further Reformation, which, in contrast to that of the century before, gave greater attention to a detailed description of inner experience.

Comrie wanted to maintain the balance between faith and experience in these writings. On the one hand, he focuses on the necessity of experience in contrast to a rationalistic view of faith. On the other hand, he sees the danger of paying too much attention to felt experiences at the expense of faith as the act whereby the soul embraces Christ. This act of faith consists not only in knowledge and assent but also in a trust that engages the entire soul.

Faith is the central pietistic theme in Comrie's works. Fundamental to his view is that faith unites the soul experientially with Christ. The genuineness of faith manifests itself in various fruits. He delineates these fruits explicitly in this work, *Distinctive Marks of Saving Faith*. Thus, faith is a

---

32. Van Valen, *Encyclopedie Nadere Reformatie*, 1:186a–89b.

grace that purifies the soul, glorifies Christ, makes a believer patient through affliction, overcomes the world, and exercises itself to attain to the sealing of the Spirit and to experience daily justification. He describes in detail the experiences that constitute the life of faith, emphasizing that the operation of the Holy Spirit is essential in all exercises of faith. The soul participates in this receptively, and when the soul is moved to exercise her faith, the sovereignty and one-sidedness of God's work of grace continue to be preeminent. Comrie is intensely fearful of self-manufactured faith and emotions not generated by faith.

The core component of Comrie's doctrine of faith, set forth in his exposition of the Heidelberg Catechism, is the distinction between the *habitus*, or propensity, of faith and the *actus*, or exercise, of faith. This distinction originated with the Greek philosopher Aristotle and was utilized within the Reformed scholasticism that flourished in the seventeenth century. The *habitus* is the propensity of faith implanted at regeneration, or the new birth. The *actus* consists of the acts, or exercises, of faith that issue forth from the *habitus*. The *habitus* is not preceded by preparation in the sense that it contributes to the Holy Spirit's implantation of one's ability to believe.

Justification is closely connected to both the *habitus* and the *actus* of faith. Although the justification of the sinner becomes a reality by the act of faith, it is anchored in the divine decree, so that one can also speak of God's purpose to justify from eternity. As such, Comrie speaks of a decree to justify *prior to* faith without denying that justification actually occurs in time *by* faith. Justifying faith becomes an assured faith by its subsequent exercises, the experiential climax being that one is justified in the court of conscience.

Comrie delineated conversion as a systematic and progressive process in which there are degrees regarding the experience of faith and justification. The distinctions used by Comrie between *habitus* and *actus* and active and passive justification serve to ground the order of salvation and its experiential application in Scripture. Hereby he wishes to erect a barrier against a superficial and rational faith and the cooperative grace of Arminianism. By these distinctions, he also wishes to accommodate believers who lack an assured consciousness of their justification.

Comrie made an important contribution to the systematization of Dutch pietistic thought. Despite his intention to hark back to the Reformation regarding the order of salvation, he did not avoid a certain rationalization of the doctrines of faith and their affiliated experience. This does not detract, however, from Comrie's intention to protect and promote a Reformed orthodoxy that harmonizes with the confessions as an expression of what the Bible confesses.

Subsequently, Comrie must be credited with a fresh assessment of the biblical experience of believers. He emphasized that faith always arises "out of the depths" and is marked by humility. Presumptive believers focus on a faith they manufacture in their own strength. Since believers are also vulnerable to doing so, Comrie distinguished between legalistic efforts believers make in their own strength and "the faith of the operation of God" (Col. 2:12). Although Comrie pointed out that the marks of grace cannot be the ground of salvation, he nevertheless addressed them in great detail. In this way, he wished to give weak believers marks of identification and to set before those who possess temporary faith what they are lacking.

In the tolerance espoused by the Enlightenment, Comrie detected a favorable view of man in which man's radical depravity and impotence were either absent or relegated to the background. The nominally religious are thereby urged to exercise faith without having been convinced of their utter inability to believe. This fits the mindset of the Enlightenment, which elevated man's reason.

How did Comrie fit within his historical context? His theological emphases were a reaction to the prevailing theological climate. He perceived much confusion, even among believers. He detected a superficiality in those who, in his opinion, arrived at the assurance of faith too easily. Nevertheless, in his pastoral letters, such as the one addressed to his much younger colleague Jean Louis Verster, he is mild and shows compassion, even for the little ones in grace.

Comrie is considered by some to be one of the most important representatives of the Dutch Further Reformation. However, that perception needs to be corrected. Comrie was more concerned about doctrinal purity than the ongoing reformation of the church and the nation. The importance of reformation initiatives, as emphasized by men such as Voetius and van Lodenstein, was not articulated by him. He was also not critical of the influence of the government, for example, in the work of calling ministers. In this respect, he was of a different mindset than his Scottish kindred spirits—such as the two Erskines who left the established church in 1733 because of patronage rights.

Comrie's Influence

Comrie's devotional writings are still influential in Reformed experiential circles in the Netherlands.[33] Reprints, as well as translations of these books into current Dutch, continue to be in demand even in the twenty-first century. The number of reprintings of his most famous works are as follows: *The ABC of Faith*, twenty-eight reprints; *Distinctive Marks of Saving Faith*, eighteen reprints; *Collection of Sermons*, sixteen reprints; *Doctrinal and Practical Exposition of the Heidelberg Catechism*, ten reprints.

The various stages of the life of faith and the experiential exercises that Comrie describes in detail are also presently endorsed by those who consider those stages as the legitimate expression of the applying work of God's Spirit. Comrie's emphasis on the passive aspect of spiritual life, such as the so-called court-of-conscience experience, influenced the piety of the Dutch conventicle community in the nineteenth and twentieth centuries.

Comrie also influenced some Dutch neo-Calvinists. The founder of the Reformed Churches (Gereformeerde Kerken), Abraham Kuyper (1837–1920), in his *Het werk van den Heiligen Geest* (*The Work of the Holy Spirit*) (1888), expresses that he prefers Comrie's view on faith and justification over that of Wilhelmus à Brakel in his *Redelyke godts-dienst* (*The Christian's Reasonable Service*) (1700). The Reformed systematic theologian Herman Bavinck (1854–1921) also opted for Comrie's view regarding the order of salvation. It is not so much Comrie's description of spiritual experiences that prevails among the neo-Calvinists but rather his view of predestination and the eternal decree regarding the justification of the elect.

Comrie's theology of the new birth, faith, and justification, especially inspired Rev. G. H. Kersten (1882–1948), the leader of the Reformed Congregations [Gereformeerde Gemeenten] in the Netherlands and North America. In his *De gereformeerde dogmatiek* (*Reformed Dogmatics*) (1950) and various prefaces to Comrie's works, Kersten expressed his great appreciation for Comrie's theology and description of spiritual life.

A Spiritual Counselor

Comrie was not only a prominent theologian but also a spiritual physician. For example, as a mature father in Christ, he gives helpful advice to a young pastor who is still somewhat unsteady spiritually. Two letters to Rev. J. L. Verster, pastor in Dordrecht, testify of Comrie's skill as a spiritual counselor.

---

33. Van Valen, *Encyclopedie Nadere Reformatie*, 1:189b–90b.

They were written in 1773–1774, shortly before he passed away. Here are some fragments:

> My dearly beloved brother in the ministry,…God, who looked upon you when you did not seek Him, permitted you to struggle so that you would die to yourself. Now He has begun to acquaint you with Jesus as a complete Savior. God has begun to teach you that, in yourself, there is no ground on which to rest, but that all is to be found in Him, and that you may confidently respond to the free offer of Christ in the gospel. This is a wonderful change. When we initially begin to learn this, we marvel at the blinding darkness and unbelief in which we found ourselves before, and we worship God for this blessed and God-glorifying transformation.…
>
> I was greatly refreshed that your letter informed me how God has led you since our recent and unforgettable encounter. Though I have but little light regarding spiritual matters, I perceived when I first spoke to you that God had graciously laid His hand upon you. For holy reasons, He was pleased to let you toil and labor in your own strength and cherish your own notions regarding how you thought you would come to spiritual liberty. And your circle of acquaintances shared your point of view.
>
> As all this conspired with your legalistic heart, you deemed such notions entirely beneficial, God glorifying, and indispensable to salvation. Yes, you thought these things were essential to make you fit for free grace and adorn you as a bride for Christ. Moved by an intense love for you, I then thought: "…It grieves and troubles me that such a sweet young child cannot suck at the breasts of pure gospel comfort." Then I thought, "…Let him experience that righteousness is not imputed to those who work but rather to those who believe. In other words, righteousness will be imputed to those who passively receive this gift and who, upon having received it, will truly rest in it."[34]

A Serious Parting Word

On several occasions, the old pastor of Woubrugge made himself free from the blood of his congregation (cf. Ezek. 33:2–9; Acts 20:26). He knew that her blood would be required of him if he did not treat souls seriously and uprightly. The following excerpts from a sermon show this clearly:

---

34. This portion, and particularly the quotations from Comrie's letters to Verster, are extracted from Gerrit H. Leurdijk, ed., *Twee pastorale brieven van Alexander Comrie* [Two pastoral letters from Alexander Comrie] (Veenendaal: uitgeverij Kool, 1985).

You know how much I have sought to promote the work of the Lord among you! Although I know my own multiple flaws, I nevertheless may know that I have the witness of a good conscience. Thus, according to my very limited talent, I have never endeavored to teach you anything other than the pure and unadulterated doctrine of the Reformed church, laying no other foundation than that which was already laid by the prophets and apostles, even Jesus Christ. He is the foundation laid in Zion, and he who builds upon Him shall never be ashamed....

Not only have we striven to maintain purity of doctrine, but above all, we have been engaged for the eternal benefit of your immortal souls. We have desired that it would please God to deliver this one and that one from the power of darkness and translate you into the kingdom of the Son of His love and to build up others in their most holy faith. To this end, we have often sought to awaken the unconverted among you from their slumber. We have confronted them with their peril and the certainty of eternal damnation as long as they do not seek to flee the wrath to come in the way of repentance.

As soon as we sensed any brokenness of heart, we have always endeavored in our sermons to engage such souls and resolve their difficulties, urging them to surrender to Jesus and bid sin and the world farewell....

We have never lost either courage or desire to unite Jesus and your immortal souls. This was so important to us that, with groaning, we have cast the net on one side and then on the other side, waiting for the time of love to arrive—that hour decreed from eternity. We have sought to maintain the simplicity of the gospel. Thus, we have never wearied the church with vain wisdom, nor have we troubled her with needless controversies, for both will yield little edification.[35]

Conclusion

Comrie was one of the more influential theologians of the Dutch Further Reformation who continues to be venerated by the Reformed-experiential segment of the heirs of the Reformation in the Netherlands. His contribution during the waning stage of the Dutch Further Reformation was forged by a complexity of circumstances that molded Comrie to be the unique pastor-theologian he was. Though he became increasingly and progressively focused on safeguarding the radical sovereignty of God's grace in both the

---

35. These quotations can be found in Comrie's preface to this work. In the Dutch edition, *Verhandeling van eenige eigenschappen des zaligmakenden geloofs* (Utrecht: De Banier, n.d), xv–xvi.

gift and exercise of saving faith, he never betrayed his rich Scottish heritage and the "Marrow" theology embedded in his soul by the Erskine brothers.

Thus, as discriminating and searching as Comrie's preaching could be, he never wavered in offering Christ unconditionally, proclaiming that this free offer is the sinner's warranty to embrace Christ by faith. Let me affirm this by concluding with a passage that highlights Comrie's experiential emphasis and his commitment to the functioning of the offer of grace in the exercise of faith: "The soul, though burning with love toward the Surety as she beholds His loveliness and necessity, is frequently and with much fear concerned whether she, being so unworthy in herself, would dare to take the liberty to appropriate Him. The offer of grace will then bear powerfully upon her heart. She will thereby perceive that the invitation is addressed to her and that God commands that she, as wretched as she is, not only may but also must believe in the Surety."[36]

---

36. See p. 17.

Bibliography

Comrie, Alexander. *Berigt nopens de waarschuwinge van de heer J. J. Schultens, professor en regent van het Staten Collegie te Leiden; tegen de catechismus-verklaringe van den heer Alex. Comrie, gegeven door een brief* [Declaration regarding the warnings of Mr. J. J. Schultens, professor and regent of the State College of Leiden, and his denunciation of the exposition of the catechism, by Mr. Alex. Comrie]. Amsterdam: N. Byl, 1755.

————. *Samuel in zyn leven zeer gelieft, in zyn doodt betreurt en hoog-geëert ofte lykreden over 1 Sam. XXV. Vs. 1* [Samuel greatly beloved during his life and mourned over and highly honored in his death, or a funeral sermon about 1 Sam. 25:1]. Leiden: J. Hasebroek; Amsterdam: N. Bijl, 1749.

————. *Stellige en praktikale verklaaringe van de Heidelbergschen Catechismus volgens de leere en gronden dere Reformatie* [...][Doctrinal and practical exposition of the Heidelberg Catechism, according to the doctrine and foundational principles of the Reformation]. Vol. 1. Leiden: J. Hasebroek; Amsterdam: N.Byl, 1753.

————. *Verhandeling van eenige eigenschappen des zaligmakenden geloofs* [*Distinctive Marks of Saving Faith*]. Utrecht: De Banier, n.d.

Honig, A. G. *Alexander Comrie.* Diss., Utrecht: H. Honig, 1892; Reprint, Leiden: J. J. Groen en Zoon, 1991.

Hooghwerff, B. *Geloofsgetuigenis van Salomo de Jood* [The testimony of faith of Solomon the Jew]. Houten: Den Hertog, 2016.

Leurdijk, Gerrit H., ed. *Twee pastorale brieven van Alexander Comrie* [Two pastoral letters of Alexander Comrie]. Veenendaal: uitgeverij Kool, 1985.

Schipper, J. *Alexander Comrie, zijn leven en werk* [Alexander Comrie, his life and work]. Apeldoorn: De Banier, 2015.

Van Es, T. *Nieuw licht: De strijd om en de prediking van het aanbod van genade in de periode 1750–1800* [New light: The battle for and the preaching of the offer of grace during the period 1750–1800]. Kampen: De Groot Goudriaan, 2005.

Van Lieburg, F. A. "De Libanon blijft ruisen: Opwekkingen in Nederland in de gereformeerde traditie' [Lebanon continues to shake: Revivals in the Netherlands in the Reformed tradition]. In *Een golf van beroering: De omstreden religieuze opwekking in Nederland in het midden van de achttiende eeuw* [A wave of emotion: The controversial religious revival in the Netherlands in the midst of the eighteenth century]. Edited by J. Spaans, 15–38. Hilversum: Verloren, 2001.

Van Valen, Leen J. "Comrie, Alexander (1706–1774)." In *Encyclopedie Nadere Reformatie* [Encyclopedia of the Dutch Further Reformation], 1:181–91. Utrecht: De Groot Goudriaan, 2015.

VERHANDELING

VAN

EENIGE EIGENSCHAPPEN

DES

ZALIGMAKENDEN GELOOFS,

ZYNDE

EEN' VERKLAARING EN TOEPASSING

VAN VERSCHEIDE UITGEKIPTE TEXTEN

DES O. EN N. TESTAMENTS;

IN WELKE

De *Zorgeloozen* en *Tyt - Geloovigen* ontdekt, gewaarfchouwt en uit-
gelokt worden, om het Leven buiten zich in een' aange-
bodenen *Jezus* te zoeken.

De *Wegen* en *Gevallen*, in welke *Godt zyn Volk* brengt, worden
voorgeftelt, en de *Oeffening* en *Kracht des Geloofs* daarin verklaart.

De *Gemoets - Gevallen* en *Zwarigheden* der *Klein - Geloovigen* worden
opgeloft, en zy worden volgens de *Kenmerken* vermaant, hunnen
ftaat vafttehouden, en naar *Vermeerdering* des *Geloofs* te ftaan.

DOOR

ALEXANDER COMRIE,

SCOTO-BRITTANNUS.

A.L.M. Philofophiæ Doctor en *Predikant te* Woubrugge.

TE LEIDEN,

By { JOHANNES HASEBROEK, EN TE AMSTERDAM, NICOLAAS BYL. } 1744.

Treatise on Several Distinctive Marks of Saving Faith

*Consisting of the Exposition and Application
of Several Selected Passages
of the Old and New Testaments in which*

- the careless and temporal believers are discovered, warned, and invited to seek their life outside themselves in an offered Jesus;

- the elucidation of the various ways in which God leads His people, as well as the exercise and efficacy of faith in such circumstances;

- the cases of conscience and perplexities of struggling believers are resolved, and they are exhorted, by way of these distinctive marks, to remain steadfast regarding their spiritual state, and to aspire after the increase of their faith.

by

Alexander Comrie

Scoto-Brittannus

A. L. M. Doctor of Philosophy and Minister
of the Gospel in Woubrugge

Dedication to My Greatly Beloved and Esteemed Congregation of Woubrugge

Esteemed and dearly beloved congregation in the Lord,

Considerable time has already passed since the blessed God began His saving work among you. So very early, and thus at the beginning of the Reformation, the Lord was pleased to illuminate you with the light of divine truths by means, as some believe, of either Jan Arendszoon Mandemaker or the Fleming, Petrus Gabriel. After Jan Arendszoon preached his first open-air sermon outside of Amsterdam near the Harlem Gate, people from Delft urged him to preach to them the sound doctrine of the gospel. As he traveled from Amsterdam to Delft, some residents of Jacobswoude asked him to do likewise, and thus he preached there also. Since then, there have always been some here who have embraced and confessed sound doctrine.

Since old times, the Lord has thus established a congregation here and sent you many eminent men. As you know, during that time, the work of powerful conversion broke forth remarkably among you through the ministerial labors of your deceased and beloved pastor, the honorable, learned, and now blessed Rev. Carolus Blom, my esteemed predecessor in the work of the Lord among you.

You are acquainted with how we have sought to further the work of the Lord among you. Although I am aware that my ministry has been deficient in many ways, I nevertheless recognize that, when asked, I can say with a good conscience that, with my minimal talent, I have never endeavored to proclaim anything other than the sound and pure doctrine of the Reformed Church. I have laid no other foundation "than that is laid, which is Jesus Christ" (1 Cor. 3:11). He is the chief corner stone in Zion, "and he that believeth on him shall not be confounded" (1 Peter 2:6). As you know, we live during a time that is very fertile ground for new sentiments and opinions—even regarding the saving operation of the Holy Spirit in the hearts of the elect. Inexperienced and unstable individuals are promoting these opinions regarding the Lord's service, and their views change almost annually because they do not experientially know the truth of the gospel as it is in Christ. Nevertheless, we declare publicly that we find so much satisfaction and peace for our soul in the old tried truth that we never crave for something new but rather are always fearful when we hear such things. We wish to warn you of this and earnestly exhort you to "contend for the faith which was once delivered unto the saints" (Jude 3). You must strive for this without yielding one jot to the right or the left, for "Jesus Christ [is] the same yesterday, and to day, and for ever" (Heb. 13:8).

We have not only striven for purity of doctrine, but we were particularly concerned about the eternal salvation of your immortal souls. Our concern was that it would please the Lord to extricate some from the power of darkness and translate them into the kingdom of the Son of His love and to build up others in their most holy faith. Therefore, we have frequently endeavored to awaken the unconverted from their slumber by confronting them with the peril and certainty of eternal damnation should they not strive to flee the wrath to come in the way of repentance and faith. As soon as we detected some brokenness of heart, we always sought to help such persons in our sermons, resolve their concerns, and urge them to surrender to Jesus[1] and bid sin and the world farewell. After that, we also sought to guide such persons by teaching them all that a Christian will encounter along the way. At the same time, we also instructed them not to succumb because of their light afflictions, which are "but for a moment" and work for them "a far more exceeding and eternal weight of glory" (2 Cor. 4:17).

And although we have much reason to complain that many have not believed our preaching, we may also acknowledge, to the praise of God's grace, that our labors have not been entirely in vain. For some time now, the Lord has opened the hearts of some here and elsewhere. In secret, we often sighed for this, and even though your spiritual fruitlessness has considerably burdened us, we have never lost either the courage or desire to persevere. To bring about the union between Jesus and your immortal soul was so important to us that, while sighing, we cast forth the net on this and then again on that side. All the while, we are waiting continually for the sacred moment to arrive, that moment decreed from eternity! My esteemed congregation, when

---

1. The Dutch reads, "Opdat zij Jezus het ja-woord zouden geven," that is, "So that they would say 'yes' to Jesus."

upon the request of many I permitted myself to be persuaded to publish the treatises recorded in this book, I immediately felt compelled to dedicate this book to you, my beloved congregation.

First, I wish thereby to express my gratitude for your love and affection for my person and ministry. Initially, I was strange and unknown to you, but my love for you has greatly increased due to my contact with you. Since I was a stranger in your midst, how could it be otherwise than that this was more than delightful for me! That caused me to forget all my sorrow, and as your pastor, this is especially a matter of joy for me, for experience teaches that when there is little respect for the pastor as a person, his message will have little effect. But on the other hand, I know myself obligated to you for your love, and thus, I experience simultaneously that my love for you continues to increase. Therefore, I pray and hope that the Lord will enable me, so to speak, to be in travail out of love for your immortal souls. Consequently, I ask you that love may continue, that you may persevere in it, and that you will diligently avail yourself of the minimal talent that God has given me on your behalf.

Second, I want to put a stop to the complaints of some that we conduct so few visits. We are hopeful that you will be somewhat understanding regarding the fact that we visit so little. That has never been our custom as it has been of others who do so with much edification. By way of this and previous works, you will perceive that, although I do not frequent conventicles, I make good use of my time. I work unobserved by myself. If others disagree with this, let them use their Christian liberty, and let me retain mine. Even though we do not visit much, we publish now and then a helpful book of which you can avail yourself. This will enable you to reflect on the substance of our sermons.

Therefore, my precious and beloved congregation, make use of this book, the contents of which we have preached for your benefit and are now publishing, praying to God that it may be a blessing for your immortal soul.

Your loving pastor and servant of the Lord Jesus Christ,
Alexander Comrie
Woubrugge, July 20, 1743

Preface Addressed to the General Public

Esteemed Reader,

For the construction of the tabernacle, everyone would voluntarily bring a gift of what he possessed. Even though the gift of the one was superior to the gift of another, everyone's gift was received and used for the service and construction of the tabernacle.

Likewise, we are hopeful that the following pages, which have been published at our initiative, may be subservient to the upbuilding of the Lord's spiritual tabernacle. We have published them as they have been spoken in the pulpit in the year 1739 and the beginning of 1740, the exception being that we have deliberately shortened the application sections so that this book would not be too expensive for those of lesser means.

We have sought to promote the simplicity of the gospel. We have never sought to occupy the congregation with a puffed-up display of wisdom or to cause confusion by addressing impertinent differences of opinion—both of which engender little edification. Nevertheless, we have expressed our disapproval toward anyone who has treated this subject erroneously. And we are hopeful that no one will disapprove of our manner of exposition and application. Indeed, we are hopeful that everyone will endeavor to carry out his task with edification to the best of his knowledge.

We do not wish to determine whether our work of constructing the spiritual tabernacle should be compared to gold or silver or the lesser gifts of camel's hair and badger skins—lest we appear to be puffed up on the one side or too belittling on the other side. Still, I trust that as *The ABC of Faith* has been approved by many, the esteemed reader will experience that these treatises fully express what is stated in the title and benefit the reader. Furthermore, I wish to commend myself to your prayers before the throne of grace.

Dear reader, I commend myself to your benevolence.

Your servant of the Lord,
Alexander Comrie
Woubrugge, July 16, 1743

CHAPTER 1

Faith, a Grace That Unites the Soul Most Intimately to Christ

But he that is joined unto the Lord [with Him][1] *is one spirit.*
—1 CORINTHIANS 6:17

That person who in some measure takes religion seriously will generally espouse the misconception and pernicious error through his innate blindness that he will please God and will indeed be saved if he can refrain from sin and practice the religious virtues demanded of him. This misconception is to be observed not only among the virtuous heathen but even among those that profess Christianity. What other purpose does the entire theological construction of the Pelagians, papists, Socinians, and Arminians serve but to stir up a man to exercise his free will in order to please God and be happy?

It is lamentable that this error has become so deeply rooted in the depraved nature of every professor of the truth even though the gospel has been placed upon the candlestick in its clarity. Every person who in some measure understands that he cannot be saved if he continues in the way of sin begins zealously to commit himself to performing duties. He is very much at peace and is confident that God is his God upon detecting some progress in this performance. Yes, this misconception has so infected fallen man as a sickness and leprosy, and none but God Himself, by His Spirit, is able to bring about some healing. Moreover, such healing progresses but slowly when it has been initiated in some measure, and it will only come to fruition upon death.

My beloved, my present objective is to warn against this misconception as much as I am able and to point out that if we are ever to practice any measure of holiness, we must first be united to Christ by a true saving faith as the

---

1. These words are inserted by Comrie for clarification.

branch is united to the vine. Such is the universal teaching of the Bible. Jesus teaches plainly that the tree must be made good before it can bring forth good fruits, for only the branch that is united to Him will bear fruit (John 15:4–5). In this text, the apostle wishes to incite the believing Corinthians to the practice of holiness through their union to Christ by faith.

The apostle indicates those that will not inherit God's kingdom in verses 9 and 10. Having spoken of fornicators as belonging to them, the apostle uses the opportunity (from verse 13 through the remainder of the chapter) to denounce the sin of fornication that was in vogue among the Corinthians. The one argument, among others set forth in the admonition of verse 15, on which the apostle dwells more than any other is most compelling: Believers are united to Christ by faith, and thus, they may not join their bodies, which are united to Christ, to a harlot. He points out in verse 16 that they who commit whoredom become one body with the harlot, whereas they who are united to Christ are one body with Christ. According to our text's words, they are to flee fornication.

In the words of our text, we find the following:

1. A description of the activity of faith whereby union between Christ and the soul is brought about: "He that is joined unto the Lord"

2. A description of the union itself, being the consequence of such an act of faith: "Is one spirit" with Him

UNION WITH CHRIST

This consists of the exposition of the following:

The first part, in which saving faith is described briefly as being united to Christ: "He that is joined unto the Lord." We have explained this activity of the soul in *The ABC of Faith*.[2]

The second part, to which we proceed where the apostle sets forth the very intimate union between Christ and believers as being consequential— that is, being immediately brought about by means of saving faith. They are one spirit with Him, which is indicative of a most intimate union according to the words of the text.

---

2. Alexander Comrie, *The ABC of Faith* (West Yorkshire, Great Britain: Zoar Publications, 1978), 12–15.

What This Union Is Not

To speak of this union, we shall establish in what this union does not consist.

First, this union is not a union that consists in the intermingling of two natures. It is not a union whereby believers would be so swallowed up in Christ as to no longer have an independent personality. Neither would believers necessarily and physically be one person with Christ, as, for example, in a mixture of similar elements, such as water and wine. Eutychus, a very dangerous heretic, understood this union to be of the two natures in Christ. Gregory of Nazianzus, however, believed the union between Christ and believers to be of a *similar* nature. He stated that Christians are "christianized" (*Christopoiein*), but contrasted that with the corrupt mysticism of the Cabalistic and Platonic school of philosophy and how they viewed this matter, asserting that the soul slips into the divine being. You understand that to maintain such a manner of teaching and instruction is a most dreadful and abominable blasphemy. Christ's personhood is never transformed into the personhood of the believer, nor is the personhood of the believer transformed into the personhood of Christ. Even in the state of glory, there is an essential distinction between the personhood of Christ and that of believers so that each retains his personhood. The Lamb (who is a distinct person) shall lead them (who again are distinct persons—distinct from both one another and the Lamb who leads them). As a distinct person, the Lord Jesus in the day of judgment will say to believers, being distinct from Him, "Come, ye blessed of my Father, inherit the kingdom prepared for you from the foundation of the world" (Matt. 25:34).

Second, we must not understand this union to mean either that believers cease from all activity or that all the actions they perform must be attributed not to them but to the account of Christ. It would then follow that a believer who is united to Christ would neither eat, nor drink, nor sleep, nor walk, nor speak, nor pray, nor believe, but that it is Christ who did so. The wickedness of some fanatics and antinomians went so far as to maintain that they did not sin when they transgressed God's law while engaging in drunkenness, fornication, and adultery, but that it was Christ (I relate this with trepidation) who committed those sinful deeds. Moreover, when they repented, it was again Christ who repented, believed, etc. Again, how blasphemous such notions are! Though the sins of believers can be called, in a sense, the sins of Christ, they are not His sins in the sense that He is the active agent. He has never known any sin, but they are His by way of imputation—that is, insofar as

(1) all the unrighteousness of God's elect has been laid upon Him as Surety and (2) He willingly took them upon Himself to satisfy the justice of God. However, believers, both before and after this union, are the actual cause of their deeds. Unless a person dispenses with all fear of God and is blinded by the devil, his conscience would witness to him that he is the cause of his deeds.

Third, this union is not to be understood as though Christ in His person, according to both His divine and human natures, makes His residence in the hearts of believers. Some entertain such carnal notions of this type of union. Howbeit, although we believe that Jesus Christ is in believers, and they in Him, we believe this is true in the spiritual sense rather than in the physical. Jesus Christ has left the earth. He is present as God-man at the right hand of His Father until that time when He will return to judge the quick and the dead.

Fourth, this union does not mean that its essence consists of the conformity believers have with Christ in sanctification, for sanctification presupposes union between Christ and the soul. Thus, John 15:4–5 teaches that one must first be in Christ by way of being united to Him, and only then will he bring forth the fruits of holiness. The expressions the Holy Spirit uses are too strong for one to understand them as referring to a mere external conformity of one's actions. Consider also that there can be similarity between two objects without there being any union whatsoever.

What This Union Is
Someone may approach this positively by asking, Wherein then does this union between Christ and believers consist? Beloved, this is a great mystery, and to expound and explain it, it is easier to point out in what it does not consist than to state in what it does consist. However, it is possible to describe this union in conformity with God's Word and the holy doctrine of our church. We thus affirm this union to be a very intimate, mysterious, most genuine, and inseparable relationship between Christ and believers whereby the person of Christ, by the Holy Spirit, is united to the person of the believer, and the person of the believer, by faith, is united to the person of Christ. This mutual union is such that believers constitute the mystical body of Christ, their Head, and thus are partakers of all the benefits He has merited.

For the better comprehension of this description, we shall consider the following matters as clearly as possible:

The Persons Who Are United

First, the essence of this union is that two persons are united, one with the other. They are Christ and believers.

The first person in this union is Christ, whom we are to consider not strictly as God nor strictly as man but as Mediator between God and man—that is, being truly God as well as truly man in two distinct natures, united to all eternity in one person. In this context, Christ is held forth (1) as the Immanuel who desires to be betrothed to sinners from among the children of men ("And I will betroth thee unto me," etc. [Hos. 2:19]); and (2) as the Husband of believers ("For thy Maker is thine husband" [Isa. 54:5]). Yes, relative to this union, Christ is compared to a vine, the branches of which are believers, and to a foundation upon which believers are laid as living stones that grow into a spiritual building.

The second person in this union is the elect, called, and believing soul. The elect, and they alone, are the genuine members of Christ's mystical body, of which He is the Head. Formal professors of the truth are not genuine members but only barren and unfruitful branches that will be cut off with the pruning knife and burned with the fire of God's wrath.

How dissimilar these persons are! The one person is the Father's eternal Son, the God-man, who is fairer than the children of men, who is white and ruddy, who is altogether lovely, and who is the chief among ten thousand. The other person is Satan's child, who by nature has neither form nor beauty and who is guilty, miserable, and utterly impotent in and of himself. Such a union would never have arisen in man's heart if God Himself had not revealed it. When the soul may behold this by faith, she will exclaim, "Who am I, Lord, and what is my father's house that I should be a member of Thy body and be bone of Thy bone and flesh of Thy flesh!"

The Bonds That Unite Them

Second, in considering this mystery, we are to note the bonds that constitute this union (*vincula unionis*).

The Bond of the Holy Spirit

First, there is the Spirit of Christ. He unites Christ to the elect sinner by efficaciously calling him out of the powers of darkness. This union of Christ with the elect sinner, wrought by the Holy Spirit, consists primarily in that Christ lays claim to and exercises the right He has to the elect by (1) the Father's gift of them to Him in the covenant of redemption and (2) Christ's actual redemption of them by means of His active and passive obedience so that they may thus be partakers of this redemption, and He may possess them in very deed as His property.

This must occur if the elect sinner, from his side, is ever to unite himself in very deed to Christ, for the sinner, though elect, is dead in trespasses and sins, even as all others (Eph. 2:1). Furthermore, this is the work of the Holy Spirit, as you will be able to ascertain from the following passages of Scripture: "And I will put my spirit within you" (Ezek. 36:27). That is the time of love. It is the hour of God's good pleasure when the Spirit comes and takes actual possession of the elect sinner. This divine initiative is expressed in Ezekiel 37:5 and must be compared with verse 14, where this mystery is explained in a most lively manner. Galatians 3:2–3; 1 Corinthians 12:13; Romans 8:9; and other texts also teach this.

We thus conclude that the elect sinner is entirely passive when this union is initially established. At the moment when Christ, by the Spirit, lays claim upon the elect sinner as His property, the elect sinner is dead in sins and trespasses and is as incapable as any dead person is to make himself alive. When the Spirit comes to unite the soul to Christ, she is as the dead bones shown to Ezekiel or as the helpless child cast out into the open field, wallowing in its blood. It follows that all preparation for this union proceeding from the sinner himself must be utterly rejected (although, in a proper sense and different respect, we can admit it), for what can he who is spiritually dead do?

We conclude, furthermore, that true spiritual life proceeds from this union. Sequentially, true spiritual life does not precede but follows it, though they transpire simultaneously, for at the very moment that the Holy Spirit unites Himself to the sinner, the elect sinner becomes alive. That one follows the other immediately and is accompanied by it is to be ascertained from the quoted Scripture passages. Thus, there is no intermediate state between death and life, for when the Spirit is bestowed upon the inner man, the soul is then alive. As we shall see, however, this life manifests itself gradually—first in weaker and then in stronger measure, and first in less and then in stronger and more sanctified activities as an affirmation of spiritual life.

The Bond of Faith

Second, there is true, saving faith. God the Holy Spirit unites Himself to the elect sinner, and the elect person, being quickened by the Spirit, likewise unites himself most intimately to the person of Christ by true, saving faith, which is the bond of union from the side of the sinner. This union is mutual, and therefore, we read, "I in them," that is, by the Spirit, "and they in me," that is, by faith. And this union is fittingly compared to the marriage bond in which the elect person is identified as the bride and wife of the Lamb. We know, however, that marriage presupposes mutual consent, and such is also the mutual bond of union between Christ and the elect sinner. It is a double knot wherewith Christ and the elect are bound to each other, a knot that will never be untied, even though all the powers of hell and the world were to conspire to that end.

Someone may ask, What are the acts of faith whereby the soul unites herself to Christ? Since this is a question of the greatest importance, we shall make this as clear as we possibly can. Take note, therefore, of the following matters:

1. The soul begins to sever her union and covenant with all her lusts and pleasures, whatever their kind, nature, name, or characteristic may be, and she bids them farewell. When the least principle of life enters the heart, the soul sees its foolishness, bondage, and slavery to sin. This engenders a thorough, heartfelt, and pervasive aversion for all sin with a heartfelt and spiritual commitment to all virtue. It is thus that believers can say in the presence of the Lord that they hate every false way. Yes, the soul is won over for the Lord so pervasively that, bound as she may have been to certain lusts, she cries out toward everything, "Depart, depart!" Such determination must necessarily precede, for no more can Christ and Belial be joined together than God and mammon can be served simultaneously. We thus detect in Paul's epistles and other Scriptures that as soon as a measure of life begins to assert itself, an aversion for sin and an inclination toward virtue manifests itself, for the first words they speak are "Lord, what wilt Thou have me to do?"

2. Moreover, the soul begins to have a lively impression of her state of separation over which she begins to mourn in secret with a most bitter sorrow before God. The soul melts away in grief because she misses Jesus, and to miss Jesus is her inexpressible misery and wretched condition. Being so grievously afflicted, this sorrow cannot be compared to any other sorrow. Yet, it is not so much caused by oppression and anxiety. This sorrow is caused by the want that it generates. It enables the soul to pour out her heart, persevering with many and repeated arguments with the Lord to look upon such a dead dog and to stretch

forth to her His gracious scepter out of pure mercy. Here the soul sows with tears, her eyes being as springs of water.

3. Daily the soul increasingly learns the necessity of being united to the Surety, for she perceives that nothing can please God apart from this union. She perceives that she has nothing wherewith to satisfy when her creditors confront her in an hour of distress. Everything is found to be insufficient and as reprobate silver for the payment of a thousand talents that she perceives she is indebted to pay. The result relative to herself, on the one hand, is that she comes to holy despair, which causes her to cry out that she is entirely without hope. She no longer can find her life in her hand, and she rejects all her righteousness as dung, as filthy rags. Thus she becomes a spiritually bankrupt soul. On the other hand, she lies prostrate at the throne of grace, hungering and thirsting and panting and yearning for Jesus Himself and for His righteousness more than a hart thirsts and pants after the water brooks. Without ceasing, she flees to Jesus as a stream of water[3] and continues to knock and to supplicate for grace rather than for justice, crying out, "Oh, let a crumb of the children's bread be given to an unworthy dog!" (cf. Isa. 26:9; Ps. 63:1–2).

4. The Lord, by His Holy Spirit, causes some rays of His divine light to shine into the soul, whereby the way of deliverance by means of a Surety is unveiled. The Surety Himself is seen in the glory and loveliness of His person, as well as in the perfection and all-sufficiency of His merits. Esteem for Him thus reaches its very zenith: "Whom have I in heaven but Thee, O God?" Love for Him is kindled in such a measure that all the affections of the soul are captivated and burn toward this incomparably glorious and precious Immanuel so that the soul can say, "How I love Thee, O Lord, my strength! This love is strong as death; this jealousy is cruel as the grave. Her coals are as coals of fire that has a most vehement flame. Many waters cannot quench this love, neither can the floods drown it. Therefore, if a man would give all the substance of his house for love, it would utterly be

---

3. The Dutch reads, "Zodat ze Jezus aanloopt als een waterstroom." Comrie here quotes Psalm 34:6 of the Statenvertaling (the Dutch equivalent of the KJV), which reads, "Zij hebben op Hem gezien, ja Hem als een waterstroom aangelopen, en hunne aangezichten zijn niet schaamrood geworden." The literal rendering of the Dutch would be "They looked unto Him, and came upon Him as a stream of water: and their faces were not ashamed." The KJV rendering of this verse (verse 5 in the KJV) is "They looked unto him, and were lightened: and their faces were not ashamed." The equivalent phrase "and were lightened" clearly does not fit the context here.

contemned." It would not be looked at with so much as half an eye (Song 8:6–7; cf. Heb. 11:24–26).

5. However, the soul, though burning with love toward the Surety as she beholds His loveliness and necessity, is frequently and with much fear concerned whether she, being so unworthy in herself, would dare take the liberty to appropriate Him. Therefore, the offer of grace will bear powerfully upon her heart. She will thereby perceive that the invitation is addressed to her and that God not only allows but even commands her, as wretched as she is, to believe in the Surety. She approves of that faithful covenant and surrenders her heart to Jesus, setting her seal upon God's testimony that He is true, exclaiming, "Oh God, since one whose sins are as scarlet and crimson may and must come to this Surety by virtue of Thine own testimony, behold, Thou art stronger than I am, and Thou hast prevailed. My heart cannot refrain itself. Be it to me according to Thy Word!" Thus, as Christ betroths her in mercy, likewise the soul, by way of this believing acquiescence, enters into this marriage covenant, and the two become one.

6. Finally, note that the soul, in all the acts and exercises here mentioned, unites herself to the person of the Surety, for nothing, neither heaven or earth nor promise or joy would be of help to her heart. She must unite herself, in very deed and essentially, to the Surety. He must be hers, and she must be His. The man did indeed buy a field (Matt. 13), but he did so because of the treasure in the field. In marriage, the heart goes out toward and for the person himself, and thus it is here the same. Everyone with an upright heart continually keeps in view not only whether he becomes a partaker of the person Himself by the acts of faith but also whether his heart unites itself to Him. Someone may say, "How shall I know this?" One ascertains this from the benefits of being a partaker and from the heart uniting itself to Him but also from what these have yielded and still do yield—namely, peace. Can you say, "It was neither my prayers nor my exercises but the Mediator, who was revealed to me, whom I received, to whom my heart was united, and who was formed within me"? Then fear not, for you have indeed united yourself to the Person.

The Characteristics of This Union

We shall now consider the characteristics of this union. They are many, but we shall only present some of them.

First, this union between Jesus and believers is a genuine or substantive relationship and is not merely an illusion. It is genuine and substantive for the following reasons:

1. It is compared in God's Word not to imaginary but rather to substantive matters. Since God's Word compares it to substantive rather than imaginary matter, it follows that this union is essential and real, for it is such a union as exists mutually not only between branches and the vine (John 15) but also between the members and the body (and whatever other examples that may be gathered from Scripture).

2. Faith, in the act of appropriation, does not so much unite itself to the benefits of Christ but first and foremost unites itself to Christ, which consequently results in being united to His benefits.

3. By virtue and in consequence of this union, Christ is said to be in believers and they in Him.

Second, this union is all-encompassing (*totalis*); that is, it encompasses the entire Christ, as God-man, as Mediator, and as Surety of a better covenant, who unites Himself to the elect as their Prophet, Priest, and King to be entirely their portion for time and eternity. They, in turn, unite themselves to Christ, according to both body and soul, in order to be eternally His and in order that He would eternally dwell in them with His Spirit as in His temple. In such a manner, God has made Christ unto them wisdom, righteousness, sanctification, and complete redemption (1 Cor. 1:30), and they can say with the bride, "My beloved is mine, and I am his" (Song 2:16).

Third, this union is very intimate. In this the Word of God guides us: "I in them, and thou in me" (John 17:23). The Holy Spirit, therefore, uses all manner of analogies to teach and to clarify the intimacy of this union, one time comparing it to the union between the members and the head (Rom. 12:5; 1 Cor. 12:12), then again to husband and wife (Eph. 5:32), and again to various other matters.

Finally, this union is indissoluble. "And I will betroth thee unto me for ever" (Hos. 2:19). These bonds will therefore never be broken. Spiritual adultery will indeed inhibit the exercise of love, but it will never result in the filing of a complete bill of divorce, for the unfaithfulness of His people will never annul His faithfulness. Upon their repentance, He will always heal their backslidings and love them freely (Hos. 14:4). Death itself will not break these bonds, for in death, their bodies remain united to Christ. God is, therefore, the God of Abraham, even according to the body, which lay in the grave and will therefore also rise again (Matt. 22:31–32).

APPLICATION

Behold, my beloved hearers, we have held before ourselves this divine truth as clearly as we possibly could. Let us, therefore, reflect for a moment upon these matters for our own use. The soul's union with the person of the Mediator is the foundation of spiritual life. Apart from this union, the soul is dead and is incapable of doing anything that pleases God. Let us, therefore, reflect for a moment upon these matters for our own use.

Lamentation

How we ought to lift our voices in lamentations when we take note of men in general and consider what they think and practice regarding this truth!

The majority of people live without God and do not think seriously about religion. They never think attentively about this truth as they live carelessly and irreligiously in their sinful course of life. Their souls are knit to their sinful ways, lusts, entertainments, and friendships without giving a thought of how or in what manner their immortal souls will be saved. I believe if I were to ask the majority of people, "Oh, what do you think of this truth? Do you know that you must experience it?" many would reply, "We do not understand the matter, for we never concerned ourselves with whether we were united to Christ." Oh, wretched and unhappy multitude! Are you so careless about a matter that ought to be so crucial to you? You should know that without it, you will never be saved. Instead, as you now are, you will remain without God and Christ, and perish eternally.

How many unite themselves to something different from this truth because they neither wish to forsake their possessions nor their service of sin, although they are at times superficially persuaded of this truth. They would rather let go of Jesus and being united to Him than to miss the enjoyment of sin. Oh, how foolish a choice it is to deem Jesus less than desirable! How foolish a choice it is to reject life and to cling to death for the short-lived pleasure of that which will be followed in this life by an accusing conscience and hereafter by gnashing of teeth!

How many, are there not, who make mockery of this truth, doing so either publicly or in secret? They gently question and carefully examine people about this truth, only to label the matter with those who subscribe to it as being the teaching of something strange.

How lamentable it is that this matter is stressed so little in formal worship as well as in the use of the special means of grace! When the truth is expounded, there is often, at best, some exposing of sin and the prescription of some religious duties in the application without confronting the sinner with his lost state and the necessity of being united to Christ before he can do anything that pleases God. When we consider this, as well as many other matters, must we not rightfully lift our voices in lamentation about the condition of most people?

Self-Examination

Many will say, "It is true indeed! Man must be reconciled to God and be a partaker of this Surety if he is to be saved, for God is a consuming fire outside of Christ." My beloved! We can indeed know this from God's Word, but the great question is, Are you united to Christ, or are you not united to Christ? Examine yourself and consider, therefore, as in the presence of the Lord, whether you have good reason to conclude that you are truly united to Christ.

Are there not many who have no other foundation but a religious life from which they conclude that they have a part in the Mediator and that they partake of His benefits? However, friends, you need to reflect on how far one can proceed in religion by one's upbringing and by having a speaking and an accusing conscience while remaining outside of Jesus, as the Pharisees and many heathen also experienced.

Are there not those who believe that they are united to Christ merely because they experienced a change? You once lived in sin, even as others, but you came to realize that the wages of sin is death. You have sorrowed over this, confessed your sins before God, and refrained from them; you are watchful against them and are displeased when any inclination toward them manifests itself. Thus you think you are now united to Christ. But do you not know as Herod knew that an awakened conscience has a great effect to make us think that we can do many things and even become an "almost Christian"? Therefore, do not build upon this.

You may say, "I do not build upon this, but having experienced sorrow for my sins, I have learned to know that there is a Jesus who with His suffering and death has satisfied God's justice. I have received Him by faith, and so I believe that I am united to Him." However, my beloved, you ought to know the vast difference between comprehending a matter and the matter itself. There is a vast difference between embracing what one perceives Jesus to be and a believing embrace of Jesus. I believe that many who do not discern this correctly deceive themselves and feed their soul with ashes, having a lie in their right hand and a deceived heart that leads them astray. Many people have had some common convictions, causing them to have much concern about their state. These people avoid and flee from sin, and they are very fervent in prayer for deliverance. They join God's people, ask for the way of salvation, and commit themselves to the searching of divine truths wherein they find delight and gain a reasonable understanding. Since their anxiety and perplexity could not be relieved by their prayers, reading, and striving against sin, they begin to understand that Jesus has merited an eternal righteousness and that one becomes a partaker thereof when the soul acquiesces in what Jesus has merited. Thus, they begin to rest in some measure on these truths that they understand, and if, at first, they are not delivered from their anxiety, they repeat these exercises. More and more they begin to find rest, thinking that they are true believers since they do not rest in anything other than the merited righteousness of the Surety. Is this not the case with many who live under the gospel? And yet, my beloved, there is nothing in this that supersedes the power of nature when the conscience is pricked with some convictions; and if not, then one is satisfied with historical faith.

Therefore, all those that have no desire to deceive themselves should search themselves very carefully, asking, Have I united myself to Him whom I perceive Jesus to be, in harmony with scriptural truth, or have I united myself to Christ by divine and supernatural light and the operation of the Holy Spirit? You can have the first and still miss Jesus and not know Jesus. If you have the latter, however, you will be saved. Regarding the first, you must realize that you could perceive much about someone's nature from hearsay— well enough to describe his characteristics—and yet, if the person himself were present, not know that it was he of whom they spoke. The Jews had a conception about the Messiah, but when He was manifested in their midst, they did not know Him; they rejected Him. There is as much concern that such is the case with many. Therefore, I beseech you to deal faithfully in this matter in the fear of God.

Someone may ask, Is it true that there are so many careless people who never think about this matter? Another may ask, Is it true that there are many who reflect upon and speak of this union who deceive themselves and build their peace upon false foundations? If these many have but a shadow instead of this precious Jesus, then would you please point out to us what the characteristics are whereby we can examine ourselves to know whether we are truly saved? If this is your desire, then give attention to the following matters:

Examine yourself in the presence of the Lord as to whether your lost state has ever been truly uncovered to you. Examine yourself whether you have clearly and explicitly seen that you were not a partaker of Christ but lived until that time without God and Christ and were subject to the wrath of God and the curse of the law. Beloved, when the gospel is preached, and Christ rides forth on His white horse, conquering and to conquer, there will be times during the worship service that His heart-piercing arrows will rain down heavily. This one is wounded, another is troubled, and yet another cries out, "What will become of me?" etc. However, it does not go deep enough. With one it is but a morning cloud; with the other, it is as seasickness, and with another, it is a sickness that is healed and daubed with untempered mortar. These, therefore, remain unsaved. But when God begins His work, He strips the soul to her very foundations. He causes her to see herself in her state of separation, the result of which is that she no longer can find her life in her hand. Therefore, she cries out, "It is without hope; it is without hope!" If you have experienced this, it speaks well of you, but if you miss it, then it is for yourself to know that you are yet still outside of salvation.

Examine yourself whether you have ever tasted and savored the bitterness of sin and then known, in that same measure, that all the bonds that knit your soul to sin and lust were broken. Were your affections, in their very root, so drawn away from sin that you hated them instead of hankering after, covering, and excusing them or in some measure allowing them to have a peaceful residence in your soul? Can you testify before God that, although they are in you, and you are often overtaken by them through weakness, they are not your friends but rather your enemies? Do you have an aversion for sin? Do you abhor sin in the very bottom of your soul? Are you able to say that nothing would be more delightful to you than if your sin, without any exception, would be indiscriminately eradicated with root and branch? Many who profess the truth taste and experience some anxiety due to their sins, which trouble the soul so much and result in such severe punishments. But they have never tasted the bitterness of sin as sin itself. Therefore, there will always be some sin to which they will continue to cling and to which they can yield when their anxiety subsides. Oh, take note! You cannot serve two masters! You cannot simultaneously be united to Christ and united to your lusts.

Examine yourself whether you, being convinced of the necessity to be united to Christ, have perceived experientially your complete impotence to exercise the faith that unites your soul to Christ. Did this frequently cause you to supplicate and to wrestle at the throne of grace for faith? Was it so that you might receive an eye of faith to see Him, that you might receive feet to walk by faith and to come to Him in response to His calling? Was it so that you might receive arms of faith to be able to embrace Him? We live in unusual times. People attain to the greatest truths of Christianity very quickly with very little strife and wrestling, which prompts me to say, "How is it that you have found it so quickly? How did you come to Jesus, engage in covenant transactions, and attain to assurance of faith so swiftly? Did it cost you many a prayer? Have you become acquainted with your impotence?" Oh, I fear for many of this generation! In the meantime, they whose impotence has been experientially uncovered to them ought not to fear because they could not exercise the faith that results in this union until God granted it to them. This proves that your faith is not imitation but rather the fruit of God's work.

Examine yourself concerning what gave you some liberty to go to Jesus in order to be intimately united to Him. The persons being united are so incompatible: the Son of God, the God-man, the King of kings being united to a guilty, poor, and leprous sinner. Therefore, if you have united yourself to such a most honorable Person, there must certainly have been something that gave you liberty to do so. What was this? Do you respond as follows? "Yes, so it was. I was so bowed down because of my burden and had such a convicting and shaming view of my unworthiness that I did not dare to think of this, being afraid that it would have been presumptuous for me to go to Jesus with my wretched soul, as ministers and the godly counseled me to do. However, while subject to my perplexity and sorrow, some words of Scripture were bound upon my heart, such as, 'Turn unto Me, and be ye saved'; 'Though your sins be as scarlet, they shall be as white as snow; though they be red like crimson, they shall be as wool,' etc. These words caused my heart to melt. In these words, the Surety was revealed to me in His suitability, all-sufficiency, and willingness—and for me, one who is most worthy of curse and damnation. Yes, these words had such efficacy that they convinced my soul and drew me in such a measure that my soul could not refrain itself from acquiescing but instead had to exclaim, "Thou art stronger than I and hast prevailed. Now I am convinced of Thy willingness that I so frequently doubted. Desirest Thou to have precisely such a one as I am? Behold, here I am, and I surrender myself to Thee for time and eternity." If you have come to Him in this fashion, then you need not fear, for the Master called you before your coming.

Examine yourself as to what followed upon your believing union to Him. Are you of one spirit with Him? Does the same mind that is in Christ manifest itself in some measure in your soul etc.? These and similar matters can be subservient as characteristics whereby we can examine our soul.

Man's Misery Identified

Wretched is the man who does not know these matters by experience, for

1. God's relationship toward you is one of an angry Judge. He is a reconciled Father only of those who are united to Christ. Oh yes, it is better to have armies and the combined forces of darkness against you than to have God against you.

2. That man does not partake of any of the benefits of the covenant of grace, since he who is not the property of Christ also does not partake of anything Christ has merited.

3. None of the religious deeds you perform are pleasing to God since they do not proceed from being united to His Son by faith.

4. All of your efforts to sanctify yourself will be fruitless as your experience indeed is. However zealous you may be, your zeal loses its vigor, and you die. However determined you may be to do battle against sin, none will be conquered. Why? Because you are not united to Christ by faith. Only he who is in Him, and he alone, bears fruits.

5. When the moment of your death arrives, you will be eternally damned despite all your imaginations and false foundations. How fearful it will be in hell to recall that these matters were pointed out to you and that they were neglected by you!

Means to Enter into This Union

Is there someone who seeks counsel, asking, "What pathway must I enter upon to be united to Christ?"

1. Seek after deep and penetrating conviction in your soul that you are not yet united to Jesus. Lay your soul bare for the conviction of the Spirit, and never be satisfied until you have been stripped of everything and all false foundations have been taken away from you.

2. Be very fearful for the diversion of your convictions because of some frames and tenderness of heart that you will experience, for they are not Jesus.

3. Especially persevere in prayer to God to receive insight into the gospel and that God Himself will call you by His gospel.

4. Seek to be convinced that if you are to unite yourself to Jesus, such an act is to be preceded by some revelation of Christ to your soul by His Word and Spirit. Such a conviction will safeguard you against deceit.

Encouragement for Souls under Conviction

I hear some convicted souls exclaim, "Oh, my soul longs that I may be united to Jesus!" One says, "I am such an insignificant, irrelevant, and unworthy person that I dare not do so." However, He has come for the very purpose of saving and redeeming those who are utterly insignificant in themselves. Another person will say, "I do desire to unite myself to Him, but I doubt whether He is willing to receive me into such an intimate union with Himself." Oh, yes, soul, He is a thousand times more willing than you are! He assures you thereof in His Word: "He that cometh unto Me, I will in no wise cast out," but He also assures by His oath-swearing as well as by the tears He sheds about your unwillingness. Another will say, "My sins are so many and my guilt is so great and heavy that I must tremble before Him." Let your sins be as scarlet and crimson; He will blot them out for His name's sake. Then again, another person will say, "I desire to unite myself to Him, but I am unable." Well, is He not the Mighty One of Jacob, a Savior to give power to the faint and to increase strength to them that have no might? Someone will finally add, "But I do not have the frame of mind of one who comes; my heart is as a stone." Such may be the case, but where can you obtain help? Has He not promised to take away the heart of stone? Therefore, convicted sinner, we proclaim to you, as an ambassador of God, "Come," for the Bridegroom says, "Whosoever will, let him take the water of life freely" (Rev. 22:17).

The Felicity of God's Favorites

Beloved of God, you who find within yourself the characteristics that you are of one Spirit with Christ, how great is your felicity! You are sons and daughters of the Most High, that is, God's children. Not only is God the God and Father of the Lord Jesus Christ, but He is also your God and Father in Him.

Being united to the Surety, everything present and future is yours, "And ye are Christ's; and Christ is God's."

Some Cases of Conscience Presented and Solved

However, I hear some among you say, "Oh yes, it is an incomprehensible privilege to be so intimately united to Jesus. But even though we cannot deny that we have experiential knowledge of some of these characteristics, there are nevertheless some matters that make us doubtful concerning our state of grace, that prevent us from enjoying the comfort that we otherwise would derive from these characteristics." Therefore, we wish to accommodate you and present some cases of conscience. While supplicating for and waiting upon God's light, give attention to the following:

Case 1: This doctrine of the union of the soul to Christ by faith has always been a very obscure doctrine for me. I cannot comprehend it, and therefore, even though I have some sweet exercises now and then, I am continually assaulted about whether my foundation is good, since no exercise or encouragement can be of any value unless it issues forth from this union.

Answer: 1. Some but not all Christians have a discerning knowledge and spiritual memory as to the nature of the transaction between Jesus and their soul. They know how the Surety appeared to them and what they did. They know which acts of faith precipitated the revelation of the Mediator and by which acts they embraced Him. However, such are generally those persons who have had profound and penetrating spiritual convictions, contrition, and humiliation of soul. If God's way in convicting you has not been thus, you may nevertheless be united to Christ, even though you cannot present the matter with such clarity.

2. You must not doubt the truth of being a partaker of, and being united to, the Mediator because you are not able to determine this a priori (ahead of time). Instead, you must do this a posteriori (reflexively) by way of the fruits. The Lord teaches this way in His Word by giving so many characteristics, enabling us to ascend to the matter itself by way of the fruits. The most infallible proofs that someone is in Christ are to be derived from the fruits. Are you in doubt? Avail yourself of the characteristics of faith. If you possess them, you may be assured that you are in Christ, for no one can have the marks of grace unless he is in Christ. For example, do you fear whether you are in Christ? The apostle states that he who is in Christ is a new creature. If,

however, you perceive within yourself renewal of heart and the endearing of your affections, then be assured that you are in Christ, even though you are without light as to how this transaction initially transpired.

Case 2: It is indeed true that one must conclude from the fruits whether one is united to Christ. This is, however, the point concerning which I am assaulted. In light of God's Word, my heart cannot deny that I have performed the essential acts of faith culminating in this union. However, it is my understanding that Jesus is not only a living Vine, but also a life-giving Vine, and that I, if I were in Him by such union, would bring forth fruits and increase in holiness. But to my regret, I do not perceive this. On the contrary, it seems as if my corruptions gain in strength, and I am becoming more impotent.

Answer: 1. The matter is so great when one's change initially occurs and growth is so evident that both we and others can perceive it. However, this may not be quite as visible later on in spiritual life, although one's growth resembles that of a young tree. The growth of the tree is visible during the initial year or two but not so readily perceived at a later time by those who see it daily. It is nevertheless growing, and another person who has not seen it for some time can detect that this is indeed the case.

2. Instead of this giving you reason to doubt, it serves to assure you that you are not a temporal believer but a true believer, for when true faith is exercised, light enters in and upon the soul. This light generally uncovers and accuses the soul reflexively, and this keeps her small and poor. Temporal faith, however, has little strife and is never affected with a heart-grieving sorrow about its lack of conformity.

3. You frequently err concerning growth and increase in grace and therefore cannot perceive the fruits you wish to have, although true fruits are to be found in you. You think that increase in knowledge, the gift of prayer, etc. must be the fruits, although these can be present without saving grace. Ask yourself, however, whether you are being made acquainted experientially with the power of indwelling corruption, with your complete impotence and the necessity of free grace for the very least of spiritual deeds, etc. Such experiential awareness is growth. Trees do not always bring forth buds, leaves, new branches, and fruit. Nevertheless, they grow in circumference and in their roots. Therefore, do not conclude from your deficiency that you are without fruit, but believe that your perception of and your mourning over your deficiency is actual growth.

Case 3: Oh, there no longer is that tender fellowship between Jesus and my soul as was previously the case, for whatever I undertake to unite myself to by renewal to Him, I cannot achieve. I now fear that everything has been deceit, for I believe that if He were the Bridegroom of my soul, He would not hide Himself as often as He does; He would not stand from afar and so rarely give Himself to be enjoyed by my soul.

Answer: 1. Although you complain of this, nothing strange befalls you. Such concerns will cause the saints to go bowed down. There is, therefore, no reason for doubt since the footsteps of the sheep are to be found upon the way on which you are.

2. You are to know that there are two special seasons in which Christ manifests Himself. The first season is in the beginning and is in order to conquer the heart in its entirety. First, He allures souls (Hos. 2); actually, He persuades the soul. The other season is when the soul herself is in difficult straits. If such is not the case with you, however, then be not surprised that Christ says to you, "Touch Me not now."

3. You are to know that God is free in His administration. Some enjoy much, whereas others are only permitted to enter the inner chamber now and then; again, some rarely enjoy a special manifestation, whereas others only see something of the Sun of Righteousness when they first place their feet upon the way but henceforth walk under a cloud.

4. You say you no longer have such intimate dealings with Him. It can be you have sinned, and sin, having been committed, can cause much harm and injury to spiritual life from which one never recovers and regains the strength he previously had. Mourn over this, and seek to be in a waiting and longing frame. Tarry for Him, for He will surely come, not when you expect Him, but at His own time.

Case 4: I heard you say in your exposition of the text that the soul unites herself to the person of the Mediator. I am now concerned whether I have done so or whether I have merely united myself to the benefits. Therefore, I wish to know how this person manifests Himself to the soul, and further, what the exercises are whereby the soul unites herself to His person, and why it is precisely the soul that must unite herself to Him.

Answer: I perceive your question to be threefold and also of great importance. Nevertheless, we shall respond to each part as much as the framework of our sermon permits. You will find a more detailed exposition of this in the parable of the sower (Matt. 13).

As to the first matter, that is, how this person manifests Himself to the soul, we respond as follows:

First, we presuppose that the soul is deeply convicted, contrite, and troubled by the working of the Spirit, for Jesus will not manifest Himself to any other but those that are brokenhearted and of a contrite spirit.

Second, when Jesus manifests Himself to the soul, He will do the following:

1. He will cause the soul to be very desirous for this manifestation, thirsting more for this than does the hart that pants after the water brooks.

2. He will grant quietness and calmness to the soul whereby she is predisposed for the reception of His operation.

3. He will use a specific promise that fits the soul's condition and serves as a mirror in which she can see herself. He will then cause such a promise, by the operation of the Holy Spirit, to penetrate the heart with an extraordinary and irresistible power whereby she perceives that this proceeds from the Lord.

4. He will cause some divine light to shine into the soul in order for light to be shed upon her darkness.

5. He will open the eyes of the understanding to behold Him in the promises of the gospel, which is called a being enlightened in the knowledge of Christ and a revelation of the Son of God in the soul.

6. He will manifest Himself to her when He thus unveils Himself to the soul in His glory, majesty, and magnificence as the God-man who is the chief among ten thousand.

7. He will grant to such a wretched one a view of His complete suitability that causes the soul to comprehend convincingly what is the essence of that which enamors her.

8. He will cause the soul that stands with outstretched arms to behold Him in His readiness and willingness to embrace not only others but also her, removing all doubt and rolling away the stone from the grave.

The second part of the question pertains to the acts of faith whereby the soul unites herself to His person. To this, we respond briefly:

1. The soul beholds His person as unveiled to her in the manner just stated, which is to behold Him in relation to herself.

2. The soul becomes exceedingly enamored with the glory and loveliness of His Person, for His arrows of love descend deeply into the soul as she beholds Him. His coals of fire that He casts into her soul set it aflame so that she burns with a love that is strong as death, a jealousy that is more cruel than the grave (Song 8:6).

3. The soul comes with the appropriating act of faith and fully embraces Him with both arms for time and eternity.

4. The soul frequently perceives upon the act of appropriation that her heart is knit to another and that her burden is removed from her shoulders.

The third part of the question pertains to the reason why the soul must unite herself to the person of Christ. We reply to this as follows:

1. None but the person of the Mediator can reconcile the soul with an angry God and pacify Him.

2. In the offer of grace, God does not merely offer peace and forgiveness, but He also offers peace and forgiveness in His Son. Thus, He first offers His Son, and then everything in and belonging to Him. If faith is to respond to this offer, she must first unite herself to the person of the Mediator.

3. Nothing but His person can satisfy the truly destitute soul.

4. The soul's uniting herself to the person of Christ will prove whether the soul is pure in her love and commitment in this spiritual marriage covenant. Temporal believers follow Christ for the bread; many hypocrites seek and serve Him and are somewhat agreeable to be His; however, it is not Jesus Himself they desire but rather that which He has and what He can deliver. Upright people, however, love Him because of His glory and desirability, which they perceive in His person. Only that is true love!

5. Without this the soul would never remain steadfast. Jesus bestows His benefits here in time sparingly. He hides Himself and frequently afflicts and chastises the soul. However, the love of a false heart will diminish, grow faint, and vanish, but the upright person will be able to say, "I have seen so much in Him, and He is so worthy so that, though He were to slay me, I shall yet cleave to Him and trust and love Him."

Exhortation to the Beloved of the Lord

Beloved of God, is it true that you are united to Jesus? Permit me to add a word of exhortation for you.

1. Oh, thank God from the depth of your heart and soul that He has made you from slaves of Satan to be His sons and daughters!

2. Frequently focus upon this relationship into which you have been brought, and it will prove to be an excellent means to sanctify you. You will then be able to perceive that nothing but great deeds are befitting for the child of a king.

3. Frequently be exercised with this union, and you will prosper. So often you pray and strive in vain. Why? You engage in this in your own strength and in reliance upon the graces you possess. If you did so, however, in union with a living and all-conquering Jesus, you would detect how strength would proceed from Him to you in such a measure that you would leap over a wall, run through a troop, and break a bow of steel with your hands.

4. Expect that Christ will care for you by virtue of this union, for the husband must provide for all the needs of the wife. Your Maker is your Husband, and He will also care for you.

5. Finally, if you are united to Him and the betrothal did take place, wait then with patience and joy for the celebration of this spiritual marriage when this hallelujah will be sung: "The marriage of the Lamb is come!" May God bless His Word. Amen.

CHAPTER 2

Faith, a Grace Whereby the Soul Is Justified

*Therefore being justified by faith, we have peace
with God through our Lord Jesus Christ.*
—ROMANS 5:1

We find when the angel of destruction went out to kill the firstborn in Egypt and saw the blood of the Passover lamb on the doorposts of the dwellings of the Israelites, he would pass by them and leave them at peace. However, the Egyptians, upon whose doorposts no blood had been sprinkled, were struck by him so that they died (Ex. 12:23). This history illustrates the spiritual truth that he whose conscience has been sprinkled by faith with the blood of Jesus Christ will not perish, because God is reconciled with him in Christ; whereas, the wrath of God will abide on them that do not believe.

The apostle teaches the first aspect of this in the words of our text when he says that they who are justified by faith have peace with God, but the second aspect we shall hold before your Christian attention in the application so that we may flee the wrath of God.

As to the context, everyone will perceive that in the four chapters preceding our text, the apostle endeavors to teach and to confirm that man is justified not by works but by faith. The apostle confirms this with many arguments and examples. He therefore concludes in our text that we are justified by faith and that we have peace with God.

We have selected these words to demonstrate to your Christian attention that faith is a grace whereby the soul is justified.

In these words, two essential matters come to the fore:

1. The benefit of which the apostle speaks—namely, justification by faith
2. The consequence that is peace with God through Jesus Christ

JUSTIFICATION BY FAITH

We shall expound the first part, where the apostle speaks of the justification of the sinner by faith: "Being justified by faith." To speak of this as clearly as possible, we must consider two matters:

1. Justification itself, and what the term means
2. The means or the instrumental cause of justification, which is faith

Justification

As to the matter of justification, you know that we annually[1] affirm over against the papists who insist that this word is indicative of an infusion of holiness or righteousness that this term instead belongs to the language of the courtroom and signifies the judicial acquittal of a guilty person charged with a crime. We shall therefore neither deal with this nor with the various remarks of theologians in this regard, which are a matter of public record.

Since the word *justification* belongs to the language of the courtroom, we shall therefore present this doctrine as a court session, because such a court is truly convened in the conscience of all who are justified. So we shall speak of (1) the judge, (2) the defendants, (3) the plaintiffs (or accusers), (4) the advocate, and (5) the sentence and its annunciation. We shall discuss each of these points briefly.

God as Judge

First, we must consider the judge and who He is as well as how He makes Himself known to the soul. This judge is neither a worldly judge nor is He a man of like passions as we are. He is rather the Creator and Preserver of all creation. He is God, whom Scripture frequently refers to as Judge: "Shall not the Judge of all the earth do right?" (Gen. 18:25; cf. Isa. 33:22); "There is one lawgiver" (James 4:12).

1. God, as Judge, is beheld in the court of conscience by divine illumination *as an awe-inspiring and majestic God*, before whom all flesh must shudder and tremble, for He is a God clothed with majesty and glory: "O LORD…glorious in holiness, fearful in praises" (Ex. 15:11), "greatly to be feared in the assembly of the saints, and to be had in reverence of all them that are about him" (Ps. 89:7). We are incapable of expressing verbally what such a clear discovery of God in His awe-inspiring majesty and reverence causes in the

---

1. The annual exposition of Lord's Day 23 of the Heidelberg Catechism.

soul. However, he who has experienced this will remember it, and we have examples in God's Word to confirm it. After Abraham acknowledges God as Judge, the patriarch exclaims that he is but dust and ashes (Gen. 18:27). Job also acknowledges God as such, and declares, "I have heard of thee by the hearing of the ear: but now mine eye seeth thee. Wherefore I abhor myself, and repent in dust and ashes" (Job 42:5–6). Isaiah was compelled to confess, "Woe is me! for I am undone; because I am a man of unclean lips" (Isa. 6:5).

When God revealed Himself to Paul in His awe-inspiring majesty on the way to Damascus, he fell down as dead (Acts 9:6)—as did the apostle John (Rev. 1:17). Such a revelation and knowledge of God is of utmost importance for man, since (1) in his state of sin, all impressions of God's majesty have nearly been worn away by the habitual inclination toward sin, and (2) this revelation and knowledge arrest and fill with awe the wanton and capricious sinner who otherwise will traverse his ways as a swift dromedary (Jer. 2:23). Everyone, therefore, needs to ask himself, What do I know of this?

2. God, as Judge, is beheld in the court of conscience by divine illumination *in His omnipresence and omniscience* as a God who fills the heaven and the earth and before whom all things are open and naked, whose eyes run to and fro throughout all the earth, so that not even the darkness hideth from Him. The soul thus perceives that it is impossible either to hide or to flee from such a God. Therefore, she says, "Whither shall I flee from thy presence? If I ascend up into heaven, thou art there: if I make my bed in hell, behold, thou art there. If I take the wings of the morning, and dwell in the uttermost parts of the sea; even there shall thy hand lead me, and thy right hand shall hold me" (Ps. 139:7–10). She perceives that God knows her to the greatest and smallest degree, for He knows even her downsitting and uprising with her most secret thoughts even before a word is in her tongue. Moreover, if God is to function as Judge, He must have such omniscience. Furthermore, if the soul is to be cured of her deeply rooted practical atheism whereby a person is inclined to think, "God does not see it," and if all of one's excuses and coverings are to be taken away from him, he must, by the light of the Spirit, become acquainted with God as an omniscient Judge. Such a soul will then acknowledge before God that the night is unto Him as the day and that the sentence God pronounces upon her is both equitable and just because He sees and knows everything.

3. God, as Judge, is beheld in the court of conscience by divine illumination *in His spotless holiness*, whereby all injustice is utterly foreign to Him.

He is so pure that He cannot have fellowship with the sinner. The soul then perceives her lack of conformity to Him and that she is entirely leprous and unclean from the sole of the foot even unto the head (Isa. 1:6).

She becomes convinced in an experiential and lively manner that God cannot have fellowship with such an unclean worm as she, and she therefore must exclaim that she is one of unclean lips (Isa. 6). Such a view of the Lord is necessary to drive a person away from all his own doings, and to cause him, spiritually, to abhor himself in such a measure so that he joins the leper in crying out loudly, "Unclean, unclean!"

4. God, as Judge, is beheld in the court of conscience by divine illumination *in His unyielding justice* whereby the soul learns to know God as a God who will set her sins in order before her eyes, who will in no wise clear the guilty, but who will pronounce a just sentence upon the violator and transgressor. The soul now perceives that God neither will nor can acquit sin without satisfaction. The soul further perceives that neither she nor angels nor people are capable of rendering such satisfaction. She sees that even though God is merciful, He cannot be so in violation of His justice, for it is His will before all things that His justice be satisfied either by her or by another who is able to do so perfectly.

The soul must learn this experientially so that she may be driven away from her last refuge, for when the awakened sinner sees that everything is falling away for her, she will be inclined to say, "But is not God merciful?" In order to strip the soul completely and to drive her from this refuge, she learns to understand the judicial nature of God in such a way that she must desist and acquiesce fully in the equitableness and appropriateness of God's way: If God is to remain God, He cannot overlook sin apart from satisfaction.

5. Finally, God, as Judge, is beheld in the court of conscience by divine illumination *as an omnipotent Judge* who not only pronounces a just sentence in conformity to truth but who also does not lack the power to execute the sentence in punishing the guilty transgressor. He is the mighty God, and when this is perceived by the soul, it causes the guilty one to tremble and puts her into a position of utmost perplexity and distress so that she despairs and sees no way of escape, having to cry out instead, "My salvation is without hope!"

The Summoned Sinner
Second, we must consider the second person present in this court, the summoned sinner. By the working of God's Spirit, the summoned sinner is

compelled to appear here and to stand before God who, as majestic Judge, solemnly summons him. This is a summons that no sinner can resist. In order to examine this calmly, we shall show how God calls the sinner and in what manner the sinner comes.

How God Calls the Sinner

As to the first—that is, how God commands the summoned sinner to appear before His tribunal—we believe that this generally occurs in the following manner:

1. God calls him *by means of His servants.* They serve as His ambassadors and heralds who faithfully declare to the sinner, in God's name and on His behalf, that the sinner stands before God as guilty and worthy of condemnation by reason of his original and actual sins whereby he has sinned against such a holy and righteous God. They declare that God, of necessity, demands payment and compensation of the very last penny of the ten thousand pounds he owes, and otherwise, the sinner will have to be punished for all eternity in both body and soul. These servants of the Lord acquaint the sinner with his guilt, open before his eyes the book of God's law and the book of his conscience in which his guilt, both concerning great and small matters, has been engraved as with an iron pen. The word that these servants speak "is…sharper than any twoedged sword, piercing even to the dividing asunder of soul and spirit, and of the joints and marrow, and is a discerner of the thoughts and intents of the heart" (Heb. 4:12). The words that they speak are to the soul as what Christ was to the Samaritan woman: men who declare to the sinner all that ever he did (John 4:29). They do not afford the soul any rest, but they call out with a loud voice as sons of thunder to make known to the soul her sin and God's judgment so that the terror of the Lord may persuade. They neither permit any delay nor accept any excuses. Instead, their objective is to use the weapons of their warfare, which are "mighty through God to the pulling down of strong holds" (2 Cor. 10:4) and are used to bring the sinner before the tribunal of God.

2. God summons the sinner before His tribunal *by the omnipotent operation of His Spirit in the soul of man.* We can delineate the operation of the Spirit as follows:

a. The Holy Spirit, as He accompanies the Word, removes the innate blindness and darkness by which one's understanding is in a stupor, and He grants the soul a clear and convicting view of her sin and misery. The first thing He does when He comes is to reprove the world (that is, worldly men) of sin, righteousness, and judgment (John 16:8). With such clarity and transparency, and with such forceful arguments that there is no room left for any doubt concerning these things, the Spirit confronts him with his sin, God's justice, and the imminent judgment. The meaning of the word in the original text expresses this and is translated as *reprove*. The effects of such reproof are to be observed in all who were savingly wrought upon on the day of Pentecost. The Spirit especially gives him a clear and penetrating view of sin in its God-dishonoring nature and manifestation. Only such conviction will engender fear and consternation in the soul as well as genuine concern for God's justice and for the imminent judgment. The faint perception such an aroused soul has of sin will readily disappear and leave little fruit behind. This view of sin causes the soul to tremble before God, to smite the breast, and to smite upon her thigh. The Spirit causes the soul to see sin as her sin, which He lays as a burden upon her shoulders and binds about her neck, causing her to say, "Against thee, thee only, have I sinned, and done this evil in thy sight" (Ps. 51:4).

b. The Holy Spirit not only illuminates and reproves but also causes that conviction to penetrate the very depths of the soul with a feeling of utmost pain as well as grief. The soul will then taste and savor how unspeakably bitter it is that she has sinned against the Lord (Jer. 3). The result of this is that pangs will take hold of the soul as a woman that travails, whereas the fiery arrows of the Almighty will penetrate so deeply that she goes bowed down with grief, mourning like doves and ostriches (Isa. 38; Job 39). This is generally referred to as the convicting ministry of the Holy Spirit (a ministry that renders the soul contrite)[2]—and rightfully so, for hereby the soul is pricked in the heart (Acts 2:37), or better, pierced as with a branding iron that penetrates the marrow of the soul and causes acute pain. Such is necessary to render the sinner a patient for the great Physician, Christ, to break the intimate union between the soul and sin and to drive the soul before God and His tribunal. For, says the Lord, "in their affliction they will seek me early" (Hos. 5:15). The measure in which everyone must experience this must be

---

2. The phrase in parentheses has been added to express the meaning of the Dutch phrase "de zielsverbrijzelende werking des Heiligen Geestes" as fully as possible. A literal, but awkward, translation would be, "The soul-contrite-making ministry of the Holy Spirit."

such to make one brokenhearted and of a contrite spirit—that is, if he has come to the years of discretion prior to having experienced justification.

c. The Holy Spirit becomes for them especially a Spirit of bondage again to fear, which, along with many eminent expositors, we understand the meaning of Romans 8:15 to be. The Holy Spirit especially exercises His influence upon the emotion of fear. We find in Romans 2:9 that the soul of every evildoer will experience tribulation and anguish. The apostle states that when fear is worked in her heart, the soul is wrought upon (2 Cor. 7:11). The Holy Spirit also will cause the soul to be conscious of matters that generate fear, anxiety, and distress. We find the same in the life of Job, who says that he had no rest during the day and that at night he was terrified by dreams (Job 7:14). We say to this that the Spirit will continually see to it that this concern neither lessens nor fades away. And although there are some intermissions, the soul will again be so stirred up that she will be driven away from creatures so that she will turn to God and cry out, "My salvation is without hope!" She will mourn and weep bitterly about her condition.

How the Sinner Comes

The soul who has been summoned efficaciously and inwardly by God's Word and Spirit to appear before God's tribunal to give an account before Him is at last compelled to appear before Him. She no longer can postpone it, for she cannot prevail against God. She can find neither a refuge nor time for delay. She comes, therefore, in the following manner:

1. As one bowed down with a heavy burden of sin and unrighteousness, a burden that she perceives and is aware of, and under which her soul is bowed down, all the while savoring and tasting the bitterness of it. She will, therefore, frequently say, "For thine arrows stick fast in me, and thy hand presseth me sore. For mine iniquities are gone over mine head: as an heavy burden they are too heavy for me. I am troubled; I am bowed down greatly; I go mourning all the day long. I have roared by reason of the disquietness of my heart" (Ps. 38:2, 4, 6, 8).

2. With deep shame as she loathes and abhors herself before God and cries out, "I am ashamed and blush to lift up my face" (Ezra 9:6); "I was ashamed, yea, even confounded" (Jer. 31:19). With the poor publican, the soul is so ashamed that she stands from afar, not having the courage to lift up her eyes, and she smites her breast, crying out, "Woe unto me, that I have sinned!" We

are thus able to imagine how this poor sinner trembles and quakes as she stands before the scrutinizing eye of such a holy God.

The Plaintiffs

The third aspect of this court session relates to the plaintiffs and the prosecutors. God will only pronounce the sentence on good grounds and, therefore, demands that the soul hear the charges that will be filed against her. We will reduce these plaintiffs to three in number, even though we could easily enumerate others as well.

The Law

We designate the law of God as the first plaintiff of the soul before God's tribunal. The Savior designates the law as such when He states in John 5:45, "There is one that accuseth you, even Moses, in whom ye trust." The apostle does likewise in Romans 2:14–15.

1. In God's tribunal, the law will give the sinner a clear and distinct view of all his sins. It will show him his original sin, saying that he was shaped in iniquity and that his mother conceived him in sin (Ps. 51:5). It will show him his actual sins from the days of his youth and that the imagination of his heart has been evil continually (Gen. 6:5). It will show him his secret sins of which no one knew except God and he himself. It frequently takes place that the law will take the sinner from commandment to commandment, pointing out that he has sinned grievously against all the commandments and has not kept one of them. Paul teaches this in Romans 3:20: "For by the law is the knowledge of sin."

2. As a plaintiff, the law, in a most emphatic manner, aggravates the sin of the accused sinner, doing so by pointing out that these sins are offenses committed not only against men but against an august, holy, righteous, and awe-inspiring Majesty. They are rebellion against God and constitute an assault upon the Almighty as with "the thick bosses of his bucklers" (Job 15:26). Sin is pointed out to be a violation of the law that is so just, equitable, holy, and good. Sin is exposed as being committed deliberately and with raised fists despite all instructions, exhortations, admonitions, threats, and convictions, and thus it constitutes an act of deliberate disobedience.

3. As a plaintiff, the law takes away all excuses and will expose all the personal righteousness of the sinner to be null and void concerning the

rendering of either complete or partial satisfaction, for the law stops every mouth and renders all the world guilty before God (Rom. 3:19).

4. Finally, the law, in addition to being a plaintiff, also makes a demand upon a holy and righteous God, namely, "the soul that sinneth" is subject to death and is to be punished in both body and soul. This demand is reasonable, for God says in His Word that "cursed is every one that continueth not in all things which are written in the book of the law to do them" (Gal. 3:10).

The Conscience

The second plaintiff and accuser is the sinner's revived conscience that renders him conscious of the deeds he has committed and brings him to the realization that all he has been charged with by the law is true and factual. His conscience will necessarily acquiesce without hesitation that he is a man who has grievously transgressed and owes a debt of ten thousand talents. His conscience will cast in his face a sharp and stinging accusation of all the sins he has committed, and thus, his sins will become a gnawing worm unto him. As God's regent, the conscience forsakes the sinner, chooses the side of God, and demands that such a one may be treated as an enemy since conscience now judges according to truth "that they which commit such things are worthy of death" (Rom. 1:32).

Satan

The third plaintiff and accuser is Satan, who is called "the accuser of our brethren" (Rev. 12:10). In Zechariah 3, he stands at the right hand of Joshua to resist him. He charges that all that is brought forth by the law and the conscience is indeed true, asserting at the same time how willing and ready the soul always was in his service. He lays claim to the sinner as his property to torment and punish him for the evil committed by him. He tries to incite God against the sinner (Job 1). He torments, assaults, and mocks the sinner by asking him how such a one would ever dare to either think about or supplicate for grace, having so grievously provoked God to wrath. His objective is to cause the soul to flee in despair from God or to bring such sinners before the countenance of God with Judas by way of suicide.

No Counterargument

Over against such accusers, whose testimony cannot be challenged and whose demands upon the sinner are just, stands the poor sinner as a child cast out in the open field, polluted in its own blood (Ezek. 16:6–7). These demands are consistent not only with the evil committed but also with God's truth and avenging justice. Were someone to ask what effect this has upon the poor sinner's soul and what the frames and inner motions are that this engenders, we shall respond as follows:

1. The sentence of death takes hold in his conscience. He acquiesces in everything and thereby must condemn himself, so that he must say, "My salvation is without hope; it is without hope!" He pronounces this sentence not only upon his person, acknowledging himself to be one worthy of condemnation, but also upon his best deeds and accomplishments, esteeming them to be nothing more than dung (Phil. 3:8). He does this so comprehensively that his entire soul acquiesces in the fact that, in and of himself, he is a child of wrath by nature (Eph. 2:3) and is worthy to be cast away eternally from before the countenance of God.

2. He neither murmurs against God nor blames Him. On the contrary, he fully accepts the blame himself, acknowledging that God created him in such a manner that he was perfectly able to render perfect obedience. He therefore says that the Lord would be righteous and just if He were to condemn him forever, since he rebelled against the commandment of the Lord (Lam. 1:18). You will discern that we do not insist on a person having to arrive at the point where he is as willing to perish as he is to be saved. This is a serious error, contradicted not only by the Word of God but also by our nature. However, the sinner must come to the point where he exonerates and justifies God.

3. He falls upon his knees before God, and with the psalmist in Psalm 32:5, he makes a sincere, heartfelt, and all-encompassing confession of his guilt in both general and particular terms: "I will confess my transgressions unto the Lord." Oh, he acknowledges that his transgressions mount up to heaven, they are more than the sand upon the seashore, they are of heavier weight than the mountains, they demand the manifestation of wrath, and if God were to enter into judgment with him, he would not be able to answer one of a thousand questions!

4. His soul begins to break and melt under it so that he becomes a true mourner—one who is broken of heart and who waters his couch with his tears (cf. Ps. 6:6). He goes mourning all the day long, sowing with tears. He is like Rachel, who wept and refused to be comforted. He concurs with the words of a poet:

Let it be as it may, oh, my grieving eye,
But let your wellspring never run dry.
As of weeping you never grow weary,
Continue to keep my cheek and bed teary.[3]

5. His soul is most deeply humbled and abased so that all the heights that exalt themselves against the knowledge of Christ and the blessed way of free grace are laid low. He becomes willing to beg as an unworthy dog for a crumb of free grace. He is made willing to buy without money and without price.

6. He is, therefore, made to cry out and to supplicate unto God for grace rather than justice. His confession is, "I have sinned; what shall I do unto thee, O thou preserver of men?" (Job 7:20). He cries out, "Oh God, is there not forgiveness with Thee that Thou mayest be feared?" The soul cries unto God for grace as a condemned person cries for pardon and as one who lies in the water cries for help that God would look upon such a dead dog.

The Surety as Advocate

The fourth matter to be considered in this judicial transaction is the Surety, the attorney or counsel, the Mediator between God and the sinner, who equally promotes God's honor and the salvation of the sinner! The apostle John says of Him in 1 John 2:1, "If any man sin, we have an advocate with the Father, Jesus Christ the righteous." This advocate, in recognition of this wretched sinner's condition, approaches the Father, saying, "O Father, I behold here a poor lost sinner lying polluted in his blood. I hear him smiting upon his thigh. My bowels are troubled for him, and My repentings are kindled together. 'Deliver him from going down to the pit: I have found a ransom' (Job 33:24). Behold, here is My active and passive obedience for the acquittal of his guilt. Is this not sufficient to make satisfaction for the greatest of sins? Thou hast set Me forth to declare Thy righteousness for the remission of sins in My blood (Rom. 3:25). Since, therefore, I have borne the punishment, let My stripes bring healing to such a stricken and wounded soul."

The Surety, having spoken well before the Judge of all the earth on behalf of the sinner who is worthy of condemnation, now draws near to the soul of the condemned sinner and makes Himself known to him in His all-sufficient suretyship as one who can save to the uttermost all those who come unto

---

3. The Dutch poem reads as follows: "Het zij, hoe het zij, mijn' droeve ogen, Laat uw springbron nooit verdrogen, Houdt, van schreien nimmer mat, Steeds mijn wang en leger nat."

God by Him (Heb. 7:25). This awareness brings forth in the soul the most inexpressible desires to be united unto Him. Meanwhile, the soul frequently frets whether He is willing to be her Surety in particular, and therefore, He draws near to the soul and reveals Himself to her in His willingness, convincing the poor sinner that all he needs to do is to surrender to Him and cast himself upon Him. The soul does so in response to the call of His voice, choosing Him and His righteousness, apprehending this alone unto reconciliation, in order thereby to be able to stand before God. Thus, the soul casts her guilt upon Jesus and appropriates His righteousness, whereby she so fully loses herself that she now becomes the property of another and acquires a solid foundation upon which she can live and die in comfort.

The Sentence

The fifth matter to be considered is the sentence that the illustrious Judge of heaven and earth pronounces in the sinner's favor. Relative to this, we wish to consider the following matters: [the contents of the sentence and its pronouncement or annunciation.]

The Contents of This Sentence

1. This sentence does not imply that the sinner is free and innocent from that of which he was accused. No; God's sentence is just and according to truth, for He is a Judge who does what is right and who, as the God of truth, speaks according to truth.

However, the sentence is twofold:

a. God acquits the soul from the guilt of sin. This acquittal encompasses all sin without exception; that is, sin committed before and after baptism, original and actual sin, and sin committed before and after conversion. Therefore, the guilty sinner will never come under condemnation for any of these sins. This first aspect of the sentence we generally refer to as the gracious forgiveness and full and free acquittal of sin. Scripture speaks abundantly of this, pronouncing the man blessed whose iniquities are forgiven and whose sins are covered (cf. Rom. 4:7–8; Ps. 32:1). Since there is no greater concern for the soul than this, there is also no matter of which Scripture speaks so abundantly to the end that all concerns about this matter may be removed. Even though man's sins are great and provoke the very heavens, yet the Lord says that even if they were as scarlet and red like crimson, He would make them white as snow and as white wool (Isa. 1:18). If the soul fears that the Lord will visit her sins and chastise her accordingly, then the Lord says, "I shall blot them out as a thick cloud. I shall cast them behind my back into the very depths of the sea so that they will be sought but not be found, as I shall never again remember them. I shall remove them from you as far as the east is removed from the west." Does the soul fear that new guilt and sins will annul this acquittal? The Lord says, "So have I sworn that I would not be wroth with thee, nor rebuke thee" (Isa. 54:9).

b. The second aspect of the sentence is that the Judge grants the soul a right unto eternal life. The justified man is made an heir of the hope of eternal life (Titus 3:7). Thus, from the time he receives forgiveness, he has a well-founded right to view God as his Father and to look forward to heaven as his native land and inheritance, for according to Romans 8:17, he is an heir of God and a joint heir with Christ Jesus.

2. This sentence is not founded upon something that man either has or can do, for all boasting is excluded, and the man who is justified stands before God as an ungodly one in himself, according to the testimony of the apostle in Romans 4:5. This sentence is founded, however, upon Christ's perfect satisfaction. Paul expressed this in Romans 3:24–26, saying, "Being justified freely by his grace through the redemption that is in Christ Jesus: whom God hath set forth to be a propitiation through faith in his blood, to declare his righteousness for the remission of sins that are past, through the forbearance of God; to declare, I say, at this time his righteousness: that he might be just, and the justifier of him which believeth in Jesus."

No less a ransom than the active and passive righteousness of Christ could have satisfied an angry God. The prophet Isaiah, therefore, states clearly that "the chastisement of our peace was upon him," and that "with his stripes we are healed" (Isa. 53:5). Oh, how precious is the way of grace! Both demands of the law, both to do and to suffer, are satisfied; all the attributes of God are glorified. The Lord, as Judge, has established His throne on the two pillars of righteousness and judgment—that is, upon righteousness as satisfied by the execution of justice upon the Surety so that, to the eternal amazement of the poor sinner, mercy and truth shall go before His face (Ps. 89:14).

The Pronouncement of the Sentence
1. The annunciation of this sentence occurs externally by way of God's precious Word in which the way of justification is taught clearly and is revealed; namely, that he who believes in Christ has life. For all the prophets bear

witness that whosoever believes in Christ will receive the forgiveness of sins in His name.

2. Nevertheless, this sentence is also made known to the justified sinner sooner or later by either the mediate or immediate operation of the Holy Spirit. The Spirit does this mediately when He illuminates the soul to discern the marks that God attributes in His Word to those who are justified, causing them to see these marks in their own soul. The apostle teaches this in Romans 8:16: "The Spirit itself beareth witness with our spirit, that we are the children of God." The Spirit does this also immediately, apart from the marks, impressing this acquittal sometimes so powerfully upon the soul that she can believe it fully and her heart is enlarged with joy, so that she can say with the words of Psalm 103:2–5, "Bless the LORD, O my soul…: who forgiveth all thine iniquities; who healeth all thy diseases; who redeemeth thy life from destruction; who crowneth thee with lovingkindness and tender mercies; who satisfieth thy mouth with good things; so that thy youth is renewed like the eagle's."

We hereby conclude the consideration of our first head [under justification by faith]: the justification of the sinner before God's tribunal.

Faith as the Instrumental Cause of Justification

We shall now proceed to consider the second head—namely, the consideration of the mediate cause of such a great benefit. Our apostle says that faith is this cause: "Being justified by faith." We have shown in the preceding that the meriting cause of justification is solely the righteousness and satisfaction of the Surety, Christ Jesus, who became a propitiation for sin so that we must now speak of faith as being the instrumental or mediate cause. In pursuance of this, we shall bring two matters to your Christian attention.

Faith, Not Works

The first matter pertains to that which is placed in opposition to faith.

1. When the apostle says that it is by faith, then it is evident that he thereby radically excludes all works of righteousness that the sinner may have performed as well as all inner dispositions of the sinner. They are without merit in this weighty matter. The entire argument of the apostle relative to the justification of the sinner makes this very clear. In Romans 3:28, he states and concludes that man is justified by faith without the works of the law. He teaches this also very clearly in Galatians 2:16 and also in Titus 3:5:

"Not by works of righteousness which we have done, but according to his mercy he saved us."

2. As the apostle excludes works, saying that it is by faith, he also excludes even faith as a work, for it is not faith itself, as a work, that justifies us but that which faith appropriates: the perfect righteousness of Christ. It is not the beggar's hand that makes him rich but rather the alms that he receives with his hand. Thus it is here. The instructor of the Heidelberg Catechism states very beautifully in his answer to the sixty-first question, "Not that I am acceptable to God, on account of the worthiness of my faith; but because only the satisfaction, righteousness, and holiness of Christ, is my righteousness before God; and that I cannot receive and apply the same to myself any other way than by faith only." Since the apostle teaches that it is by faith, we therefore conclude that all works (yes, even faith as a work) must be excluded here, and never may faith be viewed in any other way but as a means or an instrument whereby the soul appropriates Jesus Christ.

Faith as an Instrument

The second matter relates to the following question: If faith is the mediate or instrumental cause, how then does it function as such a mediate or instrumental cause? We respond to this by saying that the Lord gives us a clear understanding of this by using vocabulary in His Word that relates to the organs and senses of the body. To facilitate a clearer conception and understanding of how faith functions as such a mediate or instrumental cause, we shall follow the order of God's Word so that everyone may examine the motions of his soul.

The instrumental function of faith is frequently derived from the sense of *hearing* (Isa. 55:2; Ps. 45:11). Faith thus functions spiritually in the soul as our hearing functions in the body; that is, not only does the soul hear the external voice of the Lord Jesus when He calls, but the soul hears explicitly the voice that calls her inwardly, addressing her in the lamentable condition in which faith is to encourage her and to grant her the liberty to take refuge unto Jesus. This voice that God the Holy Spirit accompanies with power expresses itself in words similar to the following: "Be of good cheer, oh needy ones, 'the Master…calleth for thee' (John 11:28); 'Come unto me, all ye that labour and are heavy laden, and I will give you rest' (Matt. 11:28); 'Look unto me, and be ye saved, all the ends of the earth: for I am God, and there is none else' (Isa. 45:22)." The soul hears this not only as the voice of God and as the voice of God to her in particular, but the soul hears this as the voice of God to grant her liberty and to open the door of grace for her. This brings forth adoration from such a dead dog that is called. This causes one's attention to be arrested and one to approve of the divine testimony. It issues forth in a fleeing to the horns of the altar. (Cf. *The ABC of Faith*, chap. 19, "Horen or Hearing.")

The instrumental function of faith is also derived from the sense of *vision*. It is therefore referred to as seeing and beholding (Isa. 33:17). God, with His supernatural light, reveals His own Son in the souls of needy ones. They behold in Him a matchless beauty with an eminent excellence, and they behold in Him an utmost suitability and absolute necessity that issues forth in esteem for Him and stirs up love. Such a revelation causes the soul to choose Him while she rejects everything else, for she can say that she counts everything as loss and dung in order to be found in Christ (Phil. 3:1, 9).

The instrumental function of faith is also derived from *the feet*. Faith then functions as a going and coming, yes, even as a fleeing unto Jesus in order to find refuge in Him and to be placed in a high tower. (Cf. *The ABC of Faith*, ch. 21, "Komen or Coming.")

Finally, in order not to be too lengthy, this functioning of faith is also derived from *the hands* and *the arms*. From this perspective, faith apprehends Jesus and embraces Him as the offered Surety, applying Him in particular to itself in order to become a partaker of the forgiveness of sins in His blood.

Your Christian attention will thus perceive that faith, in justification, is but the mediate cause whereby the soul hears the calling voice, beholds the offered Mediator, flees to Him, and embraces and apprehends Him.

PEACE WITH GOD THROUGH JESUS CHRIST

The consequence of this eminent benefit is held before us by the apostle when he says that "we have peace with God through our Lord Jesus Christ" (Rom. 5:1). In these words we are to note the following.

Peace with God

The consequence itself is peace with God. Since the discussion of this is not so much our objective in dealing with the characteristics of faith, we shall be that much briefer. We all know that the peace that existed between God and man in the state of rectitude was disrupted. This was by virtue of the willful sin and disobedience of our first parents whereby every man by nature lives in an unreconciled state with God and remains subject to God's wrath and curse until he is united unto Christ by faith. Subsequently, however, the soul is in a reconciled state with God, which is commonly referred to in Scripture as peace with God. This peace consists in the following:

1. The complete removal of all causes of enmity—for God, being reconciled with the soul through Christ His Son, turns away from His wrath and anger. "Fury is not in me" (Isa. 27:4). He casts sin behind His back, never to remember it again. Therefore, the joyous proclamation is made to the soul: "Comfort ye, comfort ye my people, saith your God. Speak ye comfortably to Jerusalem, and cry unto her, that her warfare is accomplished, that her iniquity is pardoned: for she hath received of the LORD's hand double for all her sins" (Isa. 40:1–2).

2. The mutual exercise of friendship and fellowship by God and believers. God carries the soul, speaking figuratively, in His arms. He takes off the yoke from her jaws and lays meat unto her (Hos. 11:4). He takes her by the hand and teaches her to walk. He leads her to all the glory and fullness to be found for her in Him as the fountain of life. He makes known His ways unto her and reveals to her His secrets. Such souls walk with Him as Enoch did, with filial awe and reverence and yet with well-founded confidence that God will perform for them and deal with them as a father does with his children. They make all their ways known to Him and unburden their troubled hearts at His bosom, fleeing to Him and seeking refuge with Him on every occasion. Abraham is therefore called "the Friend of God" (James 2:23), and Christ does not call His disciples servants but rather His friends (John 15:15).

3. The quiet tranquility of the soul whereby she enjoys a quiet rest from all the vehement accusations of the conscience that has been cleansed by and sprinkled with the blood of Jesus Christ, which cleanses from all sin. Yes, the soul tastes and enjoys peace with God, which passes all understanding, since the meek will have joy upon joy, and the afflicted soul will be able to rejoice in God.

4. Finally, our being at peace with all creatures. The angels become ministering spirits unto the soul in order to keep her in all her ways and to bear her up in their hands (Ps. 91:11–12). All creation rejoices with her, for the covenant of peace, in which she is included, encompasses the stones of the field (Job 5:23) and the animals: "And in that day will I make a covenant for them with the beasts of the field and with the fowls of heaven, and with the creeping things of the ground" (Hos. 2:18). Yes, they are at peace with all

the godly, since all the godly together are united unto Christ by faith and to each other by sincere love. Oh, how blessed is the bestowal of such peace! This peace surpasses all the peace of the world.

Peace through Christ

What may be the cause of this? The apostle then explains that it is through Christ Jesus—that is, through the Son of God. He has become a Redeemer and Savior for His people in order to save them from their sins, having been anointed to be Prophet, Priest, and King so that He might be made unto His people wisdom, justification, sanctification, and complete redemption. He does so as:

1. The meriting cause—for as Mediator, He has rendered satisfaction unto God in the sinner's stead and thereby merited peace. He is therefore called the Prince of Peace in Isaiah 9:5.

2. The announcer thereof—for by His coming into the world, He has preached peace to them that were afar off and to them that were nigh (Eph. 2:17).

3. Jesus and the Christ—for by the operation of the Holy Spirit, He grants the experiential enjoyment of this peace by shedding it abroad in the soul: "For the kingdom of God is not meat and drink; but righteousness, and peace, and joy in the Holy Ghost" (Rom. 14:17).

4. Jesus and the Christ—since this peace can only be maintained in the soul when she continually makes use of Him unto the purifying of the conscience.

All this the apostle deduces from being justified by faith, and so it is indeed! All these benefits must necessarily flow forth from this justifying faith, for the handwriting of sin that was against them has been removed for those who have apprehended Christ's righteousness; and where the cause of enmity has been removed, there is peace.

APPLICATION

Behold, my beloved, that we have held this doctrine before you with some measure of clarity. Much hinges upon this doctrine, a doctrine taught and confessed in its purity in our church.[4] It is a doctrine that renders the entire

---

4. During Comrie's time there was only one Reformed Church in the Netherlands, which he here refers to as "our church."

world condemnable before God and that exalts the free grace of God to the highest. It is a doctrine full of comfort for a wretched sinner who, in himself, is condemnable, which most plainly reveals to him how God, for the sake of the only sacrifice of Christ on the cross, can justify the ungodly without any of His attributes being impugned. Let us, therefore, endeavor to make spiritual use of the truths we have considered.

Errors Refuted

First, the truth we have considered is suited to refute many pernicious errors and misconceptions, as well as to silence opponents. This truth is, therefore, suited to refute:

1. Popery, which insists that we are *justified by the works of the law*, even though the apostle concludes in Romans 3:28 that man is justified by faith without the works of the law, our best works being insufficient to merit anything, either fully or partially. Therefore, my beloved, our doctrine of free justification is the doctrine whereby the church stands or falls. Since it is the pure and comforting doctrine of God's Word for which our forefathers have sacrificed both their blood and property, let us adhere to sound doctrine and contend for the faith once delivered to the saints.

2. Arminians, who insist that *faith is imputed unto righteousness*. They misinterpret the words of the apostle, for we have shown that not faith itself but the object of faith, Jesus's righteousness, is imputed to us unto righteousness.

3. Those who maintain that man is, in actuality, *justified from eternity*. We do indeed maintain that God purposed to justify man before the world began and that He decreed to do this within the context of time. We can thus say that a man is justified *intentionaliter et in decreto*; that is, he is justified in God's purpose and decree. This is not, however, the actual occurrence of the matter, for believers would then be saved from eternity. Instead, they will only be saved in very deed when they, in actuality, enter into the full enjoyment of God. The apostle teaches that we are justified by faith, and thus, we are not justified until we have exercised faith. Furthermore, the apostle describes the natural state of believers as one contrary to the state of justification. He states in Ephesians 2:3 that they "were by nature the children of wrath, even as others." They were, therefore, subject to God's wrath and curse, as all other men are, which stands in opposition to the state of justification.

4. Those who posit that the soul is *entirely passive in justification*. This error is spawned by the previous error, for if we are justified from eternity

(as they maintain), then faith is not an extrinsic act of the soul whereby she embraces Christ as offered in the gospel but rather an intrinsic act of the soul whereby she perceives that she has already been justified. Therefore, they condemn any fleeing unto, hungering and thirsting after, yearning after, and reaching forth of the soul unto Jesus—suggesting that these are works of the law rather than acts of faith, ostensibly because, in their opinion, the soul is entirely passive.

My beloved, be on guard against such misconceptions and errors since you have discerned that faith is an extrinsic act of the soul whereby the Surety is embraced. This is how the Bible describes faith, and it is best to adhere to this biblical description.

Practical Applications

However, just as we can use this subject matter to refute error, we must also make a practical application, and as such, it can be used in a twofold manner.

Use 1: This Doctrine Applied to the Natural Man
Draw near, sinners, and reflect for a moment upon this truth, so that all the foundations and refuges of falsehood may be exposed.

Self-Examination
Examine yourself, my beloved, where you stand relative to this doctrine, not only as to your understanding and comprehension of the truth but especially as it also pertains to your experience, for that is of the utmost importance for your immortal soul.

Examine yourself whether by the light of the Spirit you have experientially become acquainted with God as a righteous and holy Judge. They who are justified have seen God as such, and oh, what a soul-stirring and grievous sight this was for them since they had nothing that they could present before the Lord to answer one of a thousand questions.

They who are justified have become acquainted with the magnitude, hell-worthiness, and God-dishonoring nature of sin, and so they had to exclaim in the grief and bitterness of their soul, "Woe unto me, for I have sinned!" Oh, my beloved, they who have never experienced grief and spiritual sorrow have also never been justified! For they whom God justifies are the sick, they who labor and are heavy laden, and yes, they who are of a broken heart and a contrite spirit. They are like Ephraim, who smote upon his thigh, and with the publican, they have smitten upon their breast, crying out, "Be merciful unto me a sinner."

They who are justified have also been driven away from all their own works and righteousness. They have been enabled to condemn their very best works, as well as subscribe to their death sentence. They have seen their works as filthy rags and, yes, even as loss and dung. Thus, they have truly understood that by the works of the law, no man can be justified. This has caused them to give it up as a case beyond hope and to crawl before God as a worm, having the cord of condemnation around their neck while crying out for grace and mercy.

They who are justified have become acquainted with the Mediator as to His absolute necessity, His readiness, and His willingness. They have heard the call of His voice internally. With their entire soul and all that is within them, they have taken refuge to the Surety in response to His call unto them and His invitation, having apprehended Him and having surrendered them-selves to Him for time and eternity.

They who are justified have experienced to a greater or lesser degree something of peace between God and their soul upon the exercise of faith. They have experienced some relief from the burden of their sin, some liberty and tranquility in their heart, and have some confidence that God will be gracious to them for the sake of His Son. Though they may neither always have the sensible awareness of this nor acknowledge it as such, they have the knowledge that it has transpired and wish that they might possess it again.

When everyone reflects upon these divine truths and examines his soul in light of them, he will be able to discern whether he has become a partaker of this benefit.

Charging the Conscience

How does your conscience respond to these matters? If you must respond that you have never experienced these things, then how lamentable is your condition if you live and die thus!

You will be summoned before the Judge of the entire earth, and you will then call out to the mountains and hills to cover you, but it will be of no avail. How will you stand before His awe-inspiring majesty? How your knees will then knock together, and how you will tremble like a leaf!

The day will come that your conscience and the book of the law will be opened to testify against you. Your conscience will then not only cast in your face but will testify that you also have greatly transgressed all the commandments of God and have kept none of them. With a strict and equitable demand, God's law will demand the execution of wrath, and this demand will be granted. Oh sinner, how dreadful this will be!

There will be no advocate for you, and no eye will pity you. There will not be one drop of mercy and grace for you, because you have despised them. In the acceptable time, you did not observe the things that belong unto your peace.

A sentence will indeed be pronounced, but its contents will be so dreadful that it will cause your hair to stand up straight, for you will hear "Depart, ye ungodly! Devils,[5] take them and bind them hand and foot, and cast them into hell!"

There you will find no peace with God, but the wrath of God will be poured out into your soul unto all eternity without any intermission. There will be no tranquility in your soul, for the worm will not die unto all eternity. There will be no peace, for your eyes will weep and you will gnash your teeth forever, doing so in the company of the devils and the damned.

Seeking Salvation

Oh, that the terror of the Lord and a belief in the things to come would persuade you to give heed today to those things that are so essential unto your salvation! With the jailor, may you be pricked in your heart and cry out, "What must I do to flee the wrath of God?" We would then prescribe the following means for you:

Strive much to become acquainted with God as your Judge, and may this engender a holy reverence for His majesty. Then you would fall at His feet and supplicate your Judge to be gracious unto you.

Seek in all manner of ways to become acquainted with your sins, but seek especially in such a manner that their weight upon your soul becomes such that you no longer can endure it. Then you would condemn yourself before God as a leprous one who confesses to having sinned grievously against all His commandments. God commands that you "only acknowledge thine iniquity" in order that you may be justified.

As great and grievous as your sins may be against all the commandments of God, nevertheless, do not despair. There is indeed a means; there is, with

---

5. Christ teaches in Matthew 13:40–42 that His angels will carry out that task.

the Father, an Advocate whose blood cleanses from all sins, even if your sins were as scarlet and crimson.

This Surety offers Himself to you in order to become for you the cause of your salvation. Yes, He offers you a perfect salvation; therefore, do not stand far away, but while the Master Christ is calling and inviting you, oh, come to Him, forsaking your own righteousness, apprehending His and His alone. Say of the Lord, "In the LORD have I righteousness and strength: even to him shall men come" (Isa. 45:24). Moreover, if you find yourself to be without strength, then He is willing to turn His hand upon the little ones; He has a mighty arm, and His desires are to draw the soul who yearns for His righteousness and strength.

Additional Arguments to Persuade Sinners

If, in addition to what we have said above, it would yet be necessary to use compelling arguments to arouse you to flee to Jesus, then note the following:

Poor sinner, there is no other way to be delivered from the heavy and unbearable burden of your sins, for salvation is in none other. "Neither is there salvation in any other: for there is none other name under heaven given among men, whereby we must be saved" (Acts 4:12). Your own righteousness and the improving and tormenting of your soul will never be able to reconcile you with God. Thus speaks the Lord: "For though thou wash thee with nitre, and take thee much soap, yet thine iniquity is marked before me, saith the Lord GOD" (Jer. 2:22). Were you to give God everything, even the very best you have, you would not be able to redeem your soul. "Will the LORD be pleased with thousands of rams, or with ten thousands of rivers of oil? shall I give my firstborn for my transgression, the fruit of my body for the sin of my soul?" (Mic. 6:7). Oh no, sinner, for the redemption of your soul is too precious, and it will cease forever (Ps. 49:8).

Do consider that the longer you postpone this, the more you will increase your guilt, and the more difficult it will be to obtain forgiveness. For the longer the soul lives in sin, the more the conscience will become calloused and the more God will be provoked to wrath so that He will say to such, "Because I have called, and ye refused;… I also will laugh at your calamity; I will mock when your fear cometh…. Then shall they call upon me, but I will not answer; they shall seek me early, but they shall not find me" (Prov. 1:24, 26, 28).

Consider that postponement is an indication that you have little regard for the precious blood of Jesus Christ, which speaks better things than the blood of Abel. Shall it then not be just when that blood will one day cry out for vengeance?

Do consider that on this very day, at this very present moment, while you may yet hear it, this Jesus who is full of love and who perceives your foolishness is calling you to buy without money and without price. Consider that He offers Himself to you as a complete Savior. Yes, He is waiting to be gracious to you. Not only does He wait, but He also weeps over you so that, on this day, you would understand the things that belong unto your peace.

Finally, however grievous, great, and persistent your sins may be, He will make them as white as snow and as white as wool, for it is His very own Word that He shall blot them out. Therefore, we entreat you to flee to Him while He yet holds forth the scepter of grace. Then, as a servant of God, we assure you that whosoever cometh unto Him shall in no wise be cast out!

Use 2: This Doctrine Applied to God's Children
You who are the children and beloved of God, how blessed you are, for your iniquities have been forgiven and are covered. God will never be wroth with you, nor rebuke you, for His wrath has been turned away from you, and His fatherly and friendly countenance has been turned toward you—and so it will be to all eternity!

Permit me to speak a word or two.

Meditation
Children of God, frequently meditate upon this truth.

Meditate frequently upon the condition in which you were when God looked upon you in mercy: hopeless and helpless, and polluted in your own blood. It was then that God said, "Live; yea, I said unto thee when thou wast in thy blood, Live" (Ezek. 16:6). Oh, it will cause your soul to melt when you consider that God has looked upon such a dead dog! It will also be to your encouragement in whatever trials may befall you, for He who has delivered you, will yet deliver you.

Frequently consider by faith how all the attributes of God have been magnified in the way of grace so that the fact that God is and can remain just and be the Justifier of those who believe in Christ, would engender in you eternal adoration and worship.

Meditate frequently upon the Surety and the ransom He has paid for you. That ransom price was not with silver and gold or the like, but with His blood and His life, doing so while you were yet enemies so that you may thereby be stirred up to magnify God with both soul and body.

If you have obtained peace through Jesus Christ, always endeavor to maintain and preserve this peace by making use of Him by faith. There is no other way, for sin will always obscure this peace, but if time and again you may by renewal take hold of Him, you will experience that by His stripes you shall be healed.

Keep especially in view that this doctrine must excite you to bear the fruits of righteousness so that you may see how your faith worketh by love.

Comfort

Children of God, let this doctrine yield comfort to you in all your circumstances, for it is indeed full of comfort.

If your situations and circumstances are trying so that you cannot see your way through and clear, then consider that you are justified and that God is to you a reconciled God and a Father in Christ. If He is *for* you, then be assured that though a woman may forget her sucking child, He will never forget you, for you are graven in the palms of His hands, and your ways are ever before Him.

Are you in darkness? Do you experience distress and anxiety, and do you frequently say, "The Lord has forgotten me; 'my way is hid from the LORD, and my judgment is passed over from my God'" (Isa. 40:27)? Then you should know that light is sown for the righteous and that God, at His time, will bring forth light out of darkness.

Here you may be taunted, despised, and slandered, but your name is nevertheless written in the Book of Life. All your enemies will not be able to erase it from there. On the contrary! "Every tongue that shall rise against thee in judgment thou shalt condemn" (Isa. 54:17).

Do your sins press you down? It is God who has justified you! The price has been paid by the Surety to the very last penny. He lives to all eternity to make intercession for you, and the Father hears Him always.

Do you fear death? Here there is comfort over against this king of terrors. If God has indeed forgiven you your sins for the sake of His Son, then death has been disarmed, and you may say with Paul in 1 Corinthians 15:55–57, "O death, where is thy sting? O grave, where is thy victory? The sting of death is sin; and the strength of sin is the law. But thanks be to God, which giveth us the victory through our Lord Jesus Christ." Amen.

CHAPTER 3

Faith, a Grace That Purifies the Soul

...purifying their hearts by faith.
—ACTS 15:9

The Lord Jesus tells us in Matthew 13:33 that "the kingdom of heaven is like unto leaven, which a woman took, and hid in three measures of meal, till the whole was leavened." It is not our objective, my beloved, to inform you as to what various writers have said in their expositions of this parable. Instead, for our purposes, we understand the "kingdom of heaven" to refer to God's gracious work or kingdom that He establishes in every gracious soul. Thus, the kingdom of heaven is nothing other than the life of grace that the believer experiences when he is quickened from death by the irresistible operation of the Spirit. This is compared to leaven that a woman hid in three measures of meal until the whole was leavened. The sole purpose of this is to show that this life of grace infiltrates all the faculties of the soul to the end that God's image might be established there.

We observe in these words when applied to the text that the apostle makes this very point when he says that faith purifies the heart; that is, faith, like leaven, is hidden in all the faculties of the soul, thereby wholly transforming her to be conformed to God's image.

Let us consider the context. We observe in the first part of the chapter of our text a grievous conflict had arisen in the congregation of Antioch due to false brethren. Therefore, Paul, Barnabas, and several other brothers traveled to Jerusalem to extinguish the fire of contention, to make this matter known, and to hear how the church would judge in this matter (vv. 1–3). Having arrived in Jerusalem, they presented the point of contention to this very first ecclesiastical assembly (vv. 4–6). Hereupon, Peter addressed this assembly and pointed out that it would be unreasonable to place a yoke upon the shoulders of the Gentiles, God having bestowed His glorious grace upon them by way of his preaching.

The words of our text, therefore, relate an extraordinary benefit that God had bestowed upon the Gentiles. In these words, we must consider:

1. The benefit itself: the purification of their hearts
2. How this is accomplished: God accomplished this by the instrumentality of faith

THE PURIFICATION OF THE HEART

First of all, we shall consider the benefit bestowed upon the Gentiles who had been converted: their hearts had indeed been purified.

The Heart Purified

The object of purification was their heart. In a literal sense, the heart is understood to be that noble organ that God has placed within the human body to be the origin and maintainer of physical life by receiving blood from all parts of the body, after which it pumps the same blood throughout the body again. In a figurative sense, however, the heart is understood to refer to the entire soul of man, this being a rational entity, endued with the faculties of intellect, will, and judgment. This can be observed in God's legitimate claim, expressed in Proverbs 23:26: "My son, give me thine heart." Sometimes it refers to the faculties of the soul, then again to the intellect—"A man's heart deviseth his way: but the LORD directeth his steps" (Prov. 16:9)—and then again to the will. In all those texts in which heart and soul are mentioned together, the heart refers to the will—this according to the great theologian John Calvin. It can also refer to one's memory as is recorded of Mary that she kept all these "things…in her heart" (Luke 2:19). Even the conscience can be designated as the heart. It is written of David that his heart smote him when he wanted to cut off the corner of Saul's robe, and John says in 1 John 3:21, "Beloved, if our heart condemn us not, then have we confidence toward God."

Therefore, we must understand the heart, for our purposes, to refer to the soul with all its faculties; however, this does not exclude the external man, for the soul or the heart represents the core aspect of the entire person. Thus, whenever the heart is purified, one's external deeds also are purified, for a good tree brings forth good fruits, and a pure fountain brings forth pure water.

Purification

The benefit bestowed upon the Gentiles was that they had been purified. To speak of this as clearly as possible, we shall show you 1) what this presupposes, 2) of what this purification consists, 3) what its characteristics are, and 4) why it is denominated a purification.

What This Purification Presupposes

Concerning the first, namely, what the term *purification* presupposes, everyone knows that only objects that are filthy and unclean need purification. This, therefore, teaches very plainly that the hearts of these Gentiles and also the hearts of all men are by nature filthy and unclean. To deal with this truth correctly, we shall deduce this matter from the following essential considerations:

Adam's guilt is transmitted to his descendants in a twofold manner, which proceeds to them via the normal channel of procreation. In and with Adam, as the covenant head, they have all fallen in his first transgression. There is an aspect of Adam's guilt that is imputed to all his descendants. It consists in this, that all Adam's descendants are conceived and born under God's wrath and curse, subject to all the miseries of this life, as well as to death itself and all the pains of hell to all eternity. This is generally referred to as imputed or hereditary guilt.

We must know that there is also inherent guilt as a consequence of Adam's imputed guilt that consists of the absence of God's image and the corruption of man's entire nature, which causes him to be incapable of any good and inclined to hate God and his neighbor. The first aspect of this guilt is removed in justification, but the second, the uncleanness referred to, is removed in sanctification, by which alone the heart is purified.

Everyone's heart is truly corrupt and unclean, as is evident from the sure testimonies of God's infallible Word in which the Holy Spirit uses various expressions to present and expound this corruption and uncleanness. In Genesis 6:5, God says concerning this that "every imagination of the thoughts of man's heart is only evil continually." Job, by way of experience, was also thoroughly convinced of this when he asked, "Who can bring a clean thing out of an unclean? not one" (Job 14:4). In Ezekiel 16, the state of nature is therefore compared to a child who is cast out into the open field and is polluted in its own blood. In Isaiah 6, Isaiah calls himself a man of unclean lips. This uncleanness is also the fountain from which proceeds all the impurity of man's deeds, since it continually casts up mire and dirt (Isa. 57:20).

Everyone's heart is truly corrupt and unclean, as is evident when we take notice of the faculties of the soul where we detect this uncleanness in all of them. The understanding is indiscreet. Not only is it ignorant, but it is darkness itself and cannot comprehend and understand the things that are of the Spirit, since its wisdom is at best enmity against God (Rom. 8:7). The conscience is polluted with unbelief and seared as with a hot iron, the result being that it is often insensitive and asleep. The will is hostile to God and to His way and is unwilling either to subject itself to the Lord or to obey Him. The affections are as untamed as unbridled horses, polluted with all manner of impure inclinations, leading the understanding and the will captive by the power of the corrupt lusts of the flesh. From all this, we conclude that man in his natural state is an unclean and abominable creature, estranged from the life of God. All this is presupposed when reference is made here to purification.

The Essence of This Purification

Second, the purification spoken of by the apostle is nothing other than sanctification, that eminent benefit of the covenant of grace. Hereby the entire man is renewed after the image of God and daily is rendered more fit to die unto sin and to live unto God, by the powerful operation of the Holy Spirit. Your Christian attention will thus perceive that this pertains to the entire man internally and externally. Internally the soul is purified in all her faculties. The intellect is enlightened, the will is sanctified, the conscience is purified, and the affections are bridled. This becomes visible in the external man since all of his members are thereby made instruments of righteousness. We have already dealt comprehensively with this, and we shall not repeat ourselves.

The Characteristics of This Purification

The characteristics of this purification are the following:

1. Sanctification presupposes justification, for thereby the conscience must first be washed in the blood of Christ before a man can serve the living God (Heb. 9:14).

2. Sanctification occurs gradually. God has appointed this for holy and wise reasons so that the soul will continually be dependent upon Him and will continue to exercise a holy longing for perfection.

3. Sanctification is subject to growth and decline, which means that many must repent and do their first works, having left their first love (Rev. 2:4–5).

4. Sanctification has but a small beginning in the most advanced. Paul himself testifies that he had not yet attained, but that he followed after [Dutch: *jaagde*, that is, "pursued"] it (Phil. 3:12).

5. Sanctification attains finally to perfection at death when souls are perfected in holiness and are immediately translated into glory.

The Reason for Designating Sanctification as Purification
This restoration of God's image in the soul is referred to as purification—as the Old Testament does—for the following reasons:

1. It results in the purification of that which is unclean and polluted (Heb. 9:14).

2. Man is thereby separated from the common lot of men and is consecrated unto the service of God (Rom. 12:1).

3. Finally, the soul is likewise purified and admitted to the congregation of the living God to serve God, who is a Spirit, in spirit and in truth. This becomes evident when we consider the purification of the leper.

THE ACCOMPLISHMENT OF PURIFICATION

In the second part of my sermon, the apostle proceeds to point out how this purification of the heart was accomplished in the hearts of converted Gentiles. It is evident from the preceding that it was God who had wrought it by faith.

God as the Efficient Cause of Purification

First, the apostle directs us to ascertain who is the efficient cause of this purification. It is God, and it is indeed man's duty to sanctify himself, to purify himself from the pollution of soul and body, to work out his own salvation with fear and trembling, and to follow after holiness. One's goal should be that he may be as holy in his entire walk as the God who has called him is holy. It is indeed an indisputable truth that without holiness, no man will see

God. The believer, in and of himself, is entirely incapable and impotent to bring this about, for he experiences that when he would do good, evil is present with him, so that he must exclaim with Paul, "For the good that I would I do not: but the evil which I would not, that I do.… O wretched man that I am! who shall deliver me from the body of this death?" (Rom. 7:19, 24). It is, therefore, a most excellent comfort for true believers that God has taken the task upon Himself to sanctify and purify His people. This is in conformity to the many precious promises He has made in the covenant of grace. Scripture clearly ascribes this work to God. Paul teaches in general terms that this is God's work: "For it is God which worketh in you both to will and to do of his good pleasure" (Phil. 2:13). In Ezekiel 34 and elsewhere, God declares that He Himself does this.

Specifically, purification or sanctification is at one time ascribed to the Father: "Holy Father…sanctify them through thy truth: thy word is truth" (John 17:11, 17). Then again it is attributed to the Son who came into this world for the very purpose to destroy the works of Satan, to purchase a holy people unto Himself, and that "[they] being delivered out of the hand of our enemies might serve [God] without fear, in holiness and righteousness before him" (Luke 1:74–75). However, this work is uniquely ascribed to the Holy Spirit, for He it is who, in the economy of grace, sanctifies and purifies the believer. This is one of the reasons why He is called the Holy Spirit (2 Thess. 2:13). This triune God purifies the soul by the infusion of holiness into all the faculties of the soul, after which He nourishes and invigorates them until the work He has begun is finished and the soul is perfected in holiness.

Faith as the Means of Purification
Second, even though God is the efficient cause of sanctification, He nevertheless uses means. Among all the mediate causes, the apostle in this text designates the preeminent one, without which all others will bear little fruit, for it is impossible to please God without faith. Faith is thus this mediate cause: "purifying their hearts by faith."

Saving Faith
Before proceeding, the following must be noted: The faith referred to here is not a temporal, historical, or miraculous faith. Such types of faith will fill the mind with much puffed up knowledge, but they will never purify the soul in conformity to the image of God. We are to understand this faith to be saving

faith, that faith that penetrates all the faculties of the soul as leaven penetrates the dough, of which we have spoken in the introduction. Meanwhile, even though we understand this faith to be saving faith, we need to consider and realize that its operation proceeds from being united with Christ and that justification issues forth in sanctification. They who are justified in the court of conscience may thus demonstrate that their faith, rather than being dead, works by love (Gal. 5:6).

The Purifying Power of Faith
In order then to get to the matter itself and to show you the purifying efficacy of faith, we shall ascertain how faith purifies every faculty of the soul and the whole life:

How Faith Purifies Every Faculty of the Soul
1. Faith works as a mediate cause to purify *the intellect* from darkness, blindness, ignorance, and sensuality.

Faith is a light in the soul, whereby blindness, ignorance, and darkness are in some measure driven out of the soul. In God's own light, the soul is enabled clearly to behold God, the way of grace, Christ, sin, etc., for "faith is…the evidence of [that is, it causes to be a present reality] things not seen" (Heb. 11:1). The disposition that is now engendered in the soul is such that she must say, "'In thy light shall we see light' (Ps. 36:9). The darkness has passed, and I am light in the Lord." This produces not only worship and adoration but also a most heart-rending abhorring and loathing of self, so that with Job, they say, "Now mine eye seeth thee. Wherefore I abhor myself, and repent in dust and ashes" (Job 42:5–6). This causes the soul to see the desirability, adorableness, and preciousness to be found in all God's attributes. She views them as so many supports for the soul upon which she may rest, so that she must exclaim, "Thou art 'glorious in holiness, fearful in praises, doing wonders'" (Ex. 15:11). This, in turn, causes her to cry out, "Who would not fear thee, O King of nations? for to thee doth it appertain" (Jer. 10:7). This purifies the soul most efficaciously. Beholding His glory as in a glass, she is "changed into the same image from glory to glory, even as by the Spirit of the Lord" (2 Cor. 3:18). Here upon this mountain, their eye cannot be satisfied. They would then desire to make tabernacles to be there forty days—yes, more than forty days! It then becomes their desire to dwell in the sanctuary, to behold there the beauty of the Lord and to always behold His might and glory. How this causes their face to shine as did the face of Moses! The soul sees in the ways of the Lord such delightful and unsearchable wisdom that she must exclaim that all His deeds are supremely majestic and glorious. When there is something in the soul that opposes this, how it is abhorred and how the soul addresses herself, "My soul, wait thou only upon God; for my expectation is from him" (Ps. 62:5). Believers, if you may have some knowledge of this to a greater or lesser degree, you will also set your seal to it that this miracle purifies the heart.

Faith, as an active propensity in the intellect, purifies the intellect from its indwelling enmity and is instrumental in casting down imaginations and every high thing that exalts itself against God and the knowledge of Christ (2 Cor. 10:5). Faith teaches and persuades the soul. Faith causes the soul to see not only her foolishness and blindness and to see that she is as a great beast before God but also to see that the essence of her salvation is comprehended in this, that Jesus may increase and that she may decrease. This causes her to be as a weaned child with the Lord. It makes her desirous to sit at the feet of Jesus and thus to deny her carnal mind, to be taught of Him, and to do nothing other than to ask, Lord, what wilt Thou have me to do? Since the soul knows that her own carnal intellect cannot comprehend the things of the Spirit of God, she desires to understand nothing apart from the Lord's own elucidation and illumination. This brings forth that activity of the soul that causes her to look unto the Lord with the eyes of faith more than a maiden unto the hand of her mistress (Ps. 123:2). Oh, how the heart is purified and cleansed of great evil in the way of humiliation when it is made small and when God causes all imaginations to be cast down (cf. Ps. 19:14) as He exercises faith!

Faith purifies the heart as an active propensity of the intellect, viewing Jesus in His preciousness and desirability as Him who "is white and ruddy, the chiefest among ten thousand" (Song 5:10). He is One who is so worthy of being loved and served. "Yes, he is altogether lovely" (v. 16)! Faith sees Jesus in the promises and does not rest until it embraces Him in her arms as did old Simeon. Having embraced Him, this lovely Jesus must lie between her breasts as a bundle of myrrh, and the soul must sit under this apple tree, under whose shadow she sits down with such delight. When she sits under this tree, the smell of her spikenard and mandrakes will drive away the stench of her sin, so that Jesus, when beholding her, says, "Thou art all fair, my love, my dove, my undefiled, my sister, my bride; there is no spot in thee"

(Song 4:7; 5:2; 6:9). The extent to which this purifies the heart is such that believers then become a "seed which the LORD hath blessed" (Isa. 61:9), and those who see them will take "knowledge of them, that they had been with Jesus" (Acts 4:13).

Faith, as an active propensity of the intellect, purifies the intellect from all the fickleness and waywardness that is to be found within the soul. Faith focuses the meditations of the soul upon Jesus and all that is to be found in Him so that Jesus has the preeminence. Oh, then Jesus will not only be the first and the last and be in our thoughts in the morning and at night, but our meditations will continually be of Him, crying out, "As the branch must abide in the vine, so I must abide in Him if I am to bear fruit." The soul will then say, "Oh, that wherever I might go or stand, near to Jesus I myself would find!"[1] This faith has such a purifying effect that believers who may possess this will be neither moved nor lightly tempted to sin. They neither can nor will play the harlot with other lovers as long as they thus dwell in the immediate presence of their Bridegroom.

2. Although faith has its preeminent seat in the intellect, it also functions as an active propensity in *the will*, cleansing and purifying it from the power and stirring of corruption, both of which reside in the will.

Faith, as an active propensity of the will, purifies the will of the residual remnant of innate enmity against God. Man in his fallen state cannot delight himself in God who reveals Himself as a holy and righteous God. Faith, however, translates the soul into the covenant of grace, in which God reveals Himself not only as a God of mercy and lovingkindness but also as a God who is able and willing to save the sinner freely by His Son, who has fully satisfied the justice of His Father. Whenever the soul beholds this, her enmity suffers defeat, for she must exclaim, "Since God did not spare His Son, but surrendered Him unto death, He thus proves that He is full of love." This engenders loving and tender thoughts toward God in the soul, for it ever remains true that love is the whetstone of love and that the love of the soul toward God issues forth from seeing that God loved her first.

Faith, as an active propensity of the will, takes away the unwillingness to come to Jesus and to buy without money and without price. Thus the will becomes willing to choose Jesus and to flee to Him when faith functions in the will, even as doves flee to their windows. In this way, the soul surrenders

---

1. Dutch: O, dat waar ik ging of stond, Dat ik mij maar dichtbij Jesus vond!

herself to God's way and to His Son. With her hand she subscribes to all things God requires from her, saying, "I desire to be the Lord's; other lords beside Thee have had dominion over me, but I will henceforth only make mention of the name of the God of Jacob."

Faith, as an active propensity of the will, purifies the will, which causes the soul to taste and to savor in very deed the love of God in Christ. Hereby the soul becomes conscious of peace with God through the Lord Jesus Christ and joy in the Holy Ghost, the love of God having been shed abroad in her heart. The soul having tasted this is no longer inclined toward sinful lust, but to the contrary, she says, "The love of Christ constrains me, judging that if one died for all (cf. 2 Cor. 5:14), I ought also to be dead to all that is not God and Jesus."

Faith also inclines the soul to embrace the will of God as being holy, wise, and good in all the circumstances He brings upon her, saying, "Thy will be done, oh Lord. Lead me by Thy counsel. Let me always be desirous, fit, and zealous to deny myself, take up my cross, and to follow Thee as a blind man in a way which I have not known. May I say this of all Thy ways:

> 'Whether they be tart or sweet.
> Let me yet be still;
> For He who is eternal Goodness,
> Makes them good in that it's His will.'"[2]

3. Faith, as an active propensity, also purifies the faculty of *the judgment*, causing it to judge correctly of the Lord and His way as being the only and safe way unto salvation. This judgment thus rendered is accompanied with such power that it becomes a settled determination for the soul to keep the judgments and institutions of the Lord, for she must rejoice in God's testimony more than in all riches. Having been united unto Jesus by faith, it thus becomes an inward joy to the soul to do well.

4. Faith purifies *the conscience*, doing so: (a) When, in the first exercise of faith, she takes refuge in Jesus's blood as the fountain opened against sin and uncleanness to be immersed in the blood of Jesus Christ, the Son of God, and to be cleansed from all sins. The conscience is thus purified from dead works,

---

2. Dutch: "Zijn ze zuurheid, zijn ze zoetheid, Laat ik toch maar zwijgen stil; Want de eeuwige Goedheid maakt ze goed met dat Hij 'twil." From the poem by Jodocus van Lodenstein, "Hert-Sterckte in Jehovah" ("The Heart Encouraging Itself in Jehovah").

and the soul is enabled to serve the living God. (b) When, in its daily activity, she allows the conscience neither to have any rest nor peace by making it sensible of committed sin, until the soul, by renewal and in actuality, beholds the Lamb of God and apprehends Jesus by faith to be acquitted of the sins she has committed. (c) As it grants the conscience liberty, based on Jesus's mediatorial righteousness, to go unto God to obtain mercy, and to find grace to help in time of need.

5. Faith also purifies *the affections*. It summons them to return from all their going to be promoted over the trees (Judg. 9:9). Then their affections are subjected to the intellect and the will, which are focused upon their proper object—a triune God—so that they might value and esteem Him above all things, for "unto you therefore which believe he is precious" (1 Peter 2:7).

6. Faith transforms *the memory* into a good treasury that brings forth those good things that have been stored there. It is here that all the words that Jesus speaks to the soul are stored so that they can bring forth old and new things to relate what the Lord has done for the soul. When faith is not in exercise, the soul perceives that she is confused and cannot lay hold of anything and that her tongue cleaves to the roof of her mouth. However, when faith shines forth into the memory, then her heart will be inditing a good matter and speak of the things she has made touching her King (Ps. 45:1).

When faith thus purifies the heart, the outward man is also purified, but I shall now not dwell upon this.

How Faith Purifies the Daily Christian Life
Having seen how faith is active in the purification of the soul and all its faculties, we shall also demonstrate to your Christian attention how faith is active in purifying the Christian life as it daily functions, for he whose soul is purified by faith will also be sanctified in all his actions by that very same faith. Note, therefore, the following matters:

1. Faith purifies the heart commensurate with the measure in which this is the case, in that *it causes the soul, in a lively and heart-melting manner, to see sin in its true nature*. Faith causes the soul not only to see how abominable and God-dishonoring sin is, but it also brings the soul to Jesus in the garden of Gethsemane, to see Jesus crawling there as a worm upon the earth and

sweating great drops of blood due to the burden of God's wrath weighing Him down. Faith leads the soul to Golgotha where the soul sees that her sins have been the thorns and nails that have pressed His divine blood from Him. She hears Jesus, so to speak, say to her, "Oh, soul, consider how much I have had to endure for you. Consider what it has cost Me before you could be redeemed! Oh, these chastisements and stripes came upon Me before you could receive peace and healing!" Faith then responds, "Beloved Jesus, hast Thou endured this for such a monster as I? Oh, let me not sin again!" With Mary, the believer comes to Him, and says, "Oh, precious Jesus, Thou hast forgiven me much, and I love Thee so very much. Let me then sit at Thy feet, and wash them with hot tears of filial sorrow, and dry them with my hair." The soul now sees Him whom she has pierced, and she mourns.

2. Faith purifies in that *it brings the believing soul who again has polluted herself with sin to see the open fountain whereby she may be cleansed* of her leprosy in that Jordan. The soul comes into darkness because of sin, not knowing how she will return.

The heart will then respond to say, "I sin so continually that I dare not think of Jesus, whom I so frequently grieve with my sins."

To this faith responds, "Yes, if He were a man of like passions as you are, it would be done with you; however, He is Jehovah, who does not change, and therefore, the children of Jacob are not consumed. He forgives abundantly, and He does not forgive but once, but with Him, there is much forgiveness so that He may be feared (Ps. 130:4)."

The soul then says, "I fear that my pollution precludes me from being numbered among His people, for my transgressions are so great."

Faith answers, "Be that as it may, He has come to save sinners, even the very chief of sinners. Oh my soul, how slow you are to believe! Do you not know that the very purpose of His coming is to glorify free grace? Therefore, the greater your sins are, the more the grace of the Lord will be magnified."

The soul responds, "At first I did believe this, but I continually go astray. I become neither purer nor holier, and I fear, therefore, that if I continually go to Him for forgiveness, I will misuse free grace and thereby render Jesus a servant of sin."

Faith replies, "Fear not, for the Father has appointed Jesus to the very office whereby He is enabled to grant repentance from sin and forgiveness (Acts 5:31). Therefore, the more you employ this lovely Jesus in His office, the better He likes it. Yes, He is offended when you do not continually come to Him."

The soul then asks, "How can I come when I have neither the disposition nor a broken, contrite, and humble heart that must characterize the one who comes?"

Faith responds, "Do you first wish to help yourself and then come to be helped? Do you want to bring some sort of payment with you to the market of free grace? That is not the way! Your tenderness does not render the blood of Jesus more effectual. Whether you are hard or tender, the blood of Jesus is equally effectual. Where else can a diamond be melted except in this blood? You will not mourn until you look and come unto Him whom you have pierced."

The soul replies, "I desire to do so, but I am groping for it as a blind man gropes for the wall."

Faith answers, "Oh, do but open your eyes! The fountain is not so far away and distant that you would have to say, 'Who will ascend into heaven to bring it down, or who will descend into the depths to bring it up?' (Rom. 10:6–7). No, it is near at hand. Behold, it has been opened wide. 'Whosoever will, let him take the water of life freely' (Rev. 22:17)."

3. Faith purifies in that *it provides the soul with eyes to see the fountain and with feet to go there in very deed.*

Faith says, "I do see the fountain; I see it is opened for 'whosoever will.' Yes, I see that it flows forth to even the chief of sinners. I hear the Bridegroom say, 'Come…and whosoever will, let him take the water of life freely' (Rev. 22:17)."

The feet are thus shod with the preparation of the gospel—that is, with obedience toward God's command to believe in His Son.

The soul responds, "Behold, at Thy word, Lord Jesus, I come to Thee!"

Oh, the feet now become lighter than hinds' feet, and the soul transcends all difficulty and begins to wash herself from top to bottom in this fountain of salvation. From this she emerges who before had "lien among the pots," even as a dove whose wings are "covered with silver, and her feathers with yellow gold" (Ps. 68:13). The soul is thus washed anew in the blood of the Lamb, and the High Priest Jesus says to one whose condition was as a leper, "I will; be thou clean" (Matt. 8:3), upon which she is cleansed immediately.

4. Faith purifies in that *it renders the soul fit, continually to surrender her heart into the hands of Jesus* to the end that He would sanctify and cleanse her, not only by His Word and Spirit but also by all the means that are employed to her benefit.

The soul says, "Oh, I am incapable of doing this. Thou hast taken upon Thyself the office to sanctify and cleanse Thy people; I do not wish to intrude upon Thy office as Mediator. Therefore, I surrender my soul into Thy hands as clay into the hands of the great Potter, doing so with the humble sigh, 'Holy Jesus, sanctify me, so that I may be holy as thou art.' Oh Lord, persist in engaging Thyself in this work, uniting my heart continually to the fear of Thy name."

5. Faith purifies in that *it causes the soul to abide in Jesus as the branch abides in the vine.* This causes her to bear fruit, for the vine bears her and continually grants life, growth, and fruitfulness to the branch (John 15). Thus, as the soul abides in Jesus, depending on Him as a poor helpless one for prevenient, enabling, and pursuing grace, she receives from Him grace for grace out of His fullness. This means that she receives the one grace to the benefit of the other—that is, grace to strengthen received grace, whereby the soul, being planted as a "vineyard in a very fruitful hill" (Isa. 5:1), brings forth good and ripe fruits to the glory of God.

6. Faith purifies in that *it causes the soul to live upon the divine promises,* laying claim to the fact that He who has spoken it will also do it. Thus, the soul comes to God in prayer with the promise, supplicating unto and wrestling with Him that He would remember the word spoken unto His servant upon which He has caused him to hope. Peter writes in 2 Peter 1:2 that believers thereby become partakers of the divine nature. More will be said concerning this when we deal with the life of faith upon the promises (chapter 14).

7. Faith purifies in that *it assures the soul that however severe the struggle may be in this battlefield, it is God's work in which she is engaged.* It reassures her that she is fighting the battles of the Lord and that He who is within her is greater than he who is against her. It reassures her that her victory, by Christ's victory, is so sure that the saints not only will conquer but will be more than conquerors. Hereby power is given to the faint, and strength is increased to them that have no might (Isa. 40:29). This causes the soul to stand firm in

faith and to quit herself like a man (1 Cor. 16:13), for she is strengthened in the LORD so that she might walk up and down in His name (Zech. 10:12).

8. Faith purifies in that *it causes the soul to focus upon heaven*, that city whose Builder and Maker is God. Oh, when the soul focuses upon this, she is made willing to endure the heat of the day and the cold of the night! Yes, she will indeed be ready to sow in tears since the time is approaching with haste that she will reap with joy. This fills the heart of the believer with zeal to lay aside every weight and the sin that so easily besets her and thus run with patience the race that is set before her (Heb. 12:1) in order that she may obtain the prize, the crown of righteousness, which the Lord, the righteous Judge, shall give her (2 Tim. 4:8). The Lord Jesus Himself encourages believers in this by way of His own obedience. In Hebrews 12:2, the apostle speaks of the Author and Finisher of faith "who for the joy that was set before him endured the cross, despising the shame" (Heb. 12:2).

The active faith of the saints of old focused also upon this recompense of the reward, and the exercise of their faith purified them. In Hebrews 11:13–16, we read of the believers preceding Moses, that by faith they "confessed that they were strangers and pilgrims on the earth. For they that say such things declare plainly that they seek a country. And truly, if they had been mindful of that country from whence they came out, they might have had opportunity to have returned. But now they desire a better country, that is, an heavenly"—that is, that city that has foundations (v. 10). It was this city they anticipated in faith, and God was, therefore, not ashamed to be called their God, having prepared a city for them. How plainly this has also been recorded concerning Moses in verses 24–26! There the apostle says of him in the last part of verse 26 that "he had respect unto the recompense of the reward." The effect upon his heart was such that he refused to be called the son of Pharaoh's daughter (v. 24), and that he would rather "suffer affliction with the people of God, than to enjoy the pleasures of sin for a season" (v. 25). However, his faith transcended even higher. For, having respect unto the recompense of the reward by faith, he esteemed "the reproach of Christ greater riches than the treasures in Egypt" (v. 26).

These are the most important exercises of faith by which the heart is purified. We would be able to add many others from our notations, but we fear that this would be too tedious for your attention.

God having thus granted salvation to the Gentiles, it would, therefore, have been entirely unreasonable to impose an unbearable yoke upon them.

APPLICATION

My beloved hearers, God bestowed this benefit upon the Gentiles, and He also bestows it upon all whom He acquits from their guilt. For even though justification and sanctification are distinct from each other, they can never be separated one from the other. As a brother and sister, they fit hand in hand. He whom God justifies He also sanctifies, so that they may be conformed to the image of Christ. We are not saved by the works of righteousness that we have done; however, he upon whom God bestows this benefit is also renewed in the spirit of his mind (Eph. 4:23). Let us, therefore, further apply the truth we have expounded so that we may use it to our benefit.

Refutation of Errors

This truth equips us to refute those who depart from the sound doctrine of the true Reformed church. It refutes:

1. *Papists*, who slander our sacred doctrine, teaching the blind in popery's domain that we dismiss good works as being entirely unnecessary and that our doctrine renders people careless and profane. But, my beloved, you perceive that the contrary is true, for even though our works are not the cause of our justification, nevertheless, the faith by which we are justified is not a dead faith but an active faith. This faith will render us diligent in adding to "faith virtue; and to virtue knowledge; and to knowledge temperance; and to temperance patience; and to patience godliness; and to godliness brotherly kindness; and to brotherly kindness charity" (2 Peter 1:5–7). Thus we will make our calling and election sure for our own soul, as without holiness, no one will see God. Paul's admonition to Titus is the word that is truly adhered to in our church: "That being justified by his grace, we should be made heirs according to the hope of eternal life. This is a faithful saying, and these things I will that thou affirm constantly, that they which have believed in God might be careful to maintain good works. These things are good and profitable unto men" (Titus 3:7–8).

2. All *Pelagians* and those who are like-minded, such as those who induce the poor, helpless soul to purify her own heart by the powers of her own free will

as though it were not dead in sins and trespasses due to sin. How lamentable it is that in many a book, nothing is prescribed to a man but a pagan morality in Christian terminology! In the final analysis, nothing but a covenant of works is to be found there: "Do this, and thou shalt live." However, the apostle teaches something entirely different here. He says that it is God who does it, not by the power of free will, but by the power of faith. By faith the soul receives everything out of the fullness of Jesus when, as a branch, she abides in Him as in the vine so that she may bear fruit. We do believe that we are under obligation to purify ourselves and that God has a right to demand this from us. However, we believe at the same time that if our deeds are to please God, they must be performed in faith, for it is God who, by His Spirit, works both to will and to do to the glory of His own name.

3. The *Antinomians* who arose at the beginning of the Reformation in Germany, who taught blasphemous things concerning God and man's duties, even as is observed everywhere in *Theologia Germanica*. This error that pertains to God and man's duties very readily was transported into England, where many have modified it to some degree and then embraced it, giving the appearance that they exalted Christ and abased man thereby that much more distinctly. The most prominent among them were (1) Dr. Tobias Crisp, who wrote three volumes bearing the title *Christ Alone Exalted*; (2) John Saltmarsh, who wrote a book that he entitled *Free Grace Flowing Forth to the Chief of Sinners*; and (3) Town and others. These errors were subsequently embraced by many in the Netherlands. And yet, my beloved, even though they pretend to exalt Christ and free grace, they are in essence nothing but practical atheists. Blessed Samuel Rutherford, in his book *Christ Dying and Drawing Sinners to Himself*, has refuted them thoroughly and has reduced their sentiments to a few main heads. He who is conversant with the language can read him on page 574 and following.

For your instruction, I will only say this: These authors view faith as being entirely passive and without any activity on man's part. They understand it to consist in being assured of God's love in Christ toward a person, concluding therefrom the forgiveness of all their sins. They think that believers need not see any sanctification or any striving after holiness in themselves since their sanctification is in Christ alone and all efforts to sanctify and purify oneself are nothing but a playing of the harlot in separation from God. They think that a believer has reached the highest level of holiness when he perceives that there is no holiness in him but that it is all in Christ, thus resting in God's will. He is fully satisfied with the fact that he has no holiness within himself but that he has everything in Jesus. He believes that his sins are subservient to the exaltation of the grace and attributes of God and that it must be equal to him whether God wants to be glorified by either sin or virtue. Thus, if Jesus permits him to sin, He is under obligation to see to it how this can redound to His glory.

I cannot permit myself to refute all these atheistic propositions. I hope and pray that you and I may detest all these abominations. May we believe and understand that we also shall never see God when we do not perceive any sanctification within ourselves. Oh, my beloved, faith is an active faith— a faith that purifies the heart!

Self-Examination

Let us now turn to ourselves a bit more to say something about this truth in accordance with everyone's condition. Consider, my beloved, that wherever saving faith is present, it will not be idle, for saving faith manifests itself in activity that purifies the heart.

A Warning to Unrepentant Sinners

When considering the common populace and examining their conduct and walk, how clearly one will be able to perceive that they are yet wallowing in the miry slough of their sins, regardless of whatever they may hope and pretend!

How many are there who live in all manner of public sin, who wear Satan's livery and boast of such sins that will bring God's righteous judgment upon the sinner! They have a countenance that refuses to be ashamed; though they are often reproved, they harden their necks and, as swine, wallow through the entire day in the mire and filth of sin. They are those who curse and continually misuse God's name. They are those who desecrate the Sabbath, spending God's day in the pursuit of vain pleasure, in the frequenting of bars, and in drunkenness. They are those who lie, who are guilty of perjury and slander, and who are unjust. If the heathen and Turks were to hear of our doctrine and holy confession and were to observe the walk of many, how astonished they would be that such things are confessed and yet are put to practice in such an ungodly manner! Must not it be a matter of shame for Christians that there are more vices in vogue among them than among the Turks? How the heathen, who have subdued so many lusts solely by the light of nature and have practiced so many good things in the material realm, will arise in the day of judgment and witness against many!

How many are there who, though they have departed from external pollution through the knowledge of the truth, nevertheless cling to secret sins and corruptions! They protect and serve them and remain so attached to them as right eyes and right hands so that they cannot be drawn away from these sins. Oh, my beloved, it is impossible to love and serve God and to sin simultaneously! It is impossible to do both. The work of purification begins in the heart, and from there, one will bid all sin farewell—not one sin excepted.

How many are there who, though they appear to have some determination to purify themselves, only do so out of concern and slavish fear for punishment! They see no desirability in the virtue itself but do everything toward their own purification in their own strength rather than by faith! Oh, poor man, you will never prosper in that way, for without faith it is impossible to please God!

How many are there who rest in having attained a certain measure of purification and so believe that all is well with them because they do certain things! If only they were properly disposed, they would instead follow after perfection, and thus they would strive to be purified from all the pollution of both the flesh and the spirit.

How many are there who misuse free grace all too often, thinking that faith is everything! They speak of faith and free grace in glowing terms. However, if faith is of the right kind, that is, if it is God's work, then such faith engenders a disposition of the soul that has a purifying effect and sanctifies the heart as to its condition.

Oh, how wretched and lamentable is your condition! May the God of all grace cause all of you to see this aright, being deeply impressed upon your soul that you are entirely unclean in God's eyes; your soul is as a cage full of unclean birds. Every faculty is polluted and corrupt, and no good dwells within you. Read Romans 3:10–18 attentively, and you will perceive what your condition is.

This uncleanness greatly cleaves to you and is deeply rooted in you. All the water of the oceans cannot remove it. Even if you were to wash yourself with soap and nitre (Jer. 2:22) and with snow water (Job 9:30), you would nevertheless not be clean.

Furthermore, whatsoever is unclean will not enter the New Jerusalem. Let this be clear: God hates all workers of iniquity, and He cannot have any fellowship with them. He will spew them out of His mouth and turn them over to Satan and his angels to be cast into that eternal fire where there is weeping, where the worm will not die, and where there will be gnashing of teeth to all eternity.

Oh, that you would be persuaded this day to consider the things that belong to your peace before it will be hidden from your eyes! Oh, may it become your concern that God would work faith in you to unite you unto Christ and so to be energized by the efficacy of that faith to be made a partaker of the inheritance of the saints in glory!

A Benefit for Believers

Believers, this is the benefit that God has bestowed upon you and which, by the activity of your faith, progresses step by step—that is, from virtue to virtue and from strength to strength until you will appear before God in Zion. There is indeed much to be said, but we shall be short, as much has been said already.

How your heart ought to be enlarged to magnify the Lord and to praise His name that He has looked upon you! He was willing to enter into such a cave, into such an unclean soul. He was pleased to establish His residence there that He might cleanse it from all pollution and conform you to His glorious image, whereas He leaves others to wallow in the mire of their sins! If you could perceive but a little of this, you would exclaim, "Oh, Lord, who am I that Thou hast loved me with such an eminent love to render me fit to be a partaker of the inheritance of the saints in glory!" You would then long to stand before the throne to join your eternal hallelujahs to those of the righteous in glory, exclaiming, "Blessing, and honour, and glory, and power, be unto him that sitteth upon the throne, and unto the Lamb for ever and ever" (Rev. 5:13).

Concern 1: Some may possibly say, "If we could believe and perceive that our faith purified our hearts, we would certainly be obligated to praise God. However, there is continual fear and concern that our faith is not good since we perceive so little of its effects." Some will say, "I perceive so much impurity in my soul, my exercises, and my actions so that I dare not think there is any purity in me."

Answer: But soul, do not dismiss yourself too prematurely! You may possibly have more purity than you think. Do you not realize now and then that your soul is stirred within about your lack of conformity and pervasive sinfulness? Do you not find it to be a delight when your soul is in some measure tender about this and you would wish you could pour out your heart like a torrent of water in wailing and bitter complaint before the countenance of the Lord? Can you say that it is the utmost desire of your heart to testify that it would please God to eradicate sin with root and branch so that you would neither spare nor cherish any sins, but instead be delivered from them all, even though sin often ambushes you? Ask yourself whether you detect any love within your heart for the pathway of godliness and whether you can say, "Lord, I find delight in all Thy commandments, without any exception." Is it not the focus of all your prayers and supplications that it would please God to enlarge your heart in the pathway of His commandments and walk therein without becoming either weary or faint? If you can discern these things, then fear not! The principles that you have heard delineated of this purification are to be found in you.

Concern 2: Another person may say, "Why must I struggle so much with corruption until the very end?"

Answer: It is God's will so that you would continually be dependent upon Jesus.

Concern 3: One will say, "If it is God's will, may I then pray that sin would be extracted with root and branch?"

Answer: Yes, indeed! You are exhorted to be holy as He who has called you is holy. Paul followed after perfection, and your uprightness becomes manifest by your desire to be delivered from all sin.

Concern 4: "I am becoming discouraged, for I do not see any progress in the purification of my heart."

Answer: Beware of despondency and unbelief. Search out the reason why you instead are making so little progress.

1. Perhaps there is a lust to which your heart cleaves too much.

2. Perhaps you strive for purification from pollution without first striving to be cleansed from your guilt.

3. Perhaps you are struggling for purification but not in the way of faith as it has been described to you.

4. Perhaps you are not exercised in prayer, for the soul will function
   as she ought when, while praying, she exercises faith, causing her to
   persevere in prayer.

Children of God, I hope I need not exhort you to purify yourself. Oh, as the dove of Jesus, it is your delight! Let this then be manifest. We have prescribed to you the pathway of faith. Strive thus for such exercises, and they will not leave you empty.

Let it be to your comfort that God has taken this matter in hand and that the time will soon come that you will become perfect in holiness and be translated into glory to serve Him in perfection to all eternity. So be it! Amen.

CHAPTER 4

Faith, a Grace That Esteems Jesus Christ Very Highly

Unto you therefore which believe he is precious.
—1 PETER 2:7

A tree is known by its fruit, whether it be good or evil. For a good tree will bring forth good rather than evil fruit, and an evil tree will bring forth evil fruit rather than good fruit. The Lord Jesus taught this in Matthew 7:20, saying, "Wherefore by their fruits ye shall know them."

So it is among men. They will, by their works and activities, be able to discern in themselves or others whether they are either converted or unconverted. An unregenerate man cannot possibly have the same exercises as does a regenerate man. The very best he can produce is but sour and unripe grapes which the Lord abhors. He says in Isaiah 66:3–4, "He that killeth an ox is as if he slew a man; he that sacrificeth a lamb, as if he cut off a dog's neck; he that offereth an oblation, as if he offered swine's blood; he that burneth incense, as if he blessed an idol. Yea, they have chosen their own ways, and their soul delighteth in their abominations. I also will choose their delusions, and will bring their fears upon them."

The righteous are like good trees that are known by their fruits, for having been grafted into Christ, they bring forth good fruits. Among them, there is no more explicit evidence than the love and esteem they cherish in their hearts for Jesus. We observe this in David: "I will love thee, O LORD, my strength" (Ps. 18:1); in Asaph: "Whom have I in heaven but thee? and there is none upon earth that I desire beside thee" (Ps. 73:25); and in Mary who loved Jesus exceedingly because He had forgiven her much. We also observe this in the words of our text: "Unto you therefore which believe he is precious" (1 Peter 2:7).

The apostle, having admonished the dispersed Jews to "desire the sincere milk of the word" (1 Peter 2:2), shows them that God has established Jesus as the only foundation of salvation to whom they were to come in order to be laid upon Him as living stones. He urges them to do so because Jesus was precious to them, even though many others had rejected Him.

In the words of our text, we observe:

1. The description of the persons of whom the apostle is speaking: they which believe

2. His testimony regarding them: Jesus is precious to them

BELIEVERS IN CHRIST

There will be an exposition of the first part of the text, giving us a description of those to whom Christ is precious: "Unto you which believe." Here God's children are described in terms of the primary and most prominent grace wrought in the heart of God's elect by the Holy Spirit, namely, saving faith. God's people are, therefore, designated as believers. Do not look for a comprehensive description of saving faith, for we have already provided one.

Suffice it to say that God's people are they who believe, for by an efficacious calling, the Holy Spirit plants this precious faith in the heart. He is therefore called the Spirit of faith (2 Cor. 4:13), and "no man can say that Jesus is the Lord, but by the Holy Ghost" (1 Cor. 12:3). Since saving faith is the unique work of the Holy Spirit, which He only works in the hearts of the elect, I wish to refer to it as the faith of the elect. Paul, therefore, says, "All men have not faith" (2 Thess. 3:2).

God's people are they "which believe" because they live by faith. Faith unites them to the second Adam, their life-giving Head, and thus unites them most intimately with the fountain of all life. Consequently, they live and abide in Jesus to bring forth fruit that is consistent with their new nature (John 15:5).

Finally, and most importantly, God's children are they "which believe" because they engage in all the exercises of faith. Let us consider the chief traits of believers:

1. Believers believe with an intense inner conviction that in themselves they are lost, being worthy of death and damnation before the countenance of God, and are thus incapable of helping themselves. The

prodigal son nearly perished for hunger, and the paralytic was incapable of getting to the pool of Bethesda.

2. Believers, by faith, acknowledge their destitute poverty, which compels them, as those who labor and are heavy laden, to go ceaselessly to Jesus as the only genuine and steadfast resting place of the soul (Matt. 11:28).

3. Believers, as poor sinners, will continue to supplicate for free grace and pure mercy, to "obtain mercy, and find grace to help in time of need" (Heb. 4:16).

4. Believers hunger and thirst after Christ's mediatorial righteousness (Matt. 5:6).

5. Believers endeavor to look away from themselves unto Jesus, and, with the prodigal son, they will arise and return. Believers will wholeheartedly embrace and appropriate an offered Jesus so that His person, and all that He has and does, may be theirs. The soul thus leans upon Jesus, trusting that He will never forsake them and that He will preserve them by His power.

This is but a short description of a believer. Should you desire an even shorter description, we would say that believers ultimately forsake their own righteousness, submit themselves to the righteousness of Christ Jesus, set to their seal that God is true (John 3:33) in response to the offer of grace, and thus entirely rely upon the Surety to be redeemed by Him alone.

THE PRECIOUSNESS OF JESUS TO BELIEVERS

As to the second part of the text, we shall now proceed to unfold for you something of the preciousness of Jesus—a matter of which we shall only be able to say the bare minimum. His preciousness transcends all our thoughts, for Jesus is the chiefest among ten thousand, and He is altogether lovely to the soul that loves Him (Song 5:10, 16).

The Meaning of the Text

The wording of the text is hardly obscure, so that linguistic insights are of little use. We would only note that the word τιμή (*timê*) in the original text has two primary meanings. Rather than being contradictory, they mutually reinforce each other. This word can either mean "precious" or "honorable." The text can therefore be translated as "Unto you therefore which believe he is precious," as our translators have done, or one can translate it as "Unto you therefore which believe he is honorable or worthy of honor." We posit that both meanings are to be considered here.

The Matter of the Text
As to the matter itself, we wish to expound these words to you as follows: It is a very sweet distinctive of saving faith that it esteems Jesus Christ very highly. He is precious to believers, for He is their exalted One and their glory. We shall address both aspects of the text as briefly and clearly as possible.

Jesus Is Precious
Regarding the first, namely, that Jesus is precious to believers, everyone ought to know at least that a matter or a person will be precious because of their essential distinctive marks and functions so that the person who is experientially acquainted with him will value and esteem him. This is so self-evident to the attentive reader that he will need no other proof in support of our argument. We shall, therefore, proceed immediately in considering the matter itself. We shall

   a. delineate how Jesus is precious to the believer;

   b. consider what constitutes the spiritual exercise of the believer when he says, by faith, "He is precious to me"; and

   c. propose briefly how faith yields such a profession.

How Jesus Is Precious to the Believer
As to the first proposition, seeking to identify the various ways in which Jesus is precious to the soul, we must note that our aim will not be to address several foundational doctrines. Thus, we will not explain at length how Jesus is precious as God and as the Son of God, as well as how precious He is in His offices and states, and whatever other matters there would be. Anyone who desires to know more of this should read the work of the godly Eversdijk, *The Glory of the Messiah* (vol. 2, p. 778).

1. *Jesus is precious to the believer in His eternal suretyship.* By faith, believers engage themselves in considering what has been purposed in the eternal counsel of peace. They will perceive how God's holiness, justice, and truth have a weighty claim upon a fallen and lost humanity due to Adam's

transgression and that the sword of God's wrath was unsheathed to execute vengeance and wrathful retribution. They will perceive that man can neither utter a word in his favor nor expect any help. They will also understand how God's Son spontaneously made a peace proposal, saying, "My heart is moved within Me; My bowels are moved within me, and I gather together all my compassion. Behold, oh Father, deliver them 'from going down to the pit: I have found a ransom' (Prov. 33:24). Let Thy sword awake against Me, Thy Friend and Thy Fellow (Zech. 13:7), so that they may escape. Let Thy sword penetrate my soul, for 'in the volume of the book it is written of me, I delight to do thy will' (Ps. 40:7–8)."

Oh, how precious He is to believers in light of that transaction! Herein is love that He took this upon Himself for His sworn enemies. He permitted the full blow to be dealt Him so that they would not have to endure it. That commitment made Him so precious to His Father that the Father exclaimed with astonishment, "Who is this that engaged his heart to approach unto me?" (Jer. 30:21). How precious He must then be to all believers! How this compels them to exclaim, "He is 'the chiefest among ten thousand'" (Song 5:10)!

2. *Jesus is precious to the believer as to His mediatorial righteousness*, having fulfilled both demands of the law on their behalf.

He is precious as to His passive obedience. The believer thus views Him as the God-man enduring the Father's wrath, who in bitter agony wrestled with all the powers of darkness. He was mocked, maligned, insulted, and subjected to the accursed death on the cross. He did so in order that by His death He would submit Himself to the threatened penalty and thereby become the fountain of life for His people. How precious He thus becomes to them—especially when they consider that it was the God-man who suffered! For whom did He suffer? For rebels and enemies. How willingly He endured such oppression, being straightened until it would be accomplished (Luke 12:50)! The awareness of their sinfulness before and after their conversion did not prompt Him to retreat from the work He had begun. They recognize that this yields for them the full pardon of all their sins. Zipporah, the wife of Moses, said to him, "Surely a bloody husband art thou to me" (Ex. 4:25). Likewise, the church may say that her Husband has redeemed her with His precious blood, as will be evident in what follows.

Jesus has done so in His active obedience, by which He rendered the obedience demanded by the law—even for them. For though a holy person must obey the law personally, Jesus must never be considered as anyone else but the God-man who committed Himself to such obedience—not for Himself but rather for others. This makes Him precious, for the believing soul perceives her actions as being inexpressibly deficient. However, the soul can respond to all accusations, saying, "Jesus's holy speech and conversation; His sleeping, eating, and drinking; His heavenly-mindedness, and His prayerful trusting in His Father is all mine when I contemplate the deficiency of all my duties." Oh, how precious Jesus then becomes to all who believe!

3. *Jesus is precious to believers, for He is the mirror in which they behold the most glorious display of God's attributes.* The soul therein beholds the inflexibility of God's justice and the impeccableness of God's holiness, as well as the non-negotiable nature of truth shining forth so transparently in punishing the sins of the elect in His own Son so that His mercy and lovingkindness could be manifested to the sinner. Paul, therefore, says, "But we all, with open face beholding as in a glass the glory of the Lord, are changed into the same image from glory to glory, even as by the Spirit of the Lord" (2 Cor. 3:18). Christ Himself says, "Neither knoweth any man the Father, save the Son, and he to whomsoever the Son will reveal him" [Matt. 11:27].

4. *Jesus is precious to believers because of the work He has done in their souls.* Whatever they may forget, they will never forget how He knocked upon their hearts, saying, "Open unto Me!" How sweetly He resolved their difficulties, allured them, and persuaded their hearts; and how all of this transpired without compulsion, drawing them "with cords of a man, with bands of love" (Hos. 11:4)!

Oh, the soul will then exclaim, "Precious Jesus! Was there so much at stake regarding me that Thou didst weep to secure the consent of such a hell-worthy wretch until Thy head was 'filled with dew,' and thy locks with the drops of the night" (Song 5:2)?

As the skill of an artist is best known from his works, likewise the incomparable and unsearchable preciousness of the Lord Jesus Christ is discerned by believers by what He has done for them. Thus, they are compelled to exclaim, "Oh, how precious must He be who has engaged Himself in such valiant and glorious deeds to deliver me from the power of darkness!"

5. *Jesus is precious to believers in having betrothed them* (Hos. 2:18–19). How astonished their souls are that He was desirous to be betrothed to such a poor,

misshapen, wretched, and profoundly guilty sinner—He who is Immanuel, God's only begotten and very beloved Son! How astonished they are that He,

- by this betrothal and marital union, is hers and she is His;
- bestows all that is His upon them and pays their vast and cumulative guilt;
- gives them His infallible Word that He will care for them as a Husband and fight their battles so that they may reside at home and share in the bounty; and
- shall never forsake them!

Yes, even though they have played the harlot with many lovers, if they but return unto Him, He will heal their backsliding and in true love remain silent. Oh, what a precious husband! He is altogether lovely to all who believe.

6. *Jesus is precious to believers in light of the work He is doing in the presence of His Father on behalf of His believing people.* Not only is He preparing a place for them in His Father's house, where there are many mansions, and wielding His scepter to cause many to surrender and to be made willing in the day of His power, but He is especially precious to them in His intercession for them with the Father. For they perceive that they sin daily and must appear before the Lord with defiled garments, and that their accusers are many and mighty. Yet, how it will invigorate them that they may behold this great High Priest who, having their names engraved upon His breastplate, steps forward with His merits and demands that however damning the sins of His people may be as such, they may not be punished but instead must be acquitted.

Oh, this renders Him so precious, for whenever they may thus behold Him by faith, the filthy garments in which they appear before this bar of faith will be taken away, and they will be clothed with a change of raiment, and a fair mitre will be placed upon their heads (Zech. 3:4–5). Yes, in that capacity, Jesus will be so precious to believers that they exclaim at times, "Oh, Lord Jesus, just as Mary Magdalene, how much I would have been delighted with Thy physical presence! However, I am willing to forego it so that in heaven Thou mayest engage in this work on my behalf. I am willing to live by faith and be patient regarding the delay in beholding Thee, for I perceive that Thou must necessarily be with the Father. By believing in Thy intercession, I reassure myself of the remission of my sins even though I may not have a clear sense of it, for Thou art praying day and night, and the Father will always hear Thee."

7. *Jesus is precious to His believing people in His sealing ministry*: "in whom also after that ye believed, ye were sealed with that holy Spirit of promise" (Eph. 1:13). The true believer is often assaulted about his spiritual state and interest in Jesus, for at times his experience appears to him either of his own making, as a work of Satan, or that he is merely a temporal believer. This can cause his soul to be in great turmoil—to be "tossed with tempest, and not comforted" (Isa. 54:11) and bring him even so far that in his haste he would say he has never known Jesus or that he has never beheld Him by faith. Such a doubting soul will resort to her closet and will engage herself in crying out to Jesus. She will say, "Lord Jesus, are my experiences of my own making, or is it Thy work? Is it of myself that I do so condemn myself and acknowledge my guilt; that, as a leper, I am abominable in my own eyes; that I do yearn after Thee; and that nothing in this world can refresh and satisfy me apart from Thee? Was I also deceived when I considered myself to have surrendered myself to Thee? Was it merely presumption that I beheld something of Thy willingness? Oh, beloved Jesus, I fear self-deception, and I find my heart to be deceitful. I know that one can come so close and yet miss the matter itself; and, yes, that Satan can transform himself into an angel of light. However, I yearn after truth within. Oh, if it is still not well with me, convict me of this so that I will not perish with a lie in my right hand. Moreover, if it is Thy work, oh, give me light to see and acknowledge it as such."

There may then be moments that such lamenting will cause Jesus to draw near and that He will set His seal upon the soul, saying, "Thou art mine," convincing the soul that her experiences are His own work. Oh, what joy this produces in the soul and how precious this makes Jesus who so graciously has given such a doubtful soul a fresh token of His love!

8. *Jesus is precious to believers by His blessed indwelling in the hearts of His people*. No truth is taught more clearly than that Jesus dwells in their hearts by faith: "Christ in you, the hope of glory" (Col. 1:27); "If any man hear my voice, and open the door, I will come in to him, and will sup with him, and he with me" (Rev. 3:20); "He that keepeth his commandments dwelleth in him, and he in him" (1 John 3:24). He is precious as the great Lord of the house who continually sustains the soul, His spiritual temple. He protects His

dwelling against all who seek to assault it. He adorns His dwelling with His spiritual presence, supplying the necessary food and shelter, for where He is present, there will be nothing lacking. He dwells there in all His fullness. How inexhaustible is that fullness! All the fullness of the Godhead dwells in Him bodily (Col. 2:9), and out of this fullness believers receive grace for grace; that is, the one grace following the other grace. Grace will thus be given to preserve the graces that have already been received, as well as to strengthen the essence and functioning of these graces so that God's spiritual house may be adorned and every upright soul may be His spiritual residence.

9. *Jesus is precious to His believing people in His blessed guidance of them as they journey through the wilderness unto Canaan.* No one will ever have a just cause to complain, and no believer has ever done so—except when they are in an unbelieving frame. Believing souls find Jesus precious as their merciful Leader. He will lead them with tender compassion. How? He will gather the lambs in His arms and carry them in His bosom, and His care will not be lacking for the ewes great with young so that in all things they will be able to proceed as prescribed. He will never send a cross of which He Himself will not carry the heaviest part. Let me put it this way: He carries both the soul and her cross, and He will repeatedly give new strength in proportion to their new crosses. He will renew the strength of believers so that they "mount up with wings as eagles" (Isa. 40:31). However dark the way of His providence may be, He will deliver the soul. At the darkest moment, He will cause the light to arise in darkness, so that with amazement and astonishment they must say, "He is a friend at midnight" (Luke 11:5). He will so lead His people that it will be evident to them that He alone is their Savior, so that with every step of the way they may praise His lovingkindness and magnify Him to all eternity.

10. *Jesus is precious to believers regarding His graces.* Not only has grace been poured into His lips (Ps. 45:2), but He has received gifts so that He might even dwell among the rebellious (Ps. 68:18). There is a multitude of such graces. There is His forgiving grace, blotting out their transgressions "as a thick cloud" (Isa. 44:22), casting "all their sins into the depths of the sea" (Mic. 7:19). There is His gracious acceptance of the very least they do, esteeming a sigh and the stammering of a child more highly than all the eloquence

of men who have the natural gift of prayer. There is such preciousness in the grace of the Lord Jesus Christ that the soul must indeed esteem Him highly who is the fountain from which all graces proceed.

11. *Jesus is precious to believers regarding the satisfaction they experience when He causes their souls to feast upon all heavenly blessings in Him, Christ Jesus.* Not only do they find in Him bread and water to strengthen them for a forty-day journey, but they will also receive wine and milk, as well as honey and the honeycomb. They may eat them to their full satisfaction, and they may drink of the river of His pleasures and be abundantly satisfied (Ps. 36:8). This is the hidden Manna, a food unknown to the world. It is a feast in which Christ, their precious Immanuel, is both the host and the food that is so sweet to the mouth of believers.

12. *Jesus is precious to the believer in being to them a delightful and refreshing shadow.* Oh, when they think that they will be smitten by the heat of the sun before they can even take refuge under this shadow, how refreshing it then is for them to sit under His shadow who is as the shadow of a large rock in a thirsty land. There they may experience a foretaste of heavenly joy and peace. They will then say with the bride, "I sat down under his shadow with great delight, and his fruit was sweet to my taste" (Song 2:3).

13. *Jesus is precious to the believer because of His excellent love and lovingkindness.* The believer will perceive how love for the elect caused Him to leave His Father's bosom to cross the Red Sea of God's wrath willingly. They will perceive that His love is immutable and that His love for His children does not fluctuate, loving them always and continually with an infinite, steadfast, and eternal love—a love in which He will rest (Zeph. 3:17). This will prompt the soul to say, "Therefore do the virgins love thee," for "thy love is better than wine" (Song 1:2–3).

14. *Jesus is precious to believers, even in His rebukes.* Oh, how tender are His rebukes! He does not raise His voice in the streets but rather lovingly confronts them with their misbehavior by pointing out to them how unbecoming such conduct is for those whom He has purchased at such a price. It is as if he says to them, "Oh, I have shed My blood to redeem you from your vain conversation! Have I bestowed all this grace upon you that you would not conduct yourself accordingly? Is that how you are rewarding Me, your

spiritual friend?" The power of that admonition will be such that it will cut deeply into the soul, causing her to melt like wax and say, "'What have I to do any more with idols?' (Hos. 14:8). I will abandon them and present my soul and body a living sacrifice to Him who has done so much for us, for that is our reasonable service (Rom 12:1)."

15. *Jesus is precious to believers in His wonderful willingness and readiness to be there for His people.* When the soul has a lively impression of this, she will be compelled to say, "I must stop with my sinful complaining and fostering such despondent and hard thoughts, as if the heart of Jesus were immovable. He has been my salvation even before I would have dared to expect this. I must say that these words are true: 'Before they call, I will answer, and while they are yet speaking, I will hear' (Isa. 65:24)." Oh, this makes Him so exceedingly precious! How delightful it is to believe this of Him!

16. *Jesus is precious to believers when He returns to them after a time of some withdrawal and the hiding of His countenance.* The soul will then be constrained to say, "I thought that Jesus had entirely forgotten me and that He would never again remember me in mercy—that the mountains of sin had become so high that He would never come across them, and that I would have to mourn until the grave, seeking Him without ever finding Him. However, wonder of all wonders, 'He brought me up also out of an horrible pit, out of the miry clay' (Ps. 40:2). 'I found him whom my soul loveth' (Song 3:4), and behold, 'His anger endureth but a moment; in his favour is life' (Ps. 30:5)." How precious He is indeed to the believer when He draws near, for "it is good for me to draw near to God" (Ps. 73:28).

17. *Jesus is precious to believers in His commitment to absolute confidentiality.* Even the best of friends will occasionally expose each other. There are things that a wife does not dare to reveal to the husband of her bosom. How wonderful it is, therefore, that believers may make everything known to Jesus. He will never make this public, nor will He rebuke them, for in a perfectly divine manner He will silently rest in His love.[1]

18. *Jesus is precious to the believer regarding all the benefits He possesses on*

---

1. Comrie here alludes to Zephaniah 3:17, "He will rest in his love." The *Statenvertaling* renders this as "Hij zal zwijgen in Zijn liefde"—that is, "He shall be silent in his love."

behalf of His believing people. He is precious to them because of justification, sanctification, and being "kept by the power of God through faith unto salvation ready to be revealed in the last time" (1 Peter 1:5). He will then openly acknowledge them as His own, satisfy them upon their awakening with His likeness (Ps. 17:15), wipe all tears from their eyes, and usher them into the full and eternal enjoyment of Himself. Oh, how precious must He be who has laid away such incomprehensible blessings that "eye hath not seen, nor ear heard, neither have entered into the heart of man," for those who fear Him and love His appearing!

19. *Jesus is precious to believers in His means of grace.* The believer neither elevates himself above the means nor substitutes these means for Christ; rather, Jesus is precious to him because He reveals Himself in those means. In the use of those means, they see the goings of God, "even the goings of my God, my King" (Ps. 68:24). Since David had beheld God in the sanctuary (Ps. 63:2), he would rather be a doorkeeper in the house of God "than to dwell in the tents of wickedness" (Ps. 84:10). The one thing he desired was to "dwell in the house of the LORD…to behold the beauty of the LORD" (Ps. 27:4).

20. *Jesus is precious to believers when they see Him reflected in His children, beholding in them the traits of His image.* There will thus be a spiritual kinship that engenders intimate love and affection, for since they have one Head and are members of the same mystical body, they experience a spiritual and mutual joy, and share each other's joys and sorrows. "To the saints that are in the earth, and to the excellent," is all their delight (Ps. 16:3).

21. Finally, not to add anything else, *Jesus is precious to believers in His return as Judge*—a day for which they long and sigh as long as they are in this wilderness. Until then, it is precious to them that, with all the saints, they have a well-founded expectation. "If in this life only [they would] have hope in Christ, [they would be] of all men most miserable" (1 Cor. 15:19).

Oh, who can explore the preciousness of Jesus, saying even a thousand times more than we have said, and not esteem Him very highly and exclaim, "He is the chiefest among ten thousand!"? After all that we have said, the best answer will be, "Come, and see!" In one moment, this would unveil more than angels and men could express in a hundred years. In having to articulate the preciousness of Christ verbally, they would be incapable of satisfactorily expressing the excellency of this subject.

Spiritual Frames of Believers

We will now proceed to address the spiritual frames of believers that enable them to say, "He is precious."

The believing soul, reflecting on all that has been said regarding Jesus's preciousness, will perceive that He is the pearl of great value, and she will, therefore, sell everything to obtain and possess this pearl. We can observe this in the parable of the gospel merchant. The soul will now say, "Whatever the cost may be, I must have this precious Jesus. I will readily dispense with wife, husband, children, friends, riches, and honor, yes, even with father and mother, and I would be prepared to endure all reproach, taunting, and tribulations in order to acquire this pearl. Oh, how blessed it is to dispense with and depart from all that would hinder the acquisition of this pearl—a pearl that can by no means be acquired in the soul's hour of death! Oh blessed acquisition of this pearl—this precious Jesus, whose value is enduring and who enriches all who possess Him so that whoever possesses Him will lack nothing and will have their treasures filled (Prov. 8:21)!"

The believing soul, having considered and acquiesced in all this, will draw near to this precious Jesus in order to behold Him. Upon getting a glimpse of Him, she will exclaim with the Samaritans (John 4), "O preacher, you have said something about Him, but now I may behold Him, and I see more in Him than angels and men could have ever told me, or that I would be able to express myself. I can say this much: that the half—even one-hundred-thousandth—has not been told me." "This is my beloved, and this is my friend, O daughters of Jerusalem" (Song 5:16).

When the soul considers all this, she will discern in herself an extraordinary esteem for Jesus, the precious Immanuel, and she will be moved to exclaim, "Whom have I in heaven but thee? and there is none upon earth that I desire beside thee" (Ps. 73:25). She does so because she discerns in Jesus a sufficiency and excellency that far surpasses everything. The soul will then say, "To what shall I compare my Beloved, for there is hardly anything that can adequately represent Him. His excellency surpasses everything, for among the roses and lilies, He is the Rose of Sharon and the Lily of the valleys. If I were to compare Him to heavenly bodies, then He is not only a star or the sun but rather the glittering Morning Star and the Sun of Righteousness under whose wings there is healing." He is thus the chiefest among ten thousand. While other men may boast of their horses, wagons, and riders, believers, due to their esteem for Him, will only boast in the Mighty One of Jacob.

The soul will rejoice with intense spiritual delight. Before this precious Jesus was their portion, there would always be something that disturbed their peace and made them dissatisfied. However, now it will be, "O magnify the LORD with me, and let us exalt his name together" (Ps. 34:3), for He has done wondrous things for me, and He has given me that which can fill and satisfy my entire soul. "The lines are fallen unto me in pleasant places; yea, I have a goodly heritage," for "the LORD [Himself] is the portion of mine inheritance," and He maintains my lot (Ps. 16:5–6). Yes, I have more joy than the ungodly, "more than in the time that their corn and their wine increased" (Ps. 4:7).

He who may see that Jesus is so precious indeed will always endeavor to make use of Him in all that renders Him precious. His life will be a continual transition from emptiness to fullness, from impotence to Jesus's power, from poverty to Jesus's riches, from his darkness to Jesus's light, and from his guilt to Jesus's righteousness. For Jesus has been made of God unto His people "wisdom, and righteousness, and sanctification, and redemption" (1 Cor. 1:30).

He who may behold the preciousness of this beloved Jesus will very keenly and carefully strive for Jesus to become more precious to him. He will see to it that his heart will never view anything else as precious and that he will neither cherish nor harbor sin in his heart. Oh, it will be his desire to part with all unrighteousness.

For the soul who esteems Jesus as precious, the hiding of Jesus will be unbearable. Oh, what sighing and groaning there will be that He would no longer hide Himself but rather return to the soul so that she may behold Him in all His glory and place Him as a bundle of myrrh between her breasts (Song 1:13)!

Finally, not to mention other spiritual frames and exercises, such a soul will be desirous that everyone would esteem this Jesus to be precious, and she will engage all her talents and abilities to bear witness to Jesus in all His preciousness so that a blind world may become enamored with Jesus. It is as a sword in his soul that the world sees no beauty in this altogether lovely Jesus that they should desire Him (Isa. 53:2).

How Jesus Becomes Precious
Someone might ask, "How does saving faith render Christ precious to the soul in all that has been addressed?" Let me respond briefly.

1. Faith will persuade the soul of the absolute necessity of Jesus in order to be saved. Whatever one deems to be absolutely essential, and without which one can neither live nor die, will become exceedingly precious.

2. Saving faith, being "the evidence of things not seen" (Heb. 11:1), is the eye of the soul by which she discerns more glory and preciousness in Jesus than words can express. No wonder Jesus is precious to such souls!

3. Faith will immediately appropriate Jesus and will claim Jesus as its own. That will make Him precious. However delightful one might perceive an object to be, if one cannot be the owner of it, it would not be precious to him. To have ownership and to be able to claim it as *mine* will make it to be of great value.

4. Finally, faith enables the soul truly to experience this preciousness. It will say to the soul, "Come, taste and relish that the Lord is good." He who has tasted of this wine will value it and will not desire former things.

Jesus Renders His People Honorable

However, we have stated earlier that our text could also be translated as follows: "Unto you therefore which believe, he will render you honor." We would be able to identify the many ways by which Jesus renders believers honorable; however, since we dare not explore that field, I will but mention the following:

1. Jesus renders honorable those who believe in Him, clothing them with His glory whereby they are made perfect in beauty (Ezek. 16:14) as "the saints that are in the earth, and…the excellent" (Ps. 16:3). Israel was perfect in her beauty by Messiah's comeliness that He had put upon her. Jesus will always clothe His people with an all-surpassing beauty so that all who observe them will recognize in them the disposition of Jesus. That disposition will manifest itself in steadfastness, reverence, uprightness, humility, and a determination to do God's will.

2. Jesus will render those who believe in Him honorable by uniting them, so to speak, to a glorious family, for to all who believe in Him, He gives power to become the sons of God (John 1:12). His Father is their God and Father in Christ Jesus (John 20:17).

3. Jesus will render those who believe in Him honorable by clothing them with His glorious garments, that is, the garments of salvation and the robe of righteousness (Isa. 61:10). The queen stands before the King in the gold of Ophir and raiment of needlework and clothing of wrought gold (Ps. 45:9–14).

4. Jesus will render those who believe in Him honorable by appointing them to special and honorable offices. Do you wish to know what they are? He will transform them into "a royal priesthood, an holy nation, a peculiar people; that [they] should shew forth the praises of him who hath called [them] out of darkness into his marvellous light" (1 Peter 2:9).

We could yet add additional matters. However, for fear of becoming too elaborate, we shall for brevity's sake forego them.

APPLICATION

Having considered, my beloved, that Jesus is very precious to believers, it has yielded many marks whereby we may truly know, by the fruits, whether we are believers. Let us, therefore, proceed by considering how we may use this.

Self-Examination

If everyone were now to examine himself, how many will perceive that they miss the root of the matter of salvation!

1. If Jesus is precious to you, you will have become acquainted clearly and sensibly with your state of misery and will have seen the absolute necessity of Jesus by the light of the Holy Spirit. One will never esteem a matter or a person unless one views it or him as indispensable. People may say that one should love Jesus for His own sake when considering the excellent glory and incomparable preciousness of His person. I am confident that neither of these two will ever be rightly perceived and known by anyone other than they who are experientially acquainted with their misery. One may presumptuously hear and speak with delight, emotion, and amazement about Jesus and all that is said of Him by the prophets and evangelists. This is similar to people reading about the life, actions, and incidents regarding a great king or general. Since, however, they do not find themselves in distressful circumstances, they will not call upon them. Such is also the case here. No one, however much he may adore and find delight in Jesus, will ever rightfully make use of Him unless he labors and is heavy-laden, perceiving that none but Jesus can give him rest. What is your response to this? Should many not conclude that Jesus has never been truly precious to them, because they have never been concerned, and their misery has never truly weighed them down?

2. If Jesus is precious to you, you will have become acquainted with Him by the light of the Holy Spirit. You will not merely have acquiesced in

your intellectual perception of Jesus; rather, Jesus will have revealed Himself to you, so that you will have been compelled to exclaim, "The half of His preciousness has not been told me!" Oh, my beloved, you need to examine yourself, for unknown means unloved.

3. If Jesus is precious to you, you will have laid the hand of faith upon Him to embrace Him and appropriate Him, and to apply Him to your soul unto wisdom, justification, and sanctification. Only when something is our own will it be precious. What benefit do we derive from seeing beautiful things if we cannot say, "They are beautiful, and they are mine. I am a partaker of them."

4. If Jesus is precious to you, you will not be able to live without Him. If He hides Himself, your heart will mourn after Him. You will hunger after Him and will thirst for His communion more than a "hart panteth after the water brooks" (Ps. 42:1). You will esteem Him so highly that you will count all other things to be "but dung" (Phil. 3:8).

5. If Jesus is precious to you, you will frequently make use of Him. You will continually resort to Him and surrender yourself to Him, and you will continually beseech Him to perform His mediatorial ministry within you.

Reflection

Lamentation over the State of Most People
When we consider all these things, the majority will perceive themselves to be void of them, and the very opposite will be true for many. How many are there not who are insensitive and hardened, and who are "rich, and increased with goods, and have need of nothing" (Rev. 3:17)? How many ignorant souls are there not who do not know Jesus and consequently do not desire Him, and who instead are at peace even when they are living apart from Him? How many are there not for whom temporal things are of far higher value than Jesus? We may rightly lament about many that they see no beauty in Him that they should desire Him (Isa. 53:2).

Appeal to the Lost
Oh, my beloved, that you would only discern your misery and that your hearts would be inclined toward Jesus, and that you would forsake all that is vain and become enamored with Jesus! What abundant reason is there that it should be so!

Jesus is the Savior, and you are a sinner. Jesus has everything that will make you happy for time and eternity. Jesus is the Object of admiration for angels and all believers. How grievous it is, therefore, that you do not deem Him to be such a precious Jesus by believing in Him!

Direction for God's Children

Children of God, you are believers unto whom Jesus is precious. You may often have doubts about this because you do not always discern the heart-felt and lively exercises of your heart. However, you should instead judge your spiritual state by your perception and sensitivity to what you are lacking and by your dissatisfaction that you do not love Jesus more heartily than you do. The natural man is never concerned about whether he loves Jesus. You should, therefore, recognize that you genuinely cherish and esteem Jesus above all else. Thus, having heard what the marks are of all to whom Jesus is precious, let me encourage you.

Believers, endeavor first and foremost to have a greater measure of the Spirit of faith so that He may strengthen your faith by working efficaciously in your hearts. As a helpless one, let your soul frequently be open to the breath of the Spirit while quietly groaning, "Awake, O north wind; and come, thou south; blow upon my garden" (Song 4:16). Faith is that grace that will enable you to love Jesus fervently, for "faith…worketh by love" (Gal. 5:6).

Believers, if you are somewhat sluggish, frequently meditate upon all that pertains to Jesus, considering all that He has suffered and done—and what He is still willing to do. This may again set your hearts aflame and stir up your souls.

Be leery of anything that would cause a separation between Jesus and your soul, for sins will have a deadening effect upon you, and the light of faith will thereby be obscured. You will then be incapable of seeing the preciousness that is in Jesus. "These things write I unto you, that ye sin not" (1 John 2:1). Oh, all who love the Lord, hate evil, and do not let sin reign in your mortal bodies (Rom. 6:12)—you are the temples of the Holy Spirit (1 Cor. 3:16).

If Jesus hides Himself for holy and wise reasons, beware of harboring hard thoughts toward Him, doubting whether He loves you, for whom He loves, He loves "unto the end" (John 13:1). Certainly, one of the signs of true love is to love a person in his absence—to esteem him highly, to long for his coming more intensely than a hart after the water brooks.

Comfort

Lovers of Jesus, let this truth comfort you amidst all of the scorn, harm, and slander to which the world subjects you. They may view you as a despised and smoking flax, saying, "This is Zion, whom no man seeketh after" (Jer. 30:17). Oh, the Jesus in whom you believe is honorable and glorious so that, in comparison, all that is of this world amounts to nothing. Comfort yourself with this: If Jesus is precious to you, you are also precious to Him. He will set you as a seal upon His heart and upon His arm (Song 8:7), and you are graven upon both palms of His hands. He will never rest until He has brought you into His Father's house in which there are many mansions (John 14:2), where you will see Him and know Him as He is. Amen.

CHAPTER 5

Faith, a Grace That Causes the Soul to Enter into True Rest

For we which have believed do enter into rest.
—HEBREWS 4:3

Everything has an innate tendency to gravitate toward a given center or focal point, and apart from any further impetus, it would remain there. With your indulgence, we would be able to affirm this in the physical realm. However, this truth is also transparent and discernible in the spiritual realm. God, in Christ, is the sole focal point of spiritual rest. He who cannot arrive at such stability will be as one being tossed with tempest and as one who labors and is heavy laden—one incapable of finding rest or genuine comfort. Our objective, therefore, will be to set before you the essential activity whereby the soul attains a spiritual equilibrium, namely, by faith. Faith is the grace whereby one enters into God's rest. The apostle teaches this in our text, saying, "For we which have believed do enter into rest."

In verse fifteen of the previous chapter, the apostle exhorted believers that they are obliged to believe and to embrace the salvation offered to them. He then proceeds to show them the dreadfulness of unbelief. Thus, having exhorted believers to embrace the promise of the gospel by true faith, he sets before them in our text the consequences of such faith, namely, that he, and all who have exercised it, will enter into rest.

In these words, the apostle speaks of this rest, designating it as

1. God's rest and
2. that into which only believers enter by faith.

GOD'S REST

We will expound that part of the text in which the apostle speaks of the glorious state into which believers enter by the lively exercise and activity of saving faith. He designates this state as a state of rest—as God's rest.

The great matter addressed here by the apostle is the rest into which believers enter. The word *rest* has various meanings. Sometimes it designates a cessation of a work with which the believer had been occupied. God rested in that sense on the seventh day (Gen. 2:2–3). Sometimes it designates a state of external peace and prosperity following a period of intense battle and fatigue. Israel rested in that sense when it entered into the land of Canaan. Sometimes it designates the blessed peace and delight found in Christ when the soul exercises faith (Matt. 11:28). Sometimes it designates the blessed state of the perfectly just residents of heaven where they rest from their labors (Rev. 14:13). Bible expositors are not of one mind what we are to understand by the word *rest* in our text. Some believe that we must understand this to be the rest of heaven. We would rather side with Dr. John Owen, who understands the rest of which the apostle is speaking as the blessed rest, peace, and joy experienced by believers upon the exercise of faith. Since one can read for himself the very learned exposition and affirmation of this truth by this godly author, we will not quote him here.

Regarding the matter itself, namely, the rest into which the soul enters by faith, we shall consider the following.

The State of Restlessness

What is implied is that a person who does not receive and appropriate Jesus by faith will be in a state of unrest.

We will demonstrate this by clearly describing three types of people, so that you, my beloved, would be made all the more desirous for the true rest to be found in God through Christ Jesus as He is set forth and offered in the gospel.

Spiritually Careless Unbelievers

The first category of people whose state is a state of unrest, being strangers of God in Christ, are all who live carelessly in their natural state. Since they still enjoy and possess so many external blessings, they live without inner turmoil.

1. That they lead very restless lives manifests itself in *the perpetually restless motion and vanity of their thoughts*. Rightfully we may say of them that vain

thoughts lodge within them (Jer. 4:14) and that they thus experience continual inner turmoil. They feed on ashes (Isa. 44:20), looking after the things of outward appearance (2 Cor. 10:7). They snort the wind like a wild ass, and that will puff them up with pride and all manner of imagination, evil lusts, and desires. They will stir each other up to yield to one of these lusts and desires, causing great inner turmoil. The poor sinner will thus be like "raging waves of the sea" (Jude 13), propelled by all manner of wind.

2. This restlessness also manifests itself in *the dissatisfaction and frustration they experience in all that they do*. Since such a man lives without God (though being unaware of this), the moisture of all that should refresh and satisfy him has been turned into the drought of summer (Ps. 32:4). That which delights him today will the next day be to him as tasteless as the white of an egg (Job 6:6). Whatever is new will quickly be old and worn out. He must immediately have something else, for his heart is like the grave that continually cries, "Give," without ever being satisfied (Ps. 30:15–16). This explains his dissatisfaction with his lot, with that which God has bestowed upon him, and with his station in life. He will be envious of the station and circumstances of others. He will, therefore, be plotting continually how he can alter his station in life, the company he keeps, the clothes he wears, the food he eats, and the things that entertain him so that, if possible, he could find yet another way to gratify his lusts and desires even more. In the end, he will discover that either they do not satisfy him, or that they do so only for a moment. A common proverb is that man lives by change. However, it is equally true that the restlessness and dissatisfaction of his heart propel this. How very evident that as yet he has not experienced the true rest to be found in God and Christ!

3. The restlessness of natural men is also evident in that they are continually *anxious about what they might lose or have to miss* and that, ultimately, they will come to poverty. In some, this restlessness can be so intense that the least disturbance will prompt them to think that someone will kill them for their possessions. They cannot trust anyone, and they are fearful of interacting with others as they seek to make a living. They will torment themselves and others with thousands of similar issues, thereby vividly affirming that they do not rest in God and His providence.

4. This restlessness also manifests itself in that natural men are *fearful of actual or potential disasters* that might afflict them, and thus they will experience

neither rest nor peace amid all their joy. "There is no peace, saith my God, to the wicked" (Isa. 57:21).

5. Finally, however favorable all things may appear to natural men, they will be in a state of unrest because they cannot get beyond *the men and circumstances they envy.* As a worm, it will consume everything else and will cause the soul to languish. Haman clearly illustrates this. Though he had everything his heart could desire, there was a Mordecai who refused to bow before him that stood in his way. This rendered all that he possessed as useless.

People in Legal Bondage
This restlessness of the natural man is superseded, however, by the restlessness of man who is in legal bondage—a man who has been awakened by the law from his careless slumber. This demands special consideration, for the rest engendered by the gospel must here be contrasted with a state of utter restlessness under the law.

1. The *awareness of sin* will render this state to be one of great unrest. Viewing herself in the mirror of the law, the soul will clearly and vividly perceive her pollution and deformity. She will be led from commandment to commandment, from one stage of her life to another, and from her actual sin to her bosom sin. She will thereby readily conclude that she owes ten thousand talents. She will discover her guilt in the book of God's Word and the book of her conscience. As she perceives her guilt, she will recognize that she does not have a single penny in payment for her comprehensive debt. Since the Mediator is still not in view for her, that perception cannot but cause her to be exceedingly restless.

2. This state of legal bondage is restless due to *the gnawing rebuke of conscience* regarding all the sins she has committed. God's Word compares this to a "worm that dieth not" (Mark 9:44) and the piercing of the heart with a hot iron (Heb. 4:12). The heart is thus pricked in the extraordinarily painful manner articulated in the original language of Acts 2:37. It transforms a man's conscience into a torturer that torments and scourges him every moment, giving him no reprieve. Day and night, the conscience of such a poor man will trouble, tyrannize, and oppress his soul. He will experience pain and sorrow that exceeds the sorrow of a woman giving birth. What do I say? It will far exceed all bodily pain, even if a man were to experience them

all simultaneously. In that state of mind, God's fiery arrows will penetrate the soul, and their fiery venom will so oppress and antagonize the spirit that a man will be at a loss as to where to find refuge. One must not think that only notorious sinners will experience this. Rather, my beloved, a single sin that is bound upon the heart, resulting in a gnawing conscience, can cause this.

I must recount the story of a Mr. Peacock, a man of God, who, on his deathbed, was reflecting on his life. He was a man whose godliness was eminent, tender, and exemplary. Nevertheless, when his perceived neglect of duty and spiritual dullness in the company of others agitated his heart, his conscience so tormented him that he exclaimed, "These have ignited a hell in my soul!" Then there would be other times that with inexpressible groanings he would cry out, "Woe is me! Oh how wretched I am! The burden of my sin weighs so heavily upon my soul that I am being pressed into the lowest hell." Those who stood around his bed asked whether they should pray for him, to which he replied, "Oh, do not desecrate God's precious name by supplicating for such a one as I am."

In his *Book of Martyrs*, John Foxe recounts the story of Mr. Glover, an eminent man of tender godliness. Upon perceiving that his love for God had cooled somewhat, he endured five years of inexpressible sorrow. Fear prevented him from eating and drinking, doing so purely to delay his anticipated damnation. Therefore, he looked like a skeleton when Mr. Foxe spoke to him.

The psalmist, being acquainted with this, writes, "My bones waxed old through my roaring all the day long" (Ps. 32:3).

I am recounting these incidents to affirm what I have been saying, and that many may be exposed and caused to fear who, though they have no use for fellowship with God, can rectify everything by an imaginary faith.

You who are careless, be assured that God has an arrow that can still strike you. If such eminent saints have endured such storms, what must you then anticipate? Do not respond by saying that these were legalistic Christians. Believe me when I say that a faith that can so readily resolve everything without first having been humbled before God, and without a subsequent tender holiness, is not the faith of God's elect. This will show a child of God what he can generally expect when he backslides.

3. The experience of many, fearful, *disturbing thoughts* will fuel the restlessness of this state of mind. Sometimes the enemy will inject the most fearful thoughts in his heart, insinuating that there is no God. When Satan perceives

that this does not accomplish anything (for the inner agitation continues), he will try to persuade a man that the Bible is not God's Word. His objective is to cause men to doubt all revealed divine truths and whether there is either a heaven or a hell.

When he cannot achieve this due to God's overruling power, he will inject grievous thoughts regarding the Almighty Himself by accusing Him of having created such a world and such a humanity, and that He is a ruthless and austere God. Such thoughts will, at times, cause people to wish that they had never been born, or that they might be an irrational animal rather than a human being. Exercised souls have been subject to this.

The enemy can also inject thoughts to persuade a poor man that everyone is familiar with his misdeeds, however hidden they may be, causing such a person to suspect that the whole world is ready to declare war on him, being of the same mind as Cain that whoever finds him will kill him. Experience teaches that some will be so fearful that they break out in cold sweat when they even remotely encounter either a judge or an officer of the law, even though only God and they know of their misdeeds. They will think that the ringing of a doorbell or a knock on the door means that they will be arrested. The intensity can be such that they will be terrified at night in their dreams. Many have even surrendered themselves to a civil judge, although they had not committed any crimes for which they could be sentenced. We know from experience that some will experience such anxiety both before and after conversion.

4. Such a state will be one of utmost restlessness due to the multifaceted distress such a person experiences regarding his sins. He not only sees them with a gnawing conscience and in light of numerous suggestive thoughts but also with *unspeakable anxiety*. Paul teaches this expressly in Romans 2:9: "Tribulation and anguish, upon every soul of man that doeth evil, of the Jew first, and also of the Gentile." He will be assaulted from every angle so that he can do nothing else but be fearful of God and man and his impending doom. Such extreme bondage will cause the soul to be "afflicted and ready to die from [his] youth up" (Ps. 88:15), causing the soul to be troubled when she remembers God (Ps. 77:3). The heart can then be so preoccupied with such terrifying thoughts and objects, that it bears more resemblance to one upon whom judgment has already been executed than one who is still in the land of the living.

Such anxiety is evident in David as a type of the Messiah: "The sorrows of death compassed me, and the floods of ungodly men made me afraid. The sorrows of hell compassed me about: the snares of death prevented me" (Ps. 18:4–5).

5. Such a state will be one of utmost restlessness due to *a lively and clear discovery of God's inflexible justice*. When a soul finds herself in such circumstances, she will not readily ask, "Is not God then also merciful?" (Heidelberg Catechism 11). God's attribute of mercy will generally be so hidden that the poor sinner appears to know nothing else about God except His inflexible and vindictive justice. The impression upon the awakened conscience will be such that the soul will perceive that God would not be God unless He would punish sin (Ps. 50:21–22). Consequently, such a soul will lose all ground under her feet. Her tearful prayers and attempts at self-improvement in order to appease God will utterly fail, and she will be more troubled than ever before. She will taste and perceive how bitter and grievous it is to sin against the Lord.

6. Such a state will be one of utmost restlessness because the enemy, Satan, will, in every conceivable way, *insinuate that deliverance is entirely impossible*. I will readily admit that many of the elect, while in such a state, still entertain a quiet hope of escape. However, experience teaches that also many, and very many, will exclaim, "There is no hope; there is no hope" (cf. Jer. 2:25). All of the above will compel the soul to engage in duty upon duty so that, if possible, she could appease God. However, when any such expectation has been cut off entirely, the enemy will then attempt to get such a poor soul to cease and desist entirely and to keep him, if possible, eternally apart from Christ as the only true rest.

7. Such a state will be one of utmost restlessness, for the soul, due to all her anxiety and tribulation, will be *unreceptive to the comfort of the gospel*. As is often true for God's church, they refuse to be comforted (Gen. 37:25; Ps. 77:2; Jer. 31:15). God's comfort will appear so minimal to them that, instead of taking note of it, their anxiety may even be significantly increased and intensified when they hear of the free offer of grace and the fullness to be found in Christ for the most wretched sinner. They will then think that God's justice is not sufficiently highlighted when His mercy is so highly exalted.

Alternatively, they will be so incapable of taking refuge to God's grace that their anxiety will increase by thinking that they are not partakers of such grace and that now it is too late for them—and, therefore, they do not possibly dare to avail themselves of it.

8. Such a state will be one of utmost restlessness due to *the temptation to commit desperate acts.* I would rather be silent than speak of them, lest the enemy tempt anyone to engage in them. Judas is an example of someone who chose to hang himself. All who have found themselves in such circumstances will say that it is only by the mercy of God that we are who we are, and that we will never be able to praise His prevenient grace sufficiently in upholding us when our soul is greatly troubled.

We have deemed it useful to address such and similar matters, abundantly affirmed by experience, to evoke a sense of awe in the soul—and to awaken the careless before it will be too late, and the Lord will say to them, "Sleep on." We want a soul who finds himself in such circumstances to understand that nothing strange is befalling him. God's ordinary way is to lead to Zion by way of Sinai—and this, so to speak, along the edge of hell—before they are led to true rest.

Restlessness in the True Believer
We shall now proceed to address a few instances about a true believer who, though reconciled with God as to his state, may experience much spiritual unrest as long as he is not privileged to exercise faith and thereby enter into rest. The experience of every believer affirms this. Furthermore, the Word of God teaches this abundantly in so many passages that I will not need to attest to this. Instead, I will immediately proceed to highlight some of the many circumstances that may cause this.

1. True believers—when they are incapable of exercising faith—will, at times, become inexpressibly anxious by *a view and representation of a given sin.* It may be a sin committed either before their conversion in their youth or following their conversion when, due to backsliding, they did not conduct themselves consistent with their state and obligations. It can be that this pertains to sin in general or also to a sin that did more violence to the conscience. Such was true in the previous examples and in David (Psalm 51), whose sin did violence upon his conscience.

This awareness of sin can be caused by a conscience that quietly and persistently accuses such believers of being guilty of certain grievous sins either before or after their conversion. Such inner turmoil can also be caused by a very sudden and intense impression of that sin upon the soul so that she is robbed of her light and liberty to deal with this in a believing manner. It can also be caused by either reading or hearing about God's punishments and judgments that He has executed upon certain persons regarding this sin, resulting in the heart being much oppressed with extreme anxiety, bringing the poor believer in inexpressible straits. Job experienced this when he lamented, "For thou writest bitter things against me, and makest me to possess the iniquities of my youth" (Job 13:26). He was fearful of being confronted with certain grievous sins (cf. Ps. 25:7). God is just in permitting the soul to experience such turmoil frequently, and no one should deny his spiritual state on account of this, for many believers have experienced and do experience this.

2. Whenever true believers are incapable of exercising saving faith, *feelings of anxiety and distress* will frequently disquiet them greatly. Consequently, their souls can be so weighed down as under a heavy burden, and they can be so oppressed that they go their way bowed down due to prevailing spiritual bondage. Such spiritual oppression can often also be attributed to one's physical condition and temperament so that one person will be more inclined than another person to be unsettled, sorrowful, despondent, and depressed.

This, in turn, can be the cause that many true and very tender believers experience less spiritual joy and sensible comfort than believers who do not live as conscientiously and carefully as they do. When, however, such anxiety has a physical cause, causing a person to be so oppressed that it feels as if the weight of the entire world rests on his shoulders, he will be unable to give a real and legitimate reason for his distress.

Occasionally this will be caused, however, by the perception of one's transgression, so that the soul cannot lay hold of the blood of Jesus Christ and so apply it to his conscience that it will be cleansed and her bonds will be broken.

It should also be noted that this distress will occasionally be accompanied by a spiritual speechlessness, causing the soul's tongue to cleave to her mouth, thereby rendering her so incapable of praying or uttering some intelligible petitions that she will frequently shrink back from prayer and look up against it as too high a mountain. It can also happen, however, that such distress of the soul can be a compelling incentive to pray without ceasing, stimulating the soul thereby to wrestle and persevere in prayer so that she cannot find rest anywhere but on her knees. Its hidden cause is that such supplicating and lamenting yields some relief to the soul, even though she does not perceive her burden to have been removed.

Furthermore, such distress and oppression of heart can be of shorter or longer duration. Some will, therefore, "through fear of death…all their lifetime [be] subject to bondage" (Heb. 2:15), whereas others must and can say, "For his anger endureth but a moment; in his favour is life" (Ps. 30:5). Carefully examine the following passages, for the person experiencing all this may extract some comfort from them: Psalm 32:3–4; Psalm 88 (in its entirety); and Isaiah 38 (nearly the entire chapter).

3. When the faith of the believer is not in exercise, he will at times be greatly distraught by this frame of mind, due to *sudden and yet very intense stirrings* from all sides—similar to the high wind that buffeted and demolished the house in which Job's children were eating and drinking (Job 1:19). This inner turmoil can be caused by

- sudden injections of Satan into the soul of the believer;
- very sudden anxiety of soul;
- the enemy very powerfully influencing the imagination by setting before the believer, as in a moment, all that is dreadful and frightful (doing the opposite to the Savior by setting before Him all the king-doms of the earth [Matt. 4:30]—something Satan can do as well); and
- a physical apparition of the enemy.

Read carefully how Satan tempted the Savior (Matt. 4:2). In 2 Corinthians 12, we read how Paul was buffeted by Satan, who appeared to him in bodily form, and elsewhere he says, "Without were fightings, within were fears" (2 Cor. 7:5). The psalmist must have experienced such sudden and troubling upheaval when he said, "The sorrows of death compassed me" (Ps. 116:3)—sorrows a person would experience when being suddenly ambushed. Experience teaches that there is much more to this than I am permitted to say.

4. A true believer, when his faith is not in exercise, can at times be greatly troubled when *tasting God's displeasure* regarding certain corruptions, lust,

or sin that they have rationalized, cherished, nourished, indulged in, and excused. I know very well that a preeminent distinctive of true believers is that they will depart from all sin and that they have a desire to live according to all God's commandments. Experience teaches, however, that when their first love begins to wane, certain sins, habitually committed in their state of nature, will again begin to appeal to them, being reminded of the pleasure such sinful indulgences would yield. Their old nature will then immediately respond with earnest desires and affections to experience such pleasure once again. When the soul begins to perceive how unbecoming this is and will, therefore, resist such desires, this sinful lust will begin to be rooted all the more deeply in the affections so that these desires will be glossed over and minimized. The soul will not be tempted to indulge in such sinful desires as she did before, but rather, she will yield to it for but one brief moment. This will be followed by the deceptive ploy of bringing to mind examples of backslidden believers, gently persuading the soul that this can be compatible with grace—and many other things that I could but will not mention. The soul will then begin to waver and will frequently give in just once. However, when her corrupt flesh has a taste of this, it will increasingly demand more.

Lust and pride will then proceed from minor to greater indulgence in sin, and when sin progresses this far, it will now demand servitude and give no rest until the soul yields to its demands, although with a speaking conscience. Her spiritual strength will now begin to decline, and a spiritual leanness will increasingly manifest itself. Prayer will now consist of words that are void of heartfelt desires and inclinations and will no longer be urgent. The yielding to such lusts will also manifest itself to others who interact with her.

One whom God loves, and is thus not a hypocrite (for a hypocrite can put on quite a show and still come to this), the Lord will then begin to fully hedge in the way of one who is yielding to a sinful desire with very sharp thorns that will cause great pain when he yields to either the right or the left to indulge in his lust. The Lord will come against him, and every obstacle will be of such a nature that he will begin to perceive the judgment annexed to his sins. Each contrary providence will exclaim to him that this is but the beginning of sorrow and that more will follow. His prayers will return into his bosom. It will begin to storm within, for there is a Jonah on board. Everything fails because there is an Achan in the camp, and God will thunder mightily with the voice of His majesty as expressed in the law, causing great inner turmoil. "He that killeth an ox is as if he slew a man; he that sacrificeth a lamb, as if he cut off a dog's neck; he that offereth an oblation, as if he offered swine's blood; he that burneth incense, as if he blessed an idol" (Isa. 66:3; cf. Hos. 2; Isa. 58).

What could be the reason of all this? I have stated it already: they choose their own ways, and, as the prophet said, their soul lusts after their own abominations. Believe me, if you intend to cherish and yield to any lust, all your best things will be transformed into abominations, for God is holy and very jealous of His honor.

5. The intense inner turmoil experienced by the believer while in this condition is because *he cannot find refuge in the blood of Christ.* Instead, as he considers his sins, he will be fearful and without courage to draw near to Jesus.

First, such a frame of mind is usually the result of all that has preceded. The reason may be that God will justly seal up for them for a season the fountain of Jesus's blood, so that they may be humbled more deeply about their sins and have a real taste of how bitter it is to depart from God—and that for the remainder of their lives they may have deep and profound impressions in their hearts of God's awe-inspiring majesty. This is by far the most common way in which God deals with this.

Thus, I wish to warn those who so readily imagine that they will enter into God's rest without first having been humbled, crying, and supplicating near the fountain to be led into it by the operation of the Holy Spirit.

Second, an overwhelming sense of sin can make a soul afraid to flee to Jesus. Having said that, when the Holy Spirit awakens the believer, He will generally do so by way of conviction. I must say, however, that the convicting ministry of the Holy Spirit is not of such a nature as to deprive a soul of liberty to flee to Jesus by an overwhelming view of his sin. On the contrary, God's Spirit aims at compelling the soul to take refuge in the blood of the covenant.

It can happen, however, that the enemy and one's heart can so conspire to focus upon sin that one would utter the wrong and unbelieving language, "Depart from me, Lord Jesus, for I am a sinful man." Let this be the rule in such cases: when the discovery of sin is such that it drives one to Christ, it is of the Holy Spirit. However, any discovery of sin that drives the soul away from Jesus proceeds from the enemy and our corrupt hearts.

Third, such turmoil can also be due to a lack of light regarding the way of free grace, the soul thinking that some great work must first be accomplished, being fearful that by a continual fleeing to Jesus and His blood, one would make Him a servant of sin. Or it can be that, without the spiritual frame she desires, she does not dare venture upon free grace alone. Whatever may be the case, the experience of the saints affirms how great the turmoil can be when one finds himself in such circumstances. Our transgressions are multiplied (Isa. 59:10–12). How shall we then live (Ps. 32:4)?

6. Believers experience much turmoil in this condition due to *being intensely assaulted about the genuineness and sincerity of their faith.* The grace of faith will often be tested. Peter writes about "the trial of your faith" (1 Peter 1:7). Such assaults will primarily consist of two things. The believer will be assaulted about the exercise of faith itself. The issue will be whether the soul in the exercise of faith has indeed ceased from self; that is, whether she, in the act of receiving, has experienced a genuine application of Jesus's righteousness to her soul and a true casting of all her guilt upon Jesus, so that the heart experienced rest rather than turmoil and enlargement rather than bondage. Faith may also be tried as to its fruits, namely, the purifying of the heart, the overcoming of the world, etc.

If the soul is in some darkness and has a tender conscience, such assaults can greatly cause her to lose her footing—especially if she lacks clarity regarding these matters. Heman may have experienced this when he lamented, "While I suffer thy terrors I am distracted" (Ps. 88:15).

7. A true believer can also be very distraught in this condition because he *cannot extract the least comfort or encouragement from previous experiences of the Lord's lovingkindness.* Asaph "considered the days of old, the years of ancient times" (Ps. 77:5). Consequently, he asked, "Will the Lord cast off for ever?" (v. 7). David reflected on God's lovingkindness in "the land of Jordan, and of the Hermonites," and he cried out, "My soul is cast down within me" (Ps. 42:6).

It may then happen that previous experiences will be hidden to the soul so that they, so to speak, will neither see the sun, the moon, nor the stars during such dark and tempestuous nights. It can also be that although the soul may perceive certain matters, she will be unable to discern that which separates the experience of God's children from that of hypocrites or temporal believers.

Finally, if they may discern this to some extent, it will not yield a measure of peace and calmness in their souls—as was the case in the examples mentioned earlier.

However, some believers experience the peculiar temptation that they, with much stirring of the emotions and due to a distorted perception, consider how hypocrites seek to be at rest with something other than turning to Jesus in order to silence their consciences when they have strife. Nevertheless, they who desire truth within will neither be able nor shall find rest when they have strife about their experiences unless they, by renewal, are led to exercise faith in Jesus, and thus wholeheartedly surrender themselves to Jesus and experience the reciprocal effects of this in their hearts.

When the soul thus seeks to exercise faith, its necessity being powerfully impressed upon her heart, and she yet fails to experience God's approbation upon her act of faith, she will be "tossed with tempest, and not comforted" (Isa. 54:11) by this temptation.

We need to know that it is not God's way always to reaffirm previous experiences with new experiences. Furthermore, we also need to know that the enemy's particular device is to persuade the soul powerfully to engage in the most essential exercises of faith, knowing full well that man is incapable of doing so. His objective is to keep the soul trapped in a frame of unbelieving despondency and imbalance, and thereby to oppress her. Only God can help in such a situation.

8. Just as the aforementioned will deeply trouble a believer, there may be some who are greatly troubled because *all the good that is transpiring within, and can be observed by others, remains hidden for him in his present experience.* Such a soul loathes herself, sets her heart on Jesus, and hungers and thirsts after Him. Though all of these are infallible marks of spiritual life, it remains hidden to her. Or else, they will think that either these are merely the stirrings of an enlightened understanding or that they issue forth from their troubled hearts—all because they cannot find any rest following and in their exercises.

A soul can become so weary of her groaning. She will be chattering all the day like a swallow and mourning as a dove (Isa. 38:14), all the while not experiencing any sensible rest. Believers can also be distressed more than usual by the manifestation of an exceptionally powerful stirring of their corrupt and sinful natures, which is still found in the best of them— either because this corruption arises from within or is powerfully agitated by Satan.

This I know: various sinful thoughts can so fill the soul that she, with the apostle, must cry out at times, "I know that in me (that is, in my flesh,) dwelleth no good thing" (Rom. 7:18). These stirrings within the soul, prompting her to do what she does not want to do, can be so intense! This will bring her into captivity to the law of sin and death, so that she will be compelled to cry out, "O wretched man that I am! who shall deliver me from the body of this death?" (Rom. 7:24).

I do not wish to address specific examples. Nevertheless, to instruct a soul in such a condition, it should be noted that when the manure pit of the heart is greatly stirred, even the most wretched stirrings will manifest themselves in certain believers who are in such a state of mind.

9. We can add to this that this condition can so overtake a believer that he will be troubled *when he begins to think about God.* When all is well, a believer will delight himself in God. He will always set the Almighty before him, saying, "How precious also are thy thoughts unto me, O God! how great is the sum of them! If I should count them, they are more in number than the sand" (Ps. 139:17–18).

However, while in this condition, there will be times when they will be unable to think of the Lord without fear. They will then think of Him as a debtor would of his creditor, as a prisoner would of his judge, as a thief would of the gallows, etc., so that the soul will be inwardly oppressed when she focuses on who God is. All who have been in this condition will know what it means to have very distorted and implausible thoughts of God. Asaph experienced what we have been discussing: "I remembered God, and was troubled: I complained, and my spirit was overwhelmed. Selah" (Ps. 77:3).

10. Add to this that a believer, while in this condition, will specifically remain troubled by being so *readily inclined to refute all the arguments that should minister comfort to him,* countering them by arguments that will increasingly fuel his unbelief. The most seasoned soul physicians will despair of comforting such souls—something that is not surprising, for only God can revive such a troubled soul.

11. Finally, true believers, being incapable of exercising faith, will be greatly troubled, *thinking that all that is happening affirms that they will never be restored.* Their prayers are not answered; they experience neither comfort nor relief; and all the waves and billows are going over them (Ps. 42:7). Thus, the

soul will frequently exclaim, "Will the Lord cast off for ever? and will he be favourable no more? Is his mercy clean gone for ever? doth his promise fail for evermore?" (Ps. 77:7–8).

I believe that these few comments should suffice, for to address everything that one might experience would be understood by very few.

The State of Rest

Just as peace and delightful sunshine follow a storm, likewise, there will be spiritual joy following troublous times for the upright in heart. What a delightful rest this will be for such as are "afflicted, tossed with tempest, and not comforted" (Isa. 54:11)! We now wish to address this matter.

Oh, that I may be able to speak of this from experience, and that you, my beloved, would be privileged to enter into this rest for the first time or by renewal!

We have already stated that we, along with many commentators, do not understand this rest to be the rest of heaven when God's children will rest from their labors. Instead, for multiple reasons (elaborated upon in-depth by the very learned and godly Dr. Owen in his exposition of this passage), we understand this rest to be experienced by the soul on this side of eternity when she may enjoy God's nearness in Jesus Christ as He may be known in the fullness of the gospel.

We could also describe it as being the spiritual state in which there is a cessation of all torment, anxiety, strife, legal fear, doubts, and mistrust. Instead, the soul may now experience a sweet calm, peace, joy, and happiness by the Holy Spirit shedding forth God's special love into the heart, so that the soul, in the appointed way of salvation, will cast herself upon God in Christ and upon His precious covenant promises. She will thus trust that God is her portion and that He will never forsake her but rather shall guide her with His counsel and afterward receive her to glory (Ps. 73:24).

Although the fathers in the Old Testament already enjoyed this in some measure, it was nevertheless greatly veiled, and therefore they did so to a lesser degree. Consequently, the apostle links this rest explicitly to the full revelation of the gospel. In the words that follow our text, the apostle quotes David as having taught this also prophetically.

The Foundation of True Rest

We will now speak of this rest more in-depth. We will thus consider the foundation of this rest, and will do so first by way of negation.

What the Foundation of This Rest Is Not
The foundation of this rest does not consist in the cessation of inner turmoil, conviction, and soul's distress. Though this will be the residual effect of this rest, one should thereby not conclude that one has found true rest. Both experience and God's Word teach abundantly that one may have, for some season, experienced intense anxiety and soul's distress that subsided after a while without such a person having had any dealings with Jesus Christ. Felix may have been such a case, for he trembled when he heard about the impending judgment. Such persons will generally become worse afterward, for the devil, having been banished for a season, will return with "seven other spirits more wicked than himself…and the last state of that man is worse than the first" (Matt. 12:45). A river that has been dammed for a season will afterward break forth all the more ferociously.

Just as the spontaneous cessation of anxiety cannot be the grounds for comfort, likewise, continual anxiety and fear cannot be the grounds for rest. Many people hope and think that they are settled upon the true foundation of rest because they live with continual sorrow and an accusing conscience. However, this proves the contrary, namely, that either they never have rested upon this foundation or that they cannot arrive at this spiritual disposition. In fact, all such anxiety and distress are but the effect of the curse of God's law, which, in and of itself, will not save anyone. Having said that, God will sanctify such anxiety to compel the souls of many of the elect to seek Jesus and to make them receptive to His sovereign and gracious lovingkindness.

Detecting some stirrings of joy and happiness within one's heart also cannot be the grounds for rest. Although one can experience this when having this true rest, it is equally true that Satan can powerfully stimulate one's imagination and stir up a man's imagination with an imaginary hope that Jesus Christ is his Savior, that his sins are forgiven, and that he will happily arrive in heaven.

We have even known people who by such stirring of Satan became almost ecstatic, and yet who afterward, as a dog, "turned to his own vomit again; and [as a] sow that was washed to her wallowing in the mire" (2 Peter 2:22). Consider only what is written about temporal believers who receive the Word with joy, etc. The devil uses two highly effective devices: he will use the gospel to seduce people by a false and unfounded joy, keeping people from the real Jesus by the false perceptions he generates, or by using the law to so focus on sin that it will lead them to despair.

The true grounds for rest are also neither determined by having a promise of God's Word impressed upon the heart, nor by various stanzas of sacred music coming to mind. Many thereby deceive themselves for eternity. They have been somewhat concerned, and then a promise or stanza came to mind. They will then immediately conclude that the Lord has been gracious to them. In their minds, they have enjoyed a great blessing, even though they had nothing more than just the words. However, for a believer it is not the promise, as such, but rather Jesus Himself in the promise that yields rest—and thus not only Jesus as they may behold Him in the promise but rather Jesus in the promise to whom they are united by faith and whom they embrace and appropriate. Let this, therefore, be the cardinal rule: all rest that one perceives before the believing embrace of Jesus in the promise is counterfeit, flawed, and deceptive. True rest is not something that precedes faith but rather issues forth from the exercise of faith.

Finally, the grounds for this rest are not to be found in a person's desires, disposition, and sincerity. Such grounds are too weak a foundation on which to base one's rest, and a soul will also lose them in the hour of temptation. Nothing can satisfy a conscience when it is weighed in the infallible scales of God's law. A truly upright soul will esteem them as less than vanity, counting them but as dung (Phil. 3:8) and as filthy rags (Isa. 64:6).

The True Foundation of Rest

Positively we may affirm that the only ground for true rest is Jehovah, the blessed triune covenant God, as He reveals Himself to the soul by His Word and Spirit, revealing Himself as the God of full salvation in His Son, Jesus Christ. Such souls will be powerfully and irresistibly wrought upon to embrace this God of salvation and to appropriate Him in exact conformity to how He offers Himself in the gospel of salvation. This is the only foundation that God has laid in Zion. He, for whom this is his rest, will never be put to shame. Woe be to them who lay other foundations! They shall not succeed. All who build upon "wood, hay, [and] stubble" will be consumed if gold is absent (1 Cor. 3:11–13). Such was the rest experienced by the Old Testament church: "The LORD is my portion, saith my soul; therefore will I hope in him" (Lam. 3:24); and Asaph confessed, "My flesh and my heart faileth: but God is the strength of my heart, and my portion for ever" (Ps. 73:26).

The Essence of True Rest

Let us now proceed to consider what the essence of this rest is. To keep your memory from being burdened with too many particulars, we will only address the following matters:

1. This rest consists of *a quietness and calmness of soul* whereby the preceding turmoil of deep despondency and despair will be quieted in some measure, and the thundering of Sinai will cease—to such an extent that the gentle voice of the divine gospel becomes somewhat discernable as a joyous message encompassing glad tidings for someone who is lost and utterly wretched in himself. In the aforementioned unrest, the soul is like a person residing in a wretched prison, who is incapable of hearing a single word that would yield comfort and rest to him due to the rattling of the chains that keep him imprisoned, and due to being beaten and scourged by a merciless jailor who roars and threatens. However, when God proceeds to create rest, this unrest will be so countered with the sound of the gospel that it will prevail over the thundering of the law, and one will become receptive to hear it. As much as Satan and one's unbelieving heart may make every effort to detract a person from hearing it, the soul will respond, saying, "I will hear what the Lord will speak to me." Anyone who is experientially acquainted with this will agree that particularly such divine speaking will pave the way to spiritual rest. Consider the experience of Mr. Peacock when he began to find rest. He says, "Truly my soul had been led astray greatly by the turmoil and gnawing of my conscience. However, thanks be to God, the storm has somewhat subsided, and I may experience a measure of quietness and refreshment. Therefore, my request is not to number me among the reprobates. I now utterly abhor such thoughts, and my prayer to God is that, in mercy, He may graciously pardon such thoughts."

2. One whose soul is troubled and assaulted will not only be quieted, but *such a soul will generally be made very desirous of experiencing some tokens of free and soothing grace.* Such a desire will be generated by the perceived possibility that free grace can be magnified in bestowing grace upon such an utterly hell-worthy sinner. Hereby the condition of the elect can be distinguished from that of the reprobates when they are in great distress. The distress of the latter will cause them to hate God, and, like Cain, they will flee from God's presence. We also observe this in Spira, who neither wanted to hear about God and Christ nor did he supplicate for mercy.

The first, however, will be groaning and supplicating for a crumb of the children's bread. They are, therefore, those who, laboring and being heavy-laden, will find rest.

3. Such rest consists of *a soul being inwardly illuminated in the way of free grace.* Such a soul may find her all-sufficiency in the most blessed God, namely, to behold God's glory with an unveiled countenance. The soul, beholding God spiritually with her soul's eye, will then be enveloped by divine glory so that she will be light in the Lord. This mystery of spiritual life is such that it cannot be expressed in words but can only be known experientially. Let me say this about it: There will be a light that will banish all darkness and ignorance regarding God, causing the soul to perceive in God's truth what she had never seen before. Such light will bring the triune God very near to the soul and the soul very near to God, resulting in genuine and reciprocal communion with a triune covenant God. Such illumination not only causes the soul to behold an inexhaustible fullness of salvation in this covenant God, but it also yields inexpressible freedom to a needy soul to partake of this salvation. Not only will the soul then be able to see the magnitude of her sins and how many doubts she has entertained, but also that she may take hold of the grace of God and the merits of Christ. Her doubts will then cease for the time being. The soul will then be able to see that there is such a fullness for her in the merits of Jesus that all her sins—even if all the sins of the world were hers—are but as a speck of dust in comparison with the infinite and bottomless ocean of God's mercy in Christ, His Son.

Consider again how the aforementioned Mr. Peacock spoke of this when this light dawned in his soul. He said, "The sea is neither so full of water nor the sun so full of light as God is full of mercy. Yes, His mercy is ten thousand times greater, giving me, an abominable worm, reason to magnify His mercy to all eternity." Oh, how pure, heavenly, and soul-enamoring, and strengthening this light is!

4. The believer's rest also consists of *a believing and sensible awareness of the gracious pardon of all his sins solely for the sake of Jesus's satisfaction,* which he has received and appropriated by faith (Rom. 5:1). It is undoubtedly a prominent component of this rest that the soul sees that her sins have been blotted out as a thick cloud (Isa. 44:22) and that God has removed them "as far as the east is from the west" (Ps. 103:12). This is the loosening of the

bonds of death whereby they were bound. This is the opening of the doors of the prison-house in which they were kept. This is a loosening of the noose around the neck of the sentenced and condemned sinner. This is a pouring of the soothing waters of grace into the soul that was being consumed by the scorching venom of the fiery darts of the Most High. This is as the oil and balm of Gilead being applied to the wounded soul, immediately removing all sorrow and pain, soothing and purifying the wounds, and fully healing her. This is the hand of the creditor who, in the presence of the poor debtor who is penniless, writes in large and legible letters, "I am fully satisfied, even to the very last penny, and I will never again be wroth with you or rebuke you" (cf. Isa. 54:9). This will yield great rest, for a peaceful conscience is as a "continual feast" (Prov. 15:15). If you have ever experienced this, you will be able to say with the apostle that this is a peace "which passeth all understanding" (Phil. 4:7).

5. This rest is also characterized by *experiencing the outpouring of God's love in the soul by the Holy Spirit* (Rom. 5:5). This metaphor is derived from the practice of pouring out precious ointment abundantly and profusely upon something in such a measure that the object being poured upon would be fully moistened—similar to the holy oil that was poured out so abundantly upon the head of Aaron, descending even "down to the skirts of his garments" (Ps. 133:2). This pouring out of love, as experienced in this rest, affects all the soul's faculties. She will experience, particularly following intense strife, that there is a height, breadth, depth, and length to this experience that is beyond comprehension. Oh, when Jesus leads the soul into the banqueting house, and the banner over her is love (Song 2:4), how this love will enamor the soul and how she will be melted by it! The soul will then be swallowed up in worship, and this pleasure will render her satiated, satisfied, and heavenly-minded. I have known someone in Christ who had to exclaim, "Lord, I cannot express what I am experiencing. I am fainting, for I am overwhelmed by such an extraordinary measure of glory. Pour this new wine no longer in such an old leather bottle, for it will burst!" A martyr once exclaimed, "Come, you superstitious papists, you are looking for miracles. Here is one. I am burning, and I feel no pain. I am bathing in the love of my God so tenderly and sweetly that I am lying on these burning coals as on a bed of roses." Olevianus said, "It is as if I am walking in green pastures in which the heavenly dew is not merely descending upon me in drops but rather by the buckets

full." Robert Bolton has left us with many examples of this. He who may enter into God's rest may experience a measure of this. In the meantime, such an abundant outpouring of God's love into the soul is generally the portion of very conscientious Christians, as well as those who must bear crosses and are engaged in much spiritual warfare.

6. This rest is also characterized by *a complete resting in and upon Christ*. The soul will commit herself fully and entirely to Him as the *Petra*, the Rock, and she will hide and abide in Him in the manner described by David. Thus, all the storms and billows will rage over the soul without moving her, for she may hide in a secure refuge. Jesus is the Rock into which she enters, and in which she abides, uniting herself ever more intimately to the Rock Christ by repeated exercises of faith.

Herein she resembles someone who resides in a castle built upon a rock amid the sea. He beholds the fury of the sea when it crashes upon the rock. He hears the roaring of the storms, tempests, and hurricanes that causes everything outside to tremble. However, he is at peace and without fear, and can say, "Therefore will not we fear, though the earth be removed, and though the mountains be carried into the midst of the sea." Let "the waters thereof roar and be troubled"; let "the mountains shake with the swelling thereof. Selah. There is a river, the streams whereof shall make glad the city of God, the holy place of the tabernacles of the most High. God is in the midst of her; she shall not be moved: God shall help her, and that right early" (Ps. 46:2–5).

He who may so rest in Christ, and upon Him alone, "shall be as mount Zion, which cannot be removed, but abideth for ever" (Ps. 125:1). I readily admit that few, yes, very few of God's beloved children experience this. Many live carelessly, and due to their sluggishness, they lack the liberty to thus rest in Christ. Others cannot rest upon Christ, and in Him alone, unless they have certain emotions and spiritual frames. Thereby they resemble a man who has one foot placed upon a rock and the other foot on a loose board floating upon the water. As soon as the board begins to move, he will begin to totter and will be ready to fall. Oh, this rest is to be found in Jesus only! Blessed are they who can put all their trust in Him alone, regardless of how low or high we are. He is always at the same level. He retains all His glory and luster, even though we often have to sit in the dark.

7. This rest is *a resting in God Himself as their Father, as their Portion, and as their All in all*. They are delivered from the spirit of bondage, and the yoke

is taken from their jaws (Hos. 11:4). God grants them the Spirit of adoption, and thus they exclaim, "Abba, Father" (Rom. 8:15–16). Viewing God as Father with a childlike disposition will yield a wonderful rest, enabling the soul to say, "Doubtless thou art our father, though Abraham be ignorant of us" (Isa. 63:16). She may say, "The LORD is my portion, saith my soul; therefore will I hope in him" (Lam. 3:24); "The lines are fallen unto me in pleasant places; yea, I have a goodly heritage" (Ps. 16:6); and "Whom have I in heaven but thee? and there is none upon earth that I desire beside thee. My flesh and my heart faileth: but God is the strength of my heart, and my portion for ever" (Ps. 73:25–26).

8. This rest consists of *a full satisfaction that the soul may experience in the Lord.* Before this experience, the soul always lacked something. However, in the enjoyment of this rest, the soul recognizes that she is now fully satisfied and that everything she needs for time and eternity is to be found in Jesus. She perceives how blessed this rest is, and she wishes to abide under His shadow, confessing, "I lack nothing; I have everything." Finally, this rest consists in the soul entrusting herself soul and body, and with all her needs, to the God of the covenant, trusting that He will sanctify them through His Word. He will guide them by His counsel even unto death, comforting them with His rod and His staff in the valley of the shadow of death, and will then satisfy them with His likeness.

Behold, these and other matters constitute this rest, and from the examples above, you will be able to conclude that this rest is emphatically referred to as God's rest, since He is the One who initiates and promises this rest, and He is the very essence of the soul's rest. More I do not wish to add at this time.

ENTERING THE REST BY FAITH

The apostle thus asserts that they who believe will enter into this rest, saying, "For we which have believed do enter into rest." The apostle connects faith and the entering into this rest, testifying that he who exercises faith does enter into this rest.

The Connection between Faith and Rest

The reasons why the apostle declares the entrance into this rest as a constituent element of faith are the following:

1. Faith brings this rest into focus, causing the poor soul who has so long been tossed with tempest (Isa. 54:11) to see that there is rest in a covenant God for the sinner who labors and is heavy laden (Matt. 11:28).

2. Faith enters into this rest by wholeheartedly acquiescing in God's testimony, setting "to his seal that God is true" (John 3:33).

3. Faith enters into this rest by casting all the causes of her concern upon the Lord, who will make all things well for time and eternity (Ps. 37:5). The soul will thus relinquish everything and surrender everything into His hands.

4. Faith will enter into this rest by way of immediate appropriation and will continually abide in this rest so that the soul "shall never be moved" (Ps. 15:5).

We will not address additional aspects since many have already been addressed and many more will be addressed.

The Promise of Rest to Every Believer

Since the apostle links this rest to the exercise of faith, he intimates that he and every believer who believes God's testimony truly enter this rest. Thus it is indeed! Every believer will enjoy and enter into this rest in proportion to the measure of his faith, and all the restlessness that some of God's children experience is due to the weakness of their faith. We who have believed do enter into rest.

APPLICATION

Behold, beloved, we have set before you the blessed rest into which God's children may enter by faith. Let us now apply these expounded truths to ourselves.

An Exhortation for Unbelievers

Unbelieving and unrepentant sinner, pause for a moment and reflect upon these truths so that you may perceive what your state and condition is before God, recognizing the vanity of all things.

Oh sinner, if you were to acknowledge this, you would recognize that you are living a life of continual sorrow and restlessness! You are without God, and you, therefore, fail to see the essence of His creation. As much as you may desire it, there is nothing that can truly satisfy you. In your very best efforts, there will be but "death in the pot" (2 Kings 4:40). Everything in your life is so accompanied by cares, concerns, and sorrows that you will be compelled to admit that the most beautiful of the world's roses have thorns and that everything is not only vanity but also "vexation of spirit" (Eccl. 1:14). Quietly reflect upon this so that your own heart may inwardly persuade you of this.

Consider the consequences of your sins. They are as honey in your mouth, and you love them so much that you would rather do without God and His communion than to part with your lusts. Oh, that you would but consider what the end shall be! Even if you were not to part with sin due to its God-dishonoring nature, consider only its grievous consequences! When the day comes that your conscience will accuse you so that its gnawing will cause your knees to knock together, how dreadful it then shall be to appear before a holy, avenging, and angry God on that great day! How you will then cry out "to the mountains and rocks, Fall on us" (Rev. 6:16), and you will not be heard! Instead, Jesus will command that all who would not enter into this rest be cast into the eternal fire, where there shall be "weeping and gnashing of teeth" (Matt. 8:12) to all eternity in a realm of eternal restlessness and "everlasting burnings" (Isa. 33:14).

Oh, see to it that your deceitful heart will not mislead you into believing presumptuously that you have indeed entered into this rest, for many deceive themselves regarding this matter. The one concludes this because he is free from distress, another because his unrest and anxiety have passed, another because God's children esteem him, another because he lives so virtuously, and another may yet have another reason. Such is the condition of the poor sinner who will always cling to something and would thus rather deceive his soul than surrender by saying, "It is without hope."

Consider, therefore, the way in which you obtain this true rest: not by doing but by believing. Now is the accepted time (2 Cor. 6:2)! Rest is being offered to you, and you are being exhorted to enter into it. Oh that none of you would have an evil and unbelieving heart but rather you would hear God's voice, endeavor to embrace God's promise, and enter into this rest!

An Exhortation for God's Children

Children of God, we have addressed these matters with such clarity that we now wish to conclude with but a word or two.

An Invitation to Restless Christians

We have a word for those who are troubled and oppressed, who are "afflicted, tossed with tempest" (Isa. 54:11). Oh, do but consider the cause of all the restlessness and distress you are experiencing: your lack of faith and your sparse exercise of this saving faith. I am confident that in proportion to the exercise of your faith you will find rest and joy in God. We have already addressed this in various ways. Oh, endeavor to believe, and may God powerfully work it in you! Frequently engage in exercising your faith, and you will increasingly profit from it and find rest for your troubled souls. As much as possible, refrain from drawing negative conclusions about yourself from the matters we have addressed because you experience so little of this rest. The fact that you experience so little of this rest and peace within your heart affirms that your faith is weak—but not that you have no faith. The opposite can clearly be concluded from the fact that you are sorrowful and fearful of deceiving yourself. This will never be observed in unbelievers.

You will be able to ascertain whether you have faith from the distinctive marks we will address below—even though you presently do not experience the rest and peace that will fully pacify your heart.

Can you affirm that you are not cherishing a particular sin but that you have turned from it? Oh, that is a token that your soul has been won for God! You will then observe a complete abhorrence of all sin. Moreover, your bosom sin, known only to God and you, which will manifest itself in the exercise of your best religious duties, will wound and trouble your soul. You will genuinely grieve over this in secret, and the condition of your soul will cause you to weep with groanings that cannot be uttered before the countenance of the Lord. It will then be true, "Blessed are they that mourn: for they shall be comforted" (Matt. 5:4).

Do you not observe that you are being bombarded by many arrows of all manner of strife? You are being emptied "from vessel to vessel" (Jer. 48:11), and many times you are being sifted as wheat. Nevertheless, as often as you may be sifted, you will remain firm in your choice to entrust yourself to the Lord. You will say, "Lord, even if I were to be slain, I will nevertheless cleave to Thee, and I will never depart from Thy way." Oh, these are evidences that it is true of you that "the eyes of them that see shall not be dim" (Isa. 32:3). This proves that you do have faith, for these fiery darts of Satan will only be aimed at the shield of faith (Eph. 6:16).

Is it not true for you that everything is void of delight and that nothing can invigorate you if you cannot find rest for your soul in God? Will it not be so until God by renewal reveals Himself to you and assures you of your portion in Him? If such is true for you, then you must not give in to unbelief.

How harmful and God-dishonoring this is—although you often do not see it! Instead, you must strive against your unbelief and give much heed to the offer of free grace. You must continually endeavor to exercise your faith and take refuge to this rest as doves take refuge to their nests during stormy weather. I am certain that upon repeatedly having labored in vain, you will say time and again, "I have done so repeatedly during the entire night of my darkness, but upon Thy Word, come what may, I will cast out my net again." You will then say, "Oh, His Word is true that he who comes to Him as a destitute sinner shall in no wise be cast out" (cf. John 6:37)! "This poor man cried, and the LORD heard him, and saved him out of all his troubles" (Ps. 34:6).

An Exhortation for Believers Already Enjoying Rest
Finally, a word for you, believers, to whom God has granted faith in a greater measure, so that you not only have entered into this rest initially, but that you may also abide in it.

Acknowledge it as a gracious gift of God that He has bestowed this favor upon you, since there are so many bowed down in grief and sorrow. The Lord alone has bestowed this upon you. May your mouth, therefore, be filled with God's praise, as you may have struggled for years before you attained to this.

Let this humble you, and be compassionate toward those who are still in bondage. Treat them with tender love. As we have observed, there have been those to whom God has given such strong faith, who now have become haughty toward others. Rather than helping those who are in distress, they judge them and do not assist them. Consequently, God has given them over to themselves. How many examples are there that pride comes before the fall (Prov. 16:18)!

Be especially on guard against sin. The smallest sin over which we do not grieve and that does not prompt the soul to take refuge to the blood of Jesus will disturb our peace. Therefore, you who love the Lord, depart from evil.

Finally, strive to abide where rest is only to be found, so that you may have full liberty in God to say upon your deathbed, "I have waited for thy salvation, O LORD" (Gen. 49:18). You may then know that you will be translated into the full enjoyment of ceaselessly praising God forever. Amen.

CHAPTER 6

Faith, a Grace That Overcomes the World

For whatsoever is born of God overcometh the world: and this is the victory that overcometh the world, even our faith.

—1 JOHN 5:4

"The elder shall serve the younger" were the words once spoken to Rebekah when she felt the children struggling within her, prompting her to say, "Why am I thus?" (Gen. 25:22–23).

Perhaps some know of a prolonged internal struggle and will often say, "Why am I thus? How will things turn out with me? What shall be the end?" Beloved, the Word of God that we have read to you assures you that grace will prevail, "for whatsoever is born of God overcometh the world."

In the previous verse, the apostle has identified as a mark of all who have been born of God that they will keep His commandments. In our text, he gives the reason: they overcome the world. Thus, in these words, we find

1. a general proposition that all who are born of God will overcome the world and

2. faith as the means whereby they overcome the world.

THOSE BORN OF GOD OVERCOME THE WORLD

First, we have the general proposition that all who are born of God will overcome the world; that is, all, without exception, who have experienced this heavenly birth will overcome the world, "for whatsoever is born of God overcometh the world."

Born of God

We must now ascertain to whom the apostle ascribes such great things: they who are born of God. When he speaks of a birth, we are not to understand this as referring to natural birth but rather to a supernatural birth, for, as we will hear, the apostle describes it as being "born of God." The Word of God speaks of this being born of God in many different ways. One time it is described as the giving of a new heart and the putting of a new spirit within, consisting of the taking away of the stony heart and the giving of a heart of flesh (Ezek. 36:26). Next it will be designated as a circumcision of the heart: "And the LORD thy God will circumcise thine heart, and the heart of thy seed, to love the LORD thy God with all thine heart, and with all thy soul, that thou mayest live." It is also referred to as a creation: "We are his workmanship, created in Christ Jesus unto good works" (Eph. 2:10). Elsewhere it is referred to as being "born of the Spirit" (John 3:8). These are the most common descriptions of the new birth.

You must know that the expression "being born of God" or "being born again" must be understood in two ways: in a narrow sense and a broader sense. In the narrow sense of the word, it refers to the omnipotent and irresistible work of God that transforms the elect sinner from being spiritually dead to being spiritually alive. Regarding this narrow sense, our godly divines teach that all preparatory work, as its cause, must be excluded and that the new birth must precede faith as the root and origin from which true faith proceeds. If faith is indeed the act and exercise of a living soul, then it follows naturally that such activity presupposes life.

However, as to its broader sense, the new birth not only refers to the resurrection of the sinner but also the renewal of God's image in him and the perfection of God's work in the soul. When viewed in that sense, faith, repentance, and all the other graces of the Holy Spirit are included as issuing forth from this fountain. To affirm this, one ought to read the great Calvin's exposition of John 1:13, or that which the godly Gijsbertus Voetius teaches in his theological *Disputationes Selectae* (vol. 2, p. 457), or Herman Witsius in his *Animadversiones Irenicae* (chapters 5 and 6). We shall not quote them, for their works are known to all lovers of true godliness. We will speak of the new birth in the broader sense of the word and will show you why this transformation is referred to as a being born of God. We will explain this in greater detail, for as Calvin points out, this birth is the fountain from which faith proceeds.

We will also do so to prompt everyone to examine himself and to tread carefully with others. Although the soul is made alive in the twinkling of an eye, the perfection of this new life happens incrementally, and various aspects will manifest themselves at various times. Our prayer, therefore, is that God would send forth His light and His truth to lead you experientially into all truth.

If someone were to ask why we refer to this transformation as a birth, or rather, as a new birth, we respond that the Holy Spirit has weighty reasons for doing so. He does so in order that our thoughts, as poor men, would be elevated to lofty and exalted matters in clearly setting before us the nature of this new birth by comparing it to natural birth. Seek to discern this carefully and thoughtfully.

The Seed of Regeneration
All who are born come forth from a carefully and suitably deposited seed. This is equally true for this great spiritual transformation, and it is therefore designated as a birth. In an incomprehensible manner God plants His Word as the seed of regeneration in the heart of man and thereby engraves upon the heart the essential meaning of that Word. It is well known that the Word of regeneration is compared to a seed (Luke 8:11). The Savior declares the seed to be the Word of God, and Peter testifies that one is "born again, not of corruptible seed, but of incorruptible, by the word of God, which liveth and abideth for ever" (1 Peter 1:23). John, therefore, states that "his seed remaineth in him" (1 John 3:9).

The Nature of the Seed of Regeneration
Should someone ask what this seed is, I will reply that it is the creative act of God's omnipotence that causes the light of nature and the voice of one's conscience to accompany the Word. Because the conscience is in a state of slumber, it will permit a man to proceed on the way to perdition without any discernible anxiety or concern. Since it is evidently God's usual way to awaken the conscience, this was likely also the case with Lydia, whose heart the Lord opened. This regenerating power will strongly affirm that which the Holy Spirit reveals—the Spirit who works with and according to the Word of God. The heart will thus be irresistibly wrought upon to acquiesce without any hesitation in that which one beholds by an illuminated conscience and the light of God's Word. This initial stirring of life is thus planted in the soul as a seed. Therefore, God's Spirit not only causes the Word of the gospel to make one wise but also becomes "the power of God unto salvation"

(Rom. 1:16). The Word will then be "sharper than any twoedged sword" (Heb. 4:12), a fire, and a hammer to shatter the stony heart (Jer. 23:29).

The Evidence of the Seed of Regeneration

Someone might ask, What would affirm that such seed has been planted into the heart? My beloved, this will be evident when a person begins to pay careful attention to his actions. He will be held back from how he conducted himself formerly. Like the prodigal son, he will come to himself, and he will be and remain restless. Worldly engagements will become to him as dung and filthy mire. This poor soul becomes aware that matters ought to be different, although he does not know how matters ought to be. There is more, but we cannot possibly enumerate all the changes that may occur—and no one will be able to rest in this.

The Planting of the Seed of Regeneration

Should someone ask how this seed of regeneration is planted in the heart, we reply that its internal aspect appears to be hidden from us (John 3:8). It is better felt than articulated. However, we can say a few things about its outward manifestation.

1. Sometimes this seed is sown into the heart by *a godly upbringing*. Parents, teachers, and instructors will then have diligently engaged themselves. Most earnestly and prayerfully they will have taught who God is and who they are, and how needful it is to be born again. This will, in some measure, take root in the heart. Such persons will be kept from committing youthful sins, and the heart will gradually and imperceptibly be inclined to serve God with love, to read and search His Word, and to be conscientious in the performance of religious duties. Such will withdraw from and abhor ungodliness and ungodly men. The heart will be strongly attracted to godly and virtuous men, and amazingly, it will be somewhat discerning as to who is truly godly and who only speaks about it. Timothy was probably such a person. Since his youth he had been instructed in the Scriptures, and after that, he had to be inclined to exercise faith.

2. Sometimes it will enter the heart by *hearing others speak* of what is necessary unto salvation. Although the person himself is not addressed, he will reflect and think, "Is this indeed how it is? Must this be experienced in the heart? Apparently, I do not know this experientially, and yet I must know it."

This will pursue him when he sleeps and when he arises. Such thoughts will continually arise in the heart throughout the day, causing such persons to be entirely different from what they were before.

3. Sometimes it will enter the heart when one becomes aware of the fact that *as long as one can remember his deeds, there have been stirrings of the soul and of the conscience*, accompanied by an oppressive sense and fear for judgments and having a heart that continually predicts impending doom—as did Agabus. Such must have been true for Heman. He said, "I am afflicted and ready to die from my youth up" (Ps. 88:15), as well as those who, according to Paul, "through fear of death were all their lifetime subject to bondage" (Heb. 2:15). Although this will not prevent you from ever breaking forth into sin, it will prompt you to live a different life from what is manifested in others. It will also cause you to grieve when you do break forth into sin, causing you to be despondent and disconsolate. Nothing will either delight or refresh you, however delightful and refreshing it may be.

4. Sometimes it will enter the heart by *dreams during the nightly hours*. It may be that a person during his entire life has been impervious to all admonition and instruction by his pastors and fellow Christians, and it can even be that inner stirrings of the conscience have been extinguished. God will then avail Himself of a person's retirement at night when one's carnal mind will not be as active. He will confront a soul with her dreadful condition by setting before her eyes the day of judgment—or something else that is fearful, beholding, as it were, the burning of the elements. It can also be, however, that Jesus will appear to him in His loveliness and by His gracious invitations. The soul then appears to embrace Him by faith and to be stirred inwardly in so doing. Such an impression will abide when the person awakes, and he will be exercised with it since he will retain everything with conviction and clarity. Job probably had this in mind when he said that God also speaks in dreams (Job 7:14; 33:15–16).

5. Sometimes it will enter the heart by *a recognition that postponement rarely turns out well*, and the soul thereby perceives that her entire life has been nothing but a postponement of conversion, having disappointed both God and the soul with lofty promises and intentions. She recognizes that the time is short and that she needs to engage herself at once. This, in summary, is

what is expressed in these words: "To day if ye will hear his voice, harden not your hearts" (Heb. 3:15).

6. It can be that one either personally experiences *God's judgments and His afflicting hand* or observes this on others. One will thus behold with utmost certainty and inner conviction that he is to be blamed for all this due to his sins, and that far more severe and greater judgments are sure to be anticipated if he does not repent. Such is the essential meaning of these words: "When thy judgments are in the earth, the inhabitants of the world will learn righteousness" (Isa. 26:9).

7. Sometimes this seed will enter the heart when one observes the *conversion of his friends* in whose presence he has frequently sinned. One will then think, "We have kept company, and will this now cease? Shall we now and forever be separated?" The soul will then be engaged, and she will begin to seek, saying with Ruth, "Thy God must be my God, and thy people must be my people." Such must have been the case with the prodigal son when he reflected on the circumstances of his elder brother (Luke 15).

8. Sometimes the seed of regeneration will enter the soul when one has *an extensive grasp of the truth* in general and of the truth of the gospel in particular. One will find great delight in being solely occupied with and endorsing such things. Upon quiet reflection, or by the testimony of a faithful friend, one will perceive that he can yet perish with such an intellectual knowledge. And indeed, having some knowledge of Jesus differs significantly from knowing Him by the illumination of the Holy Spirit. This awareness will settle deeply in one's heart, and he will be convinced that until now, everything has been merely intellectual.

9. Sometimes the seed of regeneration will enter the soul when a person is *very intent on hearing something unusual.* God will providentially send a minister or exhorter a location where one is ignorant of the work of God and the means of grace. However, the person feels compelled to go and hear him, imagining himself to be fully suited to speak of, debate, and argue about these matters. Nevertheless, there will be something that will stop him in his tracks and to which he cannot reply. This being uppermost on one's mind, the heart will consequently be moved to interact with such people and to speak about such matters. This will become the net in which one is caught, and the

great work of God will commence. Zacchaeus's curiosity became the net in which he was caught.

10. Sometimes the seed of regeneration will enter the soul *when one intends to place himself under the means of grace to hear what these babblers have to say* and what they foist upon each other. However, God will then give such awe for the ministry of the Word that a spoken word will dovetail precisely with the condition of that person. The thoughts of his heart and the perdition that awaits him will be so powerfully impressed upon him that he will tremble and be stricken in his heart—in such a manner that from that moment forward, this impression will never leave him.

11. Sometimes there will be various occasions arranged by God in His wisdom when *the words of deceased parents or friends* will be impressed upon the heart. One will then think, "They have taught me this, and they have confronted me with the danger that I am in, as well as directed me to the means whereby I can be saved. However, I never gave it any further thought, and now they can no longer either speak with me or counsel me. How grievous indeed!" These reflections will stir up love for the deceased. One will begin to weep and supplicate, for the words of the deceased will again reassert themselves and make an impression upon the heart. Consequently, this will mark the beginning of God's work. Something will be infused in the heart that will never again depart. Instead, by God's grace, it will come to full development.

When believers reflect on the matters above, they may perceive that God has thus arrested and taken hold of them.

The Transformation of Regeneration

We call this great transformation a birth or a rebirth, for just as a natural birth brings forth a living creature, likewise in regeneration, a principle of life is generated in the soul. By God's creative power, a new creature is formed and activated: "For we are his workmanship, created in Christ Jesus" (Eph. 2:10). This is the new man, the new heart, and the divine nature. Receiving a new heart does not consist of an infusion of divine attributes, but rather a conforming of the soul to the communicable attributes of God. Regeneration is thus a being created after the image of God in Christ—that is, in knowledge, righteousness, and true holiness. We wish to address a few matters regarding this transformation.

The Essence of the Transformation of Regeneration
We will consider the essence of this transformation. Since this is a great mystery, we will only set before you what God's Word and our most venerated divines teach regarding this.

First, Ephesians 2:5 refers to this new birth as a *being quickened with Christ*: "Even when we were dead in sins, hath quickened us together with Christ." In John 5:25, we read, "Verily, verily, I say unto you, The hour is coming, and now is, when the dead shall hear the voice of the Son of God: and they that hear shall live." Ezekiel 16 articulates it as follows: "I said unto thee when thou wast in thy blood, Live; yea, I said unto thee when thou wast in thy blood, Live" (v. 6). Chapter 37 sets this before us as dead bones coming to life when prophesied upon: "And the bones came together, bone to his bone" (v. 7). These quoted Scripture passages prove sufficiently that the initial work of the Holy Spirit is to bring forth life.

Second, regeneration is also *the omnipotent, irresistible, and creative act of the triune God*—Father, Son, and Holy Spirit. However, it is particularly the work of the Holy Spirit, whereby the elect vessel, the elect man, receives the initial elements of this new creation. It will be like an embryo in the mother's body that consists of all the components of the human body that are not yet fully developed into what they shall be thereafter.

Beloved, I deem this to be what the Holy Spirit is teaching us (how it behooves us to speak with great humility) in those passages that speak of a new creation, a "hidden man [or new man] of the heart," and when Peter speaks of them "as newborn babes" (1 Peter 2:2). One may thus say that before they were born, that which would be brought forth in them was, in a sense, as an embryo—the beginning of life in the mother's body— containing all the components of a child, of a young man, and subsequently, of an adult, albeit not in a full-grown form. Similarly, a seed that has germinated contains, in principle, the roots, stem, leaves, and fruit, though not in their full-grown form.

Third, when the Spirit has implanted this principle of new life in the soul as the initial components of the new creature, *a union will be established between Christ and the regenerate person.* The establishment of this union is such that Christ, as the life-giving Head and by the Spirit, is united to this embryonic new creature in order to communicate to it all life. This union is essential for all subsequent benefits that must necessarily be bestowed upon the soul, and none of them can be received other than in union with Christ and for the sake of His precious and blessed vicarious merits.

Our preeminent divines speak of this union as a passive union, for Christ is by the Spirit united to this new creature without any contribution by this new creature. Similarly, a tree unites itself to the branch that is being grafted into it. The Spirit of God Himself uses the analogy of ingrafting to describe this great mystery. However, as Christ unites Himself to this new creature, so this new principle of life will unite itself by faith and love with Christ. Since this new life is only in its initial stage, this act will be weak, feeble, and often unconscious. Nevertheless, we believe that there will always be this union, and that the union between Jesus and the soul is always reciprocal.

To be consistent with our thinking, it thus follows that there is no intermediate state between life and death—as if there could be a third condition in which one would be neither dead nor alive.

To assist you in understanding our line of reasoning, I will communicate the thoughts of my blessed great-grandfather,[1] expressed in his treatise about faith:

> This initial faith, or the seed of faith, is the hope upon salvation by the all-sufficiency of Christ and His power flowing from His gracious being and His mediatorial offices. This initial faith, or its seed, also consists of a desire and love for the riches of the covenant of grace, seeing how necessary and excellent they are, and how unworthy one is in himself. When there is such faith, its embryonic beginning will consist of being convicted of one's sins and misery. These matters are a constituent element of the work of grace and are subservient to bringing about this union.

Thus far, my great-grandfather.

Witsius speaks in like manner. I will quote from his work *Irenicae*, chapters 5 and 6:

> They will be, by an authentic and genuine union (which from their side is only passive) united to Him as soon as the Spirit of Christ takes hold of them and infuses a principle of new life within them. The beginning of this life can only proceed from a union with the Spirit of Christ. The

---

1. This was the Scottish theologian and beloved preacher Andrew Gray (1633–1656), who began his pastorate in Glasgow at the age of twenty, and who passed away at the age of twenty-three. In the original Dutch text, Comrie refers to him as his great-great uncle, whereas in reality, Andrew Gray was his great-grandfather.

Spirit is to the spiritual life of the soul (albeit in a far more glorious manner) what the soul is to the body as to one's natural and human life. Just as the union of soul and body logically precedes the life of a human being, so the union between the Spirit of Christ and the soul precedes the spiritual life of the Christian. Since faith is an activity that proceeds from the principle of spiritual life, it should, therefore, be evident that one can responsibly assert that an elect person is truly and genuinely united to Christ before he exercises faith. However, the reciprocal union is a matter in which the elect person is also very active from his side, prompting the soul to go to Christ. She will join herself to Him, accommodate herself to Him, and wholeheartedly cling to Him in conformity to her need. However, this only transpires by faith.

Thus we observe how the Word and our theologians speak of this matter.

The Evidences of Regeneration

We will now consider briefly the evidences that the person in whom regeneration transpires has been made alive.

1. This will be evident in that this person will experience in his spiritual exercises the fulfillment of one of the great promises of the covenant of grace. We read in Ezekiel 20:43, "And *ye shall loathe yourselves* in your own sight for all your evils that ye have committed." The soul will now begin to perceive who God is, and with Job, she will now abhor herself, "and repent in dust and ashes" (Job 42:6). She will see herself now as more unclean and deformed than the most unclean and deformed monster. She will exclaim, "Unclean, unclean," and with Ephraim, "I was ashamed, yea, even confounded" (Jer. 31:19).

2. Such a person will evidently have *an aversion to what formerly was his pleasure and delight.* Oh, the soul can only be troubled when she thinks about having had such delight in sin and in having indulged herself in things that had nothing to do with God! She will now say with the prodigal son, "There is such good food to be had. With God, there are the benefits of the covenant of grace: joy, peace, justification, adoption, sanctification, and glorification. Nevertheless, I have indulged myself 'with the husks that the swine did eat' (Luke 15:16)—the things of the world and sin. Oh, what nauseating food this is! Death is in the pot!" Such a person will say to sin, "Depart at once from my soul accursed brood—you who are the dreadful murderers of my God."

3. This will also be evident from the *fear and trembling* one will experience. The head will be sick, and the heart will be distraught so that a person will be entirely disconsolate and will begin to tremble when he thinks of God and himself. However, such stirrings will proceed more out of love for God than he has ever experienced before. We observe this clearly in David when we read that his heart smote him. In Hosea 11:11 we read, "They shall tremble as a bird out of Egypt, and as a dove out of the land of Assyria: and I will place them in their houses, saith the LORD." There will be a great trembling before God's majesty, causing them to approach Him with trembling.

4. The regeneration of the soul will also be evident in that her eyes will *not be as lifted up as before*. Instead, they will be cast down. David says, "LORD, my heart is not haughty, nor mine eyes lofty" (Ps. 131:1). Oh, that poor worm of the dust who formerly thought that salvation could not possibly elude him and who, with the proud Pharisee, could thank God that he was not as other men are! Now he not only comes with his upper lip curled, crying out, "Unclean, unclean," but with the publican, he does not even dare to lift his eyes or to look sideways or even open them. When he looks upward, he sees himself as being indebted to God with a debt of ten thousand talents and not even having a single penny to pay it. When he looks sideways, everything in the world will accuse him. When he looks within, he will be confronted by his conscience that will be as ten thousand witnesses against him. When he looks downward, he will perceive the place of which he is more than worthy due to his sins. He will, therefore, exclaim with a humble eye and heart, "Be merciful to me, the sinner!"

5. This new life will be evident in its breathing, for *prayer* is now detected, albeit it will now be more difficult than before. Then one prayed effortlessly, but now such a person discovers that if he could earn heaven and earth with one sigh, prayer apart from the Spirit is utterly impossible. His cry will be,

> Without Thee, I can neither sigh nor take refuge to Thee on high.
> Without Thee, I cannot rejoice, even though Thou art gracious.
> Without Thee, neither my eyes nor my heart will be inclined.
> Without Thee, my only life, I am and remain like a stone.[2]

6. This new life will also manifest itself in *the tears that now begin to flow*. One will now say with Jeremiah, "Oh that my head were waters, and mine eyes a

---

2. In the original, Comrie quotes the stanza of a poem.

fountain of tears" (Jer. 9:1), and with David, "I water my couch with my tears" (Ps. 6:6). One will say, "However it may be, my grieving eyes will never let the well be dry, and they will water my cheeks and my bed."[3]

Weeping to Jesus for Jesus will yield the utmost joy and happiness to the soul, so that she may say, "My beloved Jesus, I know that I cannot please Thee with my mourning. However, my grieving and troubled heart finds delight in Thee even in my mourning." Such souls will, therefore, say, "Thou who dost hear the groaning of poor souls, be merciful to me so that I will no longer miss the one who is so precious to my soul."

7. This new life will furthermore be evident in that one's back and shoulders will be *weighed down by a heavy burden*. Such a person will be so wearied by this oppression that he will surrender everything into God's hands. He will now be in a spiritual frame that is pleasing to Christ, who calls such persons to come to Him, saying, "Come unto me, all ye that labour and are heavy laden, and I will give you rest" (Matt. 11:28).

8. Finally, this new life will be evident in that such persons have *the capacity to hear*. Sometimes the soul will hear that Jesus came to save sinners and that there is no other way but through Him. They will hear, among other things, that He beckons and invites them so very sweetly and that particularly those who come to Him will be welcomed by Him. The soul will then also hear, "Yes, that may be so, but you have postponed this coming for such a long time. Your sins are too great, and you have enjoyed them far too much. If you were now to go to Him, He would ask you, 'How did you come to Me?' Do you wish to make Jesus a servant of sin? Your heart is not tender enough, and you do not see your sins as you should. You have not been humbled enough by the law, and you have been deficient in your spiritual duties. As a matter of fact, you are not one of the elect, and they alone are the objects of God's favor."

These considerations will cause such a person to be between a rock and a hard place. He will be "afflicted, tossed with tempest, and not comforted" (Isa. 54:11). He will be so desirous of relying upon Jesus alone, and yet he does not dare to do so. That will cause him much sorrow and restlessness.

---

3. In this paragraph and the next, Comrie is again quoting Dutch poetry.

These are evidences that the seed of regeneration has germinated in someone's soul. Other evidences of spiritual life, such as one's affections, we will bypass for now.

The Mysterious Miracle of Regeneration

Natural conception and birth are mysteries, and therefore, Job describes them by saying, "Hast thou not poured me out as milk, and curdled me like cheese?" (Job 10:10). David writes in Psalm 139:14–15, "I am fearfully and wonderfully made.… My substance was not hid from thee, when I was made in secret, and curiously wrought in the lowest parts of the earth."

In John 3:8, the Savior declares that this is equally true of spiritual birth. In Mark 4:26–27, He speaks of the kingdom of heaven "as if a man should cast seed into the ground…and the seed should spring and grow up, he knoweth not how."

1. When considering *the author or the moving cause* of this spiritual birth, all that transpires in this process is indeed mysterious and miraculous to man. Neither a man nor an angel is its author but rather God Himself by His Spirit. This divine person initiates this within the economy of God's grace by the Word of truth. It would already be a miracle if angels were to be the object of His favor. However, that the incomprehensible and blessed God would bestow this upon a sinful man, given the fact that He, in Himself, possesses all felicity and has no need of being served by men, is a wonder of all wonders! One may thus exclaim, "What is man, that thou art mindful of him? and the son of man, that thou visitest him?" (Ps. 8:4).

2. Considering *the work itself*, we deem it to be a mystery and a great wonder above all wonders. Although creation was a miraculous event, yet it does not compare to this miracle, as it only resulted in the formation of raw material. The new birth, however, produces a heavenly jewel: a creature bearing God's image, consisting of knowledge, righteousness, and true holiness. In the act of creation, there was no resistance, and there was nothing that opposed it. "He commanded, and it stood fast" (Ps. 33:9). However, in the work of re-creation, everything within man will oppose it, for "the carnal mind is enmity against God: for it is not subject to the law of God, neither indeed can be" (Rom. 8:7).

The resurrection of the dead is a great miracle, but here we have a greater miracle, namely, the resurrection of spiritually dead people. They are resurrected in the same manner as Christ was raised from the dead, namely, by God's extraordinary power "according to the working of his mighty power" (Eph. 1:19). We speak thus of the new birth because as Christ—who lay dead in the grave as to His body, was subject to the curse of the law, and had the devil as the keeper of His grave—was resurrected by the exercise of supernatural power, likewise, the elect sinner, having been killed by the law, must be resurrected from the grave and come forth.

3. It is also a wondrous work when we consider *the mediate or secondary causes* of the new birth. These are neither visible miracles, nor voices from heaven, nor visions, nor someone rising from the dead in order to arrest the attention of people but rather the simple Word of God as recorded in the Bible and frequently expounded in all simplicity. Paul writes that God has purposed to save people through the foolishness of preaching. Indeed, God places this treasure, as the seed of regeneration, "in earthen vessels, that the excellency of the power may be of God, and not of us" (2 Cor. 4:7).

4. The new birth is a wondrous work when we consider *how this seed is planted within and how it subsequently develops*. We have already seen how wondrously God achieves this by illuminating the understanding and renewing the will. However, as to how this light enters and how the will is actuated with bands of love and cords of a man (Hos. 11:4), we know no more than "how the bones do grow in the womb of her that is with child" (Eccl. 11:5).

5. The new birth is also a wondrous work when we consider *the subjects* of this miracle. Rather than angels, they are but sinful men. And among them there are "not many wise men after the flesh, not many mighty, not many noble" (1 Cor. 1:26); rather, they are the poor and the ungodly who live like the foal of a wild ass (Jer. 2:24). Upon comparing 1 Corinthians with the words of Christ, we will observe that publicans and harlots will enter. Every regenerate person must, therefore, confess that there was nothing in him that favorably distinguishes him from others, and that the thrust of these words is evident to his soul, for God did not choose him due to any attraction on his part. He will readily acknowledge that God did it for His own sake.

6. Yes, the new birth is indeed a mysterious and wondrous work when one considers *its ultimate goal*: eternal salvation. He who experiences this new birth will receive "a far more exceeding and eternal weight of glory" (2 Cor. 4:17) that will be revealed on the final day. The new birth's ultimate goal is

not achieved by heavy labor and exertion but rather by coming with the noose around our neck, by confessing our unrighteousness, and by believing instead of working. By faith one will be very willing to receive this salvation as a poor beggar out of the hand of Jesus, without money and without price (Isa. 55:1). Oh, eternity will neither impede the believer in his adoration of this, nor will it be too long to explore the greatness, mystery, and wondrous nature of this salvation.

Regeneration by Grace Alone

Natural and spiritual birth have this in common: they are both entirely passive. A brazen Pelagian may speak much of the capacity of free will, but God's Spirit, who knows us best, says that we are dead in trespasses and sins (Eph. 2:1). As noted earlier, God's Word indeed and always attributes this birth to either the Father or the Spirit. The very nature of the matter also teaches us that the one who is born must necessarily be brought forth by another. Therefore, he who experiences this transformation will be compelled to confess, "Not unto us, O LORD, not unto us, but unto thy name give glory" (Ps. 115:1). We acquiesce with the words of Paul that God alone had distinguished such souls from others when He regenerated them while they were still in their blood (Ezek. 16:6). Given its extraordinary significance, this doctrine must, therefore, in our days be believed and confessed in all its purity. How many are there not who ascribe too much to man regarding the beginning and continuation of spiritual life! Thereby they shortchange the true work of the Holy Spirit. Therefore, my beloved, I will demonstrate this succinctly to make clear to you that everything is of God and unto God so that everyone would render Him the honor due to Him.

Infinite power must be exercised to bring about this new birth—as was true in creation when there was absolutely nothing upon which to build. Paul, therefore, speaks of it as "the exceeding greatness of his power to usward who believe, according to the working of his mighty power" (Eph. 1:19). We should thus not be surprised that few are converted under the means of grace—yes, even very few were saved through Christ's own preaching. Unless "the exceeding greatness of his power" is exerted, no one's heart will be so divorced from sin that he will follow Jesus (Matt. 9:9). Augustine very correctly stated, *Sumus Dei creaturae, qua homines & qua justi,* that is, "We are God's creatures as men and as justified sinners."

Only God can achieve this work, for the observable manifestations of the new birth are of such a nature that they exceed all created powers. When the apostles performed miracles, it was an irrefutable affirmation that God was with them. Likewise, when someone loves God and obeys His precepts from a correct motive, it is proof that God is at work, for in and of ourselves, we are incapable of any good. Peter, therefore, says that when such fruits are evident, one has become a partaker of the divine nature (2 Peter 1:4).

Unless this were true, all boasting could not be excluded, thereby rendering all honor to God—as it must be, according to Paul. If it were not so, how could Christ have said, "I thank thee, O Father, Lord of heaven and earth, because thou…hast revealed them unto babes" (Matt. 11:25)?

The Completeness of the New Creature

Upon a natural birth, the child that is born will already wondrously have all the body parts it will ever have, all of which have their proper place by the arrangement of the great Creator. David undoubtedly had this in mind regarding one's natural birth, saying, "I will praise thee; for I am fearfully and wonderfully made: marvellous are thy works; and that my soul knoweth right well…. Thine eyes did see my substance, yet being unperfect; and in thy book all my members were written, which in continuance were fashioned, when as yet there was none of them" (Ps. 139:14, 16). Job speaks in like fashion regarding the preparation of this small body for birth, saying, "Hast thou not poured me out as milk, and curdled me like cheese? Thou hast clothed me with skin and flesh, and hast fenced me with bones and sinews" (Job 10:10–11). We believe that the same applies to the spiritual realm, and regeneration is, therefore, designated as a birth. We will affirm this by addressing two matters.

Components of Spiritual Life

We will first consider the essential components of spiritual life as they are established by God's power and, therefore, necessarily belong to the essence of the new creature. We will focus on their number. Some theologians deem all the fruits of the Spirit (Gal. 5:22–23) to be essential components of this spiritual life. Others arrive at an Aristotelian structure of wisdom, prudence, and virtue. Still others arrive at eight aspects in conformity with Christ's eight Beatitudes (Matt. 5:3–12). Paul, however, has the best instruction for us when he designates and limits them to those given in 1 Corinthians 13:13: "And now abideth faith, hope, charity." These aspects are essential for the new creature and also constitute the fountain from which everything else proceeds, namely, "joy, peace, longsuffering, gentleness, goodness, faith, meekness, [and] temperance" (Gal. 5:22–23). Yes, being poor in spirit, mourning, hungering and thirsting after righteousness, being pure in heart, being peacemakers, and being merciful also proceed from this fountain.

Faith as a Component of the New Creature
Faith is thus the first component. As we have stated earlier, it is not yet present in its mature and complete form; however, it is present as to its core and foundational principles.

1. One of these aspects is *knowledge*—that is, at least as to its initial principles. Such knowledge is absolutely necessary according to Christ in John 17:3: "And this is life eternal, that they might know thee the only true God, and Jesus Christ, whom thou hast sent." And that faith is wrought by the preached or read Word of God. We cannot say how minimal a measure of knowledge there must be if one can speak of the initial seeds of faith—as was true for the disciples. However, without insisting on a given measure, we maintain that the following will be such that it will not even grieve a little one in faith but rather will lift him up.

    a. You will know that through sin, you are estranged from God and the life of God so that neither you nor an angel from heaven can deliver you from this misery and make you happy.

    b. You will know the Lord Jesus to be full of grace and truth, and that He is the only Mediator given under heaven by whom you can be saved (Acts 4:12).

    c. You will acknowledge with conviction that in order to be saved, you must be united to Jesus by a true faith.

Although these matters will indeed be present concurrently in the soul, they will not all manifest themselves concurrently. Instead, there will be the one and then the other.

2. The soul that knows and acquiesces in this truth will, as a second principle and seed of faith, *hunger and thirst*. Such a soul will desire, long, and yearn intensely for Jesus, exclaiming, "Oh that He would be mine, that He would be my portion, and that I might be united to Him!" (cf. Matt. 5:6). Many deem

this to be insignificant. However, although it is not the preeminent compo-nent of faith, the initial true principles are there, for one will never exclaim in uprightness "Oh, that I might have Jesus!" unless there are attempts to take refuge to Jesus and to surrender to Him.

3. The third principle of faith is *surrender to God's will to be saved in His ordained way*. One will perceive and approve of it, for he will only be desirous to be saved in this way. With theological precision, brother Lampe[4] defines faith as a being in agreement with God regarding the way of salvation. Many eminent theologians describe saving faith as a heartfelt longing for Jesus. Although this is certainly not a complete description of the matter, it identi-fies faith's foundational principles and seeds. We would be able to enumerate additional matters as the foundational principles of faith, but we have already done so in *The ABC of Faith*.

Hope as a Component of the New Creature
According to the order established by Paul, the second aspect that defines spiritual life is hope. Although it cannot yet be designated as an immovable hope, there will, in a small measure, be a good expectation of Jesus. This small beginning of hope is expressed in the use of the word *perhaps*—such as, "Perhaps God will hear." Such souls will find themselves between hope and fear. Nevertheless, as Eliphaz counsels Job, they will endeavor to cast themselves upon God and acquaint themselves with the Lord in order to be at peace (Job 22:21).

Love as a Component of the New Creature
The third aspect of spiritual life is *love*, and this will manifest itself more strongly than the other two. This expresses itself in the restlessness of the soul and the esteeming of Jesus above a thousand worlds. The beginning believer has a high esteem and a deep inner yearning for Jesus, which are such that they exceed everything else. Granted, such a person will frequently doubt because he experiences so little from Jesus's side. Nevertheless, he will say, "Even if I had to die, I do love Jesus." Therefore, in our dealings with all who dare not speak with liberty about their own salvation, we must not seek to

─────────

4. Comrie is referring to Friedrich Adolph Lampe (1683–1729), a German Reformed professor of theology and pastor, who also served as professor in Utrecht. He was a late representative of the Dutch Further Reformation (*Nadere Reformatie*).

pressure them that they must believe. One must also not rebuke them that either they are unwilling or that they do not love Christ, for you could then sinfully oppose the work of God.

The Priority of Faith in the Heart

Furthermore, it should be noted that everything must be given its proper place. I will not detain you by proving that the heart is the *primum vivens* and the *ultimum moriens*; that is, the heart is the first to live and the last to die. Likewise, the initial grace wrought by God in the soul is faith, and the other benefits will proceed from this in the order established by God's Word. This is also essential, for faith, however weak it may be, unites the soul with Jesus so that the other benefits will manifest themselves according to the measure of faith.

New Life Fostered by Care

As a new life is nourished following a natural birth so that the newborn can develop well until it reaches maturity, likewise, the work of God will also be surrounded by great care. This care will enable this work to continue to grow and to reach maturity. This is one of the reasons why we refer to this great transformation as a birth. To consider God's hidden care in this work, we will address a few matters.

1. God's work will frequently be nourished and strengthened by *the experience of spiritual frames*. One will thus, with the most tender and lively desires of the soul, be wholeheartedly privileged to call upon God and very tenderly open one's heart before the Lord. Oh, such a soul will have it good for herself as long as such a frame lasts and as long as her heart is tender. She will then indeed be able to say, "How sweet it is to lament and to weep!"[5] One should not be too hasty in suspecting that such souls are resting in their spiritual frame. Not at all! Instead, they are so delighted that their heart is drawn to Jesus. It is wrong, however, that they again become so miserable and unbelieving when these spiritual motions cease!

2. This new principle of spiritual life will also be brought to further development when the soul begins to discover that *salvation is not impossible*. Earlier she had to say, "It is without hope." However, now that she can no longer sustain herself spiritually, God will bring to mind how Manasseh and many

---

5. Comrie is quoting an experiential poem.

others have been converted and that His grace is sufficient for the greatest of sinners. As a result, the soul will not despair but rather cling to God's tender mercies. Were the latter not the case, there could also be no exercises in the soul. Thus one should not always be suspicious toward those who cherish such a hope but rather deal with them according to the progression of God's work in them.

3. Such strengthening of the soul can also occur when she is given some *light regarding the essence of the covenant of grace*, namely, that it is immovable and one-sided, and that thus everything is offered freely to the poor sinner. Although such a soul does not yet perceive this spontaneous and conscious entering into the covenant, yet it will strengthen the soul. She frequently attempts to do so and takes some courage in doing so.

4. Such strengthening can also occur when the Word of God declares that certain traits are *marks of spiritual life*. God will, at times, so direct the one who proclaims the Word that the matters experienced by the soul—of which no one has any knowledge but God and herself—are set forth as the work of God's Spirit and as evidences of spiritual life. During this period of their lives, such souls will be encouraged to bring this before God, asking Him to shed light upon all of this.

5. Such strengthening can occur when *others think favorably of us*, although it can sometimes also be grieving when there are people who think too favorably of us. However, it can also serve as an encouragement when men judge favorably of us, making us zealous and giving us food for thought. It will also stir us up to deceive neither ourselves nor others so that we may personally perceive and experience what others deem us to possess.

6. Finally, there are *passages and promises in Scripture that so explicitly articulate their spiritual condition that they will be wonderfully moved by it.* Furthermore, although they do not quite dare to apply this to themselves for fear of this either being merely a matter of the mind or because the matter is too high for them, yet it will yield hidden support and stir them up to proceed further in this way.

Early Exertions of New Life
Before natural birth, one often observes that a child will already attempt to break forth in order to take its place among the living. Such also occurs with

a spiritual birth proceeding from God by means of the Word of truth. Such a person will exert himself, and one will frequently notice that he will make every effort to do so.

1. There will be a perceived *longing* for an authentic, clear, and transparent revelation of Jesus to the heart as being the altogether willing Mediator of the covenant. Presumptuous temporal believers are already satisfied if they, accompanied by some emotion, can engage their minds to read about Jesus. However, they are but stony-ground hearers. They receive the Word with joy, but since this seed lacks a root, it will dry up and wither when its shoot encounters distress. The root of faith will be lacking. However, living souls yearn most for those matters whereby they, with a confident heart, may take a decisive step. It is with them as it was with Rachel in an entirely different situation. They must have this Jesus, or else they will die. The observance of religious duties, the shedding of tears, the making of vows, or joyful spiritual frames will, in the end, grieve them because they neither find nor experience Jesus in these things to their comfort. Therefore, they seek Him early, and their soul will thirst for Him as "a dry and thirsty land, where no water is" (Ps. 63:1).

2. This exertion will also manifest itself in a continual *prayer* unto the Lord of one who asks that he may personally be reconciled with God. One can be in such circumstances for a long time—a time in which one fully acquiesces in the covenant of grace. Since, however, such persons do not perceive that their prayers are heard, they still deem themselves to be no partaker of these matters. They consider all to be but head knowledge, thinking that with all that they have experienced, they will yet perish—all because they cannot yet with full confidence rest in Jesus as Surety.

3. Such spiritual exertion will sometimes manifest itself in that the soul will occasionally receive some *insight* into the way of grace. They then appear to be convinced of the willingness of the Mediator and themselves. However, when they then endeavor to take the great step of faith, either light will suddenly be withdrawn or there will be a change in their spiritual frame, or they will have all manner of distressing thoughts so that they are fearful of exercising faith. Similarly, when a person has to jump across a relatively narrow stream, as he approaches, he is sufficiently confident that he can do so.

Then, however, something will come to mind, causing him to tremble. Now, as much as he desires to be on the other side, he dare not proceed.

Many do not get beyond this point. Anyone who calmly examines the ways of God with himself and others can affirm this from his own experience. Isaiah 37:3 expresses this: "For the children are come to the birth, and there is not strength to bring forth." The Lord speaks of this in Hosea 13:13, saying, "He is an unwise son; for he should not stay long in the place of the breaking forth of children." As Paul states in Galatians 4:19,[6] ministers must, therefore, labor to bring them to birth.

Grace at Work in the Whole Process

As a natural child will be born at the appointed time, so will it be in the spiritual realm. The spiritual birth of a person will also occur at God's appointed time. Before we examine this in further detail, I very much wish to affirm that we do not agree with those who claim that all that we have addressed thus far is not of a saving nature until a soul consciously engages in a real and reciprocal transaction with Christ. By no means! We believe that the saving work of God begins at the first moment that the seed of regeneration is planted in the heart and that God will see to it that such souls will come to birth—the one sooner and the other later; the one with more clarity and the other with less clarity. This is as certain as the fact that He will see to it that none who have been given to Christ in the counsel of peace will perish. Thus, it is evident that these exercises are indeed saving in nature.

The nature of the metaphor confirms this—that is, the resemblance between a spiritual birth and how natural procreation transpires. The rule governing the exposition of a metaphorical figure of speech stipulates that the metaphor must apply to the reality it represents. That reality is a spiritual one, as exemplified by a natural reality. My question is this: Is the infant not alive until it visibly appears at a natural birth and when others affirm it to be alive? Yes, it is indeed alive! Thus, if there is spiritual life in a person, it will genuinely be saving in nature—although others and the person himself may not yet perceive it to be so.

If a person truly experiences the most intimate spiritual exercises and frames that proceed exclusively from the covenant of grace, it means that there is indeed a saving work in the soul. I believe that our nature, however civilized it may be, will never produce this. Neither can our natural faculties

---

6. "My little children, of whom I travail in birth again until Christ be formed in you."

produce this, nor can this be attributed to the influence of the covenant of works whereby the naturally aroused conscience will be stirred fully to engage itself spiritually. As long as the tree is corrupt, such a person will not produce those spiritual frames promised only in the covenant of grace. That can only be attributed to those who are in this covenant.[7]

Far be it from us that we would think, let alone affirm, that the spiritual motions of temporal believers and truly gracious souls only differ as to degree. Instead, we believe that they differ fundamentally as to the essence of the matter. Has there ever been a temporal believer who has received anything experientially, however little it may be, of a genuine benefit of the covenant of grace? No, for then, such who would have received this promised benefit would yet perish forever! Anyone who maintains this contradicts the Word of God and unravels our doctrine. Living souls have the essence of the promise within their hearts, namely—as we have already seen—a loathing of self, a confessing of God to be who He is, an intense yearning for Him, and a tender willingness of heart. As you know, these are matters promised to all who are in the covenant of grace. Thus I legitimately conclude that there is indeed a saving work in the soul.

The presence of such a saving work in the soul is also evident from the spiritual frames that our great God and Savior, the infallible teacher of righteousness, pronounces to be blessed and are thus truly salvific. They proceed from the root of spiritual life planted in the heart by the Holy Spirit. We all know well how emphatically Matthew 5 pronounces as blessed all who hunger and intensely thirst after God as a hart pants after the water brooks. We read in verse 6, "Blessed are they which do hunger and thirst after righteousness." We would prove to be ignorant of God's Word if we were to say that this refers to people who already had eaten and drunk. You will find no support of this in Scripture. Jesus lifted His voice and said to the multitudes, "Blessed are they who do hunger"—whomever they may be—"for they shall be filled."

It would also be incorrect to maintain that this pertains to the future, meaning that they will not be blessed until they have been filled. No one has ever doubted the meaning of these words—neither their literal sense nor their spiritual sense. My question is, How would such a needy soul be comforted if one were to say, "When you eat, you are blessed"? It is the very intent

---

7. Here Comrie begins with a metaphor (the tree) but then immediately speaks of its fruit as being the spiritual frames of the soul. This is therefore a broken or truncated metaphor.

of the Savior in such circumstances to "lift up the hands which hang down, and the feeble knees" (Heb. 12:12), being desirous, at the right moment, "to speak a word in season" (Isa. 50:4).

If Jesus had had the future in mind, He evidently would have used the future tense rather than the present tense. For example, He would have said, "Blessed shall they be who hunger when they are satisfied." The contrary is true, however. He pronounces them blessed because they *hunger*, for it is the promised work of His life-giving Spirit that they shall eat and be satisfied. Thus the actual spiritual birth, in distinction from all that is preliminary, signifies the perfection of faith. Such a soul will, therefore, consciously and with an assured heart embrace Jesus in such a manner that she may believe that Christ is hers—that is, upon having embraced Him in response to His offer— and that she is Christ's by her act of surrender to Him. We have spoken of this in the previous treatises, and we will subsequently say more of this. We will, therefore, presently not address this.

Regeneration Produces a New Creature

As a natural birth brings forth a new creature, so does the new birth. Paul testifies of this, saying, "Therefore if any man be in Christ, he is a new creature: old things are passed away; behold, all things are become new" (2 Cor. 5:17). I propose that we now focus on this primary aspect and examine in detail several matters that are to be found in this new creature. I ask that you pay careful attention as I set them before you.

General Observations about the New Creature

A powerful transformation will manifest itself in this new creature. We have already addressed this but will now do so in greater detail.

1. Generally speaking, we can say that this transformation pertains to *the essence of one's being*. Granted, all who disagree with us will deny this. However, as a creative act brings forth a real entity resulting in a genuinely existing creature, likewise does a new creature emerge by this creative act. This new creature will be a partaker of the divine nature, will receive a new heart, and will be created in God's image. These are not merely theological terms but essential realities. Indeed, that which manifests itself in tangible activities must itself be a tangible reality.

2. The observable transformation in this new creature is *common to all*

God's children. As a result of this, they all become members of the Christian community. The same image of God will be stamped upon the heart of all believers, irrespective of whether they hail from either Africa or America. They will resemble each other as two drops of water, or as two faces reflected by a mirror. All believers, without exception, whether here on earth or in heaven, have the same new nature and the same life proceeding from God. The Spirit of adoption here on earth is the Spirit of glory in heaven. That which prompts the new creature here below to cry, "Abba, Father," causes all who are in heaven to rejoice in their Abba Father with unspeakable joy and delight. Thus it follows that this transformation is real and essential.

3. This new creature will be in a state that will be entirely *contrary to his previous spiritual state.* Is a sharper contrast imaginable than between light and darkness, between flesh and spirit, between east and west, or between the seed of the serpent and the seed of the woman? The disposition of the heart before and following this transformation is comparable to the difference between God and sin. He that now has become a new creature has a heart that is now fully inclined toward God and opposed to sin. He will be stripped of his inclination toward sin and will now be clothed with heartfelt inclinations toward God. He will now begin to hate that which he formerly loved. Formerly he was estranged from the life of God, whereas now he will be weaned from his indulgence in sinful lusts. That which formerly was as heaven to him will now be a hell to him. That ought not to be a surprise, for he "hath [been] delivered…from the power of darkness, and hath [been] translated…into the kingdom of" the Son of God's love (Col. 1:13). The apostle here uses a word rendered as "translated." This word, as originally used, describes the migration of a nation to another geographic region, resulting in its citizens now breathing a different air and living in a different climate. In short, a wolf now becomes a lamb. "Instead of the thorn shall come up the fir tree, and instead of the brier shall come up the myrtle tree: and it shall be to the LORD for a name, for an everlasting sign that shall not be cut off" (Isa. 55:13).

4. The transformation in this new creature that "is born of God" impacts *the entire man.* Having conquered Mansoul by His all-conquering power, Prince Immanuel will drive out old Diabolus. He will plant the flags of His conquering grace in every faculty of the soul without any exceptions. This transformation will introduce a purity into the soul that encompasses all the

faculties of the soul. This purity establishes a strong unity among those faculties and enables the entire soul to subject itself to God's law and to make its holiness a priority. Thus David, rather than seeking God with merely one of the faculties of his soul, seeks Him with his entire heart. His mind will now be illuminated rather than being a place of darkness, prompting such a man to submit himself to God. The will shall be tender and compliant rather than intractable. There will be humility rather than pride. Consequently, God's will becomes his will, and he will embrace God's law. His conscience, having been cleansed, will be pure, and all his faculties will function as the wings of his soul, enabling the soul to fly to the heart of God and the Rock, Christ. This lovely purity and harmony of the soul's faculties will be expressed by the continual cry, "Upward, upward, my soul, to that which is above! There is nothing here below. True life, love, and praise will only be where Jesus is!"[8] Examine yourself thereby. If such a transformation is not characteristic of all of your spiritual faculties, your claim to such a transformation will be unfounded.

A Detailed Analysis of the New Creature
We will now address several specific matters.

Transformation from the Inside Out
The observable transformation in the new creature that is born of God proceeds from the inner recesses of the soul. Not only is there a cleansing of the outside of the cup and an external plastering of the graves, but the dead man's bones are cast out. David not only desires to have clean hands but rather a pure heart (Ps. 51:10). If the hands of a clock are to function correctly, its inner mechanism must function correctly. Without the inner motion of that mechanism, the clock will stand still.

1. This transformation is internal and primarily regards *the principles by which one operates*. The natural man operates by way of natural principles. He is like a wound-up clock. However, when the weights have fully descended or when the spring has lost its tension, the clock will stand still. The natural man will only be engaged as long as it suits him, or because he thinks that it will either save him, enable him to escape judgment, or to be held in esteem by

---

8. Comrie here quotes a well-known poem by Jodocus van Lodenstein.

the godly. The Savior teaches that such are the reasons why he will not persevere. Their piety neither has any root nor proceeds from an inner principle.

Furthermore, it is precisely from that inner principle that all the activity of the new creature proceeds. The seed of God that has been sown within him will remain in him. His heart is as a fountain from which, in the words of the Savior, streams of living water will flow (John 7:38). He will spontaneously gravitate toward God and think about God. Everyone should, therefore, examine himself and ask the question, What motivates me to read, listen, and pray? If it is no more than an external form, it will amount to nothing. All fruits will only be good if the tree is good. However, if the tree is corrupt, all its fruits will be corrupt.

There are two functioning principles of this new creature: faith and love.

a. First, there is *faith*. By this gracious gift, we are united to Christ, and any fitness to achieve anything we will extract from His fullness. Apart from faith, the most excellent moral deeds are but accursed sin, for Paul says that without faith, it is impossible to please God (Heb. 11:6). As to God's commandments, apart from faith, our serving of God will only be will worship. Apart from faith in the promises, a person will be acting in his own strength and with wrong motives. This faith was the difference between Paul's praying before grace had been shed abroad in his heart and after that, for it was then that Jesus said emphatically, "Behold, he prayeth" (Acts 9:11). Paul prayed when he was still a Pharisee, but Christ accepted none of those prayers. His prayers before were those of a proud Pharisee, but then they became the prayers of a newly converted man, crying out, "Lord, what wilt thou have me to do?" (Acts 9:6). His prayers now proceeded from faith.

b. Furthermore, there is *love*. One may have many incentives to engage himself spiritually. Such incentives may either be a hope upon life in heaven and the fear of hell, the experience of losses, or the compulsion of an awakened conscience. However, the fire that will truly ignite the heart will be love. The heart will then yearn after God and will desire nothing besides God. Psalm 73:25 expresses this: "Whom have I in heaven but thee? and there is none upon earth that I desire beside thee." Asaph, therefore, adds the following: "It is good for me to draw near to God" (v. 28)—or, *God drawing near to me is my desire*. Apart from love, everything will be tasteless and void of feeling. This love, however, will be as coals of fire, as the Lord's vehement flame that "many waters cannot quench" (Song 8:6–7). One must, therefore, examine himself whether all of his spiritual life proceeds from these principles, for when Paul speaks of this new creature (Gal. 6:15), he states that "faith worketh by love" (Gal. 5:6).

2. This inner transformation does not only pertain to the principles by which we live; rather, there will also be a transformation as to *the objectives one pursues*. The old creature aims at the magnification of self, whereas for the new man, God's honor will be the objective of his life. Although the inclination toward good things will not be taken away, that inclination will now have as its focus that all things may redound to God's glory. The regenerate man will now engage his wisdom, his intellect, and all his faculties to feel and taste the incomprehensible God in His footsteps and to render Him honor in all things. The apostle exhorts us accordingly: "Whether therefore ye eat, or drink, or whatsoever ye do, do all to the glory of God" (1 Cor. 10:31). Only such a walk of life will conform to the gospel. Is it not so that the first inclination of a germinated seed will be heavenward? Likewise, the new creature, having received its life from God, will be desirous to end with it in Him.

     a. This will, first of all, be evident from the fact that God's preeminent objective with His new creation is the glorification of Himself. He does all things for His own sake: "The Lord hath made all things for himself" (Prov. 16:4). In Hosea 2:23, we read, "And I will sow her unto me in the earth; and I will have mercy upon her that had not obtained mercy; and I will say to them which were not my people, Thou art my people; and they shall say, Thou art my God." The Lord also speaks of this in the book of Isaiah, saying, "This people have I formed for myself; they shall shew forth my praise" (Isa. 43:21). Thus, he who does not have this as his life's objective has certainly also not been formed to show forth His praise.

     b. It will also be evident in that the new creature bears the stamp of the gospel that fully conforms with the gospel itself, namely, to exalt God to the highest. The gospel will teach us to live a godly life. He who does not live such a life needs to recognize that his religion is vain—that is, without content. Such may have a form of godliness, but they will deny the power thereof (2 Tim. 3:5). One will then be no better than "sounding brass, or a tinkling cymbal" (1 Cor. 13:1), and thus void of either heart or life.

c. It will also be evident in that the new creature is renewed after God's image and likeness. God is not only the creating cause of the new creature but also its Master and its example so that everything will be unto God and for God.

d. Furthermore, the objective of this birth that proceeds from God is to elevate the soul above its former disposition. And what else can this be than having God's honor in view rather than one's own?

e. Finally, one cannot possibly be a new creature without there being a change as to the purpose of one's life. A poet,[9] therefore, exclaimed: "Certainly, we solely live unto the Lord. Our salvation is to His honor, and His honor is manifested in all His works."

3. The transformation of the new creature also manifests itself in *the inner thought life*. "For they that are after the flesh do mind the things of the flesh; but they that are after the Spirit the things of the Spirit" (Rom. 8:5). Consequently, there will be no appreciation for things outside of God. The heart is inclined toward and risen with Christ. The new creature, therefore, will "seek those things which are above" (Col. 3:1), for—examine yourself regarding this point—"where your treasure is, there will your heart be also" (Luke 12:34). Everything in comparison to God in Christ is truly "but dung" (Phil. 3:8).

4. There is also a transformation regarding *the things that comfort and delight* the new creature. The old nature will grieve him, causing the new man, for the remainder of his life, to groan, "Who shall deliver me from the body of this death?" (Rom. 7:24). However, he will rejoice in God, His virtues, His Son, His Spirit, and His ways. When the prodigal son came to himself, he could no longer feed himself with the husks of the swine while there was bread in his father's house. In fact, "the kingdom of God is not meat and drink; but righteousness, and peace, and joy in the Holy Ghost" (Rom. 14:17). David could say, "Thou hast put gladness in my heart, more than in the time that their corn and their wine increased" (Ps. 4:7). He who cannot echo these words of David from the bottom of his heart should not imagine that he has experienced this transformation.

---

9. Comrie does not identify the source of this statement.

Transformation Seen in External Changes
This transformation also manifests itself outwardly. Since God is near to the new man, he will speak the language of Canaan, he will dress in conformity to the simplicity of the gospel, and his humility will be known to all. In fact, he will be "a city that is set on an hill [that] cannot be hid" (Matt. 5:14). He who sees him will observe that he belongs to the generation for whom Jacob's God is their God and for whom the Holy One of Israel is their habitation.

The Godward Disposition of the New Creature

This new creature, by divine enablement, will have the lively propensity and predisposition to be actively engaged. Having been created with an inclination toward God in the new birth, he will have the divine seed within him—a living propensity within the heart. It cannot possibly be otherwise. For the moment that the Spirit would cease to be active, this propensity would also cease to function, and every new stirring of the soul would then be a translation from death to life.

One, All-Encompassing Disposition
Generally speaking, we could remark that this propensity is not multifaceted but rather proceeds from the same principle that will manifest itself in all the faculties of the soul. Although the Spirit gives one gift to this person and another gift to that person, He will, in creating the new man, bestow a living principle that is all-encompassing, from which all things will spring forth as many grapes proceed from the same cluster or branch.

I wish to note that this propensity, this life issuing forth from one spiritual source, is described in a variety of ways.

1. As to the person in whom this spiritual propensity functions, we observe that its intellectual aspect is referred to as the knowledge of God. The exercise of the will is referred to as making God in Christ one's choice. The affections are described as the sweet motions of the soul toward God and His communion, etc.

2. When considering the one around whom everything revolves—a dying Christ who is embraced as the one giving Himself as a ransom for sin—we speak of love. Bathing His feet in tears is referred to as humility. Conformity to His will is referred to as obedience. Submitting oneself to God's rod is referred to as patience. Being grieved about having provoked Jesus to anger

is referred to as sorrow. Nevertheless, these all issue forth from the same propensity of spiritual life, or of true faith, for as regeneration is the source of faith, in turn, faith is the source of all the enumerated spiritual activities: the love of faith, the joy of faith, the humility of faith, and the patience of faith. They all proceed from the same spiritual principle and have God in Christ as their focus. Although these activities differ as to their unique connection with the object of faith—Christ—they are, nevertheless, one since they issue forth from the same principle. We observe this in the oil with which the high priest was anointed. It was a compound of various spices, and yet it was one oil.

A Disposition of Willingness

If one were to ask me what the essence of this principle is, I would ask you to note my words carefully.

1. It is a willingness to be spiritually engaged. When God calls the soul to engage in such activity, she will be inclined and ready to engage in such work with a heart willing and desirous to do so. As soon as the Lord said to Isaiah, "Whom shall I send, and who will go for us?" he responds, "Here am I; send me" (Isa. 6:8). There will then be no intent to either postpone it or to be excused. Instead, as soon as God calls the soul to go in the way of His commandments, she will go.

2. This spiritual propensity will also manifest itself in deeds.

   a. Its manifestation will first and foremost be *natural and spontaneous* as it issues forth from the nature of spiritual life itself. The sending forth of light by the sun will be no more natural than a regenerate soul manifesting his inclination toward God and His service. For such a person, the service of God will be his food and drink, for a person can indeed no longer live in sin when he has died to sin.

   b. This propensity also manifests itself in a *ready willingness*. The soul will view what God says as so just and fitting that she will most willingly embrace and observe it. As God has promised, they shall be very willing (Ps. 110:3). She cannot act contrary to the truth but will, in all things, be willing to do it. The regenerate man has joined himself unto the Lord to serve Him wholeheartedly.

   c. This propensity will manifest itself in *earnestness and devotion*. God's children do not engage in eye service. Instead, they do what their hand finds to do to the utmost of their ability. Since they have been baptized with fire and with the Holy Spirit, they will have a burning zeal in all that they endeavor to do.

d. Moreover, this propensity will *not be constrained*. The desires of the soul will be manifold, and thus they cannot be hemmed in. Since her spiritual eye is focused upon God, she cannot find satisfaction in temporal things. Furthermore, even if she becomes distracted by these things, she will time and again recover, saying, "Whom have I in heaven but thee?" (Ps. 73:25). The unrestricted focus of this principle also manifests itself toward sin. God's child will not permit any Agag to remain alive but will endeavor, if possible, to remove it with root and branch. He will bring God's children to the feet of Christ as King so that they may be crushed as the vessel of a potter.

e. This principle is also *efficacious*. God's child is invigorated according to the inner man (cf. Eph. 3:16), receiving "the spirit…of power" (2 Tim. 1:7). In fact, according to 1 Corinthians 4:20, the kingdom of God, as established in such a person, does not consist in words but rather in power, and thus he can say, "I can do all things through Christ which strengtheneth me" (Phil. 4:13).

f. This principle also *functions effortlessly*. God's commandments will be neither grievous nor an unbearable burden, because the spiritual texture of the heart is now such that it is inherently inclined to obey them. Furthermore, the yoke of Christ is easy, and His burden is light (Matt. 11:29). The soul deems it an honor and privilege to be engaged in all that pertains to God's kingdom, and thus God's commandments will not be grievous.

g. Furthermore, this principle will also engage itself with *delight*. For the regenerate man, the Word of God will be the fountain of all joy, and he will, therefore, not perish in his affliction. Consequently, Paul gloried in his weakness, and the psalmist delighted himself in God's lovely sanctuary where he could behold His power and His glory (Ps. 63:2). When, however, the soul is distracted from this, the recognition of the delight that is to be found in God prompts him to exhort himself, exclaiming, "Why art thou cast down, O my soul? and why art thou disquieted within me? hope thou in God: for I shall yet praise him" (Ps. 42:11), and, "Therefore I will look unto the LORD; I will wait for the God of my salvation: my God will hear me" (Mic. 7:7). This explains why a child of God would resolutely reject an offer to exchange all the possessions of his house for this love.

h. This propensity is also *perpetually active*. It is a fountain that continually and perpetually produces water, although not always with the same strength and intensity. It cannot be otherwise with one "in whose heart are the ways of them" (Ps. 84:5).

i. Finally, this principle functions in an *orderly manner*. First of all, it is focused on God Himself for His own sake, and secondarily, it desires to behold God in the creature and thereby render Him honor. In light of all that has been said, it should be evident that such a person will struggle with sin. Indeed, a creature cannot act contrary to its nature, and this is expressed in Proverbs 8:36: "He that sinneth against me wrongeth his own soul." In 1 John 3:9, we read, "Whosoever is born of God doth not commit sin…and he cannot sin, because he is born of God." Thus, to sin is directly contrary to his heartfelt intent. The deepest wish of the least in grace is not to walk upon the pathway of sin. He who has chosen God as his portion will find it difficult to sin. Psalm 119:57 expresses this: "Thou art my portion, O LORD: I have said that I would keep thy words." How difficult it is to engage in that which has death as its consequence! Every sin is as death to the regenerate man, and therefore, he exclaims, "Who shall deliver me from the body of this death?" (Rom. 7:24).

A New Inward Law

We have observed that in this creature—a creature that becomes a new creature by way of spiritual conception and birth—a new spiritual inclination has been implanted. We will, therefore, now consider the third matter of importance—namely, that a new rule of life has been inscribed upon the heart according to which he will act.

Each creature, contingent upon its nature and composition, is governed in its activities by laws. Physical objects will function according to the laws of motion, and man functions according to the laws of nature. Likewise, the regenerate man has a law written upon its heart according to this covenant promise: "I will put my law in their inward parts, and write it in their hearts" (Jer. 31:33). Paul refers to it as "the law of the mind" (Rom. 7:23). We will address this writing upon the heart in more detail—first, in general terms, and after that, more particularly.

General Observations about the Inward Law
Generally speaking, one must observe the following:

1. The law of the mind, written upon the heart of this new creature, is *not, as some erroneously assert, in all things synonymous with the law of nature.* They are certainly in error, for this is a law of faith or Christ's law, whereas the law of nature is the law of the covenant of works. All men are subject to the law of nature. The heathen "shew the work of the law written in their hearts, their conscience also bearing witness, and their thoughts the mean while accusing or else excusing one another" (Rom. 2:15). However, this "law of the mind" is, according to the covenant of grace, only written upon the heart of specific individuals.

2. As to its substance, this law is *the same law that was written upon Adam's heart.* As God's communicable attributes were the pattern of Adam's original righteousness, likewise, in regeneration, a person is recreated in God's image as to knowledge, righteousness, and holiness (Eph. 4:24; Col. 3:10). As Adam lost his compatibility with these divine attributes, likewise the new creature, in Christ, receives back the same that he had lost rather than something fundamentally different.

3. The *entire law* is written upon the heart. Just as God inscribed the law upon tables of stone, He likewise writes it upon the heart of the new creature, requiring true holiness Godward, true righteousness regarding one's neighbor, and moderation toward oneself (cf. Titus 2). God does not inscribe the law partially upon the heart—that is, the one commandment and not the other. No, this inscription of the entire law is part and parcel of the new creature. Should this be lacking, he would be a deficient caricature that would be inconsistent with the absolute perfection and flawlessness as mentioned in the Song of Solomon 4:7.

4. This law, as inscribed upon the heart, *does not render the written law or God's revealed will superfluous.* Instead, this will eternally be the rule for his actions. Although this internal law will not function perfectly in the imperfect state of the regenerate man, the norm for his conduct must be as perfect as the law is perfect. The law of the Lord is perfect, and if a young man desires to cleanse his way, he must take "heed thereto according to thy word" (Ps. 119:9). David, therefore, says, "Thy word have I hid in mine heart, that I might not sin against thee" (Ps. 119:11).

Detailed Analysis of the Inward Law

The inscribing of the law upon the heart, as such, consists of various matters.

1. There will be *an inward knowledge and approbation of the law* with the mind. It is a unique distinctive mark of God's children that they know the righteousness and the law of the Lord in the heart. "Hearken unto me, ye that know righteousness, the people in whose heart is my law" (Isa. 51:7). The confluence of these two forms of righteousness teaches us that mental knowledge is insufficient. Instead, there must also be a heart knowledge—a heart in which the law is embedded. Such a sanctified mind will have a spiritual propensity and ability to know the law and, as with a compass, will be governed by it.

2. Furthermore, there will be *an inner conformity to the law* that will be proportionate to the measure of inner renewal. The heart will, so to speak, be molten by regenerating grace and be cast into that form. The heart and the law will thus be as compatible as the impression made in wax by a seal. Paul's words that the law is not given for the righteous but rather for the ungodly need to be understood in that light. Yes, in that sense, Paul testifies of the Romans that they had become obedient in conformity to the mold of his doctrine to which they had submitted themselves.

3. There will also be *a strong desire to be obedient.* Just as there will be a strong inclination in the old man toward sin, so there will be an inclination in the new man toward the practice of virtue.

4. Moreover, there will be a *n unfeigned and heartfelt love for the law and the duties it demands*, for "love is the fulfilling of the law" (Rom. 13:10). "And I will delight myself in thy commandments, which I have loved. My hands also will I lift up unto thy commandments, which I have loved" (Ps. 119:47–48).

4. Finally, this principle, by God's enabling grace, will *equip the new creature to obey* the divine will. The law of God being written upon the heart implies that His children "can do all things through Christ which strengtheneth [them]" (Phil. 4:13). This will enable them to "run, and not be weary; and… [to] walk, and not faint" (Isa. 40:31). God's people will thus be "as the shining light, that shineth more and more unto the perfect day" (Prov. 4:18).

Regeneration Renews God's Image

We observe that there is some natural resemblance between parents and the children that are born to them. However, in a spiritual sense, there is every reason also emphatically to speak of such a resemblance. Man has been created in God's image as to knowledge, righteousness, and holiness (Eph. 4:24; Col. 3:10). When we may behold His glory, we will be "changed into the same image from glory to glory, even as by the Spirit of the Lord" (2 Cor. 3:18). "As we have borne the image of the earthy, we shall also bear the image of the heavenly" (1 Cor. 15:49).

General Observations about God's Image
Let me make some general comments regarding this likeness to God.

1. This likeness is *not one of essence*, as if there is a communication of the divine essence itself, or as if, according to old and new heretics, the new creature is of similar essence. The divine essence is only communicated to the Son and the Holy Spirit. Infinity cannot be exhibited, and much less can it be communicated. Thus, when God created man, He did not make him to be a God but rather a rational creature in His image and His likeness, consisting in a reflection of His communicable divine attributes. When God wanted to show Abram a token of His love, He called him Abraham, thereby inserting merely a letter of the entirely incommunicable name of Jehovah.

2. Nevertheless, this likeness, rather than being a metaphorical resemblance, is *an essential resemblance*, for Peter teaches that the new man becomes a partaker of the divine nature (2 Peter 1:4).

3. The *entire image of God* is imprinted upon the believer. By way of procreation, all the essential components of the parents are passed on to the children. In the same way, the image of God in the believer is a reflection of His communicable attributes. It may very well be that the one component of this image may stand out and manifest itself more in the one than the other, but every member of Christ's body will, in principle, be a partaker of the entire image of God.

4. This likeness encompasses *a resemblance to Christ Jesus*—not by the communication of His divine and human natures but rather by the communication of affections that conform to Christ's affections. The apostle, therefore, declares, "Let this mind be in you, which was also in Christ Jesus" (Phil. 2:5). In fact, believers have been predestinated "to be conformed to the image of [God's] Son" (Rom. 8:29); that is, bearing the image of the heavenly

one in righteousness, purity, humility, patience, longsuffering, and upright obedience. It thus follows that all who lack these characteristics are not new creatures.

5. Finally, there will be *a resemblance to the Holy Spirit*. Thus we read that this new creature is designated as "spirit," for in John 3:6, we read, "That which is born of the flesh is flesh; and that which is born of the Spirit is spirit." Consequently, whatever is born of the flesh is indeed flesh, and that which is born of the Spirit will be spirit as to its inner motions, foundational principles, and intentions. The Spirit is a Spirit of holiness, grace, love, and zeal for God's honor. It is the great work of the Spirit to magnify Christ. When someone is born again by the Word of truth, some of the marks of the Spirit will be present. The Spirit will be within him a Spirit of humility, casting down all imaginations, and a zealous Spirit, for the new man will be transformed into a person who will be engaged in the Lord's work with utmost and earnest zeal.

Detailed Analysis of the Image of God
Specifically, this likeness to God consists in three matters.

1. First, there will be *a likeness of affections*. There will not be a single trait of God's image in the soul in which this likeness of affections will not be observed. This likeness will be expressed in how intensely believers, by faith and in love, delight themselves in God. This conforms to the delight God has within Himself and to the delight He has in His image as created by Him in others. He who does not love those who have been born again cannot possibly love Him who has caused them to be born again. Arms are stretched forth, and hearts will reach out toward all who manifest even a small measure of conformity to God. However, those who are partakers of the divine nature will be recognized primarily by the affection they have for the objects of God's love. Believers will manifest their conformity to God when they have the same disposition toward the objects of God's grace as God and Christ do in dealing with their children. God is particularly well pleased when we grieve deeply over our sin—hating it as God hates it due to its vile and abominable nature—and when, above all, we pursue inward holiness of heart. "O that there were such an heart in them" (Deut. 5:29)! God rejoices when we delight in His grace—for thereby He will be supremely glorified—as well as

when we love Him and Christ above all and make everything else subordinate to this love.

2. Second, there will also be *conformity in one's behavior.* When souls, by grace, have been united to God, they will live because Christ dwells within them. That life will manifest itself tangibly in conduct that conforms to God's law. Creatures act in conformity to their nature. Likewise, the new creature that has been born of God will be engaged in conformity to this new life. That which originates with God cannot sin, it being contrary to its nature. When Paul was Saul, he was a persecutor, but when he was transformed into Paul, he became a praying man. When there is no similarity as to these matters between Paul and the believer, there is very little reason to think that one has been born of God!

3. Third, there will be *conformity to the holiness of God.* Peter's exhortation is, "But as he which hath called you is holy, so be ye holy in all manner of conversation" (1 Peter 1:15). The soul will exclaim, "Holy Jesus, make me holy so that I may be as holy as Thou art." Holiness is more important than honor, prestige, riches, and pleasure. Holiness is as precious as a jewel—yes, like heaven itself. Without that jewel, heaven would merely be a hell. A striving for holiness is the preeminent mark of our conformity to God. Oh, that we would examine ourselves! Pretense will not help us, but truth within will! Having the appearance of godliness while denying the power thereof is utterly abominable to God.

Regeneration Produces Children of God

In the realm of nature, children that are born will be the sons and daughters of their parents. This applies equally to spiritual birth. The regenerate are the sons and daughters of the Most High! "And because ye are sons, God hath sent forth the Spirit of his Son into your hearts, crying, Abba, Father" (Gal. 4:6).

The Character of God's Children

First, let us consider the character traits that will manifest themselves in these sons and daughters.

1. There will, first of all, be *a holy, childlike, and reverent fear of God.* "If then I be a father, where is mine honour?" (Mal. 1:6). Therefore, examine yourself

by the following: if, by regeneration, you are a son of God, what reverential fear and childlike trembling do you experience? What transpires within will not go unnoticed by Him. He will detect any twinge of self-exaltation or world conformity. When prayer is offered, He will perceive the frame of heart with which it was offered. Whatever means of grace we may avail ourselves of, He will perceive the principle from which they proceed and what one's intentions are. If you claim to be a son or daughter of God, your walk must then affirm it. "And if ye call on the Father, who without respect of persons judgeth according to every man's work, pass the time of your sojourning here in fear" (1 Peter 1:17).

2. One will also be *submissive to his chastisement.* "If ye endure chastening, God dealeth with you as with sons; for what son is he whom the father chasteneth not?" (Heb. 12:7). God can make our external circumstances very distressing by subjecting us to poverty and physical pain. As to one's inner life, God can make our condition bitter by subjecting us to spiritual darkness, anxiety, and the hiding of His face. If God's child were to recognize God's hand in this, it would calm the intense turmoil in the heart, and in the footsteps of God's only begotten Son, he will give his back to Him that smites, and his cheeks to Him that plucks off the hair.

3. There will also be *a childlike obedience as an expression of a tender and heartfelt love.* He who is not a child of God will conduct himself in all things as a servant, whereas a believer will conduct himself as a son. His actions will not be governed by "the spirit of bondage again to fear" but rather by "the Spirit of adoption" (Rom. 8:15). One will then obey the Lord irrespective of whether there be a hell or a heaven, "for as many as are led by the Spirit of God, they are the sons of God" (Rom. 8:14).

4. There will also be *a holy aversion toward sin,* for the believer will thereby provoke his holy Father to anger who is "of purer eyes than to behold evil, and [who can] not look on iniquity" (Hab. 1:13). "Whosoever is born of God doth not commit sin; for his seed remaineth in him" (1 John 3:9). Augustine says very aptly that we are all either *filii Dei* or *filii Diaboli,* that is, children of God or children of the devil. Therefore, examine yourself accordingly: Do you hate sin? Is there no secret inclination toward sin in your heart? Do you shun sin and sinners as you would shun hell? This clearly affirms you to be a new creature.

5. God's child will *imitate His divine goodness toward all*, even when they are hostile toward him. Observe how the Savior brings this to the fore: "He maketh his sun to rise on the evil and on the good" (Matt. 5:45); "Be ye therefore perfect, even as your Father which is in heaven is perfect" (Matt. 5:48); "If a man say, I love God, and hateth his brother, he is a liar" (1 John 4:20). When a martyr was asked what Christ had taught him, he replied, "The noble lesson of what defines me as a Christian, and that is to do good to all and to forgive and love my enemies."

6. Finally, believers are *led by an elevated spirit* that is consistent with their elevated origin. They "seek those things which are above," for their "life is hid with Christ in God" (Col. 3:1–3). And when He who is their life shall be revealed, they shall, with Him, also be "a partaker of the glory that shall be revealed" (1 Peter 5:1).

The Rights of God's Children

The right of believers to enjoy the privileges of children proceeds from all that has been stated. Paul addresses this, saying, "And if children, then heirs; heirs of God, and joint-heirs with Christ; if so be that we suffer with him, that we may be also glorified together" (Rom. 8:17). On other occasions, we have already pointed this out and discussed it. Presently I only wish to say the following:

1. They are the subjects of God's tender love. He has loved them with an everlasting love, and therefore, He has drawn them with cords of love (Jer. 31:3). As an illustration, the Lord compares this to the love of a mother for her infant, stating that His love excels that love. "Can a woman forget her sucking child, that she should not have compassion on the son of her womb? yea, they may forget, yet will I not forget thee" (Isa. 49:15).

2. Whenever God's children defile and besmirch themselves, the Lord will time and again wash and cleanse them. "Then will I sprinkle clean water upon you, and ye shall be clean" (Ezek. 36:25), and they "shall be whiter than snow" (Ps. 51:7).

3. They are dealt with gently. God looks in love upon His children and cares for them as tenderly as parents do who bestow the ultimate tokens of their love upon their children. The Lord carries them upon eagle's wings, upholds

them with His everlasting arms, gathers them into His arms, and carries them in His bosom. He will neither quench a single smoking flax nor break a single bruised reed (Isa. 42:3; Matt. 12:20). How astonishing it is that nearly all God's wisdom focuses upon assuring those who are "of a contrite and humble spirit" (Isa. 57:15) that He will "give unto them beauty for ashes, the oil of joy for mourning, the garment of praise for the spirit of heaviness" (Isa. 61:3).

4. The Lord will nourish them with the precious promises of His eternally abiding Word, which are the breasts of Zion's comfort. In these promises are comprehended the goodness of His house and the holiness of His temple (Ps. 65:4). Thereby they shall "grow up as calves of the stall" (Mal. 4:2), and from children, they will grow up to be young men, and from young men, to be fathers in Christ (1 John 2:12–14).

5. He causes them to walk upon the way that they must go, from virtue to virtue and "from strength to strength," until they will appear before God in Zion (Ps. 84:7). "I taught Ephraim also to go, taking them by their arms; but they knew not that I healed them. I drew them with cords of a man, with bands of love: and I was to them as they that take off the yoke on their jaws, and I laid meat unto them" (Hos. 11:3–4).

6. The Lord will instruct them one time through the promises and then again experientially. "I will instruct thee and teach thee in the way which thou shalt go: I will guide thee with mine eye" (Ps. 32:8).

7. The Lord will chastise them for their profit, causing them "to pass under the rod," and bringing them "into the bond of the covenant" (Ezek. 20:37).

8. The Lord will keep the benefits of salvation in abeyance until His children come of age, while at the same time protecting and bearing with them. When He will soon appear, they will appear with Him in glory. Christ will then say to them, "Come, ye blessed of my Father, inherit the kingdom prepared for you from the foundation of the world" (Matt. 25:34).

All of the above is implied in being born of God to make clear that God is the moving cause of this birth. We believe that we have abundantly proven that the triune God—Father, Son, and Holy Spirit—causes a man to be born again. We will, therefore, not elaborate any further about this.

Overcoming the World

The apostle testifies of all believers in general, and every believer individually, that they will overcome the world. The apostle speaks here of the world. The original word *kosmos* is a word that implies something that is beautiful. And indeed, when we behold the world, the *kosmos*, we will observe extraordinary beauty as a revelation of the wisdom of the great Creator. However, the word *world* in our text is not to be understood as the created world as such, but rather, it refers to what is in the world and that which affords man the opportunity to corrupt himself. The apostle expresses it as "the lust of the flesh, and the lust of the eyes, and the pride of life" (1 John 2:16). We will not attempt to address all the particulars since we have already said too much.

They who are born of God will overcome; that is, they will have the upper hand regarding the world. The world has no dominion over them. The world is beneath their feet, for "their conversation is in heaven" (Phil. 3:20), and they "seek those things which are above" (Col. 3:1).

Beloved, I know that, in addressing this overcoming of the world, much could be said regarding the world as an enemy that has to be overcome, regarding doing battle with the world, regarding the weapons to be used in this warfare, and regarding the victory to which one may attain. That victory will already be evident at the very outset of conversion; it will manifest itself by renewal in the victory to which one may continually attain, and it will, at last, be perfectly attained when all worldliness and sin will have been entirely abolished. However, we will speak no more of this, and in our second point, we will demonstrate how faith is the means whereby one overcomes the world.

FAITH, THE MEANS OF OVERCOMING THE WORLD

The apostle now proceeds to identify the means whereby those who are born of God overcome the world, for "this is the victory that overcometh the world, even our faith." We will, therefore, now proceed to demonstrate the various ways by which the faith of God's elect gains and secures this victory.

1. *Faith sees the limits of the world.* Faith is the victory that overcomes the world, for by faith, we know that the world and all that is in it is nothing more than a created entity and is, thus, finite. "Through faith we understand that the worlds were framed by the word of God, so that things which are seen

were not made of things which do appear" (Heb. 11:3). The believer thereby perceives that finite creatures are incapable of fulfilling the unfulfilled desires of the soul. The soul will, therefore, transcend all that is created and end in Him, who is the infinite Jehovah. Only then will the soul find her real and essential rest when she perceives that nothing but the eternal God alone is worthy of her love and esteem, and that all her inclinations end in the Lord. I am convinced that no one will achieve a single victory over the world until he recognizes with a calm heart that all that is of the world is no more than created matter. The things of this world will be as empty vessels in which not a drop of real and internal comfort is to be found unless God has embedded it in them.

2. *Faith sees the instability of the world.* Faith is the victory that overcomes the world because the soul learns experientially that the world and all that is in it is subject to continual change. When faith is in exercise, one will observe that one generation goes and another generation comes, that kingdoms are overturned, that princes can come so low that they sit in the dust, and that those who were dwelling in the dust attain to lofty positions. One will see that "riches certainly make themselves wings; they fly away as an eagle toward heaven" (Prov. 23:5), that friends become enemies, and that one cannot trust a single creature. In short, nothing under the sun is abiding; everything is transitory.

A person will now begin to see how foolish it is for his heart to either give itself or be unduly attached to anything that is created. He will endeavor to have and possess everything as having and possessing nothing. However lovely, however pleasant, and however invigorating things may be, he will say, "Shall I commit my heart and my affections to my possessions? They are vulnerable to the moth, the thief, and rust; and if they do not depart from me, I will certainly have to part with them and bid them an eternal farewell. Shall I commit my heart to my husband, my wife, and my children? I will once have to part with them, or they with me. 'All flesh is as grass' (1 Peter 1:24). Moreover, the more that I am affectionally bound to them and am, so to speak, intertwined with them, the more grievous it will be for me to let go of them. Shall I be sad or joyful in proportion to whether the world either mistreats me or smiles upon me? Everything is truly subject to change. He who is my friend today will be my enemy tomorrow. The appearance of all things will pass away. My soul abhors all those changes and, instead, chooses the eternal, triune covenant God who, in the midst of all that changes in creation, remains 'the same yesterday, and to day, and for ever' (Heb. 13:8)."

As long as the soul does not arrive at this point, she will be very unhappy, and she will be as changeable as the changeable creature. She will be troubled at heart. Yes, he who does not have some knowledge of such exercises of faith will be as the waves of the sea. One moment he will be ecstatically joyful, and at another moment he will melt away in sorrow. One moment he will have strong emotions of love, and the next moment he will be filled with wrath and rancor. One moment he will deem himself to be happy, and then again, he will complain about his bitter lot in life. Oh, godliness will teach one to be content under all circumstances! He who rises above all that is visible, tangible, and audible, and ends in the unchangeable Jehovah, has a great advantage, having learned to be content in whatever circumstances or situation he will find himself. How happy Paul was who, by faith, had learned so much in that regard!

3. *Faith recognizes the emptiness and trouble of the world.* Faith is the victory that overcomes the world because it is only by faith that one learns to observe, in a sanctified manner, as Solomon testified, that the world at its best is but vanity and also a troubling asset. The Preacher declares that "all is vanity and vexation of spirit" (Eccl. 2:17). When one learns by experience that sorrow increases in proportion to the increase of one's possessions, one will have achieved an enormous victory over the world. Every rose, however beautiful and lovely it may be, will have piercing thorns, and thus there will be nothing that will be *ab omni parte beatum*, that is, good in every respect. The opposite is true: the more one may delight himself in God and His communion, the more this will be experienced as being blissful. Yes, all the paths of "the way of understanding" (Prov. 9:6) will yield peace. Indeed, there will only be peace for those who walk upon those paths. This will render one content with his personal situation, and one will thus neither covet nor be envious of another person's circumstances. "The lust of the eyes, and the pride of life" (1 John 2:16) will thus be mostly mortified, and the believing soul will be overcoming the world.

4. *Faith looks to the invisible God.* Faith is the victory that overcomes the world, for this grace is the cause that enables the soul to see "him who is invisible" (Heb. 11:27). We find a noteworthy example of this in Moses's exercise of faith. He overcame the world when he left Egypt without fearing the

wrath of the king, "for he endured, as seeing him who is invisible" (Heb. 11:27). Hebrews 11:1 teaches us that it belongs to the nature of saving faith that it renders invisible things visible. In fact, in proportion to the measure of beholding the glory of God in the face of Jesus Christ, that soul will be conformed to the image of God "from glory to glory, even as by the Spirit of the Lord" (2 Cor. 3:18). When someone looks directly at the sun, he will be incapable of seeing what is around him. If that is true in the realm of nature, it is especially true in the spiritual realm. The soul will thus be able to echo the words of Asaph: "Whom have I in heaven but thee? and there is none upon earth that I desire beside thee" (Ps. 73:25).

5. *Faith rests in the covenant of grace.* Faith is the victory that overcomes the world, for the soul, by this grace, will be acquainted beyond all other things with the benefits of the covenant of grace as to their unique nature, character, and significance. The soul will thus behold the special privileges to which she may now lay claim. The believer will perceive that all that he may enjoy by this covenant has been purchased and merited by the blood of the eternal testament. This is the reason why faith overcomes the world, enabling believers to live in peace. And indeed, they have not been "redeemed with corruptible things…from [their] vain conversation…but with the precious blood of Christ" (1 Peter 1:18–19). Both body and soul are offered as a sacrifice to God as "a living sacrifice, holy, acceptable unto God, which is your reasonable service" (Rom. 12:1).

6. *Faith rejoices in the riches of Christ.* Faith is the victory that overcomes the world, for the soul views all her riches, her inner delight, her spiritual refreshment, and her salvation in light of her relationship to God. The believer will frequently pause and ask himself whether his birth, his family, his beauty, his mind, his riches, his prominent position, and the honors rendered to him above others are the focus of his life.

He can then resolutely rise above the dust and exclaim, "In former days, I was indeed that foolish, but since God has illuminated my eyes by His saving light, I deem all of that to be of no value. My Jesus is my honor, my crown, and my glory. I prefer my blessed union with Him above all the kingdoms of the entire world. All things are mine, because I am the property of Christ, and Christ is God's. Therefore, I do not desire the fleshpots of Egypt" (Ex. 16:3). Oh, "the eyes of them that see shall not be dim" (Isa. 32:3).

7. *Faith drinks from the fountain of comfort.* Faith is the victory that overcomes the world, for this grace leads the soul to the fountains of full and blessed comfort. This comfort is a wine that is so delightful that they who taste it will not immediately desire the old wine. On the contrary, such a person will testify, "Here is my comfort, my happiness, and my rejoicing. Everything else is of no value to my priceless heart."[10]

8. *Faith anticipates the glory of heaven.* Faith is the victory that overcomes the world, for it causes souls to long intensely for the full enjoyment of God in heaven, and that throughout all eternity. This faith enabled Abraham and the other patriarchs to live as strangers here below. They "looked for a city which hath foundations, whose builder and maker is God" (Heb. 11:10), looking for "an house not made with hands" (2 Cor. 5:1). He who, by faith, is truly journeying to heaven, will view all things as merely being transitory. He will not be detained but will "press toward the mark for the prize of the high calling of God in Christ Jesus" (Phil. 3:14). He will lay aside all that would impede and hinder him—all that would cause him either to succumb or slow down in the running of his race. He desires that he would go "from strength to strength" until he may appear in Zion (Ps. 84:7), that is, the place where all the saints will meet each other. He who has received a glimpse of the glory that shall be enjoyed above cannot but look forward with an intense desire "to be with Christ; which is far better" (Phil. 1:23).

9. *Faith considers the blessedness of being in Christ.* Faith is the victory that overcomes the world, for according to the apostle, believers have thereby already been "blessed…with all spiritual blessings in heavenly places in Christ" (Eph. 1:3). They will be like the eagles that make their nests on high (Job 39:27). Since they are of heavenly origin, they will lift up their hearts in the ways of the Lord. It is a joy to the righteous to do that which is good.

10. *Faith treasures becoming like Christ.* Faith is the victory that overcomes the world, for the soul thereby cherishes a desire to be fully conformed to her head, Jesus Christ. Since He was a man of sorrows and had no place "where to lay his head" (Luke 9:58), the soul will not only be willing, by faith, to dispense with the world but also to be joyfully deprived of her possessions. The

---

10. Comrie here quotes the last two lines of a poem by Jodocus van Lodenstein entitled "Heerlijkheyds loff" ("Glory and Praise").

believer will choose instead to be afflicted for his godliness rather than "to be called the son of Pharaoh's daughter" (Heb. 11:23–26).

11. *Faith turns from the world.* Faith is the victory that overcomes the world, for it will cause the soul to abhor all that the world has to offer. Even if someone were to give me all the goods of his house, I would utterly abhor him.

12. *Faith receives grace for the spiritual battle.* Faith is the victory that overcomes the world, for it will equip the believer with various graces, and thus enable her to do battle with the world and all that is to be found in it. She will continually exercise faith to receive out of the fullness of Jesus "grace for grace" (John 1:16).

13. *Faith finds strength to persevere.* Faith is the victory that overcomes the world, for the soul that becomes weary in her warfare will be greatly strengthened by faith. Faith will go to God and exclaim, "We have no might…but our eyes are upon thee" (2 Chron. 20:12). Thereby He will give "power to the faint; and to them that have no might he increaseth strength" (Isa. 40:29). The weak believer will become as David, and as a horse he will enter the battle in the strength of God's majesty. Thereby they will be "more than conquerors" (Rom. 8:37) through the victory Christ will grant to them.

14. *Faith recognizes the perils of sin.* Faith is the victory that overcomes the world, for it will enable the believer to perceive the danger of those who become thoroughly enmeshed in all that is of the world, causing them to be ensnared and to suffer shipwreck as to their faith. Such beacons will prompt believers to avoid the rocks on which Demas and others have suffered shipwreck, enabling these believers to remain "unspotted from the world" (James 1:27).

15. *Faith learns from previous experiences of victory.* Faith is the victory that overcomes the world, enabling the believer, by the power of faith, to be victorious in a given situation, and thus use it to his advantage. It will enable him to sustain and encourage his soul in its warfare, knowing that the God who has helped him will help him again and thereby equip his hands so to engage in warfare that a bow of steel will be broken into pieces. It is undoubtedly a prominent activity of faith to conclude from previous incidents that there will also be a good outcome in the future. If every believer would be enabled to do this by faith, one would take courage in the heat of the battle.

16. *Faith rejoices in spiritual progress.* Faith is the victory that overcomes the world, for it will fill the heart with extraordinary joy and satisfaction when a given temptation is entirely subdued. The believer will view this as being more significant than the conquering of a kingdom. It will prompt the soul to praise God for having delivered her out of the hand of an enemy so close at hand and that was repeatedly assaulting her.

17. *Faith keeps watch against spiritual attack.* Faith is the victory that overcomes the world, for it will expose the hidden ambushes, devices, and deceptions of the world. It will prompt the believer continually to remain watchful and sober in his station so that he will not be overcome on another occasion.

18. *Faith mortifies worldliness in the heart.* Faith is the victory that overcomes the world, for it will prompt the believer, by faith, to bring before God all the friends of this world that still reside in his heart and are allied with the world. They will then be put to death, and believers will be delivered from all their enemies, enabling them to serve the Lord fearlessly.

19. *Faith conquers in death.* Faith is the victory that overcomes the world, when, with Samson, it deals a decisive and crowning blow to the world. Faith will then cease and be transformed into beholding. The soul will then have been perfected in holiness, and she will immediately be translated into glory to be eternally satisfied with God's image.

APPLICATION

We wish to address two matters: first, we will consider the foundation upon which this application rests, and second, how it functions in the practice of godliness.

As to this foundation, my beloved, we have spoken of being born of God according to

- the measure of light granted to us by the adorable God;
- the experience of the saints; and
- the rule of God's Word in which all experience must be grounded—for if it does not conform to the rule of Scripture, it will be null and void.

We have pointed out that he who is born of God will overcome the world by faith. We have deemed it necessary and useful to add to the exposition of scriptural truth an extensive application that is consistent with the matters addressed. We will address these matters—very weighty and of great eternal consequence—so that they may all the more be impressed upon your heart.

We wish to focus on several matters that pertain to the functioning of this application in the practice of godliness.

The Necessity of the New Birth

The necessity of the new birth is affirmed by the fact that no one—whether he be prominent or insignificant, rich or poor, a slave or a free man, wise or foolish—shall ever presently be a partaker of God's kingdom in the realm of grace and hereafter in the kingdom of glory unless he is born again.

Only Two Spiritual States

Such necessity is first of all evident in that there are but two possible conditions in which Adam's descendants find themselves: a state of friendship or enmity toward God—that is, a state that culminates in either salvation or damnation. Every person belongs to one of these two categories. The human race is divided into two branches. The one segment is a branch of the true vine, Jesus Christ, that is, they who are in the Spirit and walk according to the Spirit. The other segment is a branch of the wild olive tree, that is, they who are in the flesh and walk according to the flesh (cf. John 15; Rom. 8:1, 9, 11). The one segment is referred to as light, and the other, as darkness (Eph. 5:8). You who first dwelt in darkness, He has called you "into his marvellous light" (1 Peter 2:9). Formerly you were in darkness, but now you are in the light. The one is a child of wrath, whereas the other is a child of God. There is no intermediate state. All believers—the smoking flaxes and the bruised reeds; the strong cedars of Lebanon and Thomas who could not believe without seeing, as well as Abraham who believed without stumbling—are before God in a state of life and friendship. Over against this, however, the most honorable as well as the most ungodly man, the rich young ruler with all his virtues, as well as a Judas with his provoking sins, are in a state of spiritual death and *hostility*. All men, due to the difference between these two states, are either the object of God's love or His hatred.

That presupposes that the one possesses something that the other does not possess, namely, the new birth whereby God imprints His image upon the heart of a man and writes His law upon His heart. This clearly emphasizes the necessity of the new birth, for according to Romans 8:8, "they that are in the flesh cannot please God."

The Fall of Man

Due to Adam's fall, and the consequences for all his descendants, this new birth is necessary in order to enter into God's kingdom. After all, men have all died in Adam (1 Cor. 15:22). "For…by one man's disobedience many were made sinners" (Rom. 5:19). All Adam's descendants have inherited from him, as a willfully disobedient transgressor of God's covenant, a twofold guilt: an *imputed* guilt, whereby every man is subject to God's wrath and the curse that renders the whole world damnable before God, and additionally an *inherited* guilt, whereby everyone is void of man's original righteousness. Furthermore, fallen man also is void of God's image that consists of knowledge, righteousness, and holiness. The contrary is now true for his heart, for from the womb, he now bears the image of Satan.

1. Man is by nature *incapable* of doing good and that which is pleasing to God. By nature, Adam's children are mired in deep darkness, and thus they have erroneous and carnal notions regarding all that is truly good. Paul describes man in Titus 1:16 as "being abominable, and disobedient, and unto every good work reprobate." In Ephesians 4:22, we read that "the old man… is corrupt according to the deceitful lusts," and Romans 7:14 declares that he is "carnal, sold under sin."

2. Fallen man is also *unwilling* to do that which is good. What an aversion and unwillingness there will be to think of God, to hear others speak of Him, or to hear Him speak! However, since youth, fallen man will manifest a strong attraction toward that which is morally wrong, sinful, and corrupt. Job, therefore, correctly compares man to "a wild ass's colt" (Job 11:12).

3. Furthermore, there is the complete impotence of the sinner who is *dead* in sin. He cannot possibly do anything that is good. This was all precipitated by the fall of our first parents, and it is, therefore, absolutely necessary that a sinner receives a new life if he is ever to live in communion with that God who cannot possibly have any fellowship with the workers of iniquity.

Needed For All Times and All Persons
From this emerges our third proposition, namely, that this new birth is a universal necessity for all times and all persons—kings as well as beggars, legalistic men as well as sinners, the young as well as the old, and free men as well as slaves. "If any man be in Christ, he is a new creature: old things are passed away; behold, all things are become new" (2 Cor. 5:17). "They that are Christ's have crucified the flesh with the affections and lusts" (Gal. 5:24). The mother promise (Gen. 3:15) already had the same content, namely, that there would be enmity between the seed of the woman, Christ, and that of the serpent. It is thus essential that all who are in Christ have the same characteristic, namely, that in the essence of their being, they have a disposition that is diametrically opposed to the character of the serpent. Therefore, we also read that wolves will be transformed into lambs (Isa. 11:6).

The Only Way Fitting to God's Nature
Fourthly, it follows that one who calmly and judiciously considers this cannot possibly comprehend how God could make a man happy without this transformation.

1. It would *contradict God's holiness* to designate someone to be an inhabitant of heaven and to presume that he has a bond of intimate fellowship with the Lord who has not beheld Him in grace and who has not been conformed to Him. There can be no fellowship between light and darkness, between God and Belial, and between two characters that are diametrically opposed to each other. "The LORD knoweth the way of the righteous: but the way of the ungodly shall perish" (Ps. 1:6). "For the righteous LORD loveth righteousness; his countenance doth behold the upright" (Ps. 11:7), and without holiness, no one shall see God (Heb. 12:14).

2. It would *contradict God's wisdom* if a child of God would simultaneously remain a child of the devil. It would be unbecoming of God to have a child who would have the devilish characteristics of wickedness and perversion. Though someone might claim that God would yet be able to modify his being, it would absolutely make no sense. God has purposed that the transformation from darkness to light would transpire in this time state rather than in eternity! According to God's immutable decree, "in the place where the tree falleth, there it shall be" (Eccl. 11:3).

God Will Achieve His Objective
Finally, the new birth is necessary in order that the passion of Christ and His satisfaction would not ultimately be in vain.

1. *Christ has come to save His people from their sins.* His primary concern is to save them from their sins rather than to deliver them from hell, "for he shall save his people from their sins" (Matt. 1:21). Although it is indeed implied, it is noteworthy that it is not expressly stated that He shall deliver them from hell, but rather, that He will save them from their sins. That means that He will deliver them from the cause of the first, that is, sin, and after that, of its consequences. He will first deliver them from their devilish and sinful nature, and after that, from the hellish punishment due to sin. It would be inconsistent with the excellency of a perfect Surety if He had only merited the forgiveness of sins without sanctifying the essential nature of man. Titus 2:14 affirms this: "[Christ] gave himself for us that he might redeem us from all iniquity, and purify unto himself a peculiar people, zealous of good works." Indeed, Jesus arose to that very end, namely, to bring forth new life (Col. 2:12–13).

2. *Christ has come "that he might destroy the works of the devil"* (1 John 3:8). What works are they? None other than the sin and misery that proceed from them. If man's sinful nature were not broken, the kingdom of the devil would remain entirely intact, for misery will follow sin as a shadow will trail the body. How could the Savior have been triumphant if He had not cast the devil from his throne, if He had not exerted His scepter in the soul of the regenerate man, if He had not bound the strong man and robbed him of his goods (Matt. 12:29)? However, this is precisely what happens in regeneration and never in any other way.

3. *Christ has come to bring the sinner to God,* for He "also hath once suffered for sins, the just for the unjust, that he might bring us to God" (1 Peter 3:18). The intent is not to bring a sinner to God who is still entirely clothed in his sinful and predominant corruption but rather to bring him to God with the embroidered garments of salvation. Thus the Lord will do so by granting the sinner a new nature in regeneration, thereby rendering the soul capable of having communion with God. Therefore, I must say that those who expect to be saved while their nature remains unchanged would render Jesus into a servant of sin. Such a thought would be blasphemous!

4. *The purpose for which the Holy Spirit enters the soul* confirms the necessity of this transformation. The Spirit did not come upon the dead bones of Ezekiel to affirm their deadness but rather to make them alive. Paul, therefore, says, "The spirit giveth life" (2 Cor. 3:6). His words in Titus 3:5 are, therefore, emphatic when he says, "According to his mercy he saved us, by the washing of regeneration, and renewing of the Holy Ghost."

Self-Examination

There is also the exercise of self-examination. The new birth is necessary, for it is impossible to enter into God's kingdom without being born again. Thus it follows that everyone must examine and scrutinize himself whether he genuinely is a partaker of this new birth. We read in 2 Corinthians 13:5, "Examine yourselves, whether ye be in the faith; prove your own selves. Know ye not your own selves, how that Jesus Christ is in you, except ye be reprobates?" As we will address the exercise of self-examination in this portion, I will speak to you about various matters. First, let us consider self-examination as such. The exhortation is, "Examine yourselves, whether ye be in the faith," that is, consider the nature of your faith.

The Necessity of Self-Examination

It highlights the necessity of self-examination, thus implying that the believer must examine his heart according to the touchstone of God's Word. One must, therefore, in true godliness, examine himself in light of the biblical marks to ascertain whether the spiritual frames and exercises of one's soul are to be found in him. The necessity of such self-examination will be outlined in the arguments that will follow.

1. In all of His sermons, Christ has stressed the absolute necessity of self-examination. Matthew 13 records for us Christ's first parable in which He strongly urges this by saying, "Who hath ears to hear, let him hear" (v. 9). Although the multitudes listened very attentively to Jesus, this self-examination was nevertheless necessary, for there were but few who received the Word rightly. We also read about two builders, one of whom built upon the sand. His building was torn apart and utterly collapsed. How dreadful shall the tear and breach be when one will be torn by God throughout all eternity, having assumed to have been secure! The other builder built upon a rock, and his house remained standing. If Jesus indeed so emphasized the necessity of self-examination, then its utmost necessity ought to be obvious.

2. Self-examination is necessary because a poor man can so readily be in error here. Man has such confidence in himself and his use of the means of grace and he is so full of self-love that he will readily imagine himself to be what, in reality, he is not. Ask whomever you will, everyone will be confident that he is born again, is a partaker of Christ, and shall arrive in heaven. The reason for this is that one does not examine himself honestly using the marks of free grace. One will be as the Jews who found their peace in the law and rested in external virtues and religious privileges without there being a transformation of their state before God. Therefore, these words ought to be written with capital letters upon everyone's heart and ought to be repeated verbally: "Examine yourselves, whether ye be in the faith; prove your own selves" (2 Cor. 13:5).[11]

3. Man must examine himself, for self-deception regarding the state of one's soul is very perilous. How engaged the foolish virgins were! They had their lamps and oil in their lamps, and they were going forth to meet the bridegroom. Nevertheless, they encountered a closed heaven and heard, "Verily I say unto you, I know you not" (Matt. 25:12). Oh, how dreadful is such delusion that will end in hell! What will such a person cry out? Nothing other than, "In other matters, I was so careful, but in a matter of such significance, I was so careless! If only I had examined myself, my true state might have been uncovered."

4. Self-examination is so very necessary in light of the impediments to engage in this, for man is very reluctant to be exposed in such a confrontation with himself. It is particularly necessary in light of the matter itself, for there are significant similarities between true and presumptive believers. The latter also experience joy and sorrow, and they find some delight in the Word of God. However, true believers, the recipients of grace, also experience these emotions. To define the difference is difficult indeed. And yet, the difference between these two types of persons is as vast as that between light and darkness.

---

11. The original reads, "Onderzoekt uzelven nauw, ja nauw." The words are extracted from the Dutch rendition of Zephaniah 2:1: "Doorzoek u zelf nauw, ja, doorzoek nauw." The English (KJV) rendition reads as follows: "Gather yourselves together, yea, gather together." Since the English rendition does not communicate what Comrie wishes to communicate, we have opted to quote 2 Corinthians 13:5.

5. Finally, one needs to examine himself considering the great profit it yields when one may know from personal experience what his real state is before God.

    a. One will then perceive that all his previous knowledge was null and void. Anyone who becomes experientially acquainted with himself by self-examination will observe that all that he knew previously was little more than a dream. Now, however, he will perceive matters as they are. Oh, how comforting this must be to a soul when she may observe on good grounds that God is at work in her!

    b. He who may have such experiential knowledge will have a heart that is a transcript of the Bible. Whatever he reads in his Bible, he experiences in his heart, and whatever he experiences in his heart, he reads in the Word. David and Paul say in their psalms and letters what lives in his heart; he identifies with their struggles, makes the same objections, and sets before him how he was delivered. Oh, how divine such experience is, and what affirmation this yields!

    c. Becoming acquainted with one's spiritual life by means of such self-examination will be an efficacious means to mortify the lusts of his heart radically. Rather than theoretical knowledge, it will be the experience of the heart that will mortify all sinful inclinations of the soul. It may be that you do much for Jesus and will be able to speak much about Him. However, your inner desires will never be inclined away from all manner of things unless grace has complete dominion in your heart. How sweetly Paul expresses this when he says, "I live; yet not I, but Christ liveth in me" (Gal. 2:20). Though love for the world and an external show of religion can coexist, it can never coexist with grace in the heart. Aristotle says regarding greyhounds that they cannot hunt in fields filled with all manner of sweet-smelling flowers. You cannot possibly smell the aroma of Christ's precious ointments without the inclinations of your heart immediately dying to all that is not Jesus.

    d. This knowledge will cause the soul to enjoy the personal, experiential sweetness in her use of the means of grace. Others will be as dull and sluggish as Barzillai, having no desire to minister to David or finding any delight in his music. There are others, however, who are personally acquainted with the means of grace and may experience Christ's ointment being poured out upon them so that they will love Him as did the wise virgins. They will think, "How is it possible that the minister is acquainted with the frame of my soul and speaks of things that I have experienced?" The church sanctuary will then become a Bethel; one will yearn for the means of grace, and the house of God will become a delightful place.

e. Such knowledge will keep the soul from having itching ears and being critical. She will also stay far away from unprofitable discussions about differences of opinion regarding the work of grace. I have read of an old Christian who said, "As long as Christians would align themselves with the marks of grace, and everyone would consider his own heart, there would be peace. However, when men become puffed up and no longer abide with this good custom, then many will have infiltrated the church who would spend hours and days discussing matters of faith—men in whose hearts not even a trace of it was to be found."

f. Finally, he who engages in such self-examination and experiences God's work within his own heart will persevere even unto death. On the contrary, those who only maintain an appearance will wither and fall away when tribulations arise, for they have no root within themselves.

Questions about Self-Examination

Before I proceed to address the criteria by which one must examine himself, I will first briefly answer your questions.

Question: How does God affirm the spiritual state of a soul?

Answer: By causing persons to be deeply humbled and contrite about the sin they truly sense and perceive within themselves. They alone will find true rest. Mary heard that her sins were forgiven when she washed the feet of Christ with her tears. The soul must be in spiritual labor before Christ is born within her. There will first be the spirit of bondage before there will be the Spirit of adoption. That is God's way.

There will be many doubts and much spiritual strife. Genuine assurance of faith will commonly be assaulted and battered from all sides. And although unbelief is not a mark of faith, there is nevertheless reason to question the genuineness of faith if it is not subject to assault. In fact, this is my experience: "Lord, I believe; help thou mine unbelief" (Mark 9:24).

One will also frequently experience the fiery darts and assaults of Satan. Jesus Himself was subjected to such assaults, and His followers will most certainly experience them also. Pharaoh will not oppress an Egyptian, but rather, a true Israelite.

Question: How can I properly examine my soul?

Answer:

1. Let me reply briefly by saying that a soul must set apart a specific time that will give her ample opportunity to engage in such self-examination. She must consider everything that pertains to this, realizing that such self-examination is of greater significance than to be the owner of a thousand worlds. No one will regret having engaged in this for several years. How remarkable it is that religious people can occasionally spend delightful hours in reading God's Word and other good writers, and yet can hardly spare even a quarter of an hour for self-examination!

2. Not only must a soul take time for this, but she must also do this in all quietness. Every man who deals with his heart must acknowledge that it behaves like a bird that jumps from one branch to the next, hovering from one meaningless subject to another, and will be filled with frivolous and random thoughts. Therefore, in order to examine one's heart thoroughly, one must seek to avoid the least distraction so that the soul can persevere in this task.

3. Such self-examination also requires heartfelt and persevering prayer and earnest supplication in which one wrestles with God that He would open one's eyes and send forth His light and truth, praying that they would be a light upon his path and a lamp before his feet (Ps. 119:105). This must continually be the focus of one's self-examination and conduct. In such self-examination, one is not to be concerned with marks as defined by a minister or others, for the most competent person could be mistaken here! Rather, it must conform to "the law and to the testimony," for "if they speak not according to this word, it is because there is no light in them" (Isa. 8:20).

4. He who wishes to deal honestly with himself must imagine himself as standing before God's impeccable judgment seat. In all transactions, there will not be the least hint of either persons or matters getting preferential treatment. Instead, the matter is to be judged favorably according to the standard of the sanctuary. Then it matters not what someone may pretend to be or what he can say—even if he could speak with the tongue of an angel. Instead, "if any man be in Christ, he is a new creature: old things are passed away; behold, all things are become new" (2 Cor. 5:17). One's heart must be sincerely inclined to do everything of God, through God, and unto God (Rom. 11:36), manifesting itself in the renewal of one's affections and walk of life.

5. He who does not want to err in the work of self-examination must deem the witness of the Word regarding his person, his state before God, and his spiritual exercises to be as God's sentence, pronounced by the righteous Judge of heaven and earth in His courtroom. The sentence of God's Word will not differ from the sentence issued at His very own judgment seat. They will be identical.

6. He who desires to correctly engage in the work of self-examination must endeavor to bring his heart into subjection of God's glorious majesty, His omnipresence, and His omniscience. Otherwise one will so readily be misled by his own deceitful heart, whereas the true believer will tremble when God's greatness and awe-inspiring majesty are impressed upon his heart.

7. He who does not wish to be misled in this work must, so to speak, be neutral and objective. He must be as a clean sheet of paper. His only concern should be that the truthfulness of his spiritual state before God may become apparent. Many will not be without prejudice when they begin this work of self-examination, and therefore their deceitful heart will readily cause them to go astray. Some people begin their self-examination by ascertaining that they have no grace. They will then search for anything that will affirm their assessment without calmly considering the evidences of grace that might be present in their lives, and thus they will frequently arrive at the wrong conclusion. Others will begin their self-examination by presuming that they have faith and possess grace. They will look for arguments—only God knows how founded or unfounded they may be—and disregard matters that irrefutably show them that they are void of grace as to their state before God. They feed "on ashes: a deceived heart hath turned [them] aside, that [they] cannot deliver [their] soul, nor say, Is there not a lie in [our] right hand?" (Isa. 44:20).

8. Finally, he who has examined his heart, and has carefully taken to heart everything that has been said about this, must particularly note what his conscience tells him as God's regent so that he will thereby either be encouraged or, in fact, convicted.

Inconclusive Marks of Regeneration

Having spoken of the examination of the heart itself, we now wish to assist you in this task as much as we possibly can. We will set before you the marks of the new birth as we find them in God's true and faithful Word, and we will, therefore, ask your attention—oh, that you would give heed!—for several aspects.

We will first speak of what these marks are *not*. We will do so in order that your attention will be shifted from "the refuge of lies" (Isa. 28:17), and that, instead, you would pursue the truth and act accordingly day and night. We will address all points concisely and briefly in conformity with the standard of God's Word.

Religious Privileges

Regarding the marks that do not prove that someone is born again, first of all, we must address religious privileges, for they cannot automatically be reckoned as marks of grace. "For he is not a Jew, which is one outwardly; neither is that circumcision, which is outward in the flesh: but he is a Jew, which is one inwardly; and circumcision is that of the heart, in the spirit, and not in the letter; whose praise is not of men, but of God" (Rom. 2:28–29). Thus, though you may enjoy external privileges, have the revealed Word, be circumcised, be a partaker of the Passover, it will not benefit you in the least if you are not a true worshiper of God inwardly. We shall prove that external religious privileges are no marks of saving grace.

The eternally abiding Word of God not only teaches that many shall ultimately go lost, but also that they will indeed be damned (Matt. 7:21–23). There will be many in the great day of judgment who will say, "We have eaten and drunk in thy presence, and thou hast taught in our streets." The Lord will nevertheless reply, "I tell you, I know you not whence ye are" (Luke 13:26–27). Therefore we also have the express declaration that "the children of the kingdom shall be cast out into outer darkness" (Matt. 8:12).

God posits in His Word that the condition of all who enjoy such external privileges and yet lack a true transformation of the heart is not better than the state of all who lack these privileges. Jeremiah, therefore, writes that God says regarding Israel, "All the house of Israel are uncircumcised in the heart" (Jer. 9:26).[12] Furthermore, beloved, read attentively the first chapter of Isaiah, where God testifies that He despises all external religious rituals if the transformation of the heart is lacking. How astonishing it is that the consciences of such who have no more than their upbringing, who live a moral life, who partake of the Lord's Supper, and who are diligent in the use of the means, are not awakened as to their actual state.

---

12. The Dutch *Statenvertaling* reads, "Maar het ganse huis Israels heeft de voorhuid des harten"; that is, "All the house of Israel have the foreskin of the heart."

Finally, all who have nothing more than this will not only perish, but they shall experience that even that in which they trust shall aggravate the eternal pain they shall endure. Some regions have the custom of dousing criminals with tar and oil before they are burnt at the stake to render the pain all the more unbearable.

Likewise, every ignored sermon and every unlawful partaking of the Lord's Supper will add to their hellish torment. "Woe unto thee, Chorazin! woe unto thee, Bethsaida!… It shall be more tolerable for Tyre and Sidon at the day of judgment, than for you" (Matt. 11:21–22).

Let it not annoy you that I set this before you, for the majority of men have no other ground than external privileges. Given that men carnally trust in external privileges, this was, therefore, such an essential part of the teaching ministry of Christ and the apostles. Following in their footsteps, we must say, "Even if you had all things, you will be eternally lost if you are not truly born of God."

Spiritual Gifts

Gifts and proficiencies in the exercise of true religion are in and of themselves no evidences of being truly born again. "Many will say to me in that day, Lord, Lord, have we not prophesied in thy name? and in thy name have cast out devils? And in thy name done many wonderful works? And then will I profess unto them, I never knew you: depart from me, ye that work iniquity" (Matt. 7:22–23). Paul, a multitalented man, says, "Though I speak with the tongues of men and of angels, and have not charity, I am become as sounding brass, or a tinkling cymbal. And though I have the gift of prophecy, and understand all mysteries, and all knowledge; and though I have all faith, so that I could remove mountains, and have not charity, I am nothing" (1 Cor. 13:1–2).

The truth of this will be affirmed by the fact that such excellent gifts can coexist with the works of unrighteousness. I ask you urgently, "What communion hath light with darkness?" (2 Cor. 6:14). He who is born of God will not intentionally and deliberately sin. However, what does experience teach us? Some people have the aforesaid eminent qualities who nevertheless indulged in much sin.

These eminent gifts cannot serve as infallible marks, for they do not issue forth from election. However, a person's saving faith does issue forth from election. Therefore, though they may say in the great day of judgment, "Lord, have we not prophesied in thy name…and in thy name done many wonderful works?" they will hear, "I never knew you!" On the contrary, a true believer, however little his faith may be, will hear, "Come, ye blessed of my Father" (Matt. 25:34).

Such eminent gifts are not marks of faith, for when God grants such gifts, He does not regard the person who receives them, but rather, He grants them solely for the benefit of His church. Thus, many ministers may possess great talent who, with Balaam, will yet eternally perish.

Finally, that such gifts are not marks of grace is evident from the demeanor of such men. Paul says that knowledge puffs up and that love edifies. You will observe that when one person has more gifts than another, and his heart is not kept humble by grace, he will deem himself superior to others. There will be no timidity. He will be arrogant regarding the actions and inner life of others. He will have little or no regard for his own heart and will be intolerant of anyone who contradicts him. However, humility and modesty will be the companions of true grace. Therefore, let no one rest his state before God upon a sandy foundation but instead seek to be founded upon the true rock.

Emotions about Religious Matters

Many sweet emotions and stirrings of the affections regarding sacred matters and religious exercises do not yield absolute affirmation that someone is born again. There are people who, when they are addressed, will weep, and who, while listening to sermons, will have many sad or joyful emotions. They will thus conclude and consider themselves to be born again, that God's Spirit is at work in them, and that He has done a saving work in them. My beloved, we will show you regarding both situations that such a conclusion may not be drawn, for such people can be found among those who have never been born again.

Two very clear passages affirm that emotions and many stirrings of the affections are no proof of the new birth. In Matthew 13:20, we read of hearers of the Word who are compared to stony ground who receive the Word with great joy. Hebrews 6 also teaches this, for Paul states, "But, beloved, we are persuaded better things of you" (v. 9), whereas in the preceding verses he had spoken of some having being enlightened and having "tasted the good word of God, and the powers of the world to come" (vv. 4–5). We need not mention examples of such people from the Word of God. Everyone will know how

Herod received the Word of God with joy, and how Ahab, Judas, Esau, and others repented even though their lives were entirely void of grace.

The question arises from whence such stirrings of the affections proceed.

a. First, the newness of the doctrine being taught can have an extraordinary impact on one's affections. Many went out to hear John, and for a season, they rejoiced in his light—all of which vanished quickly. When a new minister comes to a locality, many appear to be so moved that they would pluck out their right eye and would not miss any available opportunity to hear him. However, the newness will then wear off, the affections will decline, and there will no longer be any desire for the preaching or any other means of grace—showing that they remain unchanged. It proves irrefutably that however attractive the appearance of some may have been, their affections did not proceed from the Holy Spirit, but rather, they were purely an emotional response due to the newness of the matter.

b. The content of the message can also generate affections. A heavenly-minded heart can be very receptive to a joyous message, and there will be those who will be so overwhelmed with joy that it defies description. Hearing of the horrors of hell, reading the history of Christ's suffering, and reading of Joseph's mistreatment can cause many tears to flow. I have read Augustine's confession that he could never read of the grievous mistreatment of both without his heart melting into tears, while all the while, he could not shed a single tear about his own state of spiritual deadness. One must, therefore, be very careful in dealing with his own soul.

c. Such affections can also be in response to the gifts and talents of the preacher. He can be such a gifted orator and address matters in such a moving way that people will be stirred by it. I have read of speakers who, due to their extraordinary talents, could have such an impact on the emotions that there would be an immediate response of either joy or sadness. That such emotions were merely triggered in response to these talents is affirmed by the same matters and expressions having no effect when they are either read or heard by someone else.

d. Finally, such affections can proceed from the grievous depravity of the heart. Some people know that ministers and others love to see people moved. They will shed as many tears and will speak in such a manner as they know it will please the minister. However, neither their tears nor their words proceed from the heart. They only do so because they think that they can deceive God and men. This was emphatically true of the old people of Israel. They repented and sought God early. One would think that the best garment would now be put on and that the fatted calf should be killed. However, even though they did so, what followed? It was merely a lip confession, for their hearts were not upright before God—or better said, their hearts were not steadfast (cf. Ps. 78:34–37; Isa. 58). Therefore, we should not be surprised that many will rest in this! So closely do they resemble true affections. The heart appears to have been touched. For others, it will be merely a matter of natural inclination.

You must not think, however, that these are proofs of being born again, for they merely prove that there are common operations of the Spirit. They do not prove that the Spirit dwells within you, whereas a regenerate person is indeed a temple of the Holy Ghost (1 Cor. 6:19). Such dispositions can all manifest themselves in temporal believers—as is evident in the quoted passages. Oh, how careful a soul ought to be!

These affections and emotions, therefore, cannot prove that one is born of God. However, it should also be noted that man, being a wretched creature, can readily deceive himself when he views these emotions as the saving stirrings of the Spirit. You need to know that the devil is the imitator of God in his activities.

History, therefore, teaches us that when God reveals Himself to specific individuals, Satan will also concoct something similar. Due to the abundance of proof, I will only give two examples. If it was God's way in the Old Testament to make known His will by revelations and oral declarations, the devil drove people to the *oracles* which, by God's wondrous direction, ceased when God's Son was made manifest. Christ proved Himself to be God's Son and the true Mediator by His miracles. However, consider only all that *Apollonius Thyanaeus* did.[13] The devil knows that a contrite and broken heart is pre-

---

13. Comrie is here referring to Apollonius of Tyanna (AD 2–98) who was known as a neo-Pythagorian philosopher and teacher. His teaching influenced science and occultism for centuries following his death. Due to his contacts with Eastern mysticism, and by all that one of his pupils wrote about him, he earned a reputation as a magician in the classical and Christian world of the first century and, with occult powers, was able to do amazing things; therefore, he was, to a lesser or greater degree, viewed as an adversary of Jesus Christ. Comrie assumes here that everyone knows this person and, therefore, merely mentions his name.

cious in God's sight. He also knows that he cannot break the heart of man (God alone can do that), and he will, therefore, frequently stir up emotions in people that resemble such brokenness of heart. When there is much of the Spirit's work in the church, it would be very foolish to speak of the merits of good works. The wicked one will, therefore, choose another way to speak of Jesus and how one must engage himself regarding Him—all of which will merely consist of an accumulation of intellectual notions while the real work of God will be missing. Read Acts 19:13–14 to affirm this, as it speaks there of the seven sons of Sceva who were exorcists and who also spoke of Jesus and had the audacity to exorcise devils in His name.

All such affections will subside and will not produce a genuine change of heart. They will generally end in the flesh. The likelihood is one hundred to one that you will see such people turn back as "the sow that was washed to her wallowing in the mire" (2 Peter 2:22). Therefore, if one desires to deal honestly with himself (so that his soul will not perish), it is above all necessary that one examines himself to consider whether one had any affections at all, and especially from whence they proceed. The issue is what effect these affections have—whether they are affections of humility, of distrusting oneself, and a taking refuge in the blood of Jesus so that one's sinful tears may thereby be sanctified.

If such affections may indeed emerge, a person can speak of a good work. If, however, he is readily satisfied, it will be a thousand to one that the heart will become careless and unreceptive to being exposed and uncovered.

Outward Conformity to the Law

The conscientiousness of many in the keeping of God's commandments does not infallibly prove the state of grace through the new birth—even though thousands have perished for whom this was their ground. Being a matter of such importance, I wish to say a few things about it.

First, I wish to prove this from the Lord's infallible Word. In Matthew 19:20, we read of a young man having a conversation with Christ. Upon Christ's exhortation that he must keep all the commandments, he replies that he has kept them from his youth. As is evident from this history, he said this in all sincerity. Upon comparing Acts 26:5 and Philippians 3, we will observe that Paul, in all sincerity, also testified of himself that he had belonged to the strictest sect of the Pharisees and also had lived accordingly—marshaling even the witness of others. Everyone who knew Paul recognized this. In the meantime, however, everything had become but as dung to him (Phil. 3:8). Add to this the emphatic words of the Savior: "Except your righteousness shall exceed the righteousness of the scribes and Pharisees, ye shall in no case enter into the kingdom of heaven" (Matt. 5:20).

Now consider for a moment what they all had: They were Hebrews of the Hebrews, circumcised the eighth day, much in prayer—even up to seven times a day and even at midnight. They were very just toward their neighbors, abundantly generous, subdued and subjected their bodies through many prayers, engaged in much watchfulness, fasting, etc. However, it was ultimately all in vain, for we must have a righteousness other than our own, and Jesus therefore says, "Howbeit in vain do they worship me, teaching for doctrines the commandments of men" (Mark 7:7). We thus deem to have affirmed the fact that conscientious obedience is not an infallible foundation upon which to rest, for this can manifest itself without there being any true grace.

It will, however, be beneficial to show you why the majority of humanity rests in this.

1. First, it proceeds from a profound ignorance regarding the depravity of our nature. Our spiritual leprosy has not even left as much as one iota of purity in our souls. The heart of every man may be compared to a pit in which all manner of vermin is crawling. However, as long as no light shines into such a heart, it will be at peace. Therefore, oh sinner, consider your corrupt condition and exclaim that rather than having a good heart, you have an unclean and leprous heart in which any good is no longer to be found.

2. Second, people do not believe the demand of the law to be truly that strict—a law that demands perfect obedience upon penalty of death. People are generally inclined to believe that they can resolve this by being doubly compliant in their duties. However, the Word has issued forth from the mouth of God, and it shall thus not return unto Him void (Isa. 55:11). He who transgresses one commandment has transgressed the entire law, and "cursed is every one that continueth not in all things which are written in the book of the law to do them" (Gal. 3:10).

3. Third, man will disregard the full scope of God's law. Most believe that it suffices if they have obeyed the letter of the law. David said, however, "I have seen an end of all perfection: but thy commandment is

exceeding broad" (Ps. 119:96). The law not only demands compliance with the letter of the law, but everything must proceed from a truly good principle and must achieve a truly good purpose. That requires the engagement of all the faculties of the soul. The summary of the law is, therefore, that one must love God with all of his heart, all of his soul, all of his mind, and all of his strength (Matt. 22:37).

4. Fourth, the sinner does not understand how God will save a person in a way that pleases Him. The objective of this way was never to do good works for the sake of doing good works, but rather, one must do so by virtue of a covenant. Thus, if someone were to be free of hereditary sin and also would not have committed any actual sin—if he would have obeyed all commandments perfectly—even then could he not expect salvation based on his obedience. It is therefore not *ex congruo*, that is, because there is concurrence between good works and grace, and also not *ex condigno*, that is, because it is consistent with good works[14]—except when God is pleased to enter into a covenant with man in which life is promised upon the condition of obedience.

---

14. G. A. van den Brink's thoughts are helpful here: Both Latin terms are extracted from the Roman Catholic doctrine of grace. *Meritum ex condigno* would mean that God would reward works in exact conformity to their intrinsic value (*dignitas*). That would be a purely Pelagian notion that would exclude grace. Reformed theology has posited that even in the case of Adam in Paradise, he would not have received eternal life *ex condigno*. Roman Catholic theologians also rejected the *meritum ex condigno*. Instead, they defended the *meritum ex congruo*, or the *meritum ex pacto*. In that case, works are not judged by God as to their intrinsic worth or worthiness but rather upon the basis of the covenant (*pactum*) that God has made and in which He promises to graciously reward the works of man. According to this view, works have meritorious value due to God's grace. In grace, God has established an extrinsic congruence (compare: *ex congruo*) between works and merit. According to the Reformed view, the latter was true in the covenant of works but not in the covenant of grace. Comrie also rejects both views. In the covenant of grace, works do not have any meritorious value—neither *ex condigno* nor *ex congruo*. The opponents of the English theologian Richard Baxter (1615–1691) accused him of having reintroduced the Roman Catholic *meritum ex congruo* by viewing the activity of faith as an act of man that God graciously rewards by justifying him. The traditional Reformed position was to view the relationship between the act of faith and justification as an *instrumental relationship*. Baxter construed it as a *graciously meritorious (ex congruo) relationship*. Comrie was vehemently anti-Baxter, and the fact that he makes mention of this distinction in his *Eigenschappen* (this work) must undoubtedly be viewed within this context. Comrie's response to this debate was to *deny any and every meritorius relationship* between the act of faith and justification.

5. Finally, resting in one's conscientiousness will be due to a lack of self-examination. If everyone were to examine all his thoughts, intents, and deeds, he would have to exclaim, "Cleanse thou me from secret faults" (Ps. 19:12).

The latter are, therefore, to be pitied the most, since they come so very close to what it should be. However, it is precisely that proximity that hinders them, for they do not perceive the necessity of being righteous through a Surety. Only the securing of that righteousness matters in rendering payment of the ten thousand talents we owe God.

Happiness and Prosperity

Having a sense of inner joy and enjoying prosperity outwardly are also no proofs that would affirm infallibly that someone is born again. We need to address two matters regarding this.

First, enjoying inner peace is no proof, for there can be an unfounded peace that is merely an illusion. I think that Paul enjoyed that sort of peace when he lived without the law, for he writes, "For I was alive without the law once: but when the commandment came, sin revived, and I died" Rom. 7:9). Many believe that all is well as to their state before God, arguing that they are at peace and that nothing troubles them. This is, however, an evident sign that the strong one, the devil, sustains peace in his residence. Let us, therefore, carefully examine the nature of this peace.

This false peace is usually accompanied by *great tranquility*. No one will live more joyfully, and sometimes even die more joyfully, than such a person. However, he who knows true joy and has experienced it will know how difficult it was to attain such peace and how difficult it is to preserve it. Believers know that sin will disturb that peace and that it can be greatly assaulted. He who enjoys a false peace will never experience such strife.

This false peace is usually accompanied by having *an illusion regarding God's love* for men while at the same time continuing to indulge in this or that sin. In the meantime, however, for such as fear God in truth and uprightness, there is nothing that concerns them more than God's love for them. They will think a thousand times, "Am I not imagining things? Would God be able to love such an abominable, filthy, and repulsive creature as I am?"

This false peace is usually accompanied by *an inclination to avoid every occasion that could test the ground of their peace* and expose the doubtful nature of this peace. How they resent all who in faithfulness wish to examine their peace! How their hearts will rise in rebellion against sermonic applications whereby this false peace is exposed! Instead, they always want to be encouraged. An upright soul, however, will always be desirous to submit her experiences into the hands of God and man (cf. Ps. 139).

They who are governed by such a false peace will often *pretend that they are upright of heart* and live very conscientious lives. In contrast, a sincere believer will continually detect so many shortcomings in all his activity that he does not even want to talk about it.

A *careless walk* will generally accompany this false peace. The stronger their imaginary peace is, the more flighty, jolly, and rashly they will act. However, when the soul of a true believer experiences something of this peace, it will render him careful and self-controlled, and he will live before God in the fear of His name.

The second proof that a peaceful disposition does not prove that all is well regarding one's state before God is evident in that this peace does not rest upon a foundation wrought by the Spirit of adoption. Instead, their peace is imposed upon the soul, contrary to the Word of God. Many believe that they must have this peace at all costs, and their conscience will thus be seared with a hot iron. Such peace also proves to be illusionary by the fact that one does not attain this peace in God's normal way. His way is usually a way in which trouble, sorrow, and fear will first enter the heart, and only after that will peace be bestowed. Thousands ought to ask themselves the question whether they have ever grieved and been distressed regarding their sins, and whether they, for hours, even half of a night, have grieved bitterly over their sins. They would then see that the opposite is true and be convinced that their peace is carnal.

As the inner peace enjoyed by many is not an incontrovertible proof of grace, this is also applicable to the enjoyment of outward prosperity. The latter can be either a token of God's favor or His displeasure. Abraham said to the rich man in hell that he had prospered in this life, and Joseph and Asaph saw how "their eyes stand out with fatness" (Ps. 73:7). External blessings are frequently harmful to the soul, and God, therefore, often withholds external prosperity from His children.

Suffering for Christianity
Finally—not to mention other matters—*the experiences of pain, anxiety, distress, and even of dying for the cause of truth* are insufficient. They do not

prove that someone is born again. I admit that this is a rather unusual assertion, and yet it is true and conforms to the preaching of Paul. In 1 Corinthians 13:3, he says, "And though I bestow all my goods to feed the poor, and though I give my body to be burned, and have not charity, it profiteth me nothing." As good and necessary as such a surrender to Christ may be, it can be motivated by wrong intentions.

When the cause of God and worldly interests intersect, God's cause is frequently not the focal point, but rather, self-interest. One will then not be a martyr for Jesus's sake, but rather, for his own cause.

It can be that one will endure this merely because one is convinced of the truth rather than loving God and having a heart that is united to Him. This would move many to give their all in opposing Roman Catholicism. They would be motivated by a love for Reformed truth and solely because of their conviction that this doctrine is true.

Also, pride or fear can move one to undergo such trials, even if one embraces heretical teaching. After all, one can hardly find a sect that does not have its martyrs. It is as if I hear someone say, along with Christ's disciples, "Is all of the above then no evidence of the new birth? Can one endure such things and yet go lost? Who then can be saved?" Beloved, this is indeed a weighty matter; there are but few that shall be saved.

The True Marks of Regeneration

We will now proceed, however, to set before you from God's Word the infallible marks of the new birth. It should be noted that these marks may not be set too "high" so that fragile and yet true believers will be oppressed—as is sometimes the case. Tender consciences can be tormented and tossed to and fro because marks are brought forth that pertain to the quintessence rather than the essence of faith—thus focusing on the ultimate riches of faith. Instead, such a soul desires to know whether she possesses the essence of the matter, and only after that will she be intent on focusing on the quintessence of faith. However, the marks of grace may also not be too "low," so that people who presumptuously claim to have grace will appease themselves and be entrenched in their self-deceit. The latter will then continue with a lie in their right hand, and their self-deceived heart will lead them astray.

To avoid both dangerous pitfalls, we will seek to remain faithful to God's eternal Word as our guiding star and compass. Only when we take heed to the Word of God regarding every aspect of spiritual life shall we be able to cleanse our way (Ps. 119:9). We shall address more than one mark, for, as we have already observed earlier, the work of God's grace will be more evident for one believer by this mark and for another believer by that mark. Therefore, it has pleased God to set before us what faith is by various expressions, so that a soul who is not yet all that familiar with the appropriating nature of faith would recognize it as to its core activity: a taking refuge, and a hungering and thirsting after righteousness. Oh, that God would grant you and me an abundant measure of His Spirit and send forth His light and His truth so that they may both guide us in this important and compelling task!

Three Marks of Regeneration
1. A *deep and experiential inner stirring of the heart and an impression of one's spiritual poverty* are reliable evidence that someone has been made spiritually alive, for a dead person remains insensitive and will be oblivious to his condition. If your misery greatly oppresses you experientially, so that you begin to yearn for help, it will be token that the Holy Spirit, in principle, has made you alive, for you will now be aware of your condition and this knowledge will profoundly and intensely stir your heart.

2. A *hungering and thirsting after Christ and His righteousness* is one of the marks of grace. Jesus Himself pronounces such souls to be blessed (Matt. 5:6). Such hunger and thirst will occur and persist in someone who perceives his spiritual poverty, and who begins to perceive God's way by which He will save a sinner apart from any merit on the sinner's part. This will only occur if there is a genuine willingness to be saved in this way.

3. A *crying unto God* is another mark, for that will be the first thing a living soul will do. He will cry out that his great need may be met. As soon as the Spirit engages Himself, a man will be driven to his knees. We observe this in Acts 9, where it is said of Paul, "Behold, he prayeth" (v. 11).

A Fourth Mark of Regeneration: Evidence of a New Heart
A fourth mark of the new birth is a new heart. All who are genuinely born again will have a new heart. We have already observed in the expository portion of this sermon that he who is born of God will be a new creature. This mark is founded upon the infallible Word of God: "Therefore if any man be in Christ, he is a new creature: old things are passed away; behold, all things are become new" (2 Cor. 5:17). This is also the covenant promise expressed in

Ezekiel 36:26: "A new heart also will I give you." To enable you to assess the intrinsic validity of a given mark, you must note what will be the manifestation of such a mark.

1. He who is born again, having received a new heart from God, will now have *a different perception of his spiritual condition* before the Lord, and he will have different feelings about it. Two things dominated his heart before God renewed it. First, there is ignorance so that the unregenerate man will neither see, comprehend, nor believe his need and desperate plight apart from God (cf. John 8:30–47). He will, therefore, readily say with the Jews, "We…were never in bondage to any man" (v. 33). Second, such a person will manifest a very profound insensibility. His heart will be exceedingly wicked, but he will be insensible of it. His heart will be unrestrained in its pride, and he will be as careless as one who sleeps at the top of a mast. However, when God, by His grace, causes the heart to be regenerated, a person will immediately begin to perceive things differently, and he will have different affections. The poor soul will cry out, "Woe is me that I am such a sinful creature! How sinful, evil, and unyielding is my heart, all of which the Lord must punish!" How this will cause such a soul to groan (Ps. 38:4). She will complain about herself (Rom. 7:24) and will loathe herself in her own sight (Ezek. 36:31).

2. He who receives a new life from God will begin to *judge himself in a new and different way*. In his unregenerate state, his judgment regarding his state and his walk before God was entirely wrong. He thought that all was well with him and that he would happily arrive in heaven, believing that his way of life was wisely and suitably oriented toward this. He viewed choosing God and His ways as a most difficult task—not so much because of these ways as such, but rather, as to what they require. However, as with Paul, this will have changed completely. He writes, "For I was alive without the law once: but when the commandment came, sin revived, and I died" (Rom. 7:9). For such a person, it will become "without hope." He will now perceive that God is the highest good. Oh, that he could have God as his portion in Christ! He now recognizes that God's ways are delightful, and since they are so delightful, he endorses these ways in the deepest recesses of his heart. Even if God were to cast him away, and even if he were to be the object of His divine hatred, he would still desire to walk upon these ways and love God. Examine yourself!

3. As a new heart is the mark of the new birth, the regenerate man will have *new concerns and desires*. For the unregenerate man, it will be, "What shall we eat?" or "What shall we drink?" or, "Wherewithal shall we be clothed?" (Matt. 6:31); and "in what ways can I do that which pleases me?" However, he who has a new heart will, first of all, be concerned about his soul. What will he exclaim? He will cry out, "What shall become of my precious soul? What? Shall it be my experience that my soul will be 'a brand plucked out of the fire?' (Zech. 3:2). If I do not find Jesus, I will eternally perish. Let others find their delight in the world, but for me, thousands of worlds are not as precious as Christ. Others may rest in their own righteousness, but I realize that I am lost. I must receive mercy and grace in order to be saved and delivered. It would be a divine miracle if God were to look upon such a Mephibosheth, upon such a dead dog as I am." His desire will continue, however. "Would the Lord look upon such a one who has never sought after Him? Oh, that He would lift up the light of His countenance upon me. Oh, what a privilege that is!"

I perceive this mark in all who are born again. They who listened to John, said, "What shall we do then?" (Luke 3:10). They who listened to Peter said, "What shall we do?" (Acts 2:37), and the jailor asked Paul and Silas, "What must I do to be saved?" (Acts 16:30).

4. He who receives a new heart from God, as evidence of the new birth, will *live according to new principles* that will be diametrically opposed to his old principles. Do you wish affirmation of this? Ignorance regarding God and self belongs principally to the old heart. However, regeneration will result in a knowledge of both. "And have put on the new man, which is renewed in knowledge" (Col. 3:10); "For ye were sometimes darkness, but now are ye light in the Lord" (Eph. 5:8). Natural and carnal wisdom is also a principle that runs counter to the wisdom that is from above. The wisdom from above is pure and wholesome and is only exercised toward that which is good (2 Tim. 3:17). A third principle of the old heart is vanity, causing men to indulge themselves in thousands of meaningless endeavors. The internal spiritual disposition of the soul will counter this in order to "work out [his] own salvation with fear and trembling" (Phil. 2:12) before the Lord.

5. When God grants a person a new heart, the evidence will be *the immediate onset of spiritual warfare*, "for the flesh lusteth against the Spirit, and the Spirit against the flesh" (Gal. 5:17). As an exception to what we have stated earlier, there can also be such a struggle in the natural man. The difference,

however, is the principle from which it proceeds. In the natural man, this struggle issues forth from a slavish fear, whereas in the new heart from an inner love. Furthermore, this inherent struggle in the unregenerate man is between various innate principles. In contrast, in the regenerate man, there will be a struggle between the regenerate and unregenerate aspect of the same principles. Finally, as to the extent of this struggle, we note that there has never been an unregenerate man who battled against all sins, whereas the regenerate man will indeed battle against all sins.

6. Evidence of God having given a man a new heart will be that he will engage in new activities in the power of Christ, out of love for God, and with a soul entirely and intensely devoted to God.

We would be able to give you an abundance of other marks, such as the keeping of God's commandments, love for the brethren, and many more. Since, however, everyone can ascertain these from the expository portion of the sermon, we will move on. Therefore, we request that they who wish to consider additional marks would reflect on what we have already explained in the sermon.

Perplexities of God's Children about Regeneration

We will now turn to you, the children of God, who are "born of God." We wish to speak a few words to you to resolve your perplexities and to encourage you.

No Experience of Transformation

Some truly gracious souls doubt their spiritual state because they cannot recall ever to have experienced a spiritual transformation. After all, the Word of God always speaks of the new birth as a making alive of a soul that was dead in trespasses and sins (Eph. 2:1). They have heard other beloved children of God, with whom they keep company, speak of such a time in their lives—of a significant change in their lives. Since they cannot speak of such a change, they conclude that all is still not well with them. Nevertheless, they know various spiritual exercises. To resolve this perplexity, we wish to note the following:

Every descendant of Adam is dead in sin. "Wherefore, as by one man sin entered into the world, and death by sin; and so death passed upon all men, for that all have sinned" (Rom. 5:12). None can, therefore, be in a state of grace without having undergone a transformation of his state before God.

"But God…even when we were dead in sins, hath quickened us together with Christ" (Eph. 2:4–5). We must fully affirm this truth.

In the meantime, it should be noted that a powerful transformation as to sense, knowledge, and consciousness was experienced primarily by people who lived during the initial expansion of the gospel. Then the gospel came to a people that dwelt in darkness and were void of any light. It should be self-evident that their change had to be significant and discernable to themselves and others. Add to this, that immediately following their conversion, they simultaneously embraced Christ, the gallows, the torture rack, and all manner of torment. Such will also be the experience of those who have not been wrought upon unto salvation until they were older. The same is true for those who have lived sinful and ungodly lives. Such individuals frequently know precisely when and how a change came in their lives and how they were pricked in their hearts by God's Spirit. However, this is not normative for others! There are many among the godly that know of no such obvious change and whose state we may nevertheless not question due to the power of godliness manifested in them.

We are thinking of those whose heart God the Holy Spirit has begun to transform in a gentle and yet powerful manner in their early youth by planting the fear of God in them—and who, by virtue of a godly upbringing, gradually increase in love for God, Christ, and all the godly. Daily experience can yield multiple examples of such cases to those who attentively consider God's ways in this regard, and we are also not without biblical witnesses. Jeremiah, John, and Timothy were sanctified from the womb. In fact, when young children are saved—for it would be cruel to consign them all to hell— then the essence of regeneration must have been wrought in their hearts in a manner that is incomprehensible to us. The same Spirit can work similarly in one or another person, as well.

Thus, the point is not whether we know of the time and manner of regeneration, but rather, the primary concern for believers is that they know the exercises that issue forth from the new birth. As you cry out to God, examine your heart in light of these exercises.

1. Do you not occasionally experience that your heart cleaves to God in such a tender, affectionate, and warm manner? You will then value His nearness at such a moment more than a thousand worlds!

2. Do you not experience that your conscience troubles you about sins of which no one knows but God and your soul? Yes, there will then be

times that you will grieve so bitterly about the sins of your heart and your daily walk. You will grieve about the sin of being so heartless when praying and reading your Bible. You will grieve over neglecting your communion with God, viewing yourself as a great beast before God.

3. Are you not gladdened when God shows you the sins that arise in your heart? Rather than seeking to conceal them, you will openly confess them and flee from them, taking refuge to the fullness that is in Christ Jesus so that your sins may all be covered and your conscience may be at peace by taking refuge to Him.

4. Is it not your experience that your heart loves Jesus as King as much as Priest, and that you will thus frequently cry out to Him to conform you to all that is not in agreement with His will? What a matter of great joy it would be to you to perceive that there is convincing evidence that you are being renewed in knowledge, righteousness, and true holiness!

5. Is it not your experience that you are inwardly committed to all God's commandments and that you honor and esteem them in all things to be good? Moreover, with that, your soul also highly esteems and loves all who are genuinely godly.

If all this is so with you, endeavor to keep your soul no longer in a state of doubt, but rather, determine your state before God based on His Word. The essential thing is that one possesses the matters that issue forth from the renewal of one's heart, even though one may neither know the time nor the manner of that renewal.

No Experience of Wrath before Conversion
There are genuinely gracious souls who doubt their state before God, though they have experienced many inclinations toward, and spiritual exercises regarding, Jesus. The thought, therefore, arises (having heard this of ministers and other Christians), that in order to take the critical step of coming to Christ, there must first be a conscious awareness of being scrutinized by the eye of the Judge of heaven and earth—the God who has been provoked to wrath. They must also be conscious of being children of wrath outside of God and Christ. However, as the soul examines her spiritual experiences, she cannot find anything like it. They will thus arrive at the desperate conclusion

that, until now, they have deceived and deluded themselves in all things. Regarding this, you are to note the following.

If one maintains that this critical step implies that a soul can only embrace Jesus with an assured faith, it needs to be stated that this cannot possibly be true, for a truly godly person will frequently exercise a refuge-taking faith before exercising an assured faith. Therefore, he cannot truthfully say of himself that he is a child of wrath, and thus without God and Christ, when, in fact, he comes and surrenders himself to Him as a guilty sinner.

It should also be noted that God has not stipulated that a soul, before taking the critical step of coming to Christ, must either simultaneously or before that think of herself as being without God and Christ and that all her attention should be focused on this. This is not the language of the Bible, and a soul must therefore not let this either trouble or discourage her. The Bible does not explicitly say that I must first see myself as such, but rather that I must see myself as a lost and wretched man in myself. That is profitable indeed, but it does not mean that at the same time, I will see myself as being without Jesus. As true as the latter may be, the soul does not always consider this. If you wish to confer with God's Word, you will find it to be as I have stated. "Only acknowledge thine iniquity, that thou hast transgressed against the LORD thy God" (Jer. 3:13) in order that you might be justified. Not a word is said in support of the proposed notion. The publican said, "God be merciful to me a sinner," and "this man went down to his house justified" (Luke 18:13–14). The jailor said, "What must I do to be saved?" (Acts 16:30).

Therefore, let such a concerned soul ask herself if she has not often seen herself as a loathsome sinner and if it is not her desire to come, if she could, daily to Jesus as a sinner. If that is so, then none whose heart is upright should be troubled or disturbed about things that have nothing to do with the essence of the matter. Many do not experience these things and yet arrive in heaven. The only thing a soul should be concerned about is whether she seeks to come without money and without price to find help in boundless grace for Jesus's sake. This is the crux of the matter, for he who thus comes shall in no wise be cast out by Jesus.

A Lack of Joy and Peace
Many gracious souls will doubt their new birth because, to their knowledge, they have never experienced a heartfelt affirmation upon the exercise of faith whereby their souls were overwhelmed with joy and filled with a tender

peace. Though they sense that there have been spiritual exercises from their side, yet they do not know whether they were in truth.

We wish to remark that many believers are now triumphant before the throne of God who have never experienced this as is frequently assumed. They have departed in faith, finding their rest in the syllogism of faith. As extraordinary as it may be to experience such spiritual joy and enlargement, the absence of this does not prove that someone is not born again. If that were true, everyone would always experience such joy.

Such smoking flaxes must recognize that the matter discussed here is not faith itself, but rather, a consequence of faith that is not always necessarily connected to faith. As we may deduce from all its scriptural designations, faith is the yearning of the soul after Christ to obtain wisdom, justification, and a complete redemption (1 Cor. 1:30). Faith is a taking refuge to the Savior.

Such a little one in grace should note that the work of God in his life must be genuine before he receives its affirmation in the heart. That inner affirmation as such does not validate this work, but rather, it yields joy regarding God's work in him—a work that is already of God before such joy of heart will be experienced.

The Bible never uses such expressions when it speaks of faith. As to the work of God's Spirit, it is, therefore, safest to use the language of the Spirit rather than expressions different from the Word of the living God. We observe that the Word speaks of believers who "through fear of death were all their lifetime subject to bondage" (Heb. 2:15). They certainly did not consciously experience the aforesaid inner affirmation in the heart.

If this experience would be mandatory for every born-again sinner, half of God's Word would be superfluous. God's Word is filled with marks whereby one can ascertain his spiritual state. All this would be entirely of no value if the act of faith always had to be accompanied by such an inner affirmation in the heart—as if only one who has the latter would possess the matter itself. If that were true, regeneration would not have to be proven by way of marks.

Finally, anyone who doubts his spiritual state ought not to be too hasty in saying that he is void of spiritual life. Come, ask your soul whether you have ever known times when you groaned and mourned regarding your sins; when you confessed them and abhorred yourself; and when you sought to look unto the all-sufficiency of Christ's righteousness. Ask your soul whether you were not refreshed and experienced joy when you were thus exercised.

Ask yourself whether your heart was not briefly enlarged and whether you experienced some peace in your heart. Afterwards, was it not frequently your desire that such a time would dawn again? Ask your soul whether you have not experienced such power that your heart melted and thereby you, in deep humility, like wax melting in the fire, had to say to yourself that you were nothing before the Lord. Was your heart then not united with God's will, and did you not thank Him for the appointed means of deliverance? What else is this but what others call an inner affirmation of the heart? You may trust this to be true, and your soul may, therefore, be comforted and encouraged.

A Scarcity of Spiritual Exercises
Some people are genuinely born again, who yet doubt their state of grace. They dare not deny that they have seen their estrangement from God and that they have seen themselves as being lost. They then perceived that Jesus in His fullness was revealed to their soul. They could then intimately unite themselves to this Jesus and receive Him by faith. However, this experience subsided, and although they very carefully took note of their spiritual exercises, they could no longer detect anything of their previous experience. They then begin to think that if the initial spiritual exercises would have been genuine, they would still be able to detect some of this.

However, rather than extinguishing this hope, you should consider the following matters.

God's way will, at times, be that He will initially cause light to arise and then rather soon cause a cloud to come between so that such a soul will after that never again have such profound spiritual experiences. This appears to have been Heman's condition who was "afflicted and ready to die from [his] youth up" (Ps. 88:15).

Such a person ought to consider that God's way is not so much to repeatedly assure a believer by renewed affirmations of grace, but rather to assure primarily by means of the marks of true grace that prove to be a more reliable foundation than affirmations of grace. The truth of such affirmations must be validated by the results and effects they have upon the soul. He should, therefore, frequently examine himself in light of those marks that are set forth in the Word of God.

Such a person should reflect upon the course of his life. Although such persons do not experience what they so much desire to experience, they may perhaps perceive in themselves the essentials of God's grace. Dear soul, ask yourself whether you do, at times, loathe yourself. Then a promise of the covenant of grace has already been fulfilled in you (cf. Ezek. 20:42; 36:31). Is it not your experience that your heart intensely longs for Jesus? Are there not places and corners that could testify that there are those times that you long and thirst more for God than "the hart panteth after the water brooks" (Ps. 42:1)? Furthermore, how did you arrive at such a detailed knowledge of spiritual matters and frames if it were not well with your heart?

Finally, consider your character and disposition. You may discover reasons to acknowledge and embrace how God is leading you by not giving you tokens of His favor. One cause might be that you have a melancholy character, or it may be God's intent that you would know more of yourself and the depths of His ways. Else, how would you have recognized many of Satan's devices? Would you have been able to discern your indwelling and deeply felt corruption? Therefore, "be not faithless, but believing" (John 20:27).

Remembrance of Former Sins
Then there are other gracious souls who in their misery have come to Jesus, and who have experienced light, joy, and liberty in and through His work. However, dark clouds have now gathered. They are assaulted regarding their spiritual transformation as a fruit of the new birth, the reason being that sins of their former life come to mind. These sins appear to them so immense and grave that they deem it impossible that they could have ever found grace in the Lord's eyes. They now eye with suspicion all their previous spiritual experiences and present soul exercises. This will gnaw as a worm at the root of all their joy and spiritual delight. As a result, they will be bowed down, and their "moisture is turned into the drought of summer" (Ps. 32:4). Although many believers struggle with this, they often do not speak about it.

It should be noted, however, that their spiritual frame and grief are neither foreign to the spiritual experiences of the godly, nor do they contradict them. If the Lord were to affirm this by His Word and Spirit, that should be sufficient to quiet the spirit of a troubled soul. I believe that Job, the most upright and God-fearing man on earth, found himself in such a situation and was exercised accordingly. In Job 13:26, he says, "For thou writest bitter things against me, and makest me to possess the iniquities of my youth." We also have a good example in what David, the man after God's heart, says. Long after his conversion, he was so troubled that he had to exclaim, "Remember not the sins of my youth" (Ps. 25:7). How sweetly this is also expressed in the rhymed version: "Sins of youth remember not" (Psalter 64:3). If this is so, such a struggling soul should not all too readily yield to his doubts, but rather consider that this is God's adorable way to keep him small and humble.

Such a soul must also consider the biblical examples of persons who have been exceptionally godless, whom God, nevertheless, has converted and radically changed. He will then be silent. I shall not speak of Adam and Eve. Although their transgressions were a bundling[15] of all manner of unrighteousness, nevertheless, we believe wholeheartedly that they were brought into the covenant of grace. Also, consider for a moment a man like Manasseh (2 Kings 21). Though he was the son of a godly father, Hezekiah, he introduced a corrupt religion, persecuted God's true people, walked in the way of the heathen, and indulged himself in witchcraft. Your sins before your conversion may not have been as egregious as theirs. Nevertheless, just like you, they were vessels of mercy who, rather than being "fitted to destruction" (Rom. 9:22), had been appointed unto salvation. Consider also Paul who was a blasphemer and a persecutor of the church of God. His heart was powerfully changed on the way to Damascus (Acts 9). Nevertheless, both of these men have been converted.

Then why should so many be tossed to and fro and give the devil such leeway? They should keep in mind the words of the great God and Savior "that the publicans and the harlots go into the kingdom of God before [others]" (Matt. 21:31). When comparing this with current reality, they will observe that it is God's ordinary way to choose the most wicked and wretched of men to be the recipients of the riches of His grace.

Such persons ought to consider how they now think and are exercised about their former sins. Do they not think of them with grief and sorrow, and do they, therefore, not abhor themselves before the Lord? That is a certain and incontrovertible proof of a transformation of heart produced by the new birth. The affections of a presumptive believer will never be drawn away from sin. If he could, were permitted, and had the same opportunity as in former days, he would find delight in sinning.

Finally, if such a person would counter all my arguments by saying, "Yes, at my initial conversion, when I surrendered myself to Jesus Christ, these particular sins did not come to mind," My response is that this is not

---

15. Comrie uses the word "samenknoping," a word that occurs in the Dutch rendition of Acts 8:23: "Gij zijt in een gans bittere gal en samenknoping der ongerechtigheid." The KJV reads: "Thou art in the gall of bitterness, and in the bond of iniquity."

required. We are finite creatures, and we are incapable of considering all of our sins at once. No believer has ever experienced this, and when we come to Jesus as a result of the new birth, it suffices that we come as guilty men with the sins that are known to us—sins of which we are aware, and sins as yet secret or hidden (cf. Ps. 19:12). "The blood of Jesus Christ his Son cleanseth us from all sin" (1 John 1:7).

Remaining Passions and Desires

Others may be fully conscious of and know that they have experienced the new birth. However, they perceive within themselves a particular lust and corrupt inclination known only to God and themselves. These sinful desires arise time and again, and they will be overcome by them, even contrary to their prayers and good intentions. This appears to prove beyond any doubt that they are nevertheless not born again. Otherwise, according to the words of the apostle Paul, sin would not have dominion over them, for they would be under grace (Rom. 6:14).

However, it should be noted that in the quoted chapter, Paul, to reassure such persons, speaks in a twofold manner about sin's dominion in us. First, he states as a proposition, "For sin shall not have dominion over you: for ye are not under the law, but under grace." However, a bit earlier, he says by way of exhortation, "Let not sin therefore reign in your mortal body" (v. 12). Thus, a clear distinction needs to be made between these two statements. I conclude that in his first assertion, Paul states what is impossible in light of the covenant of grace, whereas in his second assertion, he tells believers what their duty is. Paul's intent, therefore, is to state first that sin shall not have dominion unto damnation, and then, in light of the preceding, that you must be zealous in doing good so that sin will not reign over you and you would break forth into sin. This text (v. 12) is, therefore, not an indictment against you.

It should also be noted that there are believers, and thus genuinely gracious souls, who experience such anxiety. Proof of this is that we read about a "sin which doth so easily beset us" (Heb. 12:1). This does not pertain to all sins, but rather, to a sin that strongly influences us. This could have been the thorn of which Paul speaks (2 Cor. 12; cf. Rom. 7). Having said that, however, no believer experiences that he is in bondage to all sins simultaneously.

The person who is troubled by such a besetting sin should avail himself of either a faithful minister or a devoted and experienced Christian who will maintain confidentiality. In speaking to him, even if one were to do so in the third person, he might hear that other beloved children of God have struggled with this as well. Such a person could thus be somewhat put at ease. I am saying this because shame will often inhibit people from being transparent.

Furthermore, such a person must consider what position he takes regarding such a sin. Does he find some delight in it, and does he give in easily when this particular sin begins to stir within him? Is he grieved and sorrowful that all his desires to be rid of this sin have not been successful and that all his prayers against this sin are not being answered? He who truly fears God will be alarmed when a bosom sin so much as rears its head.

He must also examine himself whether he is a willing accomplice regarding this sin. That would be a bad sign. The soul of him who truly fears God with his entire heart will never willingly yield, but rather, he will be dragged along and overcome by this sin.

He must consider his inner disposition when he is overcome by sin. Is this a matter of grief and regret before God? Does he set apart time to be alone with the Lord in order to overcome his sin? Does he open his heart to Christ as King so that this sin in him may be abolished and his heart may be engaged to practice true obedience? Where this is to be found, those sins which remain in his flesh, contrary to his will, shall not impact one's standing before God.

A Sense of Unworthiness

There are others who, even though a specific sin will not cause them to doubt, will nevertheless perceive their ungodly and wretched nature as such. They will thus deem themselves too unworthy to look unto Jesus. They dare not think anything of themselves when they know themselves to be in the presence of God, etc. Such a person, therefore, ought to reflect on the goodness of Christ!

- He serves an open table for hungry souls;
- He invites them;
- He invites them urgently: "Every one that thirsteth" (Isa. 55:1);
- He beseeches: "We pray you in Christ's stead" (2 Cor. 5:20);
- He commands;
- He threatens them with His displeasure if they do not come.

Let such a person also think of the dishonor he brings upon Jesus, and the sin he will be committing in so doing.

- He will be rude and ill-mannered toward Him;
- He will be prescribing to God what ought to be done;
- He despises the efficacy of Jesus's blood;
- He despises all the promises;
- He has low thoughts of God's sovereign grace and love.

The Power of Indwelling Corruption

Then there will be others who doubt their state before God because now, more than ever before, they will become conscious of their corrupt nature. They will say, "In former days, I could resist sin and be courageously victorious. However, for some time now, sin is so strong that I cannot resist it. I am therefore convinced that my state before God is not good."

Such persons should note, however, that they may not have been on the way of life that long and that therefore they may not yet have exercised senses to know what believers experience along the way. Often God will grant joy and spiritual refreshment when He draws the soul and incorporates her into the covenant of grace. He will shed abroad His love so richly in the heart that they will know and see little sin. They now deem themselves to be heroes of faith who are increasingly approaching perfection and are dying more and more to sin. However, the experience of seasoned Christians will generally teach the opposite, namely, that later they had to wrestle very much with sins that they could not subdue.

They should realize that such feelings are not to be attributed to the fact that they now commit more sin than in former days, but rather, that their souls are now possibly far more illuminated—both as to their thoughts as well as their deeds. It is light that unveils all things.

Many children of God will continue to do certain things that are wrong in and of themselves—things they do not perceive as such. Light only arises gradually, and therefore, everything will not be seen at once. Rather than rejecting one's state before God, one must retain that belief even though there are things in his life that do not line up.

They also need to know that they have something that will never be the portion of either a hypocrite, an almost-Christian, or a temporal believer. The latter will never become more sinful and miserable in their own eyes—to such an extent that they will be inwardly convinced of this and will, therefore, decrease more and more in their own estimation. They must also realize that God's way with them to keep them small, sensitive, and humble is an excellent one. They will thus be convinced experientially how inimitable God's sovereign grace is.

Finally, let all this work in us a deep humiliation before, watchfulness toward, and dependence upon the Lord. He alone can sustain us!

Deficient Sanctification

Others often doubt their state of grace before God because they are so deficient as to their growth in heavenly-mindedness and sanctification.

Such persons are to ascertain whether a given sin in them has darkened the light that ought to be emanating from them. They need to distinguish between grace in the heart and its fruit in their walk of life. They must, therefore, take note of former days and compare themselves to what they were several years ago and what they are now. One cannot daily observe whether he has made progress. Therefore, one must consider whether one's inner desires are toward sanctification. It is also good to consider that God will frequently conceal their sanctification so that they would all the more live out of their justification.

They must also learn not to murmur. Furthermore, to their comfort, they need to know that God's promises are not contingent upon the measure of grace, but upon the genuineness of that grace. The weaker they are, the more they will be the object of God's care. Moreover, they need to recognize fully that often they do more for God than they realize.

Conclusion

If you may thus acknowledge that you are born of God, then it is your duty to see to it that you will strive to overcome the world with all that is to be found in it. Others will then be able to see that you have been born of God. I know that it is your great desire and your innermost yearning to be more than conquerors in all things, and that yet you must complain and groan that you see so little of that victory. Oh, that is usually because you do not seek to overcome the world by faith! Faith is the sole means to that end. The weapons for this warfare will only be effective in the hand of faith. Having set this before you, may the Spirit enable you to do so.

Nevertheless, comfort yourself with the knowledge that the day of your redemption is drawing near. Soon the enemies will be overcome, and you will be more than conquerors through Christ who shall give you the victory. Amen.

CHAPTER 7

Faith, a Grace That Will Be Tried

That the trial of your faith, being much more precious than of gold that perisheth, though it be tried with fire, might be found unto praise and honour and glory at the appearing of Jesus Christ.
—1 PETER 1:7

To meditate upon and to search out God's ways in the sanctuary in which He leads His children yields a threefold benefit for the Christian.

First, such benefit is derived from the past—from all that has transpired. Oh, when a Christian reflects about the distresses, fears, the vicissitudes of life, and many trials he has experienced, he can say, "All thy waves and thy billows are gone over me" (Ps. 42:7). He will say, "I now view them as being primarily behind me. I have experienced sorrows, and I know what it means when one has to go his way amid trying circumstances." Frequently he will say, "I thought that I would sink away in deep waters. As a wretched man, I cried out, 'Lord, save me, for I am perishing!' The waters have come up to my lips. However, the Lord heard me in the day of my trouble, and when I called upon Him, 'He brought me up also out of an horrible pit, out of the miry clay' (Ps. 40:2). Although He permitted the water to come up to my lips, He never allowed it to cover my lips and rise above them. However dark the circumstances were, He always saved and delivered me." The believer will, therefore, be able to say, "The God who has delivered me in so many precarious circumstances and from so many mortal dangers shall deliver me again. I will, therefore, cast all my burdens and circumstances upon Him. I will surrender and entrust myself to Him. He will take care of me. I know this because my numerous experiences engender such a hope in me. This hope shall not put me to shame because 'the love of God is shed abroad in our hearts'" (Rom. 5:5).

Second, there will be a present benefit when a Christian hears of and considers the ways of God and hears others speak of experiences and trials that are similar to his own. Such a man or woman will be to him a messenger who is one of a thousand. He or she will be a person to him who will declare all that transpires within his heart and his closet.[1] The soul will then perceive that the saints have trod the same pathway upon which they must now go. Believers will observe that God has helped those who have been tried in like fashion. And although this may not at all deliver them from their present trouble, it will cause them to be still before God from whom is all their expectation. While resting in the promises of the gospel, they will trust that the Lord will perform them at His time, and by faith they will thus continue to look to the Lord expectantly and actively.

Third, there will also be a benefit that pertains to the future. When believers hear of the trials and the ways in which God leads His people, there will arise in their hearts such esteem for all who have gone through water and fire, who are thus fathers and mothers in Israel. Yes, they will have these matters within their hearts, for they do not know what shall yet befall them. This, in turn, will result in a careful, humble, and meek walk before the countenance of the Lord so that they may be kept and preserved.

So that you might experience these benefits, we will focus your attention on faith as a grace that is tried. We will not speak of the common trials regarding one's spiritual state and similar matters which would be impossible. Instead, we will focus on a few prominent examples.

To do this in an orderly manner, we will highlight and deal with two matters that you ought to consider:

1. The apostle's premise when he posits that the trial of saving faith is more precious than gold and the blessed outcome of such a trial. We will address (a) the subject of this premise, namely, the trial of faith which is more precious than gold, etc.; and (b) what the apostle says regarding this trial: that it "might be found unto praise and honour and glory at the appearing of Jesus Christ."

2. The relationship between this premise and the preceding, as expressed in the word *that*. We will thus examine the context.

---

1. In experiential parlance, the closet is the place where one withdraws himself for personal prayer and meditation.

THE TRIAL OF FAITH

First, we will explain that portion of the text in which the apostle articulates his premise that the trial of your faith is more precious than gold, for we read "that the trial of your faith, being much more precious than of gold that perisheth." As stated, this premise has two components: the subject itself, and what the apostle testifies regarding it. We will first speak of the subject: the trying of your faith which is more precious than gold that will perish upon being tried in the fire.

Faith, the Grace That Is Tested

Since the apostle speaks of the trying of faith, to have some clarity regarding this, we must recognize that the grace being tried is *faith*. Presently we will neither describe this faith nor enumerate the activity that proceeds from this faith. We only wish to note that such a trial is not so much linked to other graces wrought by the Holy Spirit within the hearts of the elect, but it is frequently connected to faith. We read of this in our text and in James 1:3, "Knowing this, that the trying of your faith worketh patience." There are numerous reasons why faith, rather than other graces, is specifically singled out as the grace that is tried.

Faith, the First of All Graces

Faith, rather than other graces, is tried because the nature of faith is such that it is according to the natural order of things the first grace wrought by the Holy Spirit. Thus faith, in conformity to the very nature of the work of grace in the soul, is the first grace activated in the soul. Faith, in turn, activates all other graces, for faith "worketh by love" (Gal. 5:6). If a general can be taken prisoner, it is very likely that it will be easy to be victorious over the entire army. When faith is wounded and defeated, experience teaches that the hands will hang down, and the soul being discouraged and distrustful must flee before the enemy as "a partridge in the mountains" (1 Sam. 26:20). However, when faith is steadfast, all other graces will be stimulated to engage in a bloody battle. The soul will then be able to say, "'For by thee I have run through a troop; and by my God have I leaped over a wall' (Ps. 18:29); 'He teacheth my hands to war, so that a bow of steel is broken by mine arms' (Ps. 18:34); I will 'not be afraid for the terror by night; nor for the arrow that flieth by day, nor for the pestilence that walketh in darkness; nor for the destruction that wasteth at noonday. A thousand shall fall at [my] side, and ten thousand at [my] right hand; but it shall not come nigh [me]. Only with [mine] eyes shalt [I] behold and see the reward of the wicked' (Ps. 91:5–8)."

The Genuineness of Faith the Integrity of All Graces
Faith, rather than other graces, is tried because the integrity of all other spiritual exercises is dependent upon the genuineness of faith. All that neither proceeds from nor is done by saving faith will be viewed by God and those who truly belong to the godly as nothing more than sin—however attractive these works may appear to the eyes of natural and unregenerate men or to people who believe that they can achieve holiness by their works. It is null and void and is no more than dung and no more pleasant than beholding a menstrual cloth. This explains why—and experience affirms it—such a person will experience little strife or conflict in his prayers, his reading, his reading of and meditation upon God's Word, his church attendance, etc. One can engage in this superficially without it being in any way detrimental to the kingdom of the devil. Also be, however, that a God-fearing person, in these activities, will so engage in the very acts of faith of embracing and receiving Jesus Christ that he will break forth in truly surrendering himself to Jesus as a poor, blind, helpless, and guilty sinner. He will then again actively surrender to the Mediator. However, it will then be as if all the forces of hell will oppose, slander, and buffet him. Why is this so? Because the integrity of one's actions is contingent upon the integrity of one's faith.

Faith, the Grace that Excludes Works in Justification
Faith will primarily be tried more than all other graces because it is a grace that conforms to the purpose of free grace in saving a poor sinner without the works of the law. God's objective is to demonstrate that in His infinite wisdom He has thought out a way to save the sinner which excludes all that man does or can do as a meritorious cause of salvation. Thus, faith, as such, is excluded as a work in the matter of justification. Faith will only function as an instrument, that is, as a means—as a beggar's hand that receives the gift of charity given him without money and without price. Faith will, therefore, radically exclude all boasting (Rom. 3), magnify free and sovereign grace, and will receive everything as a gracious gift. It will reject and set aside as a foundation upon which to rest all that does not pertain to the blessed triune God. All other graces render something to God. Since, therefore, faith supremely magnifies God in the way of free and sovereign grace, and renders

the soul willing, compliant, and submissive to be justified freely, it will be tried and sifted more than any other grace.

Faith, the Grace that Sustains All Other Graces
Faith will be tried more than any other grace because it sustains the existence, prospering, and activity of all other graces. When love is swooning due to its yearning for and the absence of the altogether lovely Jesus, saying, "I am sick of love" (Song 2:5; 5:8), faith will then engage itself. By of the precious promises of the gospel, faith will soar toward Jesus as with the wings of an eagle, transcending one's feelings and all that is visible and tangible. Faith will find Jesus in the promises and will unveil Him accordingly to the believer's heart. The languishing love of the believer will thereby be revived and invigorated. It will open his mouth and enable him to say what is expressed in the next verse (v. 8), "Though I do not perceive Him sensibly, yet, by faith, I love Him. Although presently I do not behold Him with such affection as I would desire, nevertheless I rejoice in Him by faith with inexpressible and delightful joy!" Precisely when love languishes in the believer, faith will take hold of Jesus in the promise. The one promise will bring Jesus near, and another promise will tenderly place Him in the arms of love as the Object that satisfies love, so that the believer will exclaim, "My beloved is mine, and I am his (Song 2:16); a bundle of myrrh is my well-beloved unto me; he shall lie all night betwixt my breasts" (Song 1:13). The soul will then be in the spiritual frame of old Simeon, and having the Child in her arms, she will praise God and say, "Lord, now lettest thou thy servant depart in peace, according to thy word: for mine eyes have seen thy salvation" (Luke 2:29–30). Although I could readily demonstrate how faith uniquely interacts with other graces, I will leave that for you to meditate upon.

Faith, the Grace that Distinguishes God's Children from the World
Faith will be tried more than other graces because it constitutes the essential difference between the world and God's children. Is there any person who would not agree that God must be known, served, and loved? Does not even the light of nature teach this, and even more so when this is reinforced by God's revelation? Faith teaches, however, that no one loves God, but rather, that everyone hates Him. It will teach that one must be born again by a divine and almighty power and that a man must utterly forsake himself and all that exists. Faith will teach us that man will only come to himself spiritually and

experientially when he has renounced everything and has united himself to Jesus by faith. This will discredit and render null and void all the intellectual exertion and reflections of those who derive their knowledge from books. This is so unbearable to them that some of the less experienced among them, in their intellectual reflections, will pretend to possess something other than what they have truly experienced.

Consequently, one will try to imagine himself to be converted if he or she but lives a decent life. Or they will posit that a person can love God rationally without these spiritual experiences. When God's believing children challenge this, one will observe that, rather than the majority of churchgoers, they will be the real and most bitter enemies of all heartfelt spiritual experiences.

These are but a few of the many reasons that we could enumerate as to why faith is tried more than any other grace.

The Trials or Tests

We will now address the trials themselves. As to the translation of the word, one must note that the original word *dokimion* only occurs twice in the New Testament: in our text and in James 1:3. We do not deem it necessary to elaborate on the commentary of linguists and the various translations of this word. We merely wish to remark that the best translation is rendered by those who translate it as "putting to the test." It is thus descriptive of something that is judged to be good after having been subjected to strenuous testing, thus proving it to be what one expected it to be. We could, therefore, translate the words of our text as follows: "that your faith which has passed the test, and has proven to be much more precious than of gold that perisheth, might be found unto praise and honour and glory at the appearing of Jesus Christ."

Thus, our difference with the *Statenvertaling*—for which we have the greatest respect—is not one of substance. Our varied formulation is merely expository, as you will observe in the extensive treatment of this text by Simon van Alphen.[2] You will observe that our text declares faith to have passed the test and that it has prevailed in the most intense testing. It satisfies the most stringent test to which it has been subjected.

To pursue this carefully, we shall speak of the matters whereby the faith of God's elect will be tested, so to speak, when it is subjected to fire or cast

---

2. Comrie is referring to the work *The First Epistle General of the Apostle Peter—An Analytical Exposition* (Utrecht, 1734) by Hieronymous Simons van Alphen (1665–1742), a Cocceian minister (1687) and a professor of theology in Utrecht from 1715 to 1742.

into a crucible. We will then address the nature of the faith that endures such a trial, after that when such trials occur, and finally consider why it is called a trial.

How God Tests Faith
Regarding the trials to which faith is subjected and in which such a tested faith will prevail, we will address a few particulars.

Faith Tested by Fiery Experiences
To enable us to do so, we will first explore how God Himself will try the faith of His elect as in and by means of fire. Oh, may I be enabled to speak of this! As to God's Word, one should note that it teaches with utmost clarity in many passages that God will try His children. Consider only the following passages of Scripture: "But he knoweth the way that I take: when he hath tried me, I shall come forth as gold" (Job 23:10). "The LORD trieth the righteous: but the wicked and him that loveth violence his soul hateth" (Ps. 11:5). "For thou, O God, hast proved us: thou hast tried us, as silver is tried" (Ps. 66:10). "And I will bring the third part through the fire, and will refine them as silver is refined, and will try them as gold is tried: they shall call on my name, and I will hear them: I will say, It is my people: and they shall say, The LORD is my God" (Zech. 13:9). These passages, and many others, teach abundantly that God will try and purify His children. One may not view such passages as either the imagination of despondent and mentally challenged persons or fanaticism. Such is the ridicule of the wise men of this world who merely are intellectually acquainted with these matters. One may perhaps ask *by which means* God tries faith. What are the crucibles and trying ways in which God will lead His children? If you desire to know this, consider the few remarks that we will make—that is, what we have learned from God's Word and our own experience.

1. God will sometimes try the faith of His children *by imposing a very challenging precept upon them*. It will be a precept intended explicitly for them and not for others, even though it can be that God will also impose it upon others. This would apply to the command that God gave Abraham to sacrifice his son Isaac—a history so powerfully and movingly articulated in Genesis 22:2. That command was such that it would have caused Abraham's heart to falter if his faith had not been strong, for God said, "Take now thy son, thine only son Isaac, whom thou lovest—[every word must touch our

heart]—and get thee into the land of Moriah; and offer him there for a burnt offering upon one of the mountains which I will tell thee of." In the first verse of Genesis 22 and in Hebrews 11:17, this is referred to as *tempting*, or as *testing* by others. A similarly difficult probationary command was imposed upon the young man to whom Jesus spoke, "Sell that thou hast…and follow me" (Matt. 19:21).

Although God no longer gives such probationary commands directly to anyone since the completion of His Word, yet He will impose upon some of His children in the way of His providence a precept for the testing of their faith. He may do so by impressing upon them a given portion of His Word whereby He explicitly speaks to them. He will persuade them and lead them to believe that it is His voice by which He is speaking to them through that passage of Scripture. It can also be that the Lord will cause a specific event to occur in His providence that will be very challenging and a great trial for them upon the pathway of life. In the meantime, however, this event will be so tailor-made for them that they will either see or hear in it the hand, finger, and voice of God. They will thereby perceive what God requires of them and which is so difficult to carry out.

For instance, someone may have a child of marriageable age to whom his heart is extraordinarily knit, and all his enjoyment in this world revolves around this child. The history of Abraham will then be powerfully impressed upon him. He will recognize that Abraham, in response to God's command and moved by the love and fear of the Lord, was immediately ready to sacrifice his son to God. Abraham, so to speak, gave his son back to God, even though it was his only son whom he loved. This will be impressed powerfully upon the heart of that person. It pursues him everywhere, and he must respond to it as if he is standing before the Lord, and is exercised accordingly. While he is in such a frame of mind, something extraordinary will happen soon in God's providence. I believe that in such situations, namely, in which faith is tested by a precept that is difficult to obey, God will usually prepare the heart by His Word in the manner I have already described before He causes this event actually to transpire in His providence. That event will then be a test for that person. Happy is he who then has a faith that will prevail in this trial. This may bring him to the point that he will die to everything and will part with everything that is precious to him—his possessions, his family, and his native land.[3] One will then be willing to submit to all commands that are very challenging and difficult to obey—as a trial of one's faith. In such situations, the Spirit will frequently work in the manner as described above.

Such circumstances can generate a question of conscience. An attentive believer will perceive that God's probationary commands are twofold. There are commands that God will indeed demand acquiescence in and a willingness to do what He commands, without requiring the actual execution of such a command. Such was the case with Abraham. There are commands, however, when one must not only be willing to obey but one must fully obey. Such was the case with the rich young ruler.

Someone might ask, How can I know that I am being confronted with a command that will be difficult to obey? My response is that we must not reason too much about the actual execution of the command ahead of time. Instead, we must endeavor to be prepared in our hearts to obey God. We must also conscientiously observe the ways of God's providence. When we subsequently experience that there is a willingness of heart to obey the Lord regarding this matter by faith, and we may experience free access to God, we may and must proceed upon the pathway of obedience.

Finally, if it is a command whereby the Lord solely intends to try His child, then upon observing his obedience in the way of His providence, God will wonderfully and unexpectedly find ways and means to prevent the execution of this command—even if one were at the very point of doing so. Again, such was the case with Abraham. If the Lord does not proceed and if a person has been faithful, it is an affirmation of his willingness to do what the Lord commands. I would be able to say much more, but an upright child of God can extract from this that which will yield peace to his heart.

2. God will also try the faith of His children *by postponing the fulfillment of a promise at precisely such a moment that a matter according to the typical sequence of cause and effect appears to be unattainable.* One thing is clear: "Known unto God are all his works from the beginning of the world" (Acts 15:18). In His eternal, wise, sovereign, independent, and immutable decree, God has purposed whatever shall transpire to its minutest detail, either by the execution of His power in bringing it to pass or by permitting it. This pertains even to the falling of a hair from one's head or the movement of the

---

3. It is very well possible that Comrie was here mindful of his own situation. Indeed, he had left Scotland to study theology in the Netherlands, after which he never returned.

smallest speck of dust that we can only see when the sun shines its beams into a dark place. All this He will do in such a way, and not otherwise, that it shall be to the glory of His name.

Nevertheless, it pleases the Lord now and then to give a promise about a specific matter to some of His children about a particular matter that He will fulfill either for them or their posterity. They may thereby conclude that this has been decreed "before the world began" (Titus 1:2). In the meantime, the decree cannot be the basis of one's expectation regarding a specific matter, but only the promise which God gives when it so pleases Him and is embraced by faith. However, it is God's way to give the promise at precisely such a moment when secondary causes declare that the promised matter cannot take place. That will indeed be a great trial of faith, namely, whether the soul will embrace God's testimony contrary to all probability and "set to his seal that God is true" (John 3:33)—and thus the believer expects with joy and full confidence the fulfillment of the promise in the most precarious and obscure cases.

In Genesis 17:16–17, we have another notable example of how God led Abraham. In this passage, God promises Abraham that Sarah will bear him a son. Please note that in a preceding chapter (15), there is only the promise of a seed without any further specification who that shall be. Thus, Abraham could think that this promise was fulfilled in Ishmael. However, this passage states explicitly that this seed shall be from Sarah. God fulfilled this promise when Abraham was one hundred years old, and when "it ceased to be with Sarah after the manner of women" (Gen. 18:11). Its fulfillment appeared to be entirely impossible when it was made concerning Sarah.

When we consider the experience of God's children, we will discover many similar situations whereby the desired outcome of the promise was fulfilled. I have heard from reliable sources of a godly minister who had to flee due to persecution in Scotland, England, and Ireland who finally arrived in a foreign city. The means to support himself and his family had been exhausted. His wife, who did not fear God, harassed him with the rebuke that for conscience's sake he had brought her and his children into such dire straits. When she brought one of the children to him who cried for a piece of bread so pitifully that a heart of stone would be broken by it, he went to his room to make his bitter complaint known to his covenant God. When he arrived in his room, God impressed these words upon him, "The young lions do lack, and suffer hunger: but they that seek the LORD shall not want any good thing" (Ps. 34:10). This was followed by the words, "Bread shall be given him; his waters shall be sure" (Isa. 33:16). This greatly encouraged his sanctified soul to believe God and trust in Him. Upon returning to his wife and weeping children, he joyfully said to her, "I trust God and His promise; we shall not lack." Angrily the woman said mockingly, "Why don't you take that trust to the market?" Shortly after that, during the same morning, the servant girl of this family had to cross the market, and she encountered several gentlemen who had arrived just on that day. Already from afar they saw the servant girl whom they knew, and immediately they approached her. They inquired about this minister and wanted to know how her master was doing. The servant girl who also feared the Lord told them everything upon which these gentlemen gave her money to make her purchases on the market. From that moment forward, these gentlemen saw to it that her master would lack nothing.

I will not cite additional examples—all I wish to say is that God does this in thousands and more situations. God's children should apply my account to their own situation, for this might minister relief to some of them.

For your instruction, I wish to say that the following guidelines should be observed:

a. By way of fasting and prayer, a soul should seek to ascertain whether it is God who impresses a promise upon her in such difficult circumstances.

b. Let her keep this experience to herself by not speaking to anyone about this—except later if it would prove to be beneficial.

c. The soul should reflect much on God's power.

d. Finally, let the soul quietly reflect upon God's ways while waiting upon Him without pressing her case, for what He has promised, He will most certainly perform (Rom. 4:21).

3. God will put faith to the test *by a lengthy postponement of the fulfillment of the promise—contrary to the expectation of the soul*. Abraham is a twofold example of this—concerning his posterity, as well as to the promised land. The soul that receives the promise will be very intent upon witnessing its fulfillment. Regretfully, however, experience teaches us that the best among believers have too little of the patience and submission of faith to

leave both the time and manner of fulfillment to the Lord. We have addressed this extensively in *The ABC of Faith* when we dealt with the verb "to expect."

4. God will frequently try faith *by leading His people in a way that runs directly counter to the fulfillment of His promise*. This is one of the more significant trials of faith, for believers cannot perceive in advance how these ways are linked to the ultimate outcome. God frequently achieves His objective in ways that appear to be conflicting so that one will discern very clearly His hand and finger when He grants what He has promised.

God anointed David as king, but instead of being honored accordingly, Saul became enraged against him. He had to flee to the desert, and as a partridge he was chased from mountain to mountain and from cave to cave before he could occupy the throne.

Joseph would be superior to his brothers. According to the dream he had, they and his father were depicted as bowing before him. Who could have calculated that Joseph's being bound and cast into a pit, being sold, and finally being thrown into prison would precisely be how God would bring to pass what He had shown him in that dream? On various occasions, God's children will receive a promise pertaining to the sanctification of their hearts. However, their sinful lusts will never stir so powerfully as shortly after that. Who would then be able to say, "This is how this promise will be fulfilled"? The spiritual experience of the believer will affirm this to be so, however.

Being thus led by God, this must all be subservient to stir up the soul, to adhere in quiet submission to this way and never to judge rashly how this or that could lead to the fulfillment of God's promise. Instead, follow God faithfully and, so to speak, blindly. Although you cannot see it, yet believe that every circumstance, however contradictory it may be to your mind, will be the best and most direct way leading to the ultimate outcome. May the following lines express the disposition of your heart:

> I am so engaged in blindly praising wisdom,
> That I have no time to delineate between good and evil.

You will thus find rest in God and His Word, and you will be enabled to say, "That which is consistent with God's eternal counsel can only be good."

5. God will try the faith of His children *by conducting Himself in the way of His providence as if He were their enemy*, making them the target of the arrows of His fearful judgments so that all the waves and billows will go over

them (Ps. 42:7). A loving father who loves his child most tenderly can hide the fire of love that burns within his heart, treating and chastising his child so harshly that it seems as if he does not love his child at all. Likewise, God can lead some of His own wisely and sovereignly in such ways that He not only subjects them to a cross, but also sends them cross upon cross—one great calamity after another. Thereby He, so to speak, empties them from vessel to vessel (Jer. 48:11). Unbelievers and less exercised believers will thus be inclined to think, judge, and express that such a person must be a very great sinner (cf. Acts 28:3–4).

An extraordinary example of such a God-glorifying trial experienced by one of God's most precious elect children, we will find in Job's situation. Of Job, we read "that there [was] none like him in the earth" (Job 1:8). Nevertheless, one messenger after another delivered a most grievous message. And then, after having lost all his possessions, his body was afflicted with a grievous illness. Consequently, his friends, who were indeed God-fearing men, due to their deficient exercises of faith regarding God's ways, deemed Job to be the greatest of hypocrites and the greatest evildoer in the world. This is one of the most severe trials of faith, and the faith that can withstand such hardship will perceive love burning in the heart of God even when His hand smites the believer so intensely and painfully.

Several things should be noted for our instruction:

a. Everyone needs to learn not to discredit anyone for such reasons, and he may not dismiss his neighbor as to his state before God.

b. These ways show God's children who are thus being tried by the Lord that in the Word they will find the footsteps of those who have been similarly tried. They are not walking upon ways untrod before, but upon paths which the saints have trod before them. There can be some relief upon considering that other children of God have already gone before them and that we only place our feet in their footsteps.

c. Concerning how God is leading them, they may neither draw negative conclusions about themselves nor may they conclude thereby that God either hates or loves them. Instead, they must continually adhere to God's Word.

d. It testifies of great wisdom when the Lord's people while in the furnace of affliction endeavor, reverently speaking, to impose their love upon the Lord, crying out, "Lord, it is true that Thy hand greatly presses down upon me. However, I reflect upon Thy former loving-kindness as in the days of old. Thou art not a changeable man. In all the vicissitudes of life, Thou dost remain the God 'with whom is no variableness, neither shadow of turning'" (James 1:17). The spiritual experience of God's children has taught that for such, this has been an eminent means to teach the soul to "glory in tribulations" (Rom. 5:3) while in the furnace of affliction.

e. The believer who is being tried must endeavor to conduct himself as a weaned child by giving his "back to the smiters, and [his] cheeks to them that plucked off the hair" (Isa. 50:6). Let him consider the brevity of life and the example of Christ who "for the joy that was set before him endured the cross" (Heb. 12:2). Let him also consider that "our light affliction, which is but for a moment, worketh for us a far more exceeding and eternal weight of glory" (2 Cor. 4:17).

6. God will frequently try faith *by withholding His sensible grace and comfort*. Although faith and affections are to be distinguished as cause and effect, nevertheless, they delightfully interact as a brother and a sister in the spiritual experience of the saints. The one gift is intended to strengthen and sustain the other gift. They will mutually give courage and liberty to each other. Therefore, God's children have always longed to receive both, namely, to behold Christ's glory (John 17:24), while simultaneously praying, "Restore unto me the joy of thy salvation" (Ps. 51:12).

However, it pleases God for wise reasons at times to exercise His children by withholding His loving embrace from some of them. He will do so after having allured and embraced them until they have learned to walk, spiritually speaking. Unless the Lord prevents this, this will cause great turmoil in the soul. There are others for whom God causes light to arise immediately as soon as they enter upon the pathway of life. And yet, from that moment on, God will lead them in such a way that it seems as if they live under the cloud of the hiding of God's face. Then there is a third category of believers who have had little or no sensible grace. Faith will then be very vulnerable to many attacks and will be intensely tried.

7. God will try the faith of His children *by leading and guiding them along unknown ways upon which they have not walked before*. It is true for the experience of all God's children that they must traverse ways that are variable—ways of sweetness and bitterness, of light and darkness, of going

and standing still, and of faith and unbelief. Such things are neither unusual nor unknown to experienced Christians. It can occasionally happen, however, that after having been upon the way of salvation for twenty or thirty years, God will lead in ways with which one is not experientially acquainted. (I would rather not give any concrete examples.) The soul will then not know how to conduct herself. Former spiritual experiences that were helpful in other situations are now of no avail. The general directives that faith would prescribe to guide the soul in specific situations now seem to come short so that the soul finds herself in an unusual situation. We will counsel the souls who encounter such circumstances that they must look to God "who command[s] the light to shine out of darkness" (2 Cor. 4:6). Although God is therewith trying the soul, He will also counsel them according to His own promise, "I will bring the blind by a way that they knew not; I will lead them in paths that they have not known" (Isa. 42:16). What a comfort it must be to the soul to know that, as unknown as the way may often be, she has a compassionate God who will lead her as her Guide.

8. God will try the faith of His children *by causing them to experience a measure of His wrath in their souls*. It can be that the Lord's children experience a lengthy period of being led in a delightful and soul-refreshing manner. Occasionally that can last for years so that during this season, the joy of the Lord was their strength (Neh. 8:10), and His light shone brightly upon their tents. Later, however, God would lead them in different ways. He will write bitter things against them (Job 13:26). Such a poor soul will experience the disturbance of his peace, and the sense of God's displeasure and wrath will oppress and distress his soul.

We have an example of this in God's Word. Job's spirit was very distraught and afflicted by the burning venom of the arrows of the Almighty. Jesus Christ, God's only begotten Son, experienced desertion as Mediator and Surety. There will not be a single child of God who will not experience this in some measure. This, however, will bring forth a very strong faith that will be able to endure temptation when, rather than light, one encounters distressful darkness.

To instruct you, let me say the following:

a. In such circumstances, God's children must especially reject and abhor any emerging hard thoughts toward the Lord and His ways.

b. They must particularly seek the blame with themselves so that they may fully justify God in all His dealings.

c. They must sharply distinguish between thoughts that, so to speak, are imposed upon them when they are in great spiritual distress, and the true condition of their souls when there are intermittent periods of tranquility. When they fail to do so, many tender Christians will succumb to great and bitter despair, thinking that what they discern within themselves during the darkest moments of their trial is the true condition of their souls. They will believe that what they perceive within themselves during more tranquil times does not reflect the essential condition of their souls, but rather how they presently assess themselves. Instead, however, the soul should judge her condition by what she experiences when she finds herself in very calm waters.

d. When subject to such a trial, the soul refrains from striving—a response that, at other times, is so essential. Instead, she must now first and foremost resort to prayer and lay her entire case before the Lord. She must cry out, "Oh God, hear how my enemies slander Thee and my soul. I want no part of this and, instead, protest against it, crying out, 'Rise up, LORD, and let thine enemies be scattered (Num. 10:35) and be dashed in pieces like a potter's vessel (Ps. 2:9).'" The experience of God's children teaches us that this can have a blessed effect.

e. During such a trial, the tried soul should carefully avoid anxious self-examination and seek to ascertain her spiritual state through the marks of grace. The godly will experience strong impulses that seek to compel them to do so. However, a wise person will not make too much of an effort to look for something during the dark of night, but will, instead, postpone until it has again become day time. Likewise, such a soul must not examine herself by employing the marks of grace, but rather she must focus on her exercises of faith, such as a longing for and fleeing to Jesus, entrusting herself to Him, and taking hold of Him. Although such exercises may yield little comfort at the moment, experience teaches us that light will arise in the soul when she repeatedly engages and exerts herself in such a way. Thereby such souls, with divine light, will have little difficulty in discerning in themselves the marks of grace.

f. One must not give heed to what is being interjected by the voices within, but instead, turn away from them and refuse to listen. Amid trial, a person will be all too readily inclined to focus on that which will make him even more distressed.

g. Finally, a person must bring to mind the examples of the godly and the sure promise that "his anger endureth but a moment; [and] in his favour is life" (Ps. 30:5). Such reflection can be subservient to support and sustain the soul in enduring temptation. It will enable the soul to remain steadfast toward God and His way—even when the Lord withholds all comfort and, instead, causes her to be encompassed with fear.

9. God will try the faith of His children *when He does not deal with their case, but rather, so to speak, closes His ear for all the crying, supplicating, and groaning for help.* This also is one of the greater trials that faith must endure. It will frequently be insinuated to the poor tried believer that he is no more than a natural, unregenerate man, for God does not hear sinners. It will also be suggested that he is not praying in faith, for whatever one asks in faith will be granted. Or he will think that it is in vain to call upon the Lord since He turns a deaf ear to him when he calls upon Him. I believe that the psalmist knew this experientially when he complained that he was weary of groaning and fearful of being "like them that go down into the pit" (Ps. 28:1).

The experience that is according to God's Word makes it clear that such a trial will primarily occur in two ways. It may be that the answering of prayer is postponed, even though someone may have been praying with heartfelt love and persistent wrestlings. We read that this was especially true with Jesus, who prayed three times with strong crying (Matthew 26), and with Paul (2 Corinthians 12). One can also be led into circumstances in which he clearly and intensely needs God's help, and yet cannot supplicate for it because, given his inner disposition toward the Lord, it is as if his tongue cleaves to the roof of his mouth. However much he needs God's help and however troubled and oppressed his heart may be, the matter for which he is praying will not be granted but refused. One's mouth and heart can be so closed that a person cannot pray about it as he should. He who has ever experienced such a trial, or who presently experiences it, will acknowledge that this is also not one of the lesser trials.

Let the following be to your instruction:

a. It is not always good that a man receives what he so much desires.

b. When God does not hear when one calls upon Him, He intends that such a soul remains bound to the throne of grace.

c. When someone's heart is inclined to pray, it is a good indication that the matter shall be given; that is, insofar as it is profitable. It can also be that such a prayer will be answered differently, even though one does not yet know how. This we know, however, that a person will be secretly sustained as long as he is enabled to persevere in bringing his petition before the Lord in all earnestness.

d. If you cannot pray, and it seems as if your tongue cleaves to the roof of your mouth, you need to recognize that God understands our wordless groans. He knows our thoughts before a single word has come across our lips. Moses's silent desire was considered to be a persistent supplication.

e. We need to realize that we ignorantly expect our happiness from something that would not benefit us. Such would be the case with a child who would ask for a knife with which it could cut itself. Thus, we must not set our hearts on a given matter, but must be submissive to the Lord.

f. Finally, although the revealed will of God must be the rule for our prayers, the tried soul needs to recognize that God will only give that which He has eternally decreed.

Beloved, many other things could be considered whereby God tries one's faith. However, we believe that we have addressed the most important matters, and, therefore, we will now desist.

Faith Tested by Other People

We will now address various instances in which men can try faith. I could use this opportunity to speak of the self-examination to which a person can subject himself regarding his own faith, employing the Word and the marks of grace founded upon it to determine whether his faith is genuine. That not being the intention, however, we will briefly identify several ways in which faith can be tried by other men, for that is the apostle's primary focus in our text.

1. Faith will be tried by *people who deviously attempt to disengage God's elect from the most essential foundations of their faith* by casting aspersions upon them and rendering them doubtful by subtle arguments. If possible, even the elect could be led astray by their argumentation. Such individuals may also deviously seek to distort the teaching of God's Word and seek to impress upon the godly the most brazen teachings of condemned heretics under the pretext of tender godliness. The best remedy for this is to exercise oneself in the truth and to avoid the books and company of such individuals. Instead, be continually engaged in crying out, "Lord, help my unbelief!" and be diligently and zealously engaged in exercising faith.

2. Faith will be tried by *people who will suspect and reject the faith of a true and upright Christian.* When such merciless "physicians of souls" brazenly and haughtily reject a believer, he will find himself in a very troubling situation. Oh, that everyone would see to it that he will not grieve whom God does not want to be grieved! And let everyone subject his heart and life to God's touchstone so that it will no longer matter that men judge us.

3. Faith will be tried by *people hindering a fellow believer from practicing the tender exercise of godliness.* This can be initiated by their faulty example or by their accounts regarding the backsliding of other believers. Especially the latter will have much impact when the believing soul is lax and is not on guard as Joseph was, saying, "How then can I do this great wickedness, and sin against God?" (Gen. 39:9). Balak succeeded in subjecting the people of Israel to God's displeasure whom Balaam could not curse. What a severe trial this can be! How much the world can gain with this! Happy are they who have a steadfast faith!

4. Faith will be tried by men *when the world causes the way in which God leads His people to be slandered.* One will mock them, ridicule them, and denigrate them. This would cause many to go astray if God's grace did not strengthen their hearts. Many will thereby remain "night disciples," not knowing the all-surpassing grace that shone forth in the life of Moses, who chose "rather to suffer affliction with the people of God" (Heb. 11:25) than to enjoy all the riches of the world. Yes, he even "refused to be called the son of Pharaoh's daughter" (Heb. 11:24).

5. Faith will frequently be tried by the world *when believers are threatened that they will come into disfavor if they conduct themselves faithfully* and according

to the light of their consciences. Believers will often find themselves in a situation in which they are dependent upon natural and unbelieving people for their temporal lives. When such people insist on having their way, they will threaten the godly if they decline to participate in certain situations. They will then tell the godly that they should never count on their favor again. That will bring a pious soul into thousands of straits! The conscience of such a believer will dictate to him how he is to conduct himself in a given situation, but his advantage and livelihood will speak a different language. A thousand and one pretenses will then come to the fore to quench the light of his conscience and to persuade him to obey men rather than God.

For example, a man runs a business by which he must support himself and his family. He clearly understands God's precept to keep the Lord's Day holy and that he may neither buy nor sell, but instead he must devote all his hours to public and private religious exercises. In the meantime, there will be people upon whom he depends to a large extent for his sustenance who threaten to bypass him during weekdays if he does not sell anything on Sunday.

Let me give you another example. A ministerial position becomes vacant due to either the death or the departure of a pastor and teacher. The members of the consistory are godly men who fully intend to call a godly minister. However, they are then threatened that doing so will be to their ruination.

One can make this applicable to many situations that could prove to be a temptation. For the believer, this can be a grievous trial. Happy is he who remains faithful and believes that God reigns in heaven and upon earth and has the hearts of all men in His hand. Experience has taught that they who in such circumstances have a faith that has prevailed in temptation, will, after they have thus demonstrated their faithfulness to God, be blessed by God more than they ever have before. In fact, God's blessing will be manifested to the third and fourth generation of their seed!

6. Finally, faith will be tried *by the severe and bitter persecution initiated by the enemies of Christ's kingdom for the sake of God's truth.* Their objective is to demolish and annihilate true believers by subjecting them to the severest forms of torture and torment, as well as a cruel death. This will be an intense trial of faith whereby we will be tested whether we are willing to seal our good confession with our blood and whether we do not count our lives dear unto ourselves (Acts 20:24). Although many believers tremble when they think of such a trial, we should not burden ourselves too much with fear and anxiety. God normally gives strength in proportion to our cross. He will see to it that

the soul through His divine comfort will be so extraordinarily strengthened that the believer will not only be prepared to be imprisoned, but also to die for Christ.

Where would I begin or end if I were to speak of all trials in the family and society, often inflicted by a hostile disposition? I will leave that to you.

We could also demonstrate whose faith will be tried and assaulted by Satan. However, the many things that could be said about this are of no profit, and others will be addressed annually by us when we expound the sixth petition of the Lord's Prayer. We will therefore bypass this also.

The Faith That Will Pass the Test
Having just considered what the trials of faith are, we will now briefly address what the very core and essence of the faith that can withstand trial is. If you desire to know this, please note the following:

1. A faith that can withstand trial is *a faith whereby the soul remains united to God both in times of adversity and times of prosperity*. Many appear particularly to seek God when His hand is against them, and they have to deal with many adversities. However, when affliction is removed from their loins (Ps. 66:11), they will become fat like Jeshurun (Deut. 32:15). They kick and forget God, and they serve the world. They no longer live according to the Word of God, but according to their own will. This proves that such individuals do not have the faith that can prevail in trial, and they thus grievously deceive themselves. Then there are others who, along with temporal believers and as long as there is prosperity, appear to embrace and receive the Word of God with great joy. However, they will fall away when persecution arises for the Word's sake, proving that they never possessed this faith.

2. A faith that can withstand trial, however much it may be tested, is *a true faith of which God and men will observe its essential acts and marks*. On the contrary, a disingenuous faith will evaporate like smoke upon being cast into the furnace—however attractive it may have appeared before being subjected to trial. It is not all gold that shines. Therefore, for faith to prevail in a trial, there must be found, upon thorough examination, the essential activities, distinctive marks, and fruits of faith.

3. A faith that can withstand trial is *a faith that will persevere until the end*. One often speaks of perseverance as being certain from God's vantage point

for the true believer. The power of God so preserves him that he will never fall from the state of grace. Nevertheless, God declares perseverance as an infallible touchstone of genuine faith. "He that shall endure unto the end" (Matt. 24:13), that is, who keeps the faith, shall receive the crown of righteousness (2 Tim. 4:8).

The Time of Testing

Should someone ask what the seasons are when faith is tested, we would respond that God generally postpones such trials in the beginning when His children are yet weak and inexperienced. Therefore, God's way is to cherish them tenderly for some years by carrying them in His arms. He will then not permit any trials to befall them other than the vicissitudes common to the life of grace. This is metaphorically illustrated in God's dealings with Israel by determining that He would not lead them to Canaan through the land of the Philistines—even though from Egypt, it would only have been a journey of ten days. God led them that they would not be so terrified by wars that they would return. Therefore, He led them through the wilderness so that their faith would be stimulated by the miracles He would do.

Generally speaking, the season of trial will occur at a later period. Such trials will occur when the spiritual zeal of God's church begins to wane systemically—or when this is personally and specifically true for an individual member. The latter can count on it that God will use sharp trials to restore their former zeal. Such a trial will often emerge when there is contention, discord, distrust, and disharmony among God's people. These are reliable indicators of impending dark times. This was the experience of the early Christian church. And if we are not blind, we will perceive that the groundwork is being laid to test our nation by getting drawn into a bitter and intense war. The sword has already been drawn, and it will not be put back into its sheath until blood has been shed.[4]

There can also be such a trial when it pleases the Lord to prepare someone for an important task such as being a minister or another prominent position as a Christian, thereby equipping him to encourage others. Experience teaches us that such persons will be tried more than others. They will thus be equipped with discernment to counsel, guide, and comfort others.

---

4. When the first edition of this work was published in 1744, it was a very unsettled time for the Republic of the Netherlands.

Faith can also be tried following a special and more than common manifestation of God's favor and love to the soul. Such was true for Paul when he was buffeted by a messenger of Satan so that he would not "be exalted above measure through the abundance of the revelations" (2 Cor. 12:7).

These are God's common ways. However, God is sovereign and free in His dealings. Therefore, if someone is being tried who has not experienced what we have just addressed, he should know that the Lord is not accountable to us for His deeds.

The Reasons Why Such Circumstances Are Referred to as Trials
Should someone ask why the aforementioned circumstances are designated as trials, we wish to respond as follows:

1. As gold is purified by fire, these circumstances can also be designated as a *fire*. However much such circumstances may, in retrospect, be subservient to purification, they will be very painful while one is subjected to them.

2. Gold will not change as to its essential nature, but rather, trials will only result in the *removal of all impure elements*. Likewise, in all the trials, as mentioned earlier, saving faith will not at all be impacted as to its true essence. Instead, it will be purified and cleansed from all that is deficient, fickle, and capricious—and whatever else may cleave to faith in this present state of imperfection.

3. In daily life, the hand of the blacksmith is needed to *regulate the fire* by either stirring it up or tempering it in a measure stipulated by the circumstances. Such is also applicable here. The omniscient and infinitely omnipotent God so governs all trials by His hand. He will moderate them if someone is being tempted above his capacity. He will not permit the latter to occur, and He will so wisely govern all things that they will be subservient to His glory and to the benefit of the elect and tried believers.

4. The goldsmith will be most concerned about the gold when it is *melting* in the fire. Likewise, the God who indeed loves all His children will manifest His most tender care precisely when they are being tried. In all their affliction, he is afflicted with them (Isa. 63:10)!

5. It is a fact that purified gold is *the best gold*. Likewise, that faith which is most tried will also be the best, purest, and most valuable faith. He who has

no knowledge of his faith being tried should recognize that his faith is not the faith of God's children.

The Preciousness of a Tested Faith

This faith that is being tried in various ways by God and men, and has prevailed in all trials, the apostle correctly esteems above gold, for he says that it is "much more precious than of gold that perisheth, though it be tried with fire."

Like Gold

In this text, the apostle compares faith with gold. Gold is one of the most eminent metals due to its weight, shining luster, scarcity, and durability. It also enriches all who possess it, giving them honor and prestige among men and enabling them to possess all that their eyes see and their hearts desire. One may apply all of this to the comparison between faith and gold.

1. In our present state of imperfection, faith is *the most eminent of all graces*. Faith enables one to embrace God's testimony, and thereby one is most intimately united with Jesus Christ, resulting in His mediatorial righteousness becoming the portion of the soul. All believers are clothed with this righteousness, and they are thus viewed as if they had personally secured that righteousness. By faith the soul is at peace with God and will trust Jehovah in the darkest of circumstances. Faith is, therefore, the premier and most excellent gift of grace.

2. Faith itself is extraordinarily *weighty* and therefore renders all the activity of the soul weighty. The most insignificant and feeble sigh that proceeds from faith will be accepted because of its weightiness. The most eminent deeds that are performed apart from faith will be deemed as being found wanting, for without faith it is impossible to please God (Heb. 11:6). The publican who exclaimed, "Be merciful to me a sinner," went home justified, whereas the boastful Pharisee was a vile stench in the Lord's nostrils.

3. Faith is supremely *pure* and pristine and shines forth with a pure luster. As we have seen, faith purifies the heart, and it will bring the believer in all that he does to the blood of Jesus Christ that cleanses from all sins (Acts 15:9; 1 John 1:7).

4. Faith is a *rare* jewel and precious diamond that will be found with but few. Many do indeed pretend to have faith, but with most, it is no more than

pretense. "For all men have not faith" (2 Thess. 3:2). It is a pearl that will only be found in the hearts of God's elect.

5. Faith renders its possessor *rich*, for thereby the triune God becomes the portion of his soul. All is his, for he is the property of Christ, "and Christ is God's" (1 Cor 3:23). Thus, believers have everything, for they are "heirs of God, and joint-heirs with Christ" (Rom. 8:17).

6. By faith the soul can *acquire everything it sees and that which the heart desires.* The Word says, "Open thy mouth wide, and I will fill it" (Ps. 81:10). All that one desires in a believing prayer to receive in Christ's name shall be given!

More than Gold
The apostle not only compares faith to gold, but he also elevates it far above gold and has several reasons for doing so.

1. Gold may indeed *adorn someone's body*, but faith adorns the soul before God. In whomever God detects the faith wrought by His Spirit, He will delight in them, and they will be precious in His sight. Yes, He will view them as the apple of His eye and as being graven in the palms of His hands—even if their faith was as small as that of a mustard seed.

2. Gold may *give someone pleasure as long as his conscience has not been awakened.* However, when it has been awakened, then all worldly treasures can neither remove his anxiety nor extinguish all fiery accusations. Only the blood of Jesus Christ must then cleanse the conscience, and that truth is embraced and received by faith.

3. Gold will *be of no benefit in the hour of death* when one's soul will be required. Oh, then the richest man must bid an eternal farewell to everything. However, faith will then be changed into beholding, and he who has received Jesus by a true faith shall be satisfied with His likeness when he awakes, and he will magnify God and Christ with eternal hallelujahs.

Found unto Praise
The apostle testifies that all the aforementioned and many other trials are "found unto praise and honour and glory at the appearing of Jesus Christ."

The Second Coming
He speaks of the appearing of Jesus Christ. The only, eternal, and natural

Son of God is called Jesus Christ in reference to the work He does and the offices to which He has been anointed to engage in His ministry as Redeemer. As the Son of God, He has already been manifested in the flesh (John 1:14). However, on the last day, He shall again be manifested in the flesh when He, accompanied by ten thousand of His angels, shall come upon the clouds of heaven in great majesty and glory to execute judgment. He will then judge the living and the dead according to what everyone has "done in his body" (2 Cor. 5:10). The apostle is here referring to His latter manifestation in the flesh.

The Result of Trials

The apostle then states that all trials will be vindicated; that is, a painstaking evaluation will affirm that these trials were exclusively intended to manifest God's "praise and honour and glory." A failure to do so is the sole reason why tried souls and others would have misjudged them. The apostle uses three words: "praise," "honour," and "glory." We do not have to expound each word separately, for they all have the same meaning. Their enumeration merely serves to underscore the excellency of this praise, honor, and glory. The apostle could have said that they "might be found unto praise." Thus, they are not found merely unto praise, but rather unto most extraordinary and magnanimous praise. In fact, not only unto most extraordinary and magnanimous praise but rather unto the most glorious and profound praise imaginable! Be assured that thus it shall be. All the ways in which God has led His children shall be found unto the most glorious and profound praise imaginable!

1. Then all trials will be proven to have been unto *the most glorious and profound praise of God's purpose and designs.* All that He has purposed He will have secured and achieved through all trials and a multitude of temptations. All believers who constitute God's church would often have comfortably been settled under their vines and fig trees, having said, "It is good for us to be here: and let us make…tabernacles" (Luke 9:33). However, they would then hardly have been engaged in pursuing the conversion of others and the extension of God's kingdom. God, therefore, permits the occurrence of trials and persecution. As they increase, God's children will frequently and sorrowfully complain, "Why must it be thus?" The answer is that thereby the gospel will be disseminated! They will acquire better friends and frequently also better and more enduring possessions. Jesus therefore also says, "Every one that hath forsaken houses, or brethren, or sisters, or father, or mother, or

wife, or children, or lands, for my name's sake, shall receive a hundredfold, and shall inherit everlasting life" (Matt. 19:29). The persecution spoken of in Acts 8 resulted in the expansion of the church so that the words of Daniel 12:4 would be fulfilled. Persecution in Germany and Scotland were subservient to the proliferation of sound doctrine in these and other lands. We frequently do not now perceive God's glorious purposes, and we will therefore complain when the crucible is hot. However, on the last day, it will be understood, and one will say, "Lord, was this Thy purpose when Thou didst cause me to go through fire and water? O God, Thou hast done all things well!"

2. All trials will then be found to have been subservient to *the most glorious and profound praise of God's great and extraordinary power*—and that in more than one respect.

    a. This power enables the church of God, and especially tried believers, to remain steadfast despite all the turmoil generated by men and devils whose aim it is—if they had the power to do so—to eradicate the church, as represented by her members, from the face of the earth. How it will then be observed that it was God who enabled this spark of fire to survive and burn amid the ocean of all the waters of affliction!

    b. How the glory of God's power will then be observed in having forged weak and powerless instruments to perform such wondrous deeds, having enabled His children to endure such great difficulties, torments, and vicissitudes with patience, joy, and spiritual courage! History yields many examples of this.

    c. Yes, how God's power will then be seen in all its glory in having seen to it that all that the enemies had in mind to eradicate the church, became the very means that caused the church to grow!

3. To the praise, honor, and glory of God, it will then be seen that He *had no evil intent in all the afflictions of His tried people*, but rather their purification. He thereby gave them the opportunity to exercise many virtues which otherwise would not have been exercised, enabling them to display their graces in their lively exercise.

4. Then *the Lord's tender love and concern* for them will be observed in all these things, though they did not see it at the time. They will then see how He carried them in His arms, led them in tender mercy, and continually had His

eye upon them to give them counsel and instruction. He will surely be the eternal recipient of the eternal hallelujahs. Having received all things from Him, they will render Him all honor in this and many other ways. All will "be found unto praise and honour and glory at the appearing of Jesus Christ."

The Context in 1 Peter 1

Now, something needs to be said about the relationship between our proposition and the preceding context. The apostle showed that the scattered strangers had been "kept by the power of God through faith unto salvation" (1 Peter 1:5). Thus, despite the many trials they had to endure, they had reason to rejoice in God so that He would receive the "praise and honour and glory at the appearing of Jesus Christ." All things will then be vindicated as clear proofs and affirmations of His manifold wisdom, power, and incomprehensible lovingkindness.

APPLICATION

My beloved, I have addressed in some measure the trials of faith, all of which shall "be found unto praise and honour and glory at the appearing of Jesus Christ." Let us now extract some lessons from this for further instruction.

General Lessons

From the truth set before us, we can learn four things.

1. Many do not have the faith of the elect, for they are not acquainted with trials. Oh, what quiet confidence and contentment there is to be observed with the majority of men! And they who know of no trials will ridicule all who are being tried. If such is your case, you have reason to fear, for it is the way of God's children that they will enter into glory through many tribulations.

2. Only very few people have the faith that will prevail in trials. When people are examined very conscientiously by others who are truly able to discern, their faith will often resemble that of a Roman Catholic: One believes what the church believes, even though one knows nothing of the doctrines of the faith and cannot even enumerate them. Others have a faith that rests upon imagination, the fervent insistence of others, or upon acquiescing in a general truth without knowing its essence as applicable to them. Again, others will have some desire for these things which is evident from their hungering

and yearning after them without truly and actually looking away from self and embracing Jesus as the offered Mediator and by uniting oneself to Him, so that they no longer belong to themselves, but rather, to Another. It can also be that for a season people pretend to believe, and when they are tested in affliction, their faith will dissipate and wither. My friends, if our faith is to endure, it must be wrought by the Spirit. It must prompt us to turn away from self and cause us to be united to Him. True faith must and shall persevere until the end when it causes the soul to rest upon the rock Jesus.

3. Our text will also enable us to see where all these hypercritical utterances, these careless and meddling actions, these rash judgments, and this grieving of God's children originate. People who are guilty of this think highly of themselves and therefore speak with disdain, for they have not yet been emptied from vessel to vessel in the way of many trials. Oh, if such persons had ever been in the lions' den or on the mountains of the leopards (Song 4:8), and if they would have known of the despair and despondency of God's children, they "should know how to speak a word in season to him that is weary" (Isa. 50:4) and comfort the disconsolate. In such discouragement, they will experience the pains of hell to be upon them, and they will be so overcome and tormented by anxiety that they must exclaim, "My way is hid from the LORD, and my judgment is passed over from my God" (Isa. 40:27). Oh, since we do not know to what trials we will be subjected, consider that "blessed are the merciful: for they shall obtain mercy" (Matt. 5:7). The most genuine Christians are also the most compassionate and loving Christians, and they will deal with tried believers as a tender mother deals with her weak children. They who conduct themselves otherwise will fall because of their pride.

4. We can thus deduce who are the best Christians, namely, they who have been spiritually exercised by many trials in the way in which God leads them. They are not the spiritual novices who have only recently begun to observe and traverse this way, but rather, the veterans in grace who have been tested in the heat of the day and the cold of the night. Many unexercised believers prove to be incomprehensibly foolish. They hear, for example, that either a minister or member of the congregation has been converted. That person will posit that the way in which God leads is such and such. He will endeavor to expose false foundations, and he will reject many who, in his opinion, are ignorant of the Christian faith though they are perceived to be Christians. He will point out that these individuals have no more than a legalistic zeal.

Such a converted person truly has insight into the ways of God. He intends to make everyone genuinely Reformed and thus take from them all Pelagian and semi-Pelagian foundations, etc. Such a person will be praised and elevated, even though they have been traversing the way of life briefly, or at best three or four years. The "veterans" in grace who have experienced prosperity and adversity will be dismissed for not agreeing with such spiritual novices. The shortcomings of these "veterans" will be highlighted, whereas the lofty sentiments of these novices are deemed to be gospel truth. These "veterans" will be dismissed as retired soldiers who are no longer capable of engagement, whereas the young men who have not been exercised in battle will be promoted as generals.

Oh, this ought not to be so! These old and tried Christians should be held in high esteem. You should sit at their feet, learn from them, and esteem them as fathers. You may indeed love spiritual novices, but at the same time, you must keep an eye on them. If everyone were that wise, there would not be so much unrest, and God's church would not be torn asunder by foolish disputes. It would thus be better when spiritual veterans would be rendered the love and esteem one is obligated to express to these believers. Instead, one should seek to temper these novices in their excessive zeal, impetuousness, and delusional wisdom. Nearly all errors that have troubled the church were initiated by young and spiritually inexperienced Christians who, propelled by ambition and for the benefit of their own glory, have created confusion within the church.

Lessons for God's Children
Children of God, there is also some instruction for you in all that we have considered.

1. Seek to be at peace with the way in which God is leading you, and be committed to following the Lord precisely in that way as being the way that is best and most beneficial for you. Indeed, God knows best what you need and what you can endure. There are Christians who are led by the Lord in the way of many trials. They have barely been delivered from one temptation, or another one is knocking at their door. All the waves and billows cascade upon them. Then, there are others who are led more gently, for whom the sun is always shining upon life's pathway. It may happen that those who are subjected to severe trials will doubt their state of grace, whereas others have doubts because they do not know of such ways of trial and oppression. The

latter believe that one must enter by way of many tribulations as being evidence that one is a son and not a bastard (Heb. 12:8). Then again, there are others who, upon hearing how God leads others in the way of life, will yearn to have such a way for themselves and will strenuously strive to achieve this. Oh, my beloved, strive to observe with worship and adoration the way in which God leads your neighbor, and at the same time be satisfied with how God leads you! God knows that most likely, you would not be able to endure all these trials, and therefore He will not subject you to them. Thank Him for it! God also knows that when your circumstances are more comfortable, you will not be bound to Him in such a tender and heartfelt way. Therefore, acknowledge His goodness in that by many troubles and cares, He always compels you to flee to the throne of grace as a poor worm. If we would only consider this more, we would deem the way in which God leads us as the very best, and we would not choose another way.

2. Let the trial of your faith be accompanied with patience, submission, and a quiet surrender to the Lord. Oh, how blessed it is to arrive at the point where we can say with an upright heart, "I was dumb, I opened not my mouth; because thou didst it" (Ps. 39:9). And when we detect that rebellion against God's way arises in our hearts, how blessed it would then be to say to our soul, "My soul, wait thou only upon God; for my expectation is from him" (Ps. 62:5). "Therefore I will look unto the LORD; I will wait for the God of my salvation: my God will hear me" (Mic. 7:7), and He will deliver me out of all my troubles.

3. In ways of trial, be particularly fearful of having hard thoughts about the Lord and for doubting His love. Oh, though He may slay you with His hand, He loves you in His heart! As hot as the fire of tribulation may be, yet His heart of love burns with even greater fervency, and the more troubled you will be, the more His heart will burn with love; for in all your affliction, He is afflicted with you (Isa. 63:9).

4. Finally, you must know "that the trial of your faith [shall] be found unto praise and honour and glory at the appearing of Jesus Christ." Amen.

CHAPTER 8

Faith, a Grace That Will Render the Heart Submissive and Patient before God, Even Though His Promises Are Not Fulfilled Immediately

He that believeth shall not make haste.
—ISAIAH 28:16

The words of Solomon in Proverbs 16:32 are very remarkable, for he says there, "He that is slow to anger is better than the mighty." When he speaks of one who is slow to anger, we must understand this as referring to one who exercises self-control in the circumstances he encounters, who will not permit his passions and emotions to ambush him. Instead, he will exercise self-control while calmly and wisely making use of suitable means. He will also anticipate the desired outcome with great patience, irrespective of all the calamities he might encounter. A strong person is here contrasted with one who is slow to anger. Such a mighty person has no self-control, but rather, while relying on his strength he is driven and ambushed by his emotions, and therefore rarely succeeds in what he sets out to do. Thus, the person who is slow to anger excels the strong one. Although we could affirm this through examples, this is self-evident, for the strong or mighty person relies on his own strength, whereas he who is slow to anger does not rely on himself. The strong or mighty person is propelled by his own passions, whereas the one who is slow to anger enjoys a quiet calmness and tranquility in his soul. The strong or mighty person will be motivated by various options to be either for or against something.

In contrast, he who is slow to anger will only focus on the issue itself, and when he deems it to be good, he will patiently wait for a good outcome. The strong or mighty person will often be put to shame, having boasted of himself and having caused much turmoil, all the while failing in the end to achieve his goal. However, he who is slow to anger will have a quiet disposition, and he would rather that the ultimate outcome vindicate the matter.

We will affirm this by the words we have read, "He that believeth [that is, he who is slow to anger] shall not make haste." Our text sets before us an extraordinary promise regarding the advent of the Messiah. God would lay Him in Zion "for a foundation a stone, a tried stone, a precious corner stone" (Isa. 28:16). However, since several hundred years would first transpire, it is immediately added, "He that believeth shall not make haste," so that the church would patiently await the fulfillment of this promise.

In these words, we find,

1. a description of the persons being mentioned: They who believe
2. what is said of them: They shall not make haste.

A BRIEF DESCRIPTION OF BELIEVERS

The first portion of the text describes those who do not haste, namely, they who believe. To consider very briefly who they are that believe, let us take note of the following:

1. They who believe have experientially become thoroughly acquainted with their misery by the operation of the Holy Spirit. Thus, they will become acquainted with having departed from God from the moment of their conception and will know that their sins are more in number than their hairs on their heads, making them vile and abominable before God. This knowledge will pierce their hearts and cause them, with the publican, to smite upon their breasts and cry out, "I am ashamed and blush to lift up my face" (Ezra 9:6). The soul will thus become a suitable object for Jesus as the only Physician for their soul, for the soul has wounds, bruises, and festering sores that can only be cleansed and healed by Jesus's blood.

2. They who believe will be persuaded experientially that they are incapable of delivering themselves from their misery. Thus, they will perceive that neither they nor any other creature can quench God's wrath and achieve reconciliation with the God they have provoked. This perception will prompt them to exclaim, "Asshur shall not save us" (Hos. 14:3). And no wonder, for since they can no longer find "the life of [their] hand" (Isa. 57:10), they will exclaim, "There is no hope; there is no hope."

3. They who believe have received some true saving knowledge regarding the way of salvation in and through the crucified Jesus. Through the preaching of the Word, the Holy Spirit instructs them regarding how sinners are redeemed in the covenant of grace that God has established with His own Son as the second Adam. In this covenant, God has imputed and transferred all the sins of an elect world to His Son as Surety and Goel. God imposes the full punishment of sin upon His Son in strict conformity to His avenging justice. He endured this all to secure a complete redemption. For the sake of Jesus Christ, His Son, God can manifest His mercy to a hell-worthy sinner in a way that supremely magnifies His divine justice. Every believer will receive this instruction in a greater or lesser measure by the Holy Spirit's anointing who will teach him all things.

4. From their hearts' innermost core, they who believe will hunger and thirst after blessed communion and most intimate union with Christ. In their hearts, they yearn for this even in the night, and in their innermost soul, they will seek for it. Their reins are consumed within them (Job 19:27), and they cry out, "O God, thou art my God; early will I seek thee: my soul thirsteth for thee, my flesh longeth for thee in a dry and thirsty land, where no water is" (Ps. 63:1).

5. They who believe are such upon whose hearts the offer of Jesus is personally bound. The Holy Spirit thereby causes them to see that Jesus not only calls others to blessed fellowship with Himself but also them—very personally. It is as if their first and last name are expressly mentioned in the Bible. The Lord says, "I have even called thee by thy name" (Isa. 45:4). And in Isaiah 44:1, we read, "Yet now hear, O Jacob my servant; and Israel, whom I have chosen."

6. They who believe are people whose objections due to their unworthiness, guilt, and wretched misery are resolved by the Holy Spirit who teaches them that Jesus desires to receive precisely such people who deem themselves utterly unworthy. Sovereign grace is magnified most where sin has abounded (Rom. 5:20).

7. They who believe will wholeheartedly acquiesce in the testimony God gives regarding His Son, doing so with love, esteem, and the inner engagement of their entire soul, thereby setting to their seal that God is true

(John 3:33). They fully embrace that testimony, receiving it as the most joyous tiding a lost sinner could ever possibly hear.

8. They who believe, in the day of God's power (Ps. 110:3), will freely and wholeheartedly go to Jesus Christ, doing so with inner love and esteem for His person, and with an intense desire and longing to be His property for time and eternity.

9. They who believe have experienced and still do experience that Jesus Christ, even before they could embrace Him, will give Himself altogether to them as He is. Here there will be a line of separation, especially as pertaining to the exercises of faith. Presumptive believers will also find their hearts to be inclined toward Jesus, but they never experience that Jesus responds by also revealing and giving Himself to them. Believers know experientially that, as to the nature of spiritual life, the revelation of Jesus in His willingness precedes all their acts of faith.

10. They who believe shall fully surrender to Jesus when He reveals Himself in His willingness to their souls. They do this so that He may be their reconciliation with the Father and so that He may teach them by His Word and Spirit. He will then govern them in all things that pertain to soul and body, inclining their hearts to obey His good, delightful, and holy will.

11. They who believe by this surrendering will be most intimately united themselves to the person of Jesus Himself. In all that has been said thus far, we have observed that an upright soul desires not only to experience and enjoy that which issues forth from Jesus, but they also desire the very person of Jesus. Thus they will specifically seek to unite themselves to the person of Jesus, knowing that they will also be partakers of, and have fellowship with, His benefits.

12. They who believe are such for whom Jesus Christ is the motivation of all that they do. He is in them, and they, being united to Him by faith, are in Him. Just as the branch receives everything from its root, likewise they receive out of His fullness all that they need, and they will thus bear fruit to His glory (John 15:5).

13. They who believe will commit their entire way to this Immanuel, trusting Him that as He has begun His work, He will also finish it. According to His

promise in His covenant of salt, He will provide them with everything necessary at the time, in the manner, and according to the measure that God in His infinite wisdom deems best—all to the glory of His name and their salvation.

Therefore, it is said of all who believe that they shall not make haste. These, and various other matters, are the actual reasons why God's children are called believers. He who experiences these matters and practices them is blessed. However, he who is not acquainted with them other than by intellectual reflection remains subject to God's wrath. He is already condemned because he does not receive God's testimony.

THE SUBMISSION AND PATIENCE OF BELIEVERS

We shall now proceed to our second point and reflect on what the prophet says of those who believe, namely, that they shall not make haste.

The Meaning of "Make Haste" (Isa. 28:16)

To explore this correctly, we must first clarify the text itself. The word for "haste" in the original text is *yakhish,* having *khush* as its root. It expresses a very rapid movement toward achieving one's objective. It can refer to someone who has lost his way and anxiously paces back and forth trying to find his way again. Therefore, some have translated this text as "He that believeth will not go astray." It could also possibly be a reference to someone who finds himself in trouble, distress, or danger and hastily looks for a way of escape, even though that way of escape may be as dangerous as the predicament one finds himself in (cf. Ps. 55:7–8; Acts 27:30). Better said, it speaks of someone who is in danger and to whom help is promised. However, he will expose himself to even greater danger without waiting for the promised help to arrive since it does not come soon enough to his liking.

Some expositors question whether one should view our text as an imperative, forbidding one to make haste, or as a promise linked to not making haste. However, we deem these words to be neither an imperative nor a promise, but rather as a declaration regarding that which will necessarily issue forth from the very nature of faith. Thus, they who believe and who truly may exercise the grace of faith will commit their cause to God and wait patiently for what the outcome will be at God's appointed time.

There does appear to be a measure of uncertainty, however, for our text is quoted twice in the New Testament—by Paul in Romans 9:33 ("Whosoever believeth on him shall not be ashamed") and by Peter in 1 Peter 2:6 ("He that believeth on him shall not be confounded").[1] Misguided expositors are therefore of the opinion that some errors have found their way into the Hebrew text. However, this difficulty can be solved in two ways.

The one possibility is that both apostles are focusing on the meaning rather than quoting word for word. Thus, someone who is too hasty and does not achieve his objective makes himself a fool to others by his impatience and will, therefore, be ridiculed, mocked, and condemned. Hence the apostles, by way of further explanation, have expressed themselves very accurately. It would mean that such a man will neither be ashamed nor confounded, for he will not use erroneous means in reckless haste. Instead, he will follow the Lord and wait patiently for His salvation.

Or one could say with the learned English annotations regarding this text that as the apostle combines in the first part of verse 33 two passages from Isaiah, namely, Isaiah 8:14 and 28:16, in the second part of verse 33, he likewise extracts the word *faith* from our text and "shall not be ashamed" from Isaiah 49:23. It should be clear that if he undeniably did this in the one case, what would prevent him from doing it in the second half? And Peter may have followed Paul's example.

One could also consider how the Chaldeans have formulated it: "He who believes shall not tremble; he shall not be moved at the approach of danger." One can thus do justice to both passages. We would instead choose the first option but at the same time recognize the other option.

We will now proceed to consider the matter itself. Since our text speaks of *not making haste* and the apostles of *not being ashamed* or *confounded*, we will briefly address both phrases. We wish to emphasize that saving faith is a grace that renders the soul patient and will keep it from being ashamed or confounded.

Faith, a Grace That Gives Patience

We will first consider that saving faith is neither hasty nor impatient when the fulfillment of the promises is postponed. Instead, it is a grace that renders

---

1. Comrie indicates that in the *Statenvertaling*, the language of these passages is nearly identical. In Romans 9:33, we read, "Die in Hem gelooft, zal niet beschaamd worden," and in 1 Peter 2:6, "Die in Hem gelooft, zal niet beschaamd worden." Thus the language of both passages is identical in Dutch, that is, "He who believeth in Him shall not be ashamed."

one forbearing and patient. We will now pursue several matters, and we must, therefore, first consider what is presupposed here and what one must necessarily be acquainted with. We believe that two matters in particular are being presupposed here.

Faith's Standing on the Promises
First, believers may anticipate various excellent matters based on the divine promises of the covenant of grace. As much as they may be in need of having these promises fulfilled, they have not yet experienced their fulfillment. Nevertheless, their salvation does indeed consist primarily of possessing these matters based on God's promise. Our text clearly affirms this. The first part of our text expresses the promise—the coming of the Messiah—that He would lay in Zion a cornerstone as the only ground of salvation and the foundation upon which He would build the spiritual edifice of grace. Since, however, several hundred years would expire before this promise would be fulfilled, the exercise of faith is added immediately: "He that believeth shall not make haste." We would be able to say more about these promised matters and reduce this to several prominent elements. We have done so extensively in *The ABC of Faith*, in the chapter about waiting upon the Lord.

1. Believers anticipate *intimate communion with the triune God* based on His promise, for of them is said, "If a man love me, he will keep my words: and my Father will love him, and we will come unto him, and make our abode with him" (John 14:23). Asaph's experience was that it was good for him "to draw near to God" (Ps. 73:28), for in the enjoyment of God, the soul finds light, comfort, joy, and inexpressible delight.

2. By virtue of the promise, they who believe look forward to external and internal *growth and progress in holiness*. Nothing so weighs believers down as that they come short of the requirements of God's law. However, the words of Psalm 92:13 shall also apply to them: "Those that be planted in the house of the LORD shall flourish in the courts of our God."

3. Given what has been promised, believers look forward to *God's continued and steadfast guidance* in all their ways. Their compassionate God shall lead them. But how? According to His promise, "He shall gather the lambs with his arm, and carry them in his bosom, and shall gently lead those that are with young" (Isa. 40:11).

4. They also look forward to *the Almighty Himself inclining their hearts to His testimonies*: "And I will put my spirit within you, and cause you to walk in my statutes, and ye shall keep my judgments, and do them" (Ezek. 36:27).

5. They look forward to *the demise of the old man*, the body of this death, based on this promise, "Sanctify them through thy truth: thy word is truth" (John 17:17).

6. They who believe anticipate *reviving and fructifying grace*. Their disposition can at times be so barren, and their hearts can be as hard as a stone and as fruitless as the wilderness, cleaving so much to the dust that it seems as if they are glued to it. God's promise is, however, that He will take away the stony heart and cause the soul of His people to be as "a vineyard of red wine," that He "will water…every moment," so that the wilderness will be transformed into a fruitful field (Isa. 27:2–3).

7. Trusting in the promise, they anticipate *being sustained during times of adversity* and at precisely the right moment. The Lord has promised, "When thou passest through the waters, I will be with thee; and through the rivers, they shall not overflow thee: when thou walkest through the fire, thou shalt not be burned; neither shall the flame kindle upon thee" (Isa. 43:2).

8. The promise prompts them to anticipate *the desired outcome, however dark the circumstances may be*. The Lord will cause light to arise in darkness, and He will make straight that which is crooked.

9. Based on the promise, they anticipate that *their supplications and groanings to God for His help will be received and heard*. "Before they call, I will answer; and while they are yet speaking, I will hear" (Isa. 65:24).

10. Based on the promise, they anticipate *the annihilation of their enemies*, from the smallest to the greatest, for the Lord has promised, "No weapon that is formed against thee shall prosper" (Isa. 54:17).

11. Finally, believers may anticipate the *redemption of their bodies* and

12. The *eternal and never-ending enjoyment of God*.

Faith's Need to Wait on the Lord
However, something else is implied and must be known, namely, that it is God's way to significantly delay the fulfillment of the promises. There will

therefore be no haste in believing, whereas unbelief will be in much haste. If it is indeed true that he who believes will not make haste, it must necessarily follow that unbelief, to the contrary, will make haste. Having yet spoken little of the arrogancy of unbelief, and it being profitable to be acquainted with the exercises of faith, we now wish to say something about unbelief in contradistinction to faith. There is indeed a common proverb, "*opposita juxta se posita magis elucescunt*," that is, "When two matters are contrasted, they will be all the more obvious." We wish to do so to discriminate and instruct.

The Believer's Haste from Remaining Unbelief

First, we will therefore demonstrate by way of several particulars how this unbecoming haste is to be found in God's children when they are subject to an unbelieving spiritual frame. In stating the opposite, I can therefore truthfully say, "He that believeth not will make haste."

1. He who does not experientially believe will *be distressed and distraught in his heart when he comes into troubling and difficult circumstances*. There will then be no (or very little) peace and careful deliberation, for such a person will then not know what befalls him, what course he should undertake, or what he should refrain from doing, and how he should conduct himself. Being overcome by misguided passion, he will be particularly foolish and imprudent and be someone with whom one cannot speak, but for whom one could better pray. One will find this especially in some during their initial inner stirrings when they are so troubled, and all is so obscure. His conscience will then function as a gnawing worm, acting like a tormentor who will continually accompany and accuse such a person, confronting him with God's deserved wrath. In such circumstances, it is a wonder that many do not come to an evil end.

One can also observe this in the lives of advanced and seasoned Christians when they feel that God has deserted them or when they find themselves in circumstances in which they experience excessive spiritual turmoil. Rachel is an example from the natural realm who wanted to die when she was in hard labor. Furthermore, we know from reliable witnesses how an exercised soul hazarded her eternal bliss or woe by breaking a bottle of wine.

Many more examples could be given of godly persons who were swept along by hasty unbelief in a moment when matters turned out so differently from what they had expected. This can be so grievous that they can even lose their minds and be so overcome by an overwhelming despondency that death ensues—all because they were not able to surrender their circumstances into God's hand.

2. He who does not believe will *be driven from one thing to the next* just as a hasty person. As Ruben, he will be as "unstable as water" (Gen. 49:4). Experience teaches that when true believers depart from the way of faith, they will become like Naaman. They will despise gospel remedies and, instead, avail themselves of legal remedies. They are then inclined to think that the way of faith is too simple. They want to subdue sin and receive the wish of their heart by opposing sinful inclinations in the way of fasting and earnest prayer. These are good and necessary deeds in and of themselves, provided they are engaged in by faith. However, true believers who are in the dark, by their conduct, will deem the way of faith to be suspect and will take refuge again to the law. They will also think that others who are indeed engaged by faith and will, therefore, not be engaged in such legalistic behavior do not have as tender a disposition as they have. They will deem them as ignoring their heart and helping themselves by merely engaging their minds. If discord ever arises in the church or in families—which ought to be miniature churches— then such discord will be most bitter about this. In the meantime, we should not forget that they who do not believe will be like the waves of the sea. They will be driven by all manner of wind—from the one thing to the next. They will be unstable in all their ways (James 1:8).

3. One who does not believe will *be a hasty man*. When the fulfillment of the promises is postponed, he will use illegitimate means in his unbelieving haste to secure the things he desires. Abraham's wife, Sarah, is an example of this, for she did not want to wait for God's time to fulfill the promise that she would receive a son. And indeed, she gave Hagar, her servant, to Abraham to wife so they would receive a child through her. The Lord chastised her for this by the grief that Ishmael and his mother Hagar inflicted on her. Experience teaches abundantly that some of God's beloved children are also guilty of this before God by pursuing a particular matter with unbelieving haste. They will then fail to use the God-given means to attain this and, instead, use illegitimate means.

I will clarify this by way of two illustrations. For example, a believer greatly desires to be sanctified—a very praiseworthy objective that everyone should pursue. He will receive a promise from God in which the sanctification of his heart and deeds are promised by the operation and indwelling of the Holy Spirit. He will not then seek to obtain the fulfillment of this promise by repeatedly submitting himself to the Lord as clay into the hands of the great Potter, so that he may thereby be made and shaped by God's own hand unto His glory. He also will not then seek to secure this holy frame through coming to Jesus by faith—a spiritual frame that has already been merited in and by Him. He also will not pursue this by a looking unto Jesus by faith as the divinely ordained means unto sanctification whereby the soul is "changed into the same image from glory to glory, even as by the Spirit of the Lord" (2 Cor. 3:18). Since he cannot secure his sanctification at the time, manner, and measure that he desires, he will strive to stir up his heart in such a way as to bring about the fulfillment of the promise by engaging his natural faculties and by various fruitless efforts. At one time, he will try to achieve this by searching out all the threatenings of God's Word, and then again by meditating upon the magnitude of God's wrath and the severity of His divine justice. Or he will try this by thinking upon the state of the damned, and thereby confront his sinful desire with the very sparks of hell, and as it were put a knife to his throat. Then again, he will afflict his body by watchfulness, fasting, and other severe measures—too many to enumerate!

A second example would be a believer who has been anxious for some time due to an accusing conscience, who cannot find rest in the atoning blood of Christ. He neither abides near this opened fountain nor waits for the blood of Christ to be sprinkled upon his conscience so that it may be quieted and purified. Instead, he will avail himself of other things such as drawing conclusions (i.e., using syllogisms), confessing his guilt, and similar things. We can say of this that he who thus conducts himself will first of all experience that he will exhaust himself and that sin will exert itself all the more forcefully. Furthermore, he will observe that his wound—which has not been truly healed—will after that break forth again and will be all the more grievous. This can all be anticipated when in unbelieving haste one makes use of illegitimate means.

4. He who does not believe will *behave as a hasty man*. He will cease and desist when matters do not turn out as he had wished and is thus unwilling to wait upon the Lord by using the means. Instead, he will let his hands hang down and will become careless, thinking that it is in vain to serve the Lord. You will read of this in Isaiah 58. There are but few who are resolved that they must continue to supplicate for grace, even if they would have to die. There are but few who will persevere in this for thirty-eight minutes, let alone for

thirty-eight years! Wretched unbelief is the cause of all this. If only there were faith like a mustard seed, how desirous one would be to serve God for His own sake!

5. When someone fails to exercise his faith, *his mind will be clouded and his spirit will be so listless that as a hasty man, he will forget all the good things he has enjoyed and still enjoys.* The cause of this is that such a person will only focus on the circumstances in which he finds himself and from which he wishes to be delivered. The lean years will cause the prosperous years to be forgotten, and the skinny cows will eat the fat ones. How many things will be viewed erroneously when believers dwell in darkness due to their hasty unbelief! One will then observe that they can readily elaborate about their condition and all their troubling circumstances. They will then doubt whether they have ever beheld the Lord, for He now hides Himself behind a cloud. Since it is now so dark, they will be afraid that the light will never dawn. They will then be incapable of perceiving the benefits they may enjoy, as well as the marks of grace that are so readily discernable. Instead, they will exclaim with God's church, "Is anyone's sorrow like unto my sorrow?" (Lam. 1:12).

6. He who fails to believe will act as a hasty person for whom a period of delay will appear to be so long that he will *tend to think that one moment appears to be a day, and one day appears to be as long as a century.* "How long wilt thou forget me, O LORD? for ever?" (Ps. 13:1) is the language of hasty unbelief, whereas faith will say, "For his anger endureth but a moment; in his favour is life" (Ps. 30:6). How little does one consider that salvation does not consist in the enjoyment of what one desires, but rather, in a patient waiting upon the Lord and a yearning for the God of salvation! How readily one forgets how long the Lord has waited and how He all the day stretched forth His hands to bestow His grace upon us when we did not desire it!

7. Due to his unbelieving haste, he who fails to believe will *be filled with suspicion, jealousy, and distrust regarding God's ways with him.* He will say, "If God has been for us, how could this have happened to us?" It can thus be that everything the Lord does will be misinterpreted. Such a person will view God's fatherly chastisements, being evidences of His love, as actual punishments and tokens of His wrath and displeasure. In his haste, Asaph had gone so far that he thought that he had cleansed his hands in vain. And God's church (Jacob) will say, "My way is hid from the LORD, and my judgment

is passed over from my God" (Isa. 40:27). Such a soul refuses to believe that God is moved with compassion, and beholds her sorrow with love and inner emotion, believing instead that He delights in her distress.

8. He who fails to believe will *behave imprudently*, and in his unbelieving haste, he will *frequently utter imprudent words*. In his unbelieving haste, Moses did not want the rock to bring forth water by speaking to it, even though this is what God commanded him to do. Instead, he hit it, and that was evil in the eyes of the Lord. And David said in his haste, "All men are liars" (Ps. 116:11). Oh, how it is to God's glory when, just like Job, one knows his proper place, and one neither sins with his lips nor charges God foolishly (Job 1:22).

9. He who fails to believe is *often very somber and irritated* due to his unbelieving frame. Nothing pleases him. As to both natural and spiritual things, he is entirely beside himself—even when it only appears that all is not well. It can go so far that the wife becomes a cross for the husband and the husband for the wife. It can even go so far that one's own life will become a burden. Jonah was in such a frame, for in his haste, he said, "I do well to be angry, even unto death" (Jonah 4:9). He thus preferred death over life. It may be extraordinary when someone longs for heaven and desires death. However, if this proceeds from the grievous haste of unbelief, it will be abominable before God.

Causes of the Believer's Haste
Having considered in some measure the unspiritual frames that issue forth in God's children from such unbelieving haste, we will proceed to identify the causes from which they originate. To ascertain this, we need to consider the following:

1. Such haste issues forth from great *ignorance regarding God* and His wise and adorable ways. If one were truly and deeply convinced that the Lord makes all things well according to His pleasure and that all "His work is [altogether] honourable and glorious" (Ps. 111:3), one would always quietly wait upon God (Ps. 62:1), "as a child that is weaned of his mother" (Ps. 131:2).

2. Such haste issues forth from *a faulty view of one's guilt and hell worthiness before God*. If by divine light, one would be convinced of this, one would, instead, make haste to cry out, "He hath not dealt with us after our sins; nor rewarded us according to our iniquities" (Ps. 103:10).

3. Such haste issues forth from *proud spiritual arrogance when the soul insists on having her own way*. When such high thoughts of self enter into the fray, a person will become so irritable. Oh, what a sweet disposition of the heart it would be when our own will would fully acquiesce with God's will!

4. Finally, such haste issues forth from *excessive slavish and troubling fear*. However humble such fear may present itself, it will nevertheless bring the soul into much spiritual darkness.

The Sinfulness of a Believer's Haste
Let me now briefly address the sinfulness and abominableness of such unbelieving haste.

1. Such haste is especially sinful because it is critical of God's ways and is entirely dissatisfied with them. Everyone, therefore, ought to abhor such haste.

2. Such haste will prescribe to the Almighty how He, the Sovereign One, ought to conduct Himself. The Lord is a God who "giveth not account of any of his matters" (Job 33:13).

3. Such haste will prescribe to the Lord in which manner and measure something ought to transpire, and one will thus be recalcitrant toward the Lord.

4. Such haste refuses to set to his seal that God's testimonies are true (John 3:33) and thereby makes God out to be a liar (1 John 5:10).

5. Such haste insists on God submitting Himself to our will instead of our will being inclined toward God's will. Thus, the person himself wishes to sit upon the throne.

6. Finally, such haste will open the door to all manner of vices. The hands will hang down; the soul will listen to the enemy; there will be a decline in earnestness; the heart will turn toward the world; one will flee from one's enemies, and the soul will yield to the lusts of the flesh. In a word, if one is in such an unbelieving spiritual frame, one will be vulnerable to anything.

He That Believeth Shall Not Make Haste
We will now address the matter itself, and we will thus consider the various ways in which they who believe do not make haste. We will briefly speak of the following:

1. He who believes will not make haste because he embraces God's promise as the Word of the God of truth who cannot lie, and who has "faithfulness

[as] the girdle of his reins" (Isa. 11:5). They know that sooner would "heaven and earth pass" than that "one jot or one tittle" of the promise would remain unfulfilled (Matt. 5:18). Therefore, when they truly believe, they will not be moved spiritually, but rather, they will adhere to the Word, saying continually, "Remember the word unto thy servant, upon which thou hast caused me to hope" (Ps. 119:49).

2. He who believes will expect that which is good in the bitterest of times. He will say, "My God will hear me" (Mic. 7:7), and "it will surely come, it will not tarry" (Hab. 2:3).

3. He who believes will not make haste, for it is the nature of faith to remain quiet so that the soul will not be moved. She will be as Mount Zion that shall never be moved to all eternity.

4. He who believes will not make haste, for he is convinced that his salvation consists of receiving the promised benefits—not when he wills it, but rather when God wills it.

5. He who believes therefore fully surrenders himself to the Lord's leading. He will deny his own desire and will and remain of one mind with the Lord.

6. He who believes also will not be busy in adding up and lamenting all the seasons of delay.

7. Finally, he who believes will not make haste since he knows the worth of what has been promised. He thus realizes that it is worthy of one's exercise of patience.

We will not expand this discussion by adding additional matters, for they can readily be deduced from the contrary of what has been stated.

Faith, a Grace That Will Not Put to Shame

Both apostles, Paul as well as Peter, quote our text as follows: "whosoever believeth on him shall not be ashamed" (Rom. 9:33), and "He that believeth on him shall not be confounded" (1 Peter 2:6).[2] We cannot explain this in-depth since our exposition would become too long. Let a few remarks suffice.

Believers will not be ashamed or confounded because their expectation is founded upon a sound, sufficient, and immovable foundation. Their hope is grounded in the covenant God Himself. They have embraced His Word of promise and therefore have within their hearts the powerful assurance that

____

2. As stated earlier, Comrie indicates that "in the *Statenvertaling*, the language of these passages is nearly identical."

God has associated with the great good that He has laid away for them. No one who can point toward such tokens of God's grace will be put to shame or confounded.

They will not be disappointed, even though they must wait for this to be granted, for the goodness of His house has been promised to them by that God who cannot lie. The blood of Jesus has merited these benefits, and He, as the Faithful One, is engaged in bestowing them at His appointed time. By His indwelling in their hearts, He will prepare and render them suitable to be translated into His house in which there are many mansions—mansions that He is presently preparing.

Finally, God will keep and deliver them in whatever circumstances they may find themselves in so that they will never be confounded. "Fear not; for thou shalt not be ashamed: neither be thou confounded; for thou shalt not be put to shame" (Isa. 54:4, cf. Jer. 49:23). However needy they may be, let them but look unto the Lord, as expressed in Psalm 34:5, "They looked unto him, and were lightened: and their faces were not ashamed."

APPLICATION

Behold, my beloved, we have set before you a believer as he patiently waits upon the Lord for the fulfillment of His precious promises. Let us now apply all that has been addressed thus far for your benefit and edification. Oh, that on good grounds we could and might conclude regarding each of you that you are believers and that you possess your souls in your patience (Luke 21:19) so that you will never be ashamed or confounded! However, for most of you, the opposite will be true.

A Word for the Unconverted

How few there are of whom we dare to say or think that they are believers! They have never been made acquainted with themselves, their lost state by nature, their being without God and Christ, their being subject to God's wrath and curse, and their being without hope in the world. Indeed, beloved, the first seeds of faith will never be sown into the heart until the soul has a right view of her lost state—and that with conviction, true contrition, and a deep humbling of heart. If that is lacking in you, you are not a true Christian.

How few there are who, from the bottom of their hearts and with their entire soul, desire Jesus to be their Prophet, Priest, and King! How readily some can bear to be without this Jesus and yet be joyful and satisfied!

My beloved, the very first and most tender exercises of faith are manifest in a yearning and hungering after Jesus, prompted by a true recognition of one's lost condition and the realization that Jesus is absolutely necessary so that by Him we might be reconciled with God. If you miss that, then conclude that you are not a believer.

How many there are who remain as they are without making any progress. Such souls are desirous; they yearn and long, but that will be the extent of it. And since they possess nothing else, they continue to rest in the desires and exercises they have—all without Christ. Beloved, I believe assuredly that a yearning, hungering, and thirsting for Jesus are the initial stirrings of faith. However, wherever such exercises are found in truth, such a person will not rest in them as a foundation. On the contrary, He will thereby become all the poorer and must come to Jesus Himself to embrace Him for time and eternity.

How many are there who fully expect to be saved, and yet who have never surrendered themselves to God to be saved by free grace alone—and that while the most essential and fundamental act of faith consists of the soul's full surrender to God!

Oh, how wretched is your condition as long as you do not believe! Any expectation that you may have will be swept away like a spider's web. Unless God prevents it, you will come up short and perceive that you have merely been building upon a sandy foundation, having but a lie in your right hand (Isa. 44:20). A deceived heart has led you on the wrong pathway. You will certainly be put to shame. Eternal shame and confusion shall cover you, while Christ will say, "I have not known you."

A Word for God's Children

Children of God, you have observed, however, that which unmistakably issues forth from faith. Let me also say a few words to you.

Consider attentively the harm that unbelief inflicts upon you. It will thoroughly confuse you and render you unfit for the tender exercises of communion with God. It will prevent you from having peace within your own soul. Oh, if only you would truly believe that unbelief is so harmful and detrimental to the soul, you would strive against it and not so readily give it a hearing!

You should not only consider that unbelief is harmful to you but especially that it dishonors God. As you have heard, it is one of the greatest sins.

And yet, other sins will sooner generate condemnation and shame in our conscience than this sin. How little one will be ashamed and humbled before the Lord regarding the sin of unbelief! I fear that many of God's children will not readily overcome their unbelief, for they hardly view and lament it as sin.

To act by faith and to remain still before God through endurance and patience, one must seek to rest one's faith upon the Word of promise. Only then will you, on good grounds, be able to wait while the fulfillment of the promise is postponed.

Finally, you may know that you will not be put to shame, for your God, at His time, will fulfill all your desires and satisfy your soul with His favor—all to the glory of His own name. Amen.

CHAPTER 9

Faith, a Grace That Causes One to Approach the Throne of Grace in Full Assurance to Receive Grace and Help in Time of Need

Let us draw near with a true heart in full assurance of faith, having our hearts sprinkled from an evil conscience, and our bodies washed with pure water.
—HEBREWS 10:22

How God desires to be served and feared is not a matter of indifference. He must be served in conformity to His perfect spiritual nature. The Savior teaches this clearly in John 4:24, "God is a Spirit: and they that worship him must worship him in spirit and in truth." So that you may understand this in some measure and conduct yourself accordingly, we will assist you in this by expounding the words of our text.

In the context, we must note that the apostle first has demonstrated how Christ's priestly office and sacrifice are superior to Aaron's priesthood. And indeed, Christ has by one offering "perfected for ever them that are sanctified" (Heb. 10:14), and thereby He gives liberty "by a new and living way" (Heb. 10:20) to draw near to God. Jesus is the great High Priest of the house of God. Therefore, in our text the apostle seeks to stir up himself and the believing Hebrews to engage in a duty that conforms to this gospel privilege of the New Testament church.

We are to consider two matters in the words of our text:

1. The explicit duty he exhorts the Hebrews to engage in, namely, to draw near unto the throne of grace "with a true heart in full assurance of faith." In so doing, we will address (a) the duty itself, namely, to approach or draw near; and (b) how one must draw near, namely, "with a true heart in full assurance of faith."

2. The requisites to draw near "with a true heart in full assurance of faith." It must be with (a) a heart that has been "sprinkled from an evil conscience" and (b) a body that has been "washed with pure water."

THE DUTY TO DRAW NEAR

We will first discuss the duty to which the apostle exhorts the Hebrews: "Let us draw near with a true heart in full assurance of faith."

Drawing Near to God

The duty to which the apostle exhorts is "Let us draw near," or "Let us approach."

The Persons Exhorted to Draw Near

In this exhortation, we will first consider the persons whom he exhorts. They are the Hebrews, and the apostle includes himself. They needed this exhortation so that, by God's grace, their hearts might be strengthened to endure being oppressed for the gospel's sake and that by their faith having been tested, they might remain steadfast in a good confession. By the exercise of faith, the grace of God must be prayerfully extracted from Christ. Hereby "we may obtain mercy, and find grace to help in time of need" (Heb. 4:16). However, as the apostle exhorts the Hebrews, he simultaneously exhorts himself to fulfill this duty. Thereby he gives an example to all the ministers of the church that they should never place a burden upon the shoulders of others that they will not touch with their own fingers. The apostle needed the strengthening grace of God as much as they did. In fact, in many ways he needed it more because he and all faithful ministers are, by virtue of their faith, subjected more than others to tribulation, as well as to being inwardly assaulted by Satan.

The Duty of Drawing Near

The duty to which the apostle exhorts himself and others is to draw near. To explore this further, one needs to consider the nineteenth verse of this chapter and verse 16 of chapter 4. Here this drawing near is explicitly described as an entering "into the holiest" or a coming "boldly unto the throne of grace."

The Throne of Grace

Therefore, we must first speak of the throne of grace or the sanctuary into which they are to enter. A throne is essentially a chair that symbolizes dignity upon which kings make their pronouncements, execute justice, and dispense mercy. Often Scripture speaks metaphorically of God being seated upon a throne, as, for example, in Isaiah 6:1; Ezekiel 1:26; and other passages. Noteworthy is the description of the judgment of God's throne in bestowing grace upon a hell-worthy sinner. We read in Psalm 89:14, "Justice and judgment are the habitation of thy throne: mercy and truth shall go before thy face." It is as if the psalmist says, "Oh God, Thou art seated upon a throne that has justice for its pillars. Thou art fully propitiated by having executed Thy unflinching justice toward Thy Son as Surety. Therefore, Thou art able to manifest Thy lovingkindness and truth toward a poor and hell-worthy sinner."

The Jews claim that God has two thrones: a throne of justice and a throne of mercy or of grace. The point is that we must direct you to the meaning of the metaphor used by the apostle. We must also clarify what we consider to be the essential meaning of this throne of grace. Undoubtedly, the apostle derives his manner of speech in chapter 10:19 and 4:16 from the Jewish ceremonial worship. The stipulation was that the ark of the covenant had to be placed in the Holy of Holies and that no one could enter there except the High Priest once a year. The ark was covered by the mercy seat upon which two cherubim were positioned, and above it shone forth the Shekinah glory in the cloud that symbolized God's presence. Therefore, it is said of God that He sits or dwells between the cherubim (Ps. 80:1).

On the great Day of Atonement, the High Priest would enter the Holy of Holies to make reconciliation for his own sins and those of the nation. He would enter with much fear and did not remain there very long. He would only offer a short prayer so the people would not become fearful. Upon his return, the people would rejoice greatly. We find a detailed description of the Day of Atonement in the *Tractate Joma* of the *Mishna*.[1]

Drawing Near to the Throne of Grace

The reason we are told that we must draw near to the throne of grace—or, to put it differently, that we must enter the sanctuary—is because the Shekinah glory, revealed in the cloud of God's presence, rested upon the cherubim in the sanctuary. That begs the question as to what we are to understand by the throne of grace. We concur with the best commentators that we are not to think of the throne of grace in reference to Christ but rather in reference to God the Father, for He is gracious to the sinner for the sake of His Son.

In drawing near to God, He must be viewed as Father:

---

1. Comrie refers here to the *Mishna*, the oldest Jewish doctrinal tradition that was passed on orally by way of repetition (*Mishna* means "repetition"). The *Mishna* was recorded in six major divisions that were subdivided into sixty-three tracts. The *Tractate Joma* is one of these tracts. The *Mishna* was the core around which the *Talmud* developed.

1. As the illustrious Majesty, crowned with honor and glory, before whom men are but as ants and worms, or as a drop in a bucket or a piece of dust upon a scale. One can never revere God enough; He who "is greatly to be feared in the assembly of the saints, and to be had in reverence of all them that are about him" (Ps. 89:7). After all, He is "the high and lofty One that inhabiteth eternity" (Isa. 57:15).

2. As a reconciled God in His Son Jesus Christ who has fully satisfied God's justice. Thus, in Christ, God is reconciling the world unto Himself (2 Cor. 5:19). God, in His spotless holiness and inflexible justice, is a devouring fire and everlasting burnings outside of Christ (Isa. 33:14).

3. As the God who acquits the poor, hell-worthy sinner who takes hold of Christ of the guilt incurred by his sins. He is just and will acquit those who believe in Christ (Rom. 3:26).

4. As the God who is willing and ready to help those who through Jesus Christ as the "new and living way" (Heb. 10:20) call upon Him for help and deliverance. This gives liberty to come to Him, who is a faithful God and Father who is mighty and willing to hear and answer before we call upon Him (Isa. 65:24). Such calling must occur while they draw near to Him, "for he that cometh to God must believe that he is, and that he is a rewarder of them that diligently seek him" (Heb. 11:6).

The Act of Drawing Near

The duty set forth here is a drawing near, for we read, "Let us draw near." The word used here is all the more potent because of its composition. Thus, it will never be translated simply with "to go," but rather, it expresses a drawing near as practiced in the service of God. Consequently, this word is used to describe the High Priest drawing near to God in the Holy of Holies and the drawing near to God in prayers that are sanctified in Christ. Such is the sense of this verb. This drawing near is therefore characterized as the holy activity of the soul whereby she—as an unworthy, poor, empty, helpless, utterly destitute, and insignificant creature—draws near to God through Christ as the new and living way. Such a soul is intensely desirous of receiving grace for grace out of the fullness of God's grace, proceeding solely from the weighty substitutionary actions and suffering of Jesus Christ.

We will examine this more closely by addressing the following matters:

1. It is a drawing near of the soul unto God whereby a man deems himself

to be entirely without hope, viewing all things to be utterly hopeless and despairing. As long as a person can somewhat improve his condition, he will not call upon God, his Creator, "who giveth songs in the night" (Job 35:10). The gospel records that the woman with the issue of blood was at her wit's end before she came to Jesus to touch the hem of His garment. As long as one can find life in his own hand, one will not exclaim, "There is no hope" (Isa. 57:10).

2. The Hebrews had to draw near with a deep impression of their own utter emptiness and poverty, but also an impression of the abundant fullness there is in God to help those who are bankrupt in themselves. The first must motivate the soul, whereas the second is meant to encourage her to draw near to the God of all grace.

3. The Hebrews had to draw near to the Lord with the innermost stirrings of their souls. Only the poor and needy can utter supplications. When the Lord describes in His Word how He will cause the Jews to draw near to Him, He says, "They shall come with weeping, and with supplications will I lead them" (Jer. 31:9).

4. The Hebrews had to draw near with the most affectionate esteem for the benefits of the covenant of grace, for one drop of them should be of more value than a thousand worlds.

5. They had to draw near with a persevering desire in their souls. Hosea had this in mind when he wrote in chapter 14, "Take with you words" (Hos. 14:2).

6. They had to draw near to God in such a way as to look away from themselves and to end in God. Therefore, it is described as entering into the sanctuary.

7. They had to enter the sanctuary with and by the blood of Jesus Christ as the one and only sacrifice, for the priests were not permitted into the sanctuary with anything else but blood.

The Manner of Drawing Near

We will now proceed to consider how the Hebrews had to draw near, namely, "with a true heart in full assurance of faith" (Heb. 10:22).

A True Heart

They had to draw near with a true heart, that is, with a heart cleansed from all dishonesty, hypocrisy, and duplicity, for God desires truth in the inward parts (Ps. 51:6). Since He Himself is a Spirit, He desires to be worshiped in spirit and in truth. Although such sacrifices did not have to be of pristine quality, they had to be without defect; that is, they had to be perfect. When the heart is not inclined to the fear of God's name, but rather halts between two opinions, wanting to serve both God and mammon, one then needs to know that the Lord abhors both a double-minded man and a man full of deceit. By way of several illustrations, we will point out what it means to have a true heart.

1. A true heart is a heart that has been cleansed and purified from deceit and all impurity. By nature, every man is deceitful, and everyone "speaketh deceit…to his neighbour" (Jer. 9:8). However spontaneous and upright he may be, there is no natural man who does not have hidden intentions and objectives. Their souls are teeming with sinful desires. But the true heart will be cleansed of this, as will be evident from the following.

2. A true heart is a heart where God's image and likeness have been stamped upon every faculty of the soul. There will not only be a sanctified knowledge but also holiness and true righteousness. When one has been recreated after God's image, the heart will be true and upright, being "his workmanship, created in Christ Jesus unto good works" (Eph. 2:10).

3. A true heart is preeminently a heart that engages in the important work of covenant transactions with God without guile and without the least compulsion. One will surrender himself unconditionally to God, for God requires this when He says, "My son, give me thine heart" (Prov. 23:26).

4. A true heart fully acquiesces in all that conforms to God's law. Its content is engraved upon the soul. All which God says to be a duty, the heart will not only acknowledge it to be a duty but also a privilege.

5. A true heart will not be guided by human insights to either do or not do something for the sake of people. Instead, it will be stimulated by impressions of God's majesty and the correctness of what one ought to do. Thereby the soul experiences great peace in doing all things by faith and to God's honor.

6. A true heart desires to obey God in all things. It will not merely focus on explicit commands or prohibitions but rather on all that God either commands or forbids. Thus, in all things, one will do what is pleasing to God and His will, and his conversation will be directed accordingly (Ps. 119:5–6).

7. A true heart is a consistent heart that will neither be strict in one matter and careless in another matter. Then one will not refrain from stepping across a straw while jumping across a beam. One will then not be prejudiced in what he does and will fear God both privately and publicly. One will then be as careful in the presence of worldly persons as with those who fear God.

8. A true heart will proclaim the truth at all places, in all company, and under all circumstances. Thus, one will also do this when the truth is either suppressed or when those who profess God's name are despised. One will never be like a weathervane, but one will always walk in conformity to the truth.

9. A true heart is a steadfast heart. It will not only be righteous for the moment but until the very end. It will not be so only at the outset, but it will also persevere. One will also be very alert for backsliding and lukewarmness and cry out continually, "My soul cleaveth unto the dust: quicken thou me according to thy word" (Ps. 119:25).

10. A true heart always fears deception and deceit, exclaiming, "Lord, I believe; help thou mine unbelief" (Mark 9:24). Oh, since the godly know the perversion and deceitfulness of their own hearts, their petition will be, "Search me, O God, and know my heart: try me, and know my thoughts: and see if there be any wicked way in me, and lead me in the way everlasting" (Ps. 139:23–24).

11. A true heart is distraught about its shortcomings and failures. "O wretched man that I am!" (Rom. 7:24). The sins and shortcomings of such a heart will weigh down and burden it. It cannot find rest until it is cleansed in the blood of Christ (Ps. 51).

12. A true heart yearns intensely after grace. It is not the desire of a sluggard, but rather an earnest yearning that engages both heart and soul (Isa. 26:9). It is a stronger yearning than that of a deer after the water brooks (Ps. 42:1).

13. A true heart will consciously use all means whereby God is pleased to bestow His grace. He knows that "the hand of the diligent maketh rich" (Prov. 10:4). He also knows that God does not bestow His favor upon him because of his deeds, but rather that He bestows it upon that which they do out of love, for they that seek Him shall find Him!

14. A true heart will search to uncover its secret sins. Yes, such hearts will very diligently search out the hidden corners of their souls so that not a single sin can reside there.

15. Finally, a true heart loves God—a love that will manifest itself in the most challenging circumstances in which God can bring a person. The cause of this is that the heart is fully convinced that God is so worthy to be served, loved, and feared.

Full Assurance

The second aspect of drawing near to God is to do so "in full assurance of faith." A distinctive of faith is now before us that needs to be considered in more detail, for faith is a grace whereby one draws near to God in full assurance through Jesus Christ to "obtain mercy, and find grace to help in time of need" (Heb. 4:16). To address this, we need to consider various matters.

The Meaning of the Term Translated "Full Assurance"

We need to consider the intent of the original word. This noun only occurs in this passage,[2] whereas the verb is used various times. Our esteemed translators, to communicate its strong meaning, have expressed it with two words: full assurance. This excludes all doubt and indicates that the soul finds complete rest in a given matter or declaration. Linguists are justified in inquiring about the derivation of this meaning. Some believe that *plerophoria* is a compound of two words—namely, *pleres* and *phoreo*—which means as much as the bearing or carrying away of the full burden. The word would then express the soul's inner conviction—a conviction regarding a given matter that emerges due to the persuasive weight of all the arguments that are being advanced regarding it. Others believe that this word is derived from a ship's situation, having endured many storms and dangers, finally beholding the desired harbor, entering it with full sails, and finding rest in it. The latter

---

2. Comrie is mistaken here, for the word *plerophoria* also occurs in Colossians 2:2; 1 Thessalonians 1:5; and Hebrews 6:11.

opinion is generally more accepted than the first. Having said that, the first view is not unfounded, but as to our text is also very convincing.

Full Assurance of Faith

We will now proceed to discuss the matter itself and thus the full assurance of faith. This is most certainly a very weighty matter. To discuss this briefly, we will consider the following matters.

1. We will first shed some light on this matter according to the latter meaning of the word. It clearly sets before us the state of the soul before she can attain the full assurance of faith. That state is comparable to a ship that is in great danger due to a tumultuous sea. There is no need to enumerate all these dangers. I have already mentioned many of them in the sermons in which I have expounded Hebrews 4:3 (sermon 4) and 1 Peter 1:7 (sermon 7). Such is indeed the reality of the soul's experience: the soul is often tossed with tempest and not comforted (Isa. 54:11); over which have gone all the waves and billows (Ps. 42:7); and against which the floods have lifted up (Ps. 93:3). One moment she will run into this, and then against something else. If every believer were to elaborate on these struggles, many books could be written.

2. The soul will, at last, be privileged to behold the safe haven—that is, Jesus— in the free offer of the blessed gospel. The following matters are encompassed in this:

a. The soul will be absolutely and persuasively convinced of the divine authority of the gospel, that is, of the message of salvation through a crucified Christ.

b. The soul will also have a lively and felt perception that salvation is in none other, and thus that Jesus only, by His passion and death, has fully satisfied divine justice and rendered full payment. Therefore, God can be gracious to the chief of sinners in a way that fully conforms to the strictest standard of justice.

c. This blessed offer of grace will finally be bound upon the heart of this person in particular. The call of the gospel is not only extended to others, but he, too, is called to receive forgiveness of sins by faith in Christ Jesus. The Lord will say to him, "I have even called thee by thy name" (Isa. 45:4). It is as if God's Spirit says, "Be of good comfort, rise; he [the Master] calleth thee" (Mark 10:49).

3. The Holy Spirit is especially the one who powerfully and irresistibly establishes His residence in the soul. Just as the wind blows into the sails, likewise the Holy Spirit will with a lovely breeze blow upon all the faculties of the soul. This work of the Spirit encompasses several things:

a. As a southerly breeze, He will fully warm and enliven the soul by the grace of God in Christ Jesus. Consequently, the heart will become completely quiet and peaceful and will melt away in tenderness regarding what it perceives. There will be such a peaceful serenity in the heart that no one can express this in words. You must seek to experience this, and you will then understand what we mean by these words.

b. The Spirit will see to it that the soul will be engaged as such and will cause her to be intensely engaged in drawing near to the triune God. The soul's eye will now behold something of the glory of the Lord in the face of Jesus (2 Cor. 4:6). The heart will now be engaged with a love that is stronger than death. The soul will now highly esteem the Lord. All her desires and love will actively be focused on God—not only to choose Him in Christ but especially to take hold of Him as "a bundle of myrrh" lying betwixt the breasts (Song 1:13).

c. Just as the wind, the Holy Spirit will impact the sails with an activity and influence upon all faculties of the soul that is continuing, unceasing, and uninterrupted until she will genuinely and really enter into the Rock Christ. If the Spirit were to desist, the soul, as much as she may have drawn near, would stop short. Thus, following the initial stirring, the soul would not be able to find refuge in Jesus without the subsequent, continual, and uninterrupted influence of the Spirit. The Spirit bestows upon believers the full measure of His power. Driven by the wind of the Spirit, they will readily and with ease proceed without any regard for their own burdens and opposing forces. They run through a troop with God, and by Him, they leap over a wall (Ps. 18:29).

d. The Holy Spirit will thereby bring the soul experientially to Christ Himself, and in and through Him into full and blessed communion with the triune God. The Spirit will, by an act of faith He Himself has wrought, lift her, so to speak, from the earth and cause her truly to embrace the Mediator so that she will experience true rest which she had not experienced before, namely, upon Christ as her sure foundation. She is now in a safe haven where she is secure, where the storm winds are not heard, and where one will also not be frightened by the roaring of the water billows. In that haven, there will only be quietness, tranquility, peace, and joy in the Holy Ghost. Consider how sweetly this is illustrated by God's dealings with His ancient covenant people: "As an eagle stirreth up her nest, fluttereth over her young, spreadeth abroad her wings, taketh them, beareth them on her wings: so the LORD alone did lead him" (Deut. 32:11–12). And when God becomes the eternal dwelling place of the soul by bringing her unto Him as the Rock, God's everlasting arms will be underneath the soul (Deut. 33:27), by which she is lifted up and translated into Christ.

We believe that the meaning of the word *plerophoria* is as we have described it, that is, full assurance. By the operations of God the Holy Spirit, the soul may go to this safe haven and enter into it. She may do so with raised sails and the wind at her back to find true rest in this haven. Consider also what we said about this when we instructed you as to how faith enters into rest (sermon 5).

Distinctions and Clarifications about Assurance

After having cleared up this matter by this metaphor in some measure, we will now proceed to speak of full assurance itself. My beloved, this has always been a bone of contention in the church from the beginning of the Reformation until today. Overly zealous and inexperienced men have always caused much unrest and turmoil in the church. This will especially occur when there are differences of opinion among the Reformed themselves, causing love to wane and envy, rancor, and bitterness to emerge instead. One appears to be more intent on arguing about the assurance of faith rather than being experientially exercised regarding this precious grace. How the church will be maligned by her enemies when they observe how much disagreement there is about the essence and experience of the assurance of faith as being the means whereby the soul is united to Christ! How grievously this causes the little ones in grace to be tossed to and fro! Beloved readers, we will not trouble you with this, for this is contrary to our nature. While others are striving about this, it will be most profitable for us to be exercised much about this assurance. Let it suffice that I make a few related remarks.

Faith's Essence and Exercises

First, we must make a necessary distinction between faith in the abstract and concrete sense of the word—and thus between the essence of faith and faith as it clearly manifests itself to believers themselves and others by the exercises of a believer's faith. As to its essential activities, faith is the direct opposite of unbelief. When considering faith in its essence, there is no uncertainty or even the least doubt in faith. Whatever is true regarding the contrary vice must be excluded from the nature of the contrary virtue. However, when we consider faith *in abstracto* [abstractly], is there such abstract faith without there being a subject in which it is seated? One will find it only in the fruitless speculation of contentious persons! Such a notion is a mere illusion or a *chimaera*,[3] for nothing can exist without a subject in which it resides.

Faith is not the essence of the soul, but rather a faculty planted in the soul by the Holy Spirit. As to the soul, though faith is merely accidental to its existence, it is essential to her spiritual life. For this and other accidental qualities, indeed, their existence is always defined by something else (*eorum esse est inesse*). However, where is faith operative in its essential nature? It will be operative in a subject that is entirely sinful and altogether wretched. This subject is entirely impotent and incapable of doing anything good and perfect due to that subject's inherent depravity. Therefore, however much the soul may be stimulated to practice some virtue, she will never achieve this fully in her state of imperfection. The inner disposition of the soul that opposes faith will be more or less active so that faith—which in and of itself could function with the fullest assurance—will never attain such perfection. That being said, faith will be more or less perfect in proportion to the measure in which the opposing disposition is more or less active, and this disposition may even be subdued. The obvious conclusion will be that though someone may truly have faith, it may not be functioning perfectly due to the accompanying corruptions that will be mingled with the very best deeds of the saints. Such perfection belongs to the essence of faith.

The Initial Exercise of Faith

Second, it should be noted that all the graces infused into the soul by the Holy Spirit—and that happens in conformity to the inherent essence of these graces—will only manifest themselves in their embryonic functioning and germination. As these graces are exercised, they will come to greater

---

3. A *chimaera* is portrayed frequently as a monster-like figure of Greek mythology and is often depicted as having the head of a lion, the body of a goat, and the tail of a snake.

maturity and perfection. This fact is the premise of all admonitions in which one is exhorted to be built up in the faith, to grow in grace, and other similar exhortations. Thus, we can never reasonably assume that grace will be bestowed upon the believer in the highest sense of the word at the outset of new spiritual life, for there would then be no need to grow and increase. It is, therefore, consistent with the tenor of God's Word that we are convinced that the soul, when engaged in the lesser acts of faith, will through the strengthening and comforting ministry of the Holy Spirit be led to a more mature measure of faith by its exercise.

Weak and Strong Faith

Third, we must observe that God speaks of weak and strong faith in His Word. This distinction is entirely legitimate, for the Spirit never caused anything to be recorded without reason. However, if every believer would have to be fully assured from the outset, one would have to ask what the basis for such a distinction would be. That distinction would not apply to faith as such, for everyone would then have a strong faith according to those who claim that assurance belongs to the essence of faith or is the very essence of faith itself. There would then not be any difference between a strong and a weak believer, lest the difference would be that the one retains his assurance for a more extended period and the other but for a short period. I will not address whether this distinction applies to people who fear the Lord in all quietness so that everyone might rightly reflect on this for himself.

Assurance Issues Forth from the Essence of Faith

Fourth, we must also consider that assurance must not be viewed as something that does not issue forth from the essence of faith itself. We must correctly assess where we differ with Roman Catholicism which claims that the assurance of faith does not issue forth from the essence of faith. Rather, it is the result of an immediate revelation. No, there is no distinction between weak and strong faith—as if assurance belongs to the essence of one person's faith and not of the other. On the contrary, assurance proceeds from one and the same faith, the exercise of which is at one time stronger and then again weaker—but most certainly it is not the result of an immediate revelation. To clarify this further, one must consider that where the essence of a matter is found, there will also be the innate potential (*potentia perfectibilis*) to achieve a greater measure of perfection. Granted, such perfection will not be achieved immediately but will gradually develop by removing obstacles and achieving a greater measure of perfection. For example, the eye has the potential (*potentia*) to see, but then something enters the eye that prevents it from seeing—such as the growth of a cataract or something similar. A person will then be incapable of seeing, or at least not clearly and with discernment. Nevertheless, his eye as such has *potentia vivendi*, that is, the ability to see clearly. When the impediment is removed, and light penetrates the eye, he will see clearly. How? By granting a capability that did not previously exist? No, for the potential to see was there, and the act of seeing is made possible by the removal of the impediment. Faith functions in like manner. Assurance does not come about by an immediate revelation, but rather, issues forth from the nature of faith. Herein lies imbedded the potential to conduct oneself with assurance when the impediment to doing so is removed, and the divine light shines so transparently in the soul that she can clearly perceive the matters that she embraces by faith. We may thus conclude that though not every believer is assured, the potential to be assured is embedded in the essence of faith itself. It is experientially exercised when this potential issues forth into action (*potentia ad actum*).

Furthermore, we must note that the exercises of faith in the believer are not equally strong, for sometimes the one exercise will be much more vigorous than the other. For example, it can and does happen that the seeing of Jesus results in a hungering and thirsting after Jesus—all as a result of a true sense of being troubled regarding one's deficiencies and seeing by divine illumination that God in Jesus Christ can be the God of a sinner. Jesus has fully satisfied the claims of His justice, and this Jesus is offered in the gospel! The soul will then surrender to God to be saved in that way alone. Such a soul will then melt away in the most heartfelt and tender expression of love toward Jesus, perceiving in himself love, reverence, and the full commitment of himself to the Lord. And yet, the perception of such a person can be that he has but little assured confidence.

On the other hand, someone may have much confidence and yet must complain very bitterly about his spiritual barrenness, insensitivity, and lack of zeal. If this is understood correctly, we will need much humility and sanctified wisdom regarding ourselves and in our dealing with others. Rather than questioning and judging others, we would do better by considering the Holy Spirit's leading regarding each believer. We will then worship and magnify the Lord's wise and holy ways.

Appeal to the Reformers

Fifth, it must also be noted that both schools of thought strongly appeal to the Reformers to formulate a resolution regarding this difference of opinion. They will issue bitter edicts against each other, implementing and arriving at conclusions regarding each other that are contemptuous and insulting. The one party claims that the other party is departing from the Reformation doctrine, and the other party proves with numerous quotations that the Reformers agree with him all the while heaping very bitter accusations upon his opponent. This is a matter of grief and sorrow for peace-loving and God-fearing persons, for they who as brothers ought to dwell together in peace are more embittered against each other than Roman Catholics toward Protestants. May God heal the breach of the daughter of His people, and may He take unto Himself the staves Beauty and Bands (Zech. 11:7).

If I am permitted to speak a word about this who readily wish to acknowledge myself as the least and most unworthy of all the Lord's people, I wish to say that it was an essential point of the Reformation to determine who is actually to be the judge to render a verdict in emerging differences of opinion. All the Reformers have unanimously taught that neither a man nor a human document can be the final arbiter, but rather, God alone who by His Spirit speaks in His Word—the canonical books of the Old and New Testaments. All opinions and contested issues should only be settled by an appeal to them but never by the exercise of either human authority or human writings. You will then perceive that all who seek to resolve this dispute about the assurance of faith by appealing to the opinions and writings of men—the church Fathers or the Reformers rather than exclusively to God's infallible word—dispense with a very important, yes, one of the most essential premises of the Reformation. We never think of the Reformers nor read their writings except with the greatest possible esteem and adoration. However, we certainly do not believe that they have written their books with the intent that they function as a judge in settling differences of opinion in God's church.

Rather, regarding all disputes, one must proceed in such a fashion that he will first determine whether a given doctrine is taught clearly and transparently in God's Word. Once that has been determined, one can appeal to the writings of others in affirmation of this. That has always been very beneficial and will continue to be so if done correctly and knowledgeably. Let me, therefore, ask you, "What are the arguments that are extracted from human writings?" They are merely *ad hominem* arguments, that is, arguments focused upon the person rather than yielding tightly argued and convincing proofs. Or else it must be that an erroneous representation of a given opinion is corrected and brought in line with other views, etc. If one wishes to extract a given doctrine from the writings of the Reformers, one must do so with great wisdom, circumspectness, and self-control. One must have read and reread the material many times and have a good grasp of the coherency of their systematic theology, lest one let them say things that are directly contradictory to their own sentiments.

I only wish to say that one should never arbitrarily extract a proposition from their writings without investigating the context of their argument. One should consult them when they purposefully address a certain matter and clearly articulate their opinion, but not when here and there they remark about this matter in their account. One must also carefully consider whether their proposition expresses their own opinion and whether it is clearly and unambiguously affirmed with words that are expressly extracted from the Holy Scriptures. Otherwise, it will be no more than the opinion of that writer rather than that which the Holy Spirit teaches unto salvation. Furthermore, one must note carefully their definitions and formulations—which requires that one knows the rules—to determine whether a given matter is correctly presented as to its essence. If that is the case, an essential attribute (*attributum essentiale*) will always be mentioned that can never be disconnected from the question at hand. It is the very character of that essential attribute that the matter at hand is nonexistent without that attribute. Thus we say, "*Quo posito res ponitur, quo sublato res tollitur.*"[4] If the description of the essence is correct, we will also be able to see whether the essential difference (*differentia specifica*) between two matters is clearly demonstrated in the description. Finally, one can determine whether a matter is described from the vantage point of either its effects or consequences. Everyone should be able to do so if they so desire.

Regarding the matters we are now discussing, I believe we would not hear of conflict if someone would think about this with a genuinely humble heart and a calm and godly disposition—and if it gives him joy to walk in communion with God with a calm and stable disposition, and to live in peace with his brothers. However, how harmful to the soul and our interaction with

---

4. Translation: The matter is there if the attribute is there, and the matter does not exist if the attribute is absent.

others is that cursed pride that desires to be praised above others! It will result in inordinate conduct that God will see and punish.

By way of an example, let me clarify what I have said to show how grievously we can be mistaken by letting the Reformers say things they never intended to say. Beza, who may indeed be designated as a great Reformer, says the following in his *Confession of the Christian Faith* (*Tractationes Theoliogicae*, p. 6): "*Sed fidem appellamus*," etc.; that is, "We call faith an assured kind of knowledge that the Holy Spirit, out of mere goodness and grace, increasingly engraves upon the hearts of the elect. The result of this knowledge is that everyone in his heart, being assured of his election, applies the promise of salvation in Christ Jesus to himself." Suppose you wish to interpret these words literally as descriptive of the essence of faith. In that case, it will follow that everyone must be assured of his election before he can apply the promise of salvation to himself. Instead, in describing faith here, Beza is countering the Pelagians and papists, arguing that assurance is attainable without an immediate revelation. This is affirmed by what follows when he indicates what the foundation of this assurance is, for he says on page 10, "The presupposition here is that someone is not a believer only, but that he also knows it, and that he arrives at a knowledge of the verity and uprightness of his faith. He will arrive at this knowledge by virtue of two immediate consequences of Christ dwelling in his heart by faith. The first is the witness of God's Spirit with our spirit that we are the children of God. The other is the new man in the mortification of his sins in sanctification and good works. For if we experience these two consequences within ourselves, it most certainly follows that we have faith, and thus also that we have Jesus Christ and eternal life."

Everyone can now conclude that Beza, in this quoted definition, is not speaking of faith that unites us to Christ, but instead of the exercise of faith whereby the soul is assured of its uprightness in being united to Christ. I would be able to give similar examples from the work of Calvin and others, but then this treatise would go too far afield.

Direct and Reflexive Acts of Faith

Two matters must be distinguished regarding faith: that which is received and embraced unto justification before God's tribunal, and what must be perceived to be an acquittal in the court of one's own conscience. As to the first, faith is engaged as the mediate cause (that is, as the secondary cause) by the direct exercises of faith. As to the second, faith reflects upon itself and then perceives the proofs or evidences that the acts of faith are genuine. We thus speak of the primary or *direct* acts or exercises of faith and of the secondary or *reflexive* acts or exercises of faith.

We must now consider the question of whether assurance is inherent in faith. We resolutely respond in the affirmative. If someone were to ask what sort of assurance is inherent in faith, we would not immediately respond that all my sins are forgiven or that I am a recipient of grace, but rather, that a direct assurance is inherent in the direct acts of faith and a reflexive assurance in the reflexive acts of faith. This assurance will be proportional to one's capacity to believe (*potentia perfectibilis*)—that is, to one's being engaged to a greater or lesser degree to actually believe (*ad actum*) and to the removal of obstacles and the Spirit's illumination.

Faith's Direct Exercises

To speak with clarity regarding this matter, we will first address the direct assurance of faith by considering the object of faith, or that which we believe, and secondarily, the exercises of faith.

The Object of Faith's Direct Exercises

As to the first, we believe that differences of opinion can readily be resolved if the object of faith is clearly defined.

1. By way of negation, we will first say *what the object is not*, and thus what it is not that we believe.

It is not that one believes to be one of the elect, for we may only afterward affirm our election by the marks of grace—as the apostle does when he says that we must make our calling and election sure (2 Peter 1:10). It is also not that one believes to have been justified in the death of Christ, as the Antinomians[5] in England, the so-called Hebrews,[6] and other proponents of error in

---

5. Antinomians represent a school of thought that has exerted its influence upon the church since antiquity. Comrie is here referring to the antinomianism in England and Scotland in his days, against whom, among others, Thomas Boston and the Erskines had to defend themselves. The fundamental error of the Antinomians was that they placed such an emphasis upon justification that they rendered sanctification suspect by labeling it as legalistic zeal. Comrie articulates their thinking and objectives very effectively at the beginning of the application of the sermon recorded in chapter 3 of this book.

6. The "Hebrews" were the followers of Jacobus Verschoor (1648–1700), a more or less antinomian theologian in the Netherlands. Verschoor placed great emphasis upon

our land believe. God's Word never posits this as something that one must believe unto justification. In numerous passages, faith is described as the act whereby one takes hold of and embraces Jesus to be justified by Him. The apostle Paul taught the congregation of Ephesus that in their natural state, they were children of wrath. Thus, they were not already truly justified upon appearing before God's tribunal, for he who is justified before this tribunal will at that very moment be absolved from God's wrath and curse.

Finally, it is not that one believes that all his sins are forgiven. Christ never designates this to be the object of faith. The matter itself makes it already clear that one must not believe in the *exercise* of faith that one's sins are forgiven, but rather, that one must exercise faith *unto the forgiveness of sins*. If someone is to receive the forgiveness of sins upon being united to Christ by faith, it then follows that he must first be in Christ by faith before God can view him as righteous. He can only be righteous by the righteousness of Christ being imputed to him—a righteousness he receives by faith.

2. Positively we can maintain that generally speaking, all that God has revealed in His Word is *the object of the direct exercises of faith*. This is true for both law and gospel, for faith believes the comprehensive revelation of God's will as articulated in the canonical books of the Old and New Testaments.

More explicitly, we may say that the object of faith and that which we believe is the description of the state to which we have been subjected by the fall and willful disobedience of our first parents. On the one hand, the soul will thereby be convinced of her hell-worthy state before God and will be truly contrite and humbled due to her guilt and impotence to deliver herself. She will thus have learned to look away from everything. On the other hand, she will have been made willing to give ear to the proclamation of a way in which all God's attributes are magnified in the saving of a sinner apart from any good work in herself and solely by virtue of sovereign and unmerited grace.

---

justification by faith. He went so far in his thinking that he believed that the elect, by virtue of Christ's sacrifice, came into the world as already having been acquitted (sealed by baptism), albeit that they would still have to believe and be born again. Peculiarly, Verschoor believed that one could rationally arrive at such a conclusion. He therefore believed faith to be exempt from strife and doubt. Verschoor and his followers arrived at steadfast assurance that had rationalistic overtones. His followers were called "Hebrews," for Verschoor deemed the study of the Bible's original languages, and particularly the study of Hebrew, to be of paramount importance.

That which one believes also encompasses a more or less clear revelation of God's way of grace in the heart of the deeply humbled sinner—the way that has been conceived in eternity and in which Jesus Christ, in time and by His active and passive obedience, has merited the gracious favor of God and the forgiveness of sins.

A primary aspect of what one believes is that God in His Word and in the proclamation of the gospel to all who hear it, offers all these benefits—and thus this Christ and all that He has merited. For He proclaims to them and assures them that no one shall ever be rejected who agrees with God and this way of salvation, thereby casting away everything of himself as filthy garments and thus coming to His Son to receive Him unto "wisdom, and righteousness, and sanctification, and redemption" (1 Cor. 1:30).

For me, it is beyond the shadow of a doubt that all who carefully compare the declarations of Christ and the apostles will observe that these matters will always be set forth in connection with the object of faith as to its essential exercises—that is, as it is actively engaged to secure the justification of the sinner before the judgment seat of God. However, to my knowledge, the Word of God never posits the direct object of justifying faith to be that I must believe that all my sins have been forgiven, but rather, that they who believe in Jesus have been forgiven of their sins. Why should we wish to be wiser than the Holy Spirit?

The Direct Acts of Faith

The essential or immediate acts of faith that encompass assurance in conformity to the free offer of grace are the following:

1. One will be fully convinced of these divine truths as such that the free offer of grace is intended not only for others but also for himself. This will be facilitated by the conviction of the veracity of the truth of this doctrine and also because the Holy Spirit confirms and seals these matters to the heart of an utterly helpless sinner. The pressing concerns of such a soul will then be fully resolved by God's light arising in the soul. The Heidelberg Catechism also wishes to affirm this in Lord's Day 7, for the word "given" (HC 21) can only be interpreted to mean *offered*. Thus, in the offer, something is granted. If someone meant to say that he *has* the forgiveness of sins by way of the exercise of faith, he would never use the word *given*. Instead, he would speak of *having* or *actually possessing*. For the word *given* merely means that something is being offered to me, whereas *having* or *possessing* implies and presupposes

my actual acceptance even before I possess that which is being offered. If this is the assurance one wishes to ascertain, I am certain that no one will ever challenge it. I truly believe that the Heidelberg Catechism describes this assurance. I also believe that no one will arrive at a believing reception of Jesus, thereby casting himself upon Him for time and eternity, without having been assured within his heart by the Holy Spirit that Jesus Christ is not only being offered to others, but also to him. You will thus observe that we presuppose rather than exclude these preceding acts of the soul. In the meantime, when one speaks of the uniting act of faith, you will observe that the certainty of the offer by its very nature precedes this uniting act of faith, for only that certainty will give the soul liberty to engage in this act of faith.

2. The second act or exercise of faith is the cherishing of a most intimate love and profound respect for this offered Jesus. So to speak, such love is born in the soul upon this initial exercise of faith and proceeds from the very nature and essence of faith. For as soon as the soul gets a sight of Jesus in His suitability and all-sufficiency, and thereby, through the operation of the Holy Spirit, is assured that He is given to her in the offer of grace so that she might receive Him, the entire soul will be fully persuaded with mind, will, and affections to choose Him. She will desire to have such a Savior and hunger and thirst after Him, and passionately yearn to be most intimately united to Him. The soul will do so more than watchers "that wait for the morning" (Ps. 130:6), and more than a "hart panteth after the water brooks" (Ps. 42:1). You will thus observe how these exercises of faith issue forth from the matter itself. This will enable you to affirm the sequential order of all the exercises of faith as we have expounded them in *The ABC of Faith*.

3. Following the exercises of faith as mentioned above will be the wholehearted reception [acceptance], embracing, and appropriation of the complete Christ as He is offered in the gospel. In so doing, the soul will truly be united to Him and will lose herself in Him.

    a. This reception or acceptance occurs first of all in a very tender and heartfelt manner. It issues forth from the soul seeing her absolute need of Jesus as suitable for one who in himself is deeply humbled and condemned. That believing reception will only occur after a helpless and fervent thirsting after Him. Nothing can suitably express its tenderness, fervency, and emotion. There will be a far greater fervency than when two lovers who, by virtue of their union, embrace each other when they come together again after a period of absence. Scripture says that Jesus and the soul thereby become as one spirit, for "he that is joined unto the Lord is one spirit" (1 Cor. 6:17).

b. It is also a reception or acceptance of the entire Jesus, without any exception, for the sinner perceives that he needs Him in every aspect of His person. Everything about Jesus will therefore be equally precious and desirable. Thus, the sinner will receive or accept Him with a most heartfelt fervency unto "wisdom, and righteousness, and sanctification, and redemption" (1 Cor. 1:30).

c. Furthermore, it will be an acceptance with the entire soul and all her faculties. Each faculty of the soul will be engaged as to its unique nature and function. This is entirely consistent with God's intent and the nature of things.

d. Finally, it is an acceptance of what God offers the sinner—and thus not only to others but also to *him*. Therefore, the soul will receive or accept Jesus in a most personal manner and truly appropriate Him with all His benefits, doing so for the duration of this life and for eternity. This is the sinner's personal appropriation, and that appropriation must necessarily be so in response to the offer being made by the Lord not only to others but also to *him*.

4. This appropriating act of faith is followed by a resting in Jesus—a trusting in and reliance upon Him for time and eternity since He is mighty and willing to bring the matter to full fruition. Consider only how entirely consistent this is with article 22 of the Belgic Confession.[7]

Regarding these direct acts of faith, you will observe that the immediate focus is not so much upon one's state before God—and thus whether I am a recipient of grace. Rather, the soul has direct dealings with the Surety to be found in Him. If someone, while thus engaged, also manages to reflect on the act of faith itself, let him take no offense if another person, who at that moment is engaged in actual and direct exercises of faith, will not take the

---

7. Belgic Confession, Article 22: "We believe that, to attain the true knowledge of this great mystery, the Holy Ghost kindleth in our hearts an upright faith, which embraces Jesus Christ with all His merits, appropriates Him, and seeks nothing more besides Him. For it must needs follow, either that all things which are requisite to our salvation are not in Jesus Christ, or if all things are in Him, that then those who possess Jesus Christ through faith have complete salvation in Him."

time to analyze everything and ask himself whether his sins are forgiven and whether he is a child of God.

You will perceive that the one act of faith, consistent with its inherent nature, will follow upon the other. We do not wish to stipulate a specific time frame, for the Bible also does not specify this. Experience teaches us that the one person experiences these acts of faith in rapid succession, whereas the other person experiences them gradually and is, so to speak, led step by step. If, therefore, God has been so good to you that you were privileged to receive all of this within a short period, then do not look down upon someone else, for God deals with us according to His wise counsel.

From what has been stated thus far, you can conclude how the soul in this way draws near to God with full assurance. We do not wish to repeat ourselves but merely state that we have a beautiful description of this in question and answer 117 of the Heidelberg Catechism. The question is, "What are the requisites of that prayer, which is acceptable to God, and which He will hear?" The answer is, "First, that we from the heart pray to the one true God only, who hath manifested himself in his Word, for all things, he hath commanded us to ask of him; secondly, that we rightly and thoroughly know our need and misery, that so we may deeply humble ourselves in the presence of his divine majesty; thirdly, that we be fully persuaded that he, notwithstanding that we are unworthy of it, will, for the sake of Christ our Lord, certainly hear our prayer, as he has promised us in His word."

Faith's Reflexive Exercises

Having spoken of the immediate and direct acts of faith and the assurance of faith associated with them, we will now address reflexive assurance. Thus, we will speak of the soul's assurance of faith resulting from the reflexive or intrinsic acts of faith. To enable us to speak of this, we must first have some clarity regarding the object of faith: the matters on which faith focuses, and subsequently on the acts of faith.

The Object of Faith's Reflexive Exercises

As to the object of this reflexive assurance of faith, we note that this is not the truth of the gospel and its inherent offer of Christ—an offer which God's Spirit reveals and applies marvelously to the soul, enabling her simultaneously to accept this offer with convincing certainty and as specifically applied to herself. No, as we have already seen, this is the focal point of assurance that issues forth directly from faith itself. Instead, the focal point of this reflexive assurance is one's state of grace, that is, that one is a child of God and that all his sins are forgiven him.

Much could be said regarding this, and, therefore, take note of the following. In the way of deep conviction, wrought by the Holy Spirit, the soul must be uncovered before God and be thoroughly convinced of her sinful and wretched state before Him. If the soul does not perceive this with some clarity, she will very rarely be assured of her state before God despite the grace she may possess.

I have always stated three important reasons why a soul will remain uncertain of her portion in Christ. A concerned soul will ask herself (1) whether the conviction of her sin and misery has been deep enough; (2) whether in surrendering herself to all that is encompassed in the covenant of grace she truly has experienced the tokens of God's love in her heart, and (3) whether her faith has indeed brought forth good fruits.

The sinner must therefore experience that his sins have been fully exposed, that he has genuinely grieved over them, that he has become thoroughly acquainted with his misery—and finally, that he has been cut off from everything so that as a poor sinner, with the noose around his neck, he will supplicate for the unmerited remission of his guilt.

The soul must truly and most intimately be united to Jesus Christ by an upright and unfeigned faith. This is one of the most important elements that necessarily belongs to the state of grace. Apart from this union, there can be no justification, for when the judicial acquittal is granted, the soul will be viewed as she is by faith in Christ and thus clothed with His righteousness. Furthermore, apart from union with Christ, a person cannot perform a single good deed in a manner that pleases God. Every branch must first be in the vine, and only after that will there be the bearing of fruit. And indeed, "whatsoever is not of faith is sin" (Rom. 14:23). We can, therefore, conclude that "without faith it is impossible to please [God]" (Heb. 11:6). If, therefore, one is to be assured of being truly a partaker of divine grace, one must be able to perceive that he belongs to Another by virtue of an upright and unconditional surrender of himself to the Lord Jesus and that this surrender has forged a true bond between Jesus and the soul. Paul saw this clearly when he described the certainty of his state before God, saying, "I live; yet not I, but Christ liveth in me" (Gal. 2:20).

Before the judgment seat of God, the soul, standing before the supremely righteous Judge of heaven and earth, must have been acquitted of the guilt of her sin and thus have been admitted to the number of God's people. Darkness regarding this manner will result in darkness regarding everything else. However, clarity regarding this matter will give the soul liberty before God and cause these words to be fulfilled, "Therefore being justified by faith, we have peace with God through our Lord Jesus Christ" (Rom. 5:1).

Finally, the soul must manifest the authentic marks of God's children and of a true faith. The matters mentioned above are particularly precious when they may be discerned. However, it can also happen—and experience confirms this—that these marks often cannot be ascertained except by way of a conclusion drawn from the distinctive marks of faith. Therefore, we add this point as a matter of utmost necessity. If, indeed, we may conclude "that we have passed from death unto life, because we love the brethren" (1 John 3:14), we can also know from the true and infallible marks of grace that we believe and are in Christ and that by virtue of His righteousness we have been acquitted when we stood before the judgment seat of God.

The Reflexive Acts of Faith
We shall now consider the reflexive acts of faith whereby a person may conclude that it is well regarding his state before God.

First, we wish to clarify that one cannot arrive at this conclusion employing pure intellectual reasoning—such as is asserted by some theologians who attribute too much to the intellect. It is indeed true that the primary or major premise is clearly articulated in God's Word and the lesser or minor premise in the heart. Nevertheless, we believe that a special work of the Holy Spirit is needed to enable one to draw a conclusion for himself. For example, one who hungers and thirsts after righteousness shall be saved. That is the major premise as stated in God's Word. The soul dares not deny that she does this, and that is the minor premise to be found in the heart. Yet, the soul is entirely incapable of concluding this and of having the courage to say, "I shall be saved." However, if she does so, she will learn by spiritual experience that this conclusion can neither overcome her fear and doubt nor yield for her a quiet assurance. Thus, it is true what Paul teaches us in Romans 8:16, "The Spirit itself beareth witness with our spirit, that we are the children of God."

Second, one will be assured of his portion in Christ by reflexive and inwardly oriented acts of faith. As the eye of the soul, faith will be affirmed, notified, and arrested by earlier or present spiritual experiences of God's favor toward her and being exercised thereby. That will render the soul receptive and fit for the matters we will subsequently address. Without such experiences, the soul will always remain as a tumultuous sea.

Faith observes the essential acts in her own activities whereby the soul has taken hold of Christ, or is presently taking hold of Him, and will detect these acts and their fruits within herself.

Faith will behold God's own stamp of approval imprinted upon all that is transpiring, for if grace may be observed by divine illumination, the soul will perceive this to be the very work of God and not as something proceeding from her own heart.

Faith will perceive this as God's work without the soul having to condemn herself and without powerful inner whisperings demanding one to "have lived in all good conscience before God" (Acts 23:1).

Faith will thereby fill the heart with inner happiness and joy so that everything affirms that this assurance may be present by the soul being inwardly persuaded by the Spirit. To that end, He will use the reflexive acts of faith so that one may believe to be truly a child of God and that one will assuredly arrive in eternal glory. This will set the soul at liberty and cause her to be full of joy because she may now know whom she has believed (2 Tim. 1:12).

The acts of faith in approaching the throne of grace in the full assurance of one's being in Christ are, among others, the following:

1. The soul will then not approach God in a general sense, but rather, as her own God and Father in Christ Jesus by virtue of His covenant and one's surrender to the Mediator of the covenant. Viewing God as *her* God will deliver the soul from fearful anxiety in her approach to Him. Thereby she may already, from a distance, perceive expressions of her Father's love and be assured of His love and willingness to help her. This will stimulate the soul and give her a great desire and intense yearning to be embraced by both of His arms—arms that are full of mercy and compassion. This cord of love has such a strong pull that the soul will not merely engage herself, but she will also walk rapidly toward Him as a child does to his father.

2. With such assurance, the soul will approach God with the heart of a child. She will then call upon God not as a servant exclaims "lord" or "master," but rather, as a child that continually cries out to its father, saying, "Abba, Father." God delights in hearing this, and therefore He promises repeatedly that the

soul may say, "Thou art my God." That will engender much believing trust in the heart.

3. With this assurance, the soul will approach God to ask Him reverently and believingly to fulfill His divine promise. This, in turn, will prompt the soul to plead upon this promise and be exercised with God's covenant.

4. With this assurance, the soul will approach God with the believing expectation that she will be helped and receive grace for grace, for it is an absolute certainty that her prayer "is more assuredly heard of God, than [she] feel[s] in [her] heart that [she] desire[s] these things of Him."[8]

Differences Between Direct and Reflexive Acts of Faith
Having spoken of these things according to our small measure of light, we will now submit the matter to your judgment. However, before we conclude our discussion, we will, for the sake of further self-examination, point out several differences between the direct and reflexive acts of faith so that some things may be better understood.

First, it must be noted that the direct and extrinsic acts of faith, and the immediate assurance of faith affiliated with them, precede the reflexive or intrinsic acts of faith, for the latter presuppose the former. We are thereby saying that the extrinsic act of faith, as to the nature of the acts of faith, has preeminence, although this is not always true chronologically. In His infinite goodness, God can grant to this or that person both acts of faith simultaneously, so that by virtue of a direct and extrinsic act of faith, they unite themselves to Christ while simultaneously experiencing powerfully in their soul the reflexive act of faith. They will then know at the same moment that by faith they are united to Christ and reconciled with God, and will also have the assurance in their souls that all their sins are forgiven them "as if we had in our own persons suffered and made satisfaction for our sins to God" (HC 79). Since some people experience both acts of faith simultaneously, they arrive at the erroneous conclusion that they are merely one and the same act. They will then measure God's way and leading regarding saving faith by their experience—something that regrettably suits us well.

---

8. Heidelberg Catechism 129.

But no, beloved, the direct, intrinsic act of faith precedes, and the reflexive act follows if it pleases God to grant this, for we may not impose limitations upon the Almighty.

Second, we must posit that the primary act of faith is requisite unto salvation, for only he shall be saved who is acquitted before the judgment seat of God and receives a right to eternal life between the cradle and the grave. And no one will be justified except he who is in Christ and is united to Him. From the side of the sinner, this union takes place by a true saving faith that engages itself directly in response to God's call by embracing Jesus and rests in Him unto salvation as He is offered in the gospel. However, the reflexive act of faith is not requisite unto salvation in the absolute sense of the word, but rather, is needed to have a joyous consciousness of that salvation, for no one will be saved by believing that he is in Christ. One will only be saved by being ingrafted into Christ, as a consequence of which he may be in Jesus. Being in Christ is inseparably connected with salvation.

Third, we maintain that the initial and direct act of faith will always be inherent in faith itself to a greater or lesser degree, whereas the secondary or reflexive act of faith can be lacking for a long time. This is confirmed by God's Word and the spiritual experience of the saints.

The Testimony of the Westminster Confession
These truths have been beautifully formulated in the confession and (larger) catechism of the Scottish church. As to their doctrinal purity, these standards do not have to yield one inch to the standards of any other church on the face of the earth! We will quote a portion, not to prove something, but rather to affirm our complete agreement.

> 1. Although hypocrites and other unregenerate men may vainly deceive themselves with false hopes and carnal presumptions of being in the favor of God, and estate of salvation (Job 8:13; Mic. 3:11; Deut. 29:19; John 8:41) (which hope of theirs shall perish [Matt. 7:22–23]): yet such as truly believe in the Lord Jesus, and love Him in sincerity, endeavoring to walk in all good conscience before Him, may, in this life, be certainly assured that they are in the state of grace (1 John 2:3; 3:14, 18–19, 21, 24; 5:13), and may rejoice in the hope of the glory of God, which hope shall never make them ashamed (Rom. 5:2, 5).

> 2. This certainty is not a bare conjectural and probable persuasion grounded upon a fallible hope (Heb. 6:11, 19); but an infallible assurance of faith founded upon the divine truth of the promises of salvation (Heb.

6:17–18), the inward evidence of those graces unto which these promises are made (2 Peter 1:4–5, 10–11), the testimony of the Spirit of adoption witnessing with our spirits that we are the children of God (Rom. 8:15–16), which Spirit is the earnest of our inheritance, whereby we are sealed to the day of redemption (Eph. 1:13–14; 4:30; 2 Cor. 1:21–22).

3. This infallible assurance [this reflexive salvation—A.C.] doth not so belong to the essence of faith, but that a true believer may wait long, and conflict with many difficulties before he be partaker of it (1 John 5:13; Isa. 50:10; Mark 9:24; Pss. 77:1–12; 88): yet, being enabled by the Spirit to know the things which are freely given him of God, he may, without extraordinary revelation, in the right use of ordinary means, attain thereunto (1 Cor. 2:12; 1 John 4:13; Heb. 6:11–12; Eph. 3:17–19). And therefore it is the duty of everyone to give all diligence to make his calling and election sure (2 Peter 1:10), that thereby his heart may be enlarged in peace and joy in the Holy Ghost, in love and thankfulness to God, and in strength and cheerfulness in the duties of obedience, the proper fruits of this assurance (Rom. 5:1–2, 5; 14:17; 15:13; Eph. 1:3–4; Pss. 4:7–8; 119:32); so far is it from inclining men to looseness (1 John 2:1–2; Rom. 6:1–2; Titus 2:11–12, 14; 2 Cor. 7:1; Rom. 8:1, 12; 1 John 3:2–3; Ps. 130:4; 1 John 1:6–7).[9]

We may thus observe how the Westminster General Assembly dealt with these matters in the year 1645.[10] Hopefully, no one will counter this, for every statement is supported by the Word of God.

THE REQUISITES TO DRAW NEAR

We will proceed to consider two matters that are requisite for a drawing near with a true heart in full assurance of faith, namely, "having our hearts sprinkled from an evil conscience, and our bodies washed with pure water."[11] Since, however, this treatise has already become very lengthy, we will now proceed with brevity. Thus, there are two requisites for drawing near.

---

9. Chapter 18 of the Westminster Confession has four paragraphs. Comrie did not include the fourth paragraph, as it was not as pertinent to his argument.

10. December 4, 1646, marked the completion of the Westminster Confession, and it was published in May 1647.

11. After his extended discussion of the doctrine of assurance, Comrie now returns to the exposition of Heb. 10:22.

The Sprinkling of the Heart

First, the heart must be sprinkled from an evil conscience.

An Evil Conscience

We will therefore address several distinct matters to show you what an evil conscience consists of. To do so, beloved, we must recognize that the conscience is a capacity planted into the soul by God whereby we have a conscious knowledge of all the deeds we have committed. As God's "regent" and "viceroy," the conscience accuses of that which is evil and absolves regarding that which is good. The conscience in and of itself is not evil. However, since it has been corrupted by sin, as is true for all the soul's faculties, it is called an evil conscience. This pertains to us as human beings in a twofold way.

An Accusing Conscience before God

It is an *evil* conscience insofar as it troubles and accuses man due to having sinned against the Most High Majesty of God. In His adorable goodness, God can sometimes—and yes, frequently—use it as a means to confront His elect with themselves, to recognize the absolute necessity of a Surety, and to prompt the soul to cry out, "What must I do to be saved?" We observe this with the jailor and those who came to conversion on the day of Pentecost. Nevertheless, the conscience functions as such merely as a consequence of committed sin and as a just punishment upon it. Thus, the conscience already manifests some traits of hell—some of which we will now mention.

1. The conscience *vividly depicts the God-dishonoring and despicable nature of sin* before the eyes of the soul, thus rendering the sinner worthy of death and damnation. It will display sin as a painting to be observed and, therefore, will bring sin very near to the soul. The weight of sin will then become a heavy burden to be borne by the soul and under which she must be bowed down.

2. The conscience *will speak loudly and clearly and pronounce the threatened curses so ominously that it will cause fear, and utter distress.*

3. The conscience is as a continually gnawing worm, for it *continually demands restitution as well as the vindication of God's honor which one has so grievously impugned.* There will be nothing one can use to counter this legal indictment, or that could be considered a form of restitution. Thus, as to committed sins, the conscience will be, as we have shown, an evil conscience. The blood of sacrificial animals could neither cleanse nor purify the conscience, for those

offering the sacrifices would retain a conscience that in one way or another would yet be contaminated by sin in light of the handwriting that was against them (Col. 2:14).

A Malfunctioning Conscience

However, an evil conscience is also a conscience that does not function correctly, either being deficient in executing its task or being entirely in error.

1. That being the case, we speak of *a sleeping conscience* that resides in man as a silent dog that does not bark and leaves man alone, enabling him to walk according to the imagination of his own heart. He will always be actively sinning, and his heart will be filled with dreams, vain imaginations, and sinful fantasies. He will feed on ashes and will have so deceitfully seduced his heart that he will be incapable of either seeing or saying that he has a lie in his right hand and a seductive heart that leads him astray (cf. Isa. 44:20).

2. One can also have *a misleading conscience* that will impose obligations on a person and demand rigorous obedience of that to which God does not at all obligate us in His Word. Or it will either obscure essential duties that are requisite for the service of God or draw erroneous conclusions from what God's Word teaches us.

3. One can also have *a seared conscience* that has been silenced either by sin having become so commonplace or as a result of God's righteous judgment.

4. Finally, one can also have *a conscience that is too particular or scrupulous*. One would encounter this primarily in the early church, and presently with recent converts who will condemn the least little thing, are very strict about what they eat or how they dress, and various other things.

The Sprinkling of the Heart from an Evil Conscience

The heart, that is, the soul, must be sprinkled or cleansed regarding this. Such cleansing can only be achieved by the blood of Jesus Christ which is received by faith and applied to the conscience. The conscience will then be cleansed from dead works, thus enabling a man to serve the living God, for the blood of Jesus Christ does indeed cleanse from all sins! This cleansing of the conscience by the blood of Jesus Christ was already depicted during the Old Testament era. Since, however, in the New Testament era, the type has been replaced by the matter itself, this must also be experienced in the lives of all who as spiritual priests draw near unto God by Christ as the only High Priest.

The Washing of the Body

The second requirement is the cleansing of the body with pure water. My beloved, you know that the ceremonial law prescribed many purifications that depicted the cleansing of believers. Rather than addressing this or quoting the exposition of others, we concur with various other writers that we must view the washing mentioned in our text as referring to one's outward walk. When we draw near to God, both the inward cleansing of the heart and the external cleansing of our walk are requisite. Our entire person must be cleansed and washed in the blood of Jesus Christ.

APPLICATION

Behold, beloved, I have in some measure set before you what is indeed required and what the proper disposition of the soul must be to draw near to God. Though our treatise has become somewhat more elaborate than we are accustomed to, the weightiness of the matter required this. In our application, we will therefore be a bit briefer.

Conviction for the Unconverted

The preaching of the Word must convince the unconverted how bereft they are of these spiritual exercises and how insufficient and fruitless the performance of all their duties and spiritual activities are.

The Lack of These Spiritual Exercises

Let us avail ourselves of the preached Word to be convinced and to show how many are strangers of the truth of our text. My beloved, though we believe that you excel many others as to your religious disposition, you must nevertheless know that your religious activities are meaningless if they come short of the requisites as mentioned above and without the necessary disposition of the heart. Let us now consider whether we have both.

No Desire for Cleansing
As to the requisites for drawing near, we must say that there are but few who seek to have their "hearts sprinkled from an evil conscience" and to have their "bodies washed with pure water."

Most people are spiritually sick or slumbering and insensitive to their guilt—a guilt they increase daily with a measure that exceeds the sand of the seashore. My beloved, as long as you have an evil conscience that slumbers and does not accuse you, you will never draw near to God in true sincerity. Consequently, all exhortations and admonitions will be without effect.

Most people will sustain themselves with superficial thoughts and imaginations, even though they do not have the slightest ground to live quietly and peacefully.

There are many, having spent their entire day irreverently and carelessly, who draw near to God in prayer without careful reflection or meditation. Thus, they do so without first preparing their hearts and having any impression of their guilt.

Some people are more serious about this than others who yet do not get beyond their own conceit in which they manufacture some distress and emotion about their life not conforming to the will of God. However, this does not issue forth in a genuine appropriation of the blood of Jesus that He shed as Surety, and thus they do not traverse this new and living way to draw near to God.

No Disposition to Draw Near to God

Considering the duty itself and the disposition of the heart with which one engages in this duty, we must conclude that its practice is inexpressibly deficient and lacks conviction.

Most people do not know the God to whom they draw near; they are blind, and their understanding is darkened. And if they know anything about God, it will only be what they have heard of Him rather than by the true illumination of the Spirit. Therefore, the inscription of the Athenian temple may also be stamped upon all their religious duties: "TO THE UNKNOWN GOD" (Acts 17:23). What irreverence, sluggishness, and listlessness this generates so that one is satisfied with a religious routine! There is no impression of God's majesty upon the heart, and one can also not detect any reverence or stirring in response to His majesty.

Most people do not long for the blowing of the wind of the Spirit, that is, for His influences to invigorate their prayers which causes them to yearn with inexpressible groanings after God and stirs them up to be exercised with it. They also do not perceive this to be a deficiency, for they are satisfied when the progression of their argumentation flows well or when a sufficient number of Bible texts come to mind. They are neither accustomed to being beggars nor do they know what it means to be dependent upon external influences. In all that they do, they are governed by what proceeds from within, whereas the influences of the Spirit, being as wind in the sails, are required to bring a soul, through Christ, unto God.

How many there are whose heart is not upright, but rather, duplicitous and insincere! Many who make a great impression by their external appearance and demeanor have a heart that is as cold as a rock. Others cry with their lips for the mortification of sin while their hearts are unwilling. With their mouths, so to speak, they vomit things out while with their hearts and inner inclinations, they lick up what they have vomited out. They continue to live with a heart that cherishes sin. And again, others are neither serious nor persevering. They can easily submit to having to wait for the manifestation of grace and are satisfied with it. The latter is a sign, however, that they are not really interested.

What lack of faith there is! And yet, everyone that comes to God must believe that He is (Heb. 11:6). And we also know that "he that wavereth [doubts] is like a wave of the sea" (James 1:6). Such people will receive nothing, for God will only hear and answer those prayers uttered by faith in the name of Christ.

The Futility of Such Religion

My beloved, the religion of one who lacks these matters is vain and however earnest and zealous he may be, God will be displeased with it. It is no better than the practice of pagan morality whose best efforts and virtues are but as splendid sins since they are neither done by faith in Christ, nor through Christ, nor focused upon Christ. If only you would become weary of your laborious efforts so that you would cease and desist, saying, "In this way, it is without hope!" And may God then move you and truly incline your heart to make you willing to surrender to the righteousness of Jesus as a poor and needy one.

An Exhortation for God's Children

Children and beloved of God, this exhortation is primarily intended for you. You are living under the better and much clearer administration of God's covenant of grace. The veil has been rent. A new and living way has been opened through the blood of Christ, our only High Priest. Thereby you may draw near to God who is fully well-pleased with His Son "that we may obtain mercy, and find grace to help in time of need" (Heb. 4:16). How this should prompt you to draw near to God in conformity to the apostle's exhortation in our text; that is, "with a true heart in full assurance of faith, having our hearts sprinkled from an evil conscience, and our bodies washed with pure water" (Heb. 10:22). I know not only that you desire to do so but also that you complain about your deficiencies and that you recognize your absolute impotence to come as such. Permit me, therefore, to remove some of your obstacles regarding this and speak a word of exhortation.

Objections Refuted
Upon hearing all of this, true believers will undoubtedly respond with many and various concerns and make mention of heart issues that they cannot possibly resolve.

The Deceitfulness of the Heart
Among them, there may be those who say, "I have listened to the description of an upright heart, and also to what is found in an upright heart. How sad is my condition, and how far I am from what I ought to be! If I were to describe my heart, I would not know of a better description than the one given by Jeremiah in chapter 17:9, 'The heart is deceitful above all things, and desperately wicked: who can know it?' Thus, I do not even begin to approximate the disposition of heart whereby I can draw near to God with a true heart." My beloved, though it is good that you perceive your deficiency, you should therefore not deny the truth of the matter that is to be found in you.

1. Are you conscious of the deceitfulness of your heart, and does that weigh you down? That is a trustworthy sign that you have an upright or true heart, for temporal believers will never perceive the heart's depths of deceit and its ulterior motives. And when their conscience sheds some light on this, it will not trouble them, and they will not be bowed down by the fact that they feel like they actually have two hearts. It will not cause them to cry out in secret, with continual groaning, "Oh God, I am double-minded. 'Unite my heart to fear thy name'" (Ps. 86:11).

2. Does your heart truly concur with all that it must do toward God, and is it opposed to every sin? If that is the case, you may believe that your heart is upright irrespective of the sinful deficiencies in your walk. Every insincere

heart has some sins to which it continues to be knit, and it will habitually neglect to perform certain duties.

3. Is it not your desire to live your life more in secret than to appear in public and be seen of others? Oh, that is also a sign that you are upright, for they who are not upright want to appear to others more than they actually are. Their intent is to be seen of men as worthy of fame, honor, and praise. However, your words and all by which you manifest yourself are less than you truly do experience. Instead, you are afraid that others will think more of you than you really are.

No Perception of Assurance

Others will say, "How will it benefit me to be sincere and upright if it does not proceed from faith? This is indeed the crux of the matter. We are concerned about having this full assurance, for we do not sense it at all in our spiritual exercises." But, my beloved, such a notion can result from ignorance as to the nature of assurance, for you are not paying attention to the distinction we have just made. You are confusing matters that are distinct as to the essence, object, deeds, and fruits of faith. We only wish to say with this that you must meditate on all that we have said thus far, and you will then probably recognize that you have more assurance than you think you have. For the assurance of faith is, in essence, not being assured of one's state of grace. Rather, it is an assurance wrought by the Spirit regarding the offer of Jesus in the heart whereby the soul engages in the true exercise of those direct acts of faith of which we have written. If you consider this carefully, you will observe that you truly have engaged and still engage in such acts. If time would permit me, regarding each of the four enumerated acts of faith, we could illustrate their distinctive marks by way of their fruits.

Uncertainty about How to Draw Near

Another person may say, "Oh, my heart has such a longing for this drawing near by faith. But how shall I proceed as such?" We respond that this is the work of God whereby faith works efficaciously in your soul. Though many people want to force themselves into this way, God Himself places His children upon this pathway. Having said that, the following matters could be to their blessed benefit.

Meditate much on the offer of grace that is made to you so generously, unconditionally, and sincerely. The greatest confusion regarding the act of drawing near proceeds from a serious misunderstanding regarding the offer of Jesus. When you hear the offer being made in the gospel, then do not ask yourself, Am I the person for whom this is intended? Do I have a suitable spiritual frame of mind? Am I capable of embracing this offered salvation? However suitable such questions may appear to you and however good your point of reference may appear to be, you will experience that the light of the gospel which you may enjoy in some measure will be obscured, and your heart will be reluctant to entrust itself to Jesus. Instead, seek to believe the Word of God without asking your heart various questions. Then what happened to the man who stretched forth his paralyzed arm to Christ may happen to you.

Oh, how good it is when we attempt to do so! Endeavor often to engage in the receptive act of faith, and assurance will naturally issue forth without any exertion. Many upright souls are often going about this in the wrong way. They wish to ascertain first whether their state before God is good, and only then will they embrace an offered Jesus. However, at that place they will not arrive. At one time they have more courage, and at another time they are more doubtful—all contingent upon their assessment of their state before God. Oh, how you are to be pitied that you so rob yourself of light and are roaming about in a desert place and that while the door and entrance to a land overflowing with milk and honey is open to whoever desires to come! And indeed, if you were to receive Jesus upon His offer to you, then this Sun of Righteousness would illuminate your heart to see what God has bestowed upon you; and that would warm your soul and cause you to melt within.

Assurance Fading Away

Someone else may say, "I know that in former days I had this assurance, but it has now faded. The most that I still have is a faint memory of it. What must I do to regain it?" My response: If your question expresses a heartfelt longing for your former enjoyment, you need to realize that you will not experience it with that intensity after having been on the way for some time. That is reserved for young believers. Perhaps there is also a specific sin that has brought you into spiritual darkness. Do your utmost to acknowledge this sin and to be humbled accordingly. With David, cry out prayerfully whether God will cause you to taste the joy of His salvation and endeavor to obtain those things of which we have just spoken. God's light may then possibly arise in your soul.

Closing Exhortation

Finally, a word of admonition. Since you have such a High Priest (Heb. 8:1), we urge you to draw near to Him. However, since you are inclined to do so, we say, "Oh, how this way is to the glory of God! For this way is secure—a way upon which a fool cannot go astray. How advantageous this way is for you! All that you are seeking shall be given to you, for you are drawing near to a Father who is well pleased with His Son."

May God grant to you and me that we may often draw near to the God of the covenant in this prescribed way to receive out of His fullness grace for grace. Amen.

CHAPTER 10

Faith, a Grace That Will Be Sealed

In whom ye also trusted, after that ye heard the word of truth, the gospel of your salvation: in whom also after that ye believed, ye were sealed with that holy Spirit of promise.
—EPHESIANS 1:13

Just as there is an inner transaction between the Lord and His people, there is likewise an inner affirmation of this transaction. There is a transaction between the Lord and His people that is reciprocal. God initiates this by visiting them, inclining their hearts to enter into a spiritual betrothal with Jesus, His Son. The Lord will then so overpower the soul that she can no longer decline this delightful offer. She will be made willing in the day of His power (Ps. 110:3) to surrender herself truly and fully to the Lord Jesus and to be united to Him (Hos. 2:18–19). An affirmation of this transaction will follow, for the Lord says, "I am delighted that you have chosen my Son, and I have, therefore, heard your supplications. You are now to Me a beloved child, and I will surely be merciful to you. You may be assured of this, and I will affirm this with My seal."

In our text, the apostle highlights this when he says, "In whom also after that ye believed, ye were sealed." In verse 3, the apostle has shown that the Ephesian believers had been blessed "with all spiritual blessings in heavenly places in Christ." He then proceeds to mention each of these blessings individually, among which is that they have been sealed—by no means the least blessing.

Two matters are addressed in our text:

1. The exercise of the Ephesians: they believed.
2. That which followed this exercise: they were sealed etc.

THE EXERCISE OF BELIEVING

First, the apostle highlights the most excellent exercise of these Ephesians, namely, that they had believed. *Faith* can be understood in a twofold manner.

Faith as Assent to the Gospel

To believe is when one assents to the divine gospel, the glad tidings of the doctrine of salvation, as the most definitive truth and joyous tiding a poor sinner will ever be able to hear. From this vantage point, we speak of faith when one "hath received [God's] testimony [and] hath set to his seal that God is true" (John 3:33). One thereby confesses that "this is a faithful saying, and worthy of all acceptation, that Christ Jesus came into the world to save sinners; of whom I am chief" (1 Tim. 1:15). It is beyond doubt that many in the city of Ephesus had exercised such faith. As God's ambassador, Paul had indeed labored extensively to experientially acquaint the citizens of Ephesus with their state of misery by nature. We read of this in the second chapter, where he says to them that they "were by nature the children of wrath" (Eph. 2:3). Due to Adam's transgression, they were therefore guilty of sins imputed to them and that clave to them inwardly. They had thus been as sinners worthy of wrath. Yes, along with all Gentiles, they "were without Christ…having no hope, and without God in the world" (Eph. 2:12).

However, it must be noted that Paul, having stricken their hearts with this message regarding their misery, also unveiled to them the essential contents of the gospel of Christ. That gospel proclaims the day of God's good pleasure, a free pardon for rebels, and the forgiveness of sins offered to all—however great their sins would be, even if they were fornicators, mockers, drunkards, and publicans—who in response to God's call and His offer of grace come to Him in and through Christ. As an affirmation that many thus believed, we direct you to the first verse of our chapter. And you should also recall that Paul speaks of "a great door and effectual [having been] opened unto me" (1 Cor. 16:9) in Ephesus.

Faith as Receiving and Surrendering

Faith can also be viewed as the soul's activity that issues forth from this assent whereby the convicted sinner, responding to God's call, turns away from self and receives Jesus, surrendering himself with his entire heart and soul to Jesus to be His property for time and eternity. The Ephesians also believed in this sense, for they were saved by grace through faith. That faith did not proceed from themselves due to the proper use of their free will, but rather, as stated in Ephesians 2:8, it was God's gift.

If someone were to ask why it is said that this sealing follows upon the exercise of faith and not upon the exercise of other graces, we would give a twofold response. First, it is God's good pleasure and His divine order that all spiritual blessings, such as justification, adoption, and sanctification, issue forth from faith, and to this we can and must wholeheartedly surrender. Second, one can say that sealing is a consequence of faith because faith surrenders itself fully to God in Christ. Then, after the soul has entirely entrusted herself to the Lord, the Spirit will impress upon her the mark of God's ownership.

THE SEALING THAT FOLLOWS FAITH

We will now consider our second point; that is, we will consider more closely the benefit received by the Ephesians following the exercise of their faith. The point is that after they had believed in Christ, they were sealed with the Holy Spirit of promise. To address this as clearly as possible, we will not trouble you with too many subdivisions, avoid all subtle distinctions, and respond briefly and from the heart to the following questions.

Question 1: Who Seals Believers?

Answer: Generally speaking, all God's extrinsic works are the joint work of the three persons of this one and only adorable Being. However, in the economy of God's grace, this sealing is the unique and special work of the third person, God the Holy Spirit. Therefore, it is said of Him that He testifies with our spirit that we are the children of God and that He enables us to cry out as children do to their father, "Abba, Father—my God and Father" (cf. Rom. 8:15–16). Consequently, it is also said of Him, "Now he which stablisheth us with you in Christ, and hath anointed us, is God; who hath also sealed us, and given the earnest of the Spirit in our hearts" (2 Cor. 1:21–22). Therefore, He is frequently called a *Parakletos*, a Comforter, and an Advocate (John 14–16; Rom. 8:26). And in Ephesians 4:30, the apostle teaches clearly that the Spirit seals us and that we must not grieve the Spirit since He seals us until the day of redemption. Thus, the Spirit is the One who seals us, and consequently He has names of profound significance.

In the words of our text, the sealing person is expressly identified in three ways.

First, He is identified as *Spirit*. God is commonly designated as a Spirit. We read in John 4:24, "God is a Spirit: and they that worship him must worship him in spirit and in truth." Thus it must be, for God is a purely spiritual Being. The notion of any physical dimensions must be utterly banished concerning the most perfect God. Therefore, they who wish to unmask the erroneous views of the secret followers of Spinoza[1] do well by describing the Spirit as an infinite, independent, simple, immutable, eternal, omnipotent, and absolutely perfect Being who must be sharply distinguished from the created world. We are inclined to have carnal views regarding God, and therefore we must praise His goodness that we know with certainty from His revelation to us that God is a Spirit. That being said, the third person of the Trinity bears the name of Spirit—but not because He is a more spiritual Being than the Father and the Son. Far be it from us to imply this! Although all three persons are of one divine essence, the third person is designated as Spirit because of the manner of His personal subsistence within the divine Being. From eternity to eternity, He proceeds from the Father and the Son in a manner expressed as the movement of wind (John 16:13). He is thus called the Spirit of the Lord and the breath of His mouth. I address this in more detail in my exposition of the Heidelberg Catechism.

Second, He is identified as the *Holy Spirit*—not because He is holier than the Father and the Son, for God is the thrice-holy God. Many expositors before us have thought that the third person of the Trinity is designated as Holy Spirit because of His work in the economy of grace: the sanctification of elect, called, and justified believers. However, a very subtle theologian[2] has abused

---

1. The Spinozians are the followers of Baruch (later Benedictus) de Spinoza (1632–1677). He was born in Amsterdam as the son of Jewish parents who belonged to the Portuguese Synagogue. He came in conflict with the Jewish community and was consequently expelled from this synagogue. Spinoza became infamous as a radical philosopher. He was the first to challenge the existence of miracles and the supernatural. Though he did not deny the existence of God, he viewed God as an impersonal force. This viewpoint was articulated in his work *Ethica* that was published posthumously (1677) in which he posits that there is no such thing as a personal God. Spinoza assumes that there is but one existing substance that he designates as either nature or God. Spinoza is viewed by some as the father of atheism; others view him as a pantheist.

2. It appears probable that Comrie is referring to F. A. Lampe (see footnote 4 in chapter 6). This Cocceian professor had published his *Exposition of the Gospel of John*. In his exposition of John 5:26, he emphasized that the Father gave life to the Son only economically. According to Lampe, there is a parallel with John 15:26 where the Spirit in His operations proceeds from the Father only in regard to the economy of grace. Lampe

this proposition to cover up his detestable error regarding the sonship of the second person of the Trinity. He maintains that the Spirit is called the Holy Spirit in light of His economic activity and that the Son is only referred to as Son because of His economic activity as Mediator. He argues that one must use the same line of reasoning when assigning names to the divine persons. To dismantle this argument, careful theologians have inquired more in-depth why the word *holy* is used in God's Word. As everyone ought to know, its essential meaning is "to set apart or to consecrate." The distinction of being separate or consecrated is thus pertinent regarding the Holy Spirit. The Spirit has His unique and distinct manner of subsistence in the divine Being. And indeed, one person is thus distinguished from the other persons by personal attributes that are distinct from those of the other persons.

Regarding the Spirit, it should specifically be noted that He has His own manner of subsistence within the divine Being. The Son comes forth from the Father by eternal generation, and the Spirit proceeds in a manner resembling the blowing of the wind. The Son only comes forth from the Father, whereas the Spirit proceeds from both the Father and the Son. The divine essence communicated to the Son by eternal generation is also communicated to another person, namely, the Spirit who proceeds from both the Father and the Son. Such is the ontological functioning of the divine essence, and that essence cannot be communicated to anyone else. Thus, it can be said of the Spirit that He is the *Holy* Spirit because of His unique subsistence within the divine Being. Having stated what several theologians teach, we will now leave the matter to rest.

Third, He is identified as the *Spirit of promise*, and we will give the most prominent reasons for this.

1. He is the most prominent object promised to the church of the New Testament. God shepherded the church of the Old Testament by the promise of the coming Messiah. However, He has come into the world and has perfectly completed His redemptive work. He has returned to His Father and has been highly exalted as a reward upon His mediatorial labors. He is seated at His Father's right hand until

---

believed that the communication of the divine essence to the Son and to the Spirit presupposes imperfection in God. The Voetian Jacobus Fruytier took Lampe to task regarding this in 1728. Lampe did indeed defend himself, but that was insufficient to erase distrust toward him. Though Comrie has some appreciation for Lampe, here he resolutely rejects his teaching.

He shall come to judge the living and the dead. However, the great promise to the New Testament church is that the Holy Spirit would come and be sent forth to apply the accomplished redemption efficaciously and irresistibly to all the elect. To that end, Christ had to return to heaven so that the Spirit could come, and thus Christ, upon His departure, would send forth this Comforter. He also delineated what His work would be, namely, to "reprove the world of sin, and of righteousness, and of judgment" (John 16:8). He is therefore called the Spirit of promise.

2. He is also called the Spirit of promise because, having inspired the entire Scripture, He will see to it that all the promises of God's Word are fulfilled. He has inspired not only the histories, the threats, and the prophecies but also all the words of comfort—and is therefore called the Comforter.

3. Finally, He is called the Spirit of promise because He uses the promises to seal believers. In this way, He speaks to the hearts of God's children, sheds forth joy into their souls, prevails over their doubts, and assures them of being partakers of God's grace. To achieve this, He does not use the law, which would be a ministry of death. Rather, He uses the gospel that consists exclusively of a collection of precious and sovereignly bestowed promises and is thus designated as the ministry of the Spirit.

Question 2: At What Occasion Does This Sealing Take Place?

Answer: We could readily respond by highlighting many ancient practices from antiquity and speak of national rituals, but that would not be very edifying in a sermon. We will leave that to others and say only, based on God's Word, that sealing takes place at the time of a sale. In biblical times, when a sale had been finalized, a sales contract would be composed, to which one would attach a seal (cf. Jer. 32:11, 14). Slave masters and cattle owners were accustomed to branding their seal and mark as proof of ownership and as a mark of distinction for their cattle and employees. We read in Revelation 7:3 that the servants of God were sealed on their foreheads. Furthermore, one would seal particular objects, such as letters, to conceal secrets or protect and keep them as securely as possible. An example of the latter would be the sealing of Christ's grave by the Jewish Council. Similar matters could be mentioned here, but we will presently not do so.

Question 3: What Does This Sealing Consist Of?

Answer: When we speak of believers being sealed, we must not think of a literal act of sealing. No, this is a metaphorical way of speaking derived from what occurs among men in various circumstances. Therefore, we will now address the following matters:

A Symbol of Separation

This seal distinguishes believers from all others. They have been set apart as God's property. He has a special claim upon them due to their having been redeemed by His Son and due to their being truly dedicated to Him by the Holy Spirit. So to speak, the world is a great ship that carries a full load of all manner of merchandise. God's property is in this ship, and He places His mark upon His goods so that He can carefully unload the ship when it arrives. This metaphor is extracted from the practice of businesspeople who place their own stamp upon the goods that belong to them. Oh, how comforting this is to the elect! None upon whom God's stamp has been imprinted shall perish. Though one shipment of goods may be more valuable than the other, the least and most insignificant of God's properties belongs as much to Him as the most valuable of them. God desires to demonstrate and exercise His right of ownership and to act accordingly. Thus, He will neither permit His property to perish nor to remain obscure among unmarked goods.

Evidences of Conformity

This sealing will also result in some tokens of conformity to the Spirit being impressed upon the souls of believers. Thus, it is stated that the Spirit seals them—as is stated in Ephesians 1 and chapter 4:30. When someone impresses his signet or seal upon wax or lacquer, the same image carved into this seal will then be visible. Thereby the seal of one person will be distinguished from that of another. Thus, this sealing consists of God's image and likeness being impressed in some measure by the Spirit upon the souls of believers. Consequently, Galatians 5:22 designates this as one of the fruits of the Spirit, and in 2 Corinthians 3:18, it is stated that they "are changed into the same image from glory to glory, even as by the Spirit of the Lord." As a result, they now belong to God and Christ—just as formerly they belonged to the devil as his slave and bore the image of the first Adam. The image of Christ has now in some measure been impressed upon their souls, for they have indeed been recreated in His image, consisting of knowledge, righteousness, and true holiness.

Strengthening of the Believer
Since we wish to address only the most essential aspects of this sealing, we will conclude by saying that this sealing encompasses the strengthening and reassuring of the believer concerning the hope of eternal glory and his knowledge that he is God's property and His "merchandise." To assure them of this, God impresses His own mark upon them, and He attaches the prominent seal of heaven to the spiritual transactions between Him and the soul. This action will affirm that it is decidedly true and certain that God has accepted and endorsed the soul's transaction that she has often proposed with weeping and supplication. The soul's union with Christ will thus be affirmed, and she will be encouraged with the knowledge that, no matter how much the ship may be tossed to and fro, "the Lord knoweth them that are his" (2 Tim. 2:19). They may know that they shall be elevated from their sorrows to the full possession of the heritage of which they now have a sure and certain pledge. The devil may roar like a lion and attempt to deceive them as an angel of light, and the world may oppress them, but all whom the Lord has purchased shall come to Zion with joy and gladness. Then "everlasting joy shall be upon their head" (Isa. 51:11), for the tears of all who have been sealed shall be wiped from their eyes.

Question 4: How Does the Spirit of Promise Seal the Believer?

Answer: Much is to be gleaned from learned expositors of Scripture. The reader can quietly explore this, and by each of them leave it for what it is and consider the following matters.

A Pledge
Receiving the Spirit, or some operations of the Spirit, will be a pledge of one's inheritance (cf. 2 Cor. 1:21–22). God's giving a pledge affirms that He intends to bring the matter to fruition, that He has accepted the "merchandise," and that He intends to keep it. The Jews would be assured of the harvest by the firstfruits. A servant would be assured of impending employment upon receiving a monetary advance. It was an ancient custom that a notary public would remove earth and stones from the land that someone had purchased upon selling a property or an inheritance. He would then place it into the hands of the one who purchased it, thereby publicly affirming that the buyer was the lawful owner of this parcel of land, even though the land's rent and fruit yield were not yet his.

Likewise, when God the Holy Spirit works in the soul the characteristic disposition that proceeds from and is promised in the covenant of grace, He thereby gives the believer a trustworthy and reliable pledge that he has a right to all the benefits of the covenant. Thus, even though he does not yet actually possess these benefits, he has a sure pledge that the other benefits will follow.

Feeble believers would be greatly encouraged if they were to observe this. It could teach them to value more the work of the Spirit, even if it were but the initial stirrings. It would also encourage them to anticipate additional benefits—yes, assure them that they will follow in due season, albeit not immediately.

If someone were to ask me what fruits of the Spirit serve as a pledge, one should read Galatians 5:22, Matthew 5:3–12, and other passages. There they are identified as hungering and thirsting after righteousness, mourning, a loathing of self, and a sincere and ready condemnation and accusation of self before the Lord. In so doing, one will pronounce his own sentence and indict himself as a rebel, as someone worthy of death and judgment, while simultaneously pleading upon God's infinite mercy in Christ Jesus.

Gracious Gifts
The Spirit of God seals the soul of believers when He strengthens and revives the gracious gifts in the soul, causing them to be exercised in conformity to the nature of these gifts. Thereby He strengthens faith—a faith that is as a spark buried by ashes, as small as a mustard seed, and as weak as a bruised reed and a smoking flax. In fact, this faith is weighed down by a great measure of fear and timidity, as well as thousandfold anxieties and doubts. However, the Spirit enables the soul to overcome all of this. He engenders liberty in the soul to flee to the Lord Jesus. And as they flee to Him, He sees to it that they may behold the Lord Jesus in some measure in His all-sufficiency, His absolute necessity, and His willingness to receive such persons as they are. Thus, the soul will be enabled to hide in Jesus as the only hiding place and covert (Isa. 32:2). She will embrace Him and will again surrender herself to Him.

In so doing, as did old Simeon, the soul will embrace Jesus Christ with the arms of faith. Love and deep reverence for Jesus will be exceptionally fervent so that believers may lay Him, whom they have embraced by faith, as "a bundle of myrrh...betwixt [their] breasts" (Song 1:13). They can never sufficiently behold, meditate upon, and explore His matchless beauty, for He is "fairer than the children of men" (Ps. 45:2), and He is "white and ruddy, the chiefest among ten thousand…yea, he is altogether lovely" (Song 5:10, 16).

The exercises and deliberations of the soul regarding Christ, wrought by the Holy Spirit, will always be accompanied by the Spirit granting a measure of assurance and sealing in proportion to the clarity and transparency experienced during those exercises. However, the soul will doubt this when her tender affections have subsided, for she does not yet know what it is to believe and to adhere to the covenant without such a tender disposition.

The Holy Spirit of promise seals many of God's children in this manner—as can also be deduced from the words of our text, for there we read: "after that ye believed, ye were sealed with that holy Spirit of promise."

Illumination

The Holy Spirit of promise seals believers, for He illuminates them and enables them to spiritually consider, observe, and examine the true work of the Spirit within them, as well as their rightful claim to the divine promises of the covenant of grace. Thereby they understand the will of God as expressed in these promises. They hear, discern, and obey God's voice speaking to them, and they will apply what He says to themselves.

Someone may have known of a work of God within them and have a rightful claim to the promises without ever having been able to draw a conclusion from them or to plead upon these promises. However, it is the Spirit's explicit work to enable a sealed soul to ascertain that she possesses the marks of grace in conformity to the Word of God. The soul thereby becomes acquainted with God's covenant, as well as how she has entered into this covenant. Therefore, upon considering that she has thus entered the covenant, she may conclude that she is a partaker of God and the benefits of the covenant. Paul teaches this plainly in 1 Corinthians 2:12.

Indwelling

The Holy Spirit seals by His indwelling ministry when He renews the soul and conforms the believer to Christ as her Head. In 2 Corinthians 3:18, we read, "But we all, with open face beholding as in a glass the glory of the Lord, are changed into the same image from glory to glory, even as by the Spirit of the Lord." The soul will thereby be encouraged—a soul that doubted as to whom she belonged and who exclaimed, "Oh, I do not know what I must think of myself!" The Spirit will then cause her to look within, and she may then perceive that her spirit strives with her flesh. She loves what Christ loves, and she hates what Christ hates. The Spirit will therefore witness with her soul, "You do not have this of yourself, for these are the traits of God's image that I have imprinted upon you. You may thereby be assured that you are a child of God and that you are thus sealed until the day of redemption."

Witness

The Spirit also seals when He witnesses with the spirit of believers that they are God's children. In Romans 8:15–16, we read, "For ye have not received the spirit of bondage again to fear; but ye have received the Spirit of adoption, whereby we cry, Abba, Father. The Spirit itself beareth witness with our spirit, that we are the children of God." Thus, when a believer vacillates between hope and fear and dares to neither affirm nor deny his state before God, and he has but one witness (the witness of his own spirit), the Holy Spirit will come. He knows what lives in the soul because He Himself is the author of it. He will bear witness to the truthfulness and genuineness of faith, love, and other matters. By His speaking in the heart, He will testify, "I assure you with the deepest conviction that this is true faith and upright love. You may take Me at My Word, for I am the Spirit of truth!" Thus, the genuineness of the graces in the heart will be sealed by the Spirit's own witness.

Liberty

Finally, the Spirit seals and affirms the believer by setting his heart at liberty to draw near to God as his Father in Christ with a childlike, believing, and trusting disposition of the heart. He will do so as a child goes to his father. Galatians 4:6 expresses it as follows: "And because ye are sons, God hath sent forth the Spirit of his Son into your hearts, crying, Abba, Father."

However, lest you be misled in any way, you need to carefully consider two things:

1. We must keep together the matters we have addressed and thus not separate the one from the other. That means that we must not divorce the Holy Spirit in His sealing work and His testifying with our spirit that we are God's children from the Word, for He does all of this with and by the Word of God. We must also not divorce the Word from the powerful operation of the Holy Spirit and its fruits. When that happens, there will be the great danger of self-deceit, fanaticism, and extremism!

2. In what has been said, we can observe the difference between the witness of the Spirit of the Lord and the witness of the spirit of delusion. The Spirit of the Lord indeed illuminates the soul, transforms her into God's image, mortifies sin, and grants her a comfortable and filial inner disposition to draw near to God in prayer and by faith expects everything from Him. However, the spirit of delusion—a spirit that is sensual, puffed up, and impetuous—makes one to be at peace without there being ground for this in the Word of God. Therefore, the conversation of such individuals is neither stable nor tender, but rather is intermittent and irregular; for one moment, they serve God and then again the world.

Question 5: When Are Believers Sealed?

Answer: The apostle teaches that this occurs after they have exercised saving faith and thus after they have believed. To explore this further, we must consider the following matters:

A Distinct Work that Follows Faith

The sealing of the Spirit does not precede faith. It does not belong to the essence of faith, but rather it is a distinct work of the Holy Spirit that follows the exercise of faith in Christ. Hopefully, you will now perceive the error of those who posit that the assurance of one's portion in Christ belongs to the essence of faith. Rather, it is a work of the Spirit that manifests itself following the actual exercise of faith, for our text states, "after that ye believed."

The Initial Sealing Immediately upon the Exercise of Faith

Thus, we must view the sealing of the Spirit as distinguished from and following upon faith. One who receives this benefit will live a life of separation from the world. Furthermore, God's image will have been imprinted upon the soul whereby she is "changed into the same image from glory to glory, even as by the Spirit of the Lord" (2 Cor. 3:18). When viewed as such, this sealing is the common possession of all who believe in Christ and it is bestowed immediately following the exercise of saving faith. All who believe, insofar as it has been a work of the Spirit, are thereby separated from the common mass of worldly and unconverted men. For sanctification or the renewal according to God's image, though distinct from being justified by faith, can never be separated from justification but rather will immediately follow it.

The Subsequent Sealing in Christian Experience

We can also view the sealing of the Spirit as His work whereby He affirms and seals to believers their being partakers of grace. He will affirm and seal that they are God's children, that all their sins have been forgiven, and that upon death they will be the recipients of the joy of salvation. When we speak thus of this sealing, it remains true that this occurs "after that ye believed," but how soon and how long this will take we dare not stipulate. Neither does the apostle do so, nor is there a single passage in God's Word in which the interval following the exercise of faith is stipulated. On the contrary, God's Word speaks of believers who have lacked such sealing for an extended period, such as Heman, who said, "I am afflicted and ready to die from my youth up" (Ps. 88:15). Experience also teaches us that during the time of the early New Testament church, there were many "who through fear of death were all their lifetime subject to bondage" (Heb. 2:15). Experience also teaches us that some God-fearing persons, who undoubtedly manifest more tender godliness than many others who speak much about this matter, must nevertheless live for years without such sealing as we have just described. We now frequently meet those who belong to a generation to whom tried and godly persons could pose the question, "How is it that thou hast found it so quickly?" (Gen. 27:20).

We now wish to address this in conformity to God's Word and the experience of the saints.

1. We believe that following every act of faith that is exercised with a measure of clarity there will be *a measure of sealing*—even though believers may often be unconscious and unaware of this and will therefore frequently be in doubt regarding their state before God. Your experience will affirm this if you are a believer. Recall some of your best spiritual seasons. As you drew near to God, did you not experience a sweet enlargement of heart that was more than you usually experienced? Was it then not your desire that this would never fade, and did you not desire to build a tabernacle there (Matt. 17:4)? Then it lived in your heart, "Oh, all is now well with me. I desire nothing else in heaven or on earth." Were your experiences not such at that time that you had much freedom to make your desires known? That was a sealing of the Spirit—even though you did not perceive it as such and still often doubt your portion in Christ.

2. The *conscious sealing* of one's portion in Christ is generally granted following many struggles and trials to which God subjects His children for holy and wise reasons, and it is generally bestowed upon a tender walk before God's countenance. God usually bestows His love and His gift to enjoy Him more frequently to those believers who have such an inner disposition rather than to others. After having fasted and prayed, Daniel heard that he was a greatly beloved man (Dan. 10:11), and Paul, following his trial and subsequent struggles, heard Christ's voice: "My grace is sufficient for thee" (2 Cor. 12:9).

Question 6: In Whom Are Believers Sealed?

Answer: In our text, the apostle speaks of "in whom." We will not engage you with the thoughts of those who believe the antecedent to be the gospel itself as the glad tidings and the doctrines of truth. This would indeed be an acceptable interpretation. Instead, we concur with those who believe this to refer to Christ. Believers are sealed in Christ as the Head of His spiritual body so that they will so abide and be preserved in Him that the union between them will never be broken.

APPLICATION

Beloved, you will thus perceive what an eminent benefit the Ephesian believers received upon the exercise of faith: they were sealed with the Spirit of promise.

Evidence of Lacking God's Seal

It should be noted that many who claim to believe and to have the hope of salvation are merely deceived and deluded because the seal of the Spirit, God's stamp of approval, has not been imprinted upon them. Thus, God has not accepted what they have proposed to Him since He has not given an earnest or pledge as its affirmation. Oh, my beloved, if a bill of sale lacks a seal as an affirmation of the sale, we cannot lawfully avail ourselves of the purchased goods and lay claim to them as our property. Such is also true here. However much one may flatter himself with the hope of heaven, upon further investigation, it will be discovered that the seal and stamp of the Spirit have not been attached to God's work, and Christ will then say, "'I never knew you: depart from me' (Matt. 7:23). My seal has not been imprinted upon you, and you are therefore not one of Mine." From what follows, it will be evident that many lack this seal.

1. The purpose of a seal is to set apart and distinguish the persons or objects from other persons or objects. Therefore, beloved, as we observe the majority of people, we must ask, "Wherein are they set apart, and how do they distinguish themselves from the world?" Is it not true that many live like the world and are outwardly fully conformed to the world so that one cannot discern any difference? Should one not be able to discern even outwardly who serves the world and who serves God as a people that are His property? Is it not true that the majority of men dwell among and keep company with the world rather than with "the saints that are in the earth, and…the excellent" (Ps. 16:3)—that is, God's children? That proves that one belongs to the world, for he that is born of God will love the brethren (1 John 3:14). However, he who keeps company with the world and avoids the communion of saints is not born of God, for they who are like-minded will be attracted to each other just as "birds of a feather will flock together." Even though one may not have personal knowledge of such individuals, one will nevertheless recognize them from the company they keep and the people with whom they prefer to interact. Is their language also not the language of the world? In any event, it is not the language of Canaan! And the majority of them engage themselves in nothing else but worldly entertainment and pleasure. They do not know what it is to rejoice in the Lord and find their joy and delight in knowing, loving, and serving this great God. Thus, there are evidently few who are sealed, for sealed believers will in all respects be so different than and separate from the world.

2. When a seal is impressed upon an object, there will be a visible impression and image of that which is recorded on this seal. Thus, when the Holy Spirit of promise has sealed someone, God's image will be imprinted upon all his faculties, resulting in his mind being infused with light and knowledge—that is, true, saving knowledge—regarding God, Christ, and himself. His will is engaged in holiness, and there will be a strong inclination to be perfectly holy. His affections will be regulated and focused upon the Lord and His service. In a word, the same mind that was in Christ will also be in them (Phil. 2:5) so that they will love what Jesus loves—and that with a love that is stronger than death. All that Jesus hates, they will hate with a perfect hatred and view it as hostile for them. Considering this, how small is the number of sealed believers among us!

3. A seal will not be attached to an object unless a genuine transaction has preceded this. A seal will be attached to ratify and affirm this transaction. How few are there indeed who have truly interacted with God in confessing their unworthiness, hungering and thirsting after His communion, assenting to His covenant, giving their hearts to the Lord, and committing themselves with body and soul to God so that in both life and death they may be His property! In fact, the God of heaven will not attach His seal to something that does not exist.

4. Finally, how obvious it is with many that they are, so to speak, encapsulated in hardness and obstinacy of heart and spiritual insensitivity! It is as if they bear the mark of the devil upon their foreheads, for they engage in his work and keep company with those who are his bondservants. They are kept until the day of God's wrath when His righteous judgment will be executed.

Consequences of Lacking God's Seal
Oh, my beloved, if you have not been sealed, your condition is lamentable and wretched. You may be a confessing member of the church, have a great deal of intellectual knowledge, and have made frequent use of God's covenant seals. If, however, the Spirit's seal is lacking, you are wretched indeed!

1. The truth you profess to believe and also acknowledge as truth, you will help suppress when oppression and persecution arise for the sake of the truth. You will then blaspheme because of your apostasy (Matt. 13:20–21), for you have not been sealed, and the truth has never been sealed upon your soul with divine light. This explains why we so often observe with amazement that a believer with but little knowledge—who perceives himself to be but a worm—who so often is overcome with anxiety and fear of death, will be steadfast when called upon to suffer for the sake of the truth. He will then say, "Although I cannot debate about Jesus and His truth, I can, by the grace of God, submit myself with joy to the cruelest death" (Heb. 11:36–38).

In contrast to that, we observe others who, though they are very knowledgeable (and who make that known), yet readily change their viewpoint. When new viewpoints emerge, one will embrace them, but what is embraced one year will be rejected the following year. Such individuals resemble a weathervane that moves as the wind blows. Such can turn from being a defender to a bitter persecutor of God's people and the holy truth of the gospel. We could support this with many examples.

Why is this so? Oh, some people have been sealed, and the truth has been sealed to them. They have experienced its power and have tasted its sweetness and comfort, and the truth has made them free. However, others merely reflect on the truth very superficially. They have never experienced its power, and consequently, they readily conform to current thought, new fads, and other morals. Therefore, they will never remain steadfast in the hour of temptation. How dreadful this is, for one must remain steadfast until the end. A Christian must always remain consistent. Both today and tomorrow he must always espouse the same sentiments. He must remain steadfast about what he has heard and learned of God the Father (John 6:45), and he must abide in it.

2. How dreadful it shall be for you if you lack the seal of the Spirit on the great day of judgment when we must all appear before the judgment seat of Christ! Oh, my beloved, Christ and His angels will then carefully ascertain who they are that are either sealed or not sealed. Those who are sealed and upon whom the mark of God will be found shall be embraced by the angels who will carry them to meet Christ in the air. Christ will behold His own seal, and when He finds a genuine seal rather than an imitation seal, He will openly acknowledge them and receive them with a joyous welcome as His own, saying, "Come, ye blessed of my Father [upon whom is My seal], inherit the kingdom prepared for you from the foundation of the world" (Matt. 25:34).

However, those who do not bear God's mark, or who have imitated it, will be numbered on His left hand among the goats and will be subjected to eternal punishment. And though they may cry out, "Have we not taught in our streets, and have we not prophesied in Thy name, and have we not eaten and drunk with Thee?" it will be of no avail. Rather, Christ will speak a final word to them in His wrath, saying, "Depart from me into the eternal fire prepared for the devil and his angels where there will be weeping and gnashing of teeth, for I do not know you—that is, I do not acknowledge you because my mark and seal is not to be found on you."

Pursuing God's Seal

My beloved, how desirable it would be that this would bring you into a bind and that your heart would be pricked! Therefore, we exclaim to you: Seek to acquire an experiential and saving knowledge of the truth. Pray for saving faith, for he who believes in the Son has eternal life (John 3:16, 36).

Applications for Believers

Children of God, you have received this benefit. The Holy Spirit, the Spirit of promise, has sealed you following your exercises of faith. We will consider and address this in some detail.

Evidence of God's Seal

First, that you are a sealed person can be evident from the following marks:

1. Do you not perceive that from the moment that God dealt with your soul and became too strong for you, you have separated yourself from your former acquaintances and friends, as well as from your former pleasures? Do you also not perceive that you then visited God's people since you valued them more than the most prominent persons in the world? And have you not thought hundreds of time, "Though the world may slander God's people and look down upon them, and trouble them in every way possible, they are, however, the people with whom I wish to live and die. Their God shall be my God, and their people my people. I would rather be ridiculed along with God's people than choose all the treasures of Egypt." Where do these thoughts originate? Why is it that you now depart from your former bosom friends and, instead, love the people you formerly hated? It can only be that God has drawn you out of the world! Therefore, you love the brethren.

2. You may know yourself to be a sealed one because God's image has in some measure been restored, and it is your inner delight to live to God's honor. The most minor sin will now wound your soul and cause much inner unrest! A token that God's seal rests upon you is that you hate the things the Lord hates and also have an aversion for them.

3. You may also know this from the battle that rages within you: the battle of the Spirit against the flesh and of the flesh against the Spirit (Gal. 5:17). This proves that there is a law within your heart that battles the law that is in your members. And that also means that Christ will give you the victory!

Obligation Not to Offend the Spirit Who Sealed You

When the Holy Spirit of promise has sealed you, you will have the special obligation to follow the Spirit in all things and not to grieve Him with your sins. And indeed, the Spirit testifies with your spirit that you are a child of God (Rom. 8:16). If that witness were to cease, what dreadful distress would then come upon you!

1. It is the Spirit who also in your prayers aids you in your weakness. He enables you to pray with groanings that cannot be uttered (Rom. 8:26), to seek after the Lord, to chatter as a swallow and mourn as a dove (Isa. 38:14) until you are by renewal led to communion with Him.

2. The Spirit is the earnest and firstfruits of your inheritance who grants you the beginning of heavenly joy and enlarges and lifts your heart to walk in the ways of the Lord. When reflecting upon these matters, how one ought to keep his soul and maintain a conscientious walk so that the witness of God's Spirit with his spirit may remain clear and lively!

Comforts for the Sealed
The fact that you are sealed can yield comfort in many circumstances.

1. When the enemy assaults you and seeks to destabilize you, then you must think upon this sealing so that thereby you may be comforted and lifted up. When you cannot discern the witness of the Spirit within you, by the Spirit you must go to the fountain of sanctification. You will then detect the reflection of some traits of God's image and experience a desire to mortify all sin. And though this may not be as evident and be distorted by various sins and corruptions, you must therefore not cast this away. Are there not many legitimate coins upon which the seal is not all that visible, and which are nevertheless genuine? However, if you cannot detect the witness of water and the Spirit, it would be wise to take refuge in the blood of Jesus Christ by faith. You will thereby observe that the two previously mentioned exercises will be cleared up by using this third means. For it is God's way to grant the seal of His Spirit to those who exercise faith in Christ.

2. The sealing of the Spirit is also a source of comfort when God causes His judgments to come upon the earth. These judgments will not harm those who may have this divine seal. And indeed, the Lord knows them, and the fire and water through which they must pass will neither consume them nor swallow them up.

3. Finally, here is comfort for the hour of death. As dreadful as death may be, it has been disarmed by God's seal that rests upon you. The Lord's rod and staff will comfort you so that you need not fear when you must go through the valley of the shadow of death (Ps. 23:4), for you will be translated that very moment into God's immediate fellowship to be satisfied eternally with His likeness (Ps. 17:15). Amen.

CHAPTER 11

Faith, a Grace That Sustains the Life of the Christian

I am crucified with Christ: nevertheless I live; yet not I, but Christ liveth in me: and the life which I now live in the flesh I live by the faith of the Son of God.

—GALATIANS 2:20

Saving faith is compared rather effectively to a root (Job 19:28). As a root is hidden, so faith is hidden in the heart, "for with the heart man believeth unto righteousness" (Rom. 10:10). A root gives and communicates life to plants and trees so that they live and bear fruit by their roots. Likewise, faith is the root of spiritual life. Since faith unites itself to Christ as the fountain of life, spiritual life receives everything from Jesus, and the believer lives by this his faith.

The apostle teaches this in our text when he says, "I am crucified with Christ: nevertheless I live; yet not I, but Christ liveth in me: and the life which I now live in the flesh I live by the faith of the Son of God."

My beloved, you will observe how Paul here challenges those who were slandering the doctrine of justification by implying that it leads to carelessness. He proves the opposite in verse 19 and supports this by the arguments given in our text. Here we find two essential matters:

1. The apostle's description of grace: "I am crucified with Christ: nevertheless I live."

2. The causes of the life he lived: "Yet not I, but Christ liveth in me: and the life which I now live in the flesh I live by the faith of the Son of God."

PRELIMINARY REFLECTIONS ON THE LIFE OF FAITH

The apostle first indicates that the grace he partakes of consists of two matters: (1) I am crucified with Christ, and (2) I live.

Having come this far in our treatment of the marks, fruits, and circumstances of faith, you need to know from the outset that we deemed it advisable to address the fact that faith is the principle that governs the life of the righteous. Our frequent intention has been to instruct you regarding this from the words of Habakkuk 2:4: "The just shall live by his faith." These words must be of profound significance, for Paul quotes them three times to support two crucial aspects of the Christian faith. First, he thereby affirms that justification is by sovereign grace and apart from the works of the law (Rom. 1:17; Gal. 3:11). Then he quotes them in connection with the perseverance of the saints (Heb. 10:38).

It appeared to us that everything needed for our objective could be articulated in a concise summary. We realized, however, that the apostle quotes the words of the prophet to establish two distinct components of the doctrine of faith. Nevertheless, we believe that God's Word only permits one interpretation of the word *faith*. Furthermore, in the quoted Scripture passages, the apostles never relied upon allegorical interpretations, but rather they let the truth of these passages be consistent with the intent and meaning of the Holy Spirit. Therefore, we have carefully consulted various translations, learned expositors, and the original text. We did so to determine the subject and predicate of this declaration. In the meantime, the very scholarly work of Thomas Boston regarding Hebrew syntax[1] has been published in which the godly author demonstrates that "the just" (or the one justified by faith) is the subject, and the phrase "shall live" is the predicate. Thus, the text states that he who is justified by faith *shall live*. You will perceive that Paul justifiably identifies two components of the doctrine of faith in these passages. However, it affirms that we can hardly speak about the life of faith by way of this text.

We have chosen our text as the preferred passage in light of the many practical and experiential truths expressed in it. And indeed, these words teach us that they who live must first be crucified and that all who live, live by Christ and a true saving faith.

---

1. Thomas Boston, *Tractatus stigmologicus, Hebraeo-biblicus* (Amsterdam: Apud J. Westenium and G. Smith, 1738).

Upon considering the first portion of the text, we will observe that the apostle says two things regarding himself: first, that he is crucified with Christ, and second, that he lives.

CRUCIFIED WITH CHRIST

As to the first, namely, being crucified with Christ, we must note two matters: what the apostle clearly presupposes, namely, that Christ has been crucified, and subsequently, he speaks of a being crucified with Christ.

Christ Crucified

The apostle identifies Christ as the person who has been crucified. His name means "Anointed One" and is identical in meaning to the Hebrew word *Messiah*. "We have found the Messias, which is, being interpreted, the Christ" (John 1:41). It is common knowledge that Jesus is called the Christ or the Anointed One due to the Holy Spirit having anointed him. Thereby He was equipped to administer His three offices for the benefit of and instead of the elect as their Surety, Goel,[2] and Redeemer. We will not address this any further since we have recently addressed this extensively by way of the Heidelberg Catechism.

The apostle states that Christ has been crucified. And indeed He was. As the Surety of His elect, He had to obey the law in a twofold manner. In His person, He had to keep God's commandments meticulously and perfectly to the very end, for by His vindication of the law, eternal life could be granted to all who believe in Him. This is commonly referred to as His active obedience. Though some deny this, it is a source of great comfort to all souls who seek salvation. However, the law threatens death as a punishment, for disobedience as sin is the impugning of God's majesty. Therefore, the Surety had to be subject to a most bitter, grievous, shameful, and accursed death. Jews and Gentiles were of one mind that this was to be death by crucifixion. Jews would view crucified persons as so accursed that they had to be buried before sundown as an additional degree of punishment so that the land would not be defiled. Therefore, it is written, "Cursed is every one that hangeth on a tree" (Gal. 3:13). We have recently considered that Christ was subjected to

---

2. A Hebrew word meaning the next of kin upon whom devolved the duty of avenging the death of a relative, the payment of a kinsman's debt, or the redemption from slavery. Thus, one who was a Goel was a redeemer.

this death on behalf of His elect, and thus we should not have to reaffirm this to all who are "determined not to know any thing…save Jesus Christ, and him crucified" (1 Cor. 2:2).

The Believer Crucified with Christ

The apostle says regarding himself that he has been crucified with the crucified Christ. To explain this as clearly as possible, we will first consider what it means to be crucified, then what it means to be crucified with Christ, and finally, that the apostle had indeed been crucified with Christ.

Spiritual Crucifixion

Regarding the first, and thus what it means to be crucified, you can readily grasp in light of what crucifixion and its consequences entailed that it is descriptive of mortification, dying, and total abandonment. When we consider the witness of God's Word, we will observe that this crucifixion primarily pertains to two matters, namely, the dying to all that pleases and delights the unregenerate man and the dying to all that a religious man in his blindness and ignorance adheres to as the ground of his righteousness before the judgment seat of God. We will, therefore, now address these two aspects of being crucified.

Dying to That Which Pleases the Flesh

Regarding the first, that is, the dying to all that pleases and delights the unregenerate man, God's Word demands that we "mortify therefore [our] members which are upon the earth" (Col. 3:5). The apostle strove to keep his body under and "bring it into subjection," lest he "should be a castaway" (1 Cor. 9:27). Here and elsewhere, he testifies of himself that "the world is crucified unto me, and I unto the world" (Gal. 6:14). This is indeed the basic "ABC" of the Christian faith, namely, to deny all that pertains to the world and to have so died to it that it is as if it no longer exists. Oh, how sweet it is to practice this so that we, too, may say, "I am crucified!"

However, to practice this, we must know what this consists of. Let me, therefore, propose to myself and you of what this self-denial consists so that our souls may fall in love with it. Therefore, with me, let us consider the following matters:

1. Being crucified is expressive of *one dying to his own intellect, understanding, will, and wisdom.* Such a person will not be wise in his own eyes; he

will esteem his wisdom to be foolishness and his intellect to be as blindness and a being inclined toward the world. Moreover, the better he becomes acquainted with God and Christ, the more he will exclaim with Agur, "Surely I am more brutish than any man, and have not the understanding of a man" (Prov. 30:2). When one thus truly dies to the world, the high places will be cast down, and the soul will be enabled to esteem the other higher than himself. Her abiding sense of utter foolishness and ignorance will cause the soul to surrender herself to Christ to be instructed by Him. And the more such a person may learn upon the school of Christ, the smaller, humbler, and more mortified he will become day by day. There are many who grow above everyone's head when they begin to acquire some knowledge. They neither can nor are willing to learn from others. However, that merely proves that they only possess a knowledge that puffs up and that they have never been crucified with Christ.

2. Being crucified also implies that *one distances himself from himself and, so to speak, abandons himself* so that he ceases to be who he was and becomes what he was not. You can easily deduce this conclusion from the nature of dying and being crucified. Thus, he who is being crucified will be illuminated with supernatural light. His own mindset and will are no longer the norm for his obedience, but rather the law of His God as written upon his heart. In proportion to his being crucified, he will cease to cherish his own opinions. He will have holy thoughts regarding God and will always set the Almighty before His eyes so that he may live and walk in uprightness (Gen. 17:1). He will abandon and die to his own pleasures. As much as they may have formerly entertained him, they will become to him as tasteless as the white of an egg when he is crucified. Moreover, when there are things that still cause him to yearn for the fleshpots of Egypt, he will denounce them and indict himself regarding them. He will bring this before God as an enemy so that it may be shattered and broken in pieces as a potter's vessel. He will no longer find delight in vain honor and glory whereby others flatter him and trumpet his praise. Instead, he will desire to serve God in secret and to walk with the Lord.

3. Being crucified also implies *a heartfelt and voluntary surrender to Christ* and a surrender to Him as Lord. He who dies to himself becomes the property of another. He will embrace Christ as his Guide to show him the way, as a Rock to give him courage and security, and as the only fountain of all his comfort. He will take refuge to the wisdom of Christ to be instructed by Him,

to the authority of Christ to be subject to Him, to the truth of Jesus to have always a foundation for his faith, and to the fullness of Christ to be filled with all comfort. Jesus will then become all and he nothing.

4. Being crucified also implies that in a heartfelt, humble, and God-fearing manner, *one will ascribe to the sovereign grace and unmerited mercy and compassion of God all that one is, possesses, and does.* He who is crucified will ascribe all that is evil in him to himself. Simultaneously he will acknowledge the triune God as the sole Cause of all the good he may perform as a secondary cause. Paul did indeed say that he had labored more abundantly than others. However, did Paul desire to be honored for this? Not at all, for he immediately adds in the same breath, "Yet not I, but the grace of God which was with me" (1 Cor. 15:10). Only by grace he was what he was. He who is crucified is fearful and filled with holy zeal when he is privileged to do something special. He is, after all, fearful that men will attribute more honor to him as an instrument rather than to the Lord. Consequently, he cannot tolerate being praised. Consider only two passages: Acts 3:12–13, 16 and Acts 14:14–15. When the apostles realized that people wished to ascribe some good to them, they objected very much, and the quoted passages tell us that they even rent their clothes.

5. Being crucified also means that *the soul will consider all to be of little value and even contemptible compared to Christ.* She will view herself as crucified and thus as someone in whom there is neither beauty, desirableness, nor excellence. Because of and with Christ, she will joyfully view all vilification as an honor. Yes, compared to Christ, she will esteem all the glory of this earth as something insignificant, vain, and perishable, and therefore there is nothing in heaven or upon earth that she desires beside Him (Gal. 6:14; Ps. 73:25).

6. Being crucified means that *one will be entirely willing to part with all things*—just as Ruth said to Naomi, "Thy people shall be my people, and thy God my God" (Ruth 1:16). Thus, the believer will part with everything: father, mother, wife, children, and whatever else could be mentioned. Only then will the believer become delightful in the eyes of Jesus. Such a person will view Christ as the Vine, as the Plant of Renown, as the bright Morning Star, and as the Sun of Righteousness. He will view the world as no more than a thorn and a thistle, and as a dark cave. Thus, being a stranger and pilgrim on this

earth, he will seek that which is to come: an unchangeable and incorruptible inheritance (1 Peter 1:4).

7. Being crucified will also *include a delight and rejoicing in Christ amid all trials and tribulations*. He who is crucified can deem himself, in his poverty, to be rich in Christ, the pearl of great value. In seasons of darkness, he can delight himself in the light of the Sun of Righteousness. When he stumbles, he can remain immovably secure in the cleft of the rock. Christ will reward him for the loss of all things, and thus he can leap for joy in his God and sing with delight. What an extraordinary touchstone this is by which we can examine our hearts! Is our heart satisfied with Christ, even when we are deprived of all things? That will be irrefutable evidence that we have indeed died to all things. However, if Christ alone cannot quiet the heart and it insists on having something beside Him, it will prove that we are halting between two opinions and that one's heart is divided.

8. He who is crucified will not only delight himself in Christ in all his tribulations, but *he will even esteem the cross of Christ as a badge of honor*. Moses esteemed "the reproach of Christ greater riches than the treasures in Egypt" (Heb. 11:26), and therefore, as a crucified one, he gloried in affliction (Rom. 5:1–11). He thanked God that He deemed him worthy of being afflicted for Christ's sake. Therefore, read 2 Corinthians 6:9–10 attentively.

9. Finally, for him who is crucified and has died to himself, *it will be the greatest honor to glorify Christ*. His soul will be so aflame with love for Jesus that he is prepared to go through fire and water should Jesus call him to do so. To serve Christ is his delight; it is as a paradise to him due to the delightful joy he experiences in doing so. It is like being in a treasure chamber due to the hidden treasures to be found therein. In the keeping of His commandments, "there is great reward" (Ps. 19:11). It is as a secure wall of fire surrounding him, for the doing of Christ's will is his only food and drink.

Dying to One's Own Righteousness

He who has been crucified to all that delights the unregenerate man, that is, the world and sin, will also have died to all that the religious man ignorantly establishes as the foundation of his righteousness before God's judgment seat. In the preceding text, the apostle refers to this as dying to the law. This means that he neither expects his salvation from the law regarding his justification nor does he fear its curse. Dying to the law consists of these two matters, for the believer who is crucified with Christ continues to be entirely bound to the law as a rule of obedience. Much could be said about this, but we would rather publish a helpful booklet entitled "Dying to the Law" for the benefit of the reader.[3]

The Metaphor of Crucifixion

A second matter that demands our attention is why the apostle refers to his spiritual experiences as a crucifixion, and then specifically a being crucified with Christ.

Why It Is Called Being Crucified

Regarding this crucifixion, the apostle designates it as such for the following reasons:

1. It is designated as a crucifixion since the dying to all carnal delights, sin, and self-righteousness is very difficult and painful—all of which is descriptive of death by crucifixion. The delights to which one is accustomed, and which so pleasantly flatter our corrupt nature, must be eradicated. One must transcend them and die to them to such an extent that one will no longer delight in them. The moment these desires and longings initially arise, one must resist them and be continually armed against any further temptations. Our flesh and blood will then have to be crucified! Scripture, therefore, compares it with the plucking out of the right eye and the cutting off of the right hand. When Paul speaks of this, he calls it a subduing of the body so that in so doing, it may be useful (1 Cor. 9:27). He who is most determined to be crucified with Christ will have to exclaim from time to time, "I am oppressed; undertake for me" (Isa. 38:14).

2. It is also designated as a crucifixion because death does not occur immediately upon being crucified, as is true for other ways of dying. Rather, it is a slow process. This is also true when one must die spiritually to all things. The sinful nature, the old man, is nailed to the cross, and though the crucified one receives a deadly wound from which he will surely die, he will die very slowly. The most advanced in grace must acknowledge that they have but a

---

3. Comrie is referring to an extensive treatise of the Scottish preacher, Ralph Erskine, which was published and reprinted numerous times. Its complete title is "Dying to the Law and Living According to the Gospel." This treatise is an exposition of Galatians 2:19: "For I through the law am dead to the law, that I might live unto God."

small portion of the desired matter. To his sorrow, he will observe that inner lusts to which he believed to have died can rear their head with greater force than before. That being said, the completion of sanctification and the dying of the old man will not occur until the death of believers. Then their souls will be perfected in holiness and will be translated immediately into glory while their bodies, in union with Christ, will rest in the grave until the day of the resurrection.

Why It Is Called Being Crucified with Christ

However, the apostle does not only speak of being crucified, but rather of being crucified *with Christ,* for he says, "I am crucified with Christ." Everyone will understand that this must be interpreted metaphorically rather than literally, for only the two malefactors were crucified with Christ. Moreover, Paul's conversion on the way to Damascus occurred after Christ's exaltation. Thus, being crucified with Christ means the following:

1. When Christ was crucified publicly as Surety and the second Adam, He represented His spiritual children so that all the elect are viewed judicially by God as comprehended in Him. Thus, they have been crucified with Him, and they have died with Him. His actions and suffering on their behalf must be reckoned as their actions and suffering. Likewise, the actions of the first Adam must be viewed as the actions of his natural children. Consequently, the apostle says in Romans 5:12, "for that all have sinned." Likewise, all believers have been crucified with Christ.

2. Being crucified with Christ also means that Christ by His death on the cross has merited the dying of the old man for His spiritual seed. In 2 Corinthians 5:15, we read, "And that he died for all, that they which live should not henceforth live unto themselves, but unto him which died for them, and rose again."

3. Finally, being crucified with Christ signifies the similarity between the crucifixion of believers and the crucifixion of Christ. The apostle expresses this in a lovely way in Romans 6:5, where he speaks of having "been planted together in the likeness of his death." We will clarify this by exploring some of these similarities.

    a. Christ was betrayed by one of His disciples and delivered into the hands of those who crucified Him. This commonly happens when one is crucified with Christ. When a person is convicted by being confronted with a given bosom sin, resulting in a soul being spiritually arrested, the process of spiritually dying begins. For although God's Spirit convinces of all sin, the penetrating conviction in the conscience generally begins by being made aware of a specific sin. Though one cherishes this sin, the damnable nature of this will be brought to light. Consider only the conversion of Paul. The focus was not on sin in general, but rather on one sin: "Why persecutest thou me?"

b. Christ was brought before the judge by force. Likewise, the soul who is being crucified will be summoned before God as the Judge of all the earth. A person will frequently resist and be unwilling to submit, but when having to die becomes a reality, he will be brought before the countenance of God against whom he has sinned so gravely and grievously.

c. Christ was led from one judge to the next. Likewise, the soul will be led from one commandment to the next so that she might see her iniquities and believe with conviction that she has sinned against *all* God's commandments.

d. As Christ did not open His mouth and remained silent, likewise, the person who is being crucified with Him will not be able to say anything in his defense. On the contrary, he will verbalize his death sentence, saying, "I have sinned; what shall I do unto thee, O thou preserver of men?" (Job 7:20), and "God be merciful to me a [poor] sinner" (Luke 18:13).

e. As the death sentence was pronounced upon Christ, so it will be with those who are crucified with Him. Their conscience, as God's subordinate judge, will pronounce the death sentence in light of their being worthy of damnation. Therefore, they will surrender and say, "There is no hope," for they can no longer find their life in their hand (Isa. 57:10).

f. As Christ was stripped until He was naked, so they who are crucified with Him will truly and fully be emptied and stripped of all their own virtues so that they will no longer have anything whereby they can cover the shame of their nakedness.

g. Finally, as Christ gave up the spirit when He died, so they who are crucified with Him are crucified to the world and the world to them (Gal. 6:14).

Paul's Crucifixion with Christ

The description of Paul's life proves that he indeed had been crucified with Christ. In Acts 9, this crucifixion began on the way to Damascus. As of that moment, he had surrendered himself to the service of Jesus. He denied himself and disciplined his body so that he could be beyond reproach and thus live before God and the Gentiles without offense. This is so self-evident that we no longer have to dwell on it.

ALIVE WITH CHRIST

The second aspect of the apostle's description of his state of grace is "and I live." To address this with all clarity, we will address the following matters:

Spiritual Life

We will address what the life about which the apostle speaks consisted of when he says, "And I [Paul] live." Everyone will recognize that we are here dealing with spiritual rather than natural life—and thus the life of grace. To understand in some measure the nature of this life, we must note the following distinctive marks that we have explained in detail on other occasions.

Awakened from the Sleep of Death

It demonstrates that the soul has been awakened from the mortal sleep of sin and has been made alive by the regenerating and irresistible operation of God the Holy Spirit. After all, it is the Spirit who quickens. By nature, everyone is dead in trespasses and sins. Therefore, the very thing the Spirit will do is to infuse by His creative power a principle of spiritual life into the sinner who is, by nature, dead and worthy of damnation. This will manifest itself in the soul's restlessness regarding her natural state before God. Such a sinner will resemble the dove of Noah, which also could find no rest. That will last until she enters into the true Ark, Christ, her heart's intent being to go, as a prodigal son, to God. Such souls will then say with the prodigal son, "I will arise and go to my father" (Luke 15:18). They will confess their guilt and condemn themselves because of their sins: "I have sinned; what shall I do unto thee, O thou preserver of men?" (Job 7:20). After Ephraim repented, he grieved in dust and ashes. He smote upon his thigh and "was ashamed, yea, even confounded" (Jer. 31:19). These and similar experiences affirm that a person has been made spiritually alive.

United to Christ the Lifegiver

"I live" also indicates that the soul, by the Spirit and through faith, is united to Christ Jesus as the fountain of life and her life-giving Head. Although we maintain that regeneration precedes this union with Christ, this sequence is logical rather than chronological. They who are alive are made alive by virtue of their union with Christ, for in regeneration, they are united to Him. Those who are united to Christ must necessarily be alive. There are no dead branches in the living Vine; there are no dead or decayed members in the mystical body of Christ. Since He lives, they will live also, for He has come "that they might have life, and that they might have it more abundantly" (John 10:10). He who has been ingrafted into Him by a true faith "though he were dead, yet shall he live" (John 11:25). In a natural sense, one lives as long as soul and body are united. Thus it is also in a spiritual sense. By virtue of this union, Christ dwells in the hearts of believers. Once He has entered the heart and has transformed the soul into a temple or house of God, He will never depart.

Made Alive in All the Soul's Faculties

"I live" indicates that all the faculties of the soul have been touched and made alive, for the life of grace will influence all the functions of the soul. It will bring about a spiritually active disposition and generate activities consistent with the nature of the spiritual life that has been infused into the soul by the Spirit upon the regeneration and conversion of the soul. We will briefly explore this.

A Disposition toward Spiritual Activity in the Mind

This spiritual life in the mind consists of spiritual illumination. In Ephesians 1:18, the apostle prays for the believers in Ephesus that God would give them enlightened eyes of their understanding. When he wishes to describe the state of a regenerated soul before God, he says, "For ye were sometimes darkness, but now are ye light in the Lord: walk as children of light" (Eph. 5:8). "The night is far spent, the day is at hand" (Rom. 13:12). When spiritual life enters the mind, "the light of the moon shall be as the light of the sun, and the light of the sun shall be sevenfold, as the light of seven days" (Isa. 30:26). By this light of life, the soul will be instructed.

1. The believer may *know God in His being* and His essence as the triune covenant God. He may know Him in His virtues as the spotless and thrice-holy God (Isa. 6), as the just God who can by no means clear the guilty (Ex. 34:7), as the gracious and merciful God who for His name's sake blots out sin (Isa. 43:25), and as the august and majestic God who is "to be had in reverence of all them that are about him" (Ps. 89:7). That will cause the soul to exclaim, "I have heard of thee by the hearing of the ear: but now mine eye seeth thee. Wherefore I abhor myself, and repent in dust and ashes" (Job 42:5–6).

2. This light of life will descend deeply into the dark cave of the believer's abominable and darkened soul. It will then illuminate the most hidden recesses of his heart in such a manner that he will begin to *view his heart as more evil, cunning, and deceitful than anything else.* He will perceive that he cannot possibly plumb his heart as to the depth of its sinful corruption and hostility toward God. That uncovering light will cause him to cry out, "O wretched man that I am! who shall deliver me from the body of this death?" (Rom. 7:24).

3. This lively and brightly shining light that illuminates his mind teaches him *how much he needs a Surety to reconcile him with God.* It will reveal to him how this Surety in all respects is suited for his wretched soul. He is as balsam for his wounds, as eyesalve for his blindness, as the All-Sufficient One for his emptiness, and as a garment for his nakedness. He is the Mighty One of Jacob, who brings him up from the horrible pit and makes His strength perfect in weakness. Consequently, such a regenerated soul will wholeheartedly agree with the way of salvation through a crucified Savior, approve of this way, and praise and worship God for it.

A Disposition toward Spiritual Activity in the Will
The will functions in this spiritual life preeminently in conformity to God's will. This conformity primarily manifests itself in that the born-again Christian exercises his will to practice the holiness that becomes God's house.

1. One's natural and deadly *impotence is thereby removed.* The regenerated man is made willing in the day of God's power (Ps. 110:3). To this impotent

one who was mourning in his misery, power is given so that upon the proclamation of the blessed tidings of salvation, he must hastily rush toward a crucified Jesus. Due to his unworthiness he will frequently come trembling "as a bird out of Egypt, and as a dove out of the land of Assyria" (Hos. 11:11).

2. Where such life is present, *a love for and consenting to sin will be taken away*. The regenerated soul has an all-encompassing love for all God's commandments. She delights in the careful observance of God's precepts and rejoices in God's testimonies more than in all riches (Ps. 119:14).

3. Wherever this holy life functions in the will, *the soul will no longer cherish her own delight and will*. Instead, the more this new life functions within her, the more she will exclaim, "May Thy will be done, oh my God, for it is wise, holy, and elevated above all things. 'Guide me with thy counsel, and afterward receive me to glory'" (Ps. 73:24). Whether Thy ways be either sour or sweet, I will always remain silent, for Thou art able to make all things well according to Thy will.[4]

A Disposition toward Spiritual Activity in Other Faculties
This animated spiritual frame of one who is spiritually alive will manifest itself in a lively manner in all the other faculties of the soul: in the *conscience* that has been cleansed from all dead works to serve the living God; in the *memory* that retains all the wondrous deeds of God so that one may continually have substance for lively spiritual meditation out of the good treasury of one's heart in order to be continually engaged in holy activity; and in all *affections* so that with love, esteem, and intense yearning the soul longs to enjoy God and heartily love Jehovah.

Though this spiritual life is seated in the soul and its affections, it will also manifest itself in words, conversations, facial expressions, the company one keeps, clothing, and all things. After all, a good tree cannot bring forth evil fruits.

The Qualities of Spiritual Life
The second matter we now wish to explore is what life the apostle was living when he said, "Nevertheless I live." Much could be said about this, but we will limit ourselves to the following matters:

---

4. This is a paraphrase of a poem by Jodocus van Lodenstein quoted earlier by Comrie in chapter 3.

1. As one can see in the previous verse, he lived *unto God*.

To live a life devoted to God is to live out of God by the exercise of faith. Being thus enlivened by God Himself, one will by new and repeated acts of faith continually abide in God as the fountain of life, as the Sustainer of life, and also as the Preserver of life. Yes, these are acts of faith whereby one repeatedly takes refuge to the fullness of Christ to receive from Him both Spirit and life.

To live a life devoted to God also means that one in all things will aim for God's glory. Oh, just as God does all things for His own name's sake, so the soul who lives unto God, in eating and drinking, desires to do all things to God's honor and glory.

To live a life devoted to God also means that one, in conformity to God's will, endeavors continually to be a man "of His right hand" (Ps. 80:17) regarding all that pertains to His institutions and that one will order his life in conformity to God's Word.

Finally, to live a life devoted to God means that one will view God as the Counselor and the Pattern of one's life, thereby having nothing else in view but Peter's admonition, "But as he which hath called you is holy, so be ye holy in all manner of conversation" (1 Peter 1:15).

2. The life the apostle lived was *a hidden life*, saying, "[My] life is hid with Christ in God" (Col. 3:3). It is a hidden life as far as the world is concerned. The world does not understand the things of the Spirit, for they are foolishness to it. It is a hidden life as to the beginning and development of spiritual life. Such is also true for the wind, for no one knows where it originates and where it goes—as is true for someone who is born of God.

It is also a hidden life due to the hidden manner in which it is maintained. Though the devil and the world conspire to destroy it, the gates of hell will not prevail against it. Furthermore, it is a hidden life because it is primarily practiced in seclusion. Many people live a public life, causing them to traverse the land, but this life chooses solitude where one can have an intimate relationship with God, enjoy the hidden manna, and commune with Him.

3. The life of the apostle was also *a life of holiness*. All who are spiritually alive belong to a holy people called the "saints of the most High" (Dan. 7:18, 27). It is impossible to be spiritually alive and not to be serious about sanctification, for, without holiness, no man will see God (Heb. 12:14).

4. Finally, the life of the apostle was, as he subsequently states, *a life of grace* that excluded all boasting. Moreover, this life of grace will always increase and will culminate in perfection. Other aspects of this life may also come to mind.

Why These Spiritual Activities Are Called Life

Third, we wish to explore why the activities we are currently discussing are referred to as "life." Among many things, we wish to note the following: These spiritual activities are correctly designated as life:

1. Because of *the living principle that keeps them lively and active*. A watch will have a gear that by its motion will set all other gears in motion. Natural life has inherent warmth that will be present as long as one lives. Likewise, when there is the seed of regeneration in the soul, it will influence the entire man.

2. Because there will be *a continual activity* consistent with the nature of such life. Granted, although there will be times that this will manifest itself more strongly than at other times, it will never cease to be active. Since Christ lives, all who belong to Him will live also!

3. Because there is *the potential and striving for growth*. And although such growth will not be visible during seasons of backsliding, the soul will nevertheless grow in self-knowledge and humility. Such is the case with trees during winter, for though there will be no new branches, and there will be neither blossom nor leaves, their root systems will nevertheless grow. And indeed, "Those that be planted in the house of the LORD shall flourish in the courts of our God" (Ps. 92:13).

4. Because there will be *a strong attraction toward all that will stimulate the growth and increase of the work of grace*. Where such life is present, the soul will greatly desire "the sincere milk of the word [of God]" (1 Peter 2:2). She will thirst after God "as the hart panteth after the water brooks" (Ps. 42:1), and she will exclaim, "O God, thou art my God; early will I seek thee: my soul thirsteth for thee, my flesh longeth for thee in a dry and thirsty land, where no water is" (Ps. 63:1).

5. Because by its very nature, there will be *an inherent antipathy and aversion toward all that would be detrimental toward such life*. When grace is lively, one will flee from sin as if it were hell itself. One will avoid all unrighteousness

and endeavor to be watchful and sober, having one's loins girded about and one's lights burning (Luke 12:35). David could say, "I hate every false way" (Ps. 119:128).

6. Because, finally, this life will *never culminate in death*. It begins here, and though it is not without beginning, it shall nevertheless be and remain endless and eternal.

The Excellency of This Life

Fourth, we will now consider the multifaceted excellency of this spiritual life. The very nature of this life is that it excels all other forms of life. It is excellent for the following reasons:

1. Because it is a spiritual life that is *the sole possession of God's elect people* whose names are written in the Book of Life. They have become partakers of the divine nature (2 Peter 1:4), and thus their life issues forth from God.

2. Because of its *origin*. In Colossians 3:4, we read that Christ Jesus, as Mediator, is our life. What an excellent river it is that flows forth from such a fountain of life (Ps. 36:9).

3. Because of its *comfort*. This life knows of a joy that others cannot experience who are strangers to it. The most bitter aspect of this life is full of comfort, for we read in Romans 5:3, "And not only so, but we glory in tribulations also." What a glorious, incomprehensible, and inimitable joy there must then be in such comfort! The apostle, therefore, says that it "passeth all understanding" (Phil. 4:7).

4. Because of its *security*. It is, with Christ, hidden in God (Col. 3:3). The devil can neither extinguish this life, nor can he pluck a single sheep out of the hands of Christ. And indeed, all believers are preserved by "the power of God unto salvation" (Rom. 1:16). One may therefore rightly say, "He that trusts in the LORD, shall be as Mount Zion, and 'shall not be moved for ever" (Ps. 112:6).

5. Because of its *outcome*. This life will spring up into eternal life where there shall be joy, and where all sighing, mourning, and weeping shall forever vanish. Blessed Paul and blessed are all believers with him who can and may say, "I live!"

Having described his state of grace, namely, that he was crucified with Christ, the apostle proceeds to identify the origin from which issues forth the life he had received whereby he died daily to himself.

LIFE IN CHRIST BY FAITH

Therefore, he highlights the fact that Christ alone is the origin of this life and that in light of this, he lived solely by faith in the Son of God. And indeed, he writes, "Yet not I, but Christ liveth in me: and the life which I now live in the flesh I live by the faith of the Son of God." Thus, the apostle here highlights two matters.

First, he identifies the cause of this life and who sustains it, namely, Christ who lives in him. Christ lives in His people by His Word and Spirit. He gives them life, enables them to live, and continually administers all that is necessary for the strengthening and sustenance of this life. We will not enlarge upon that now because we desire to do so further on when by way of Ephesians 3:17 we will declare faith to be a grace whereby Christ dwells in the soul of believers.[5]

Having considered who the moving and sustaining cause is of the life that the apostle lived, namely, Christ who lived in him, we must now consider the so-called mediate cause that resulted in this life, namely, "the faith of the Son of God," for he says, "And the life which I now live in the flesh I live by the faith of the Son of God." In this context, the apostle speaks of two matters: "the faith of the Son of God," and subsequently what the apostle did by way of this faith.

Christ, the Object of Faith

As to the first, we must consider the object of faith, namely, the Son of God. Hopefully, everyone knows that God has eternally generated His Son and communicated the divine essence to Him. We read of this in Psalm 2:7; Proverbs 8:24; Micah 5:1; and John 5:26. Annually we receive detailed instruction regarding this subject,[6] and then related errors are refuted. Therefore, we will

---

5. Comrie is here referring to a sermon he still intended to preach in his congregation. In any event, this sermon was not included in this work.

6. Comrie is here referring to his annual exposition of the Heidelberg Catechism, and he is particularly referring to Lord's Days 5–8 and 11–13.

not enlarge upon this. However, we will consider the phrase "the faith of the Son of God." Faith in the Son of God is:

1. The faith whereby one will be fully assured within his heart that Jesus Christ is the eternal, only begotten, and natural Son of the Father, having been generated by the Father. He has life within Himself and is the express image of His person (Heb. 1:3). Therefore, John explicitly wrote his glorious gospel so that one "might believe that Jesus is the Christ, the Son of God" (John 20:31). He "is the true God, and eternal life" (1 John 5:20).

2. The faith whereby one believes that Jesus Christ Himself, as the Son of God, willingly became the Substitute of all whom God has chosen unto life. He did so because the entire human race is condemned due to the covenant breach of the first Adam. He died and suffered on their behalf all that God's law and His justice demanded, and thereby He reconciled them with God and redeemed them. By this faith, one will see that this Interpreter, "one among a thousand," has said, "Deliver him from going down to the pit: I have found a ransom" (Job 33:23–24).

3. The faith whereby one believes that the eternal Son of the eternal Father was made of a woman in the fullness of time (Gal. 4:4). This means that He took a genuine body and a rational soul into a most intimate union with His divine person. Though He is the Lawgiver, He was thereby "made under the law." He willingly was made under the law to accomplish a perfect and actual obedience—not for Himself, but rather on behalf of the elect. He did so also to subject Himself to the wrath of God and an accursed death so that the chastisement that was upon Him would yield peace to His elect and that for their wounded souls, they would find healing in His stripes (Isa. 53:5).

4. The faith that God has raised His Son as Surety from the dead by His almighty power unto the justification of the sinner who believes in Him. By this faith, one will be assured that He is highly exalted and has an infinite and divine fullness out of which He most willingly bestows His gifts. This faith is certain that He ceaselessly waits to be gracious. This faith also knows that he who comes to Him to be taught by Him and to be reconciled with God, and who willingly submits to Him, shall in no wise be cast out (John 6:37).

5. The faith whereby the believer upon serious consideration not only highly esteems and chooses the Son with all of his heart and soul but also actually

goes to Him with the most tender and intense desire to be united with Him so that the believer may be in Christ and Christ in him. This is a hungering and thirsting after His righteousness (Matt. 5:6) and a cleaving of the soul to Christ.

6. The faith whereby the soul with both arms embraces and receives the Person of Jesus Christ whom the Holy Spirit unveils to her by divine illumination in His all-sufficiency, suitability, and willingness. By Word and Spirit, Christ will thus be offered to the soul.

7. The faith that, finally, makes use of Jesus Christ in all possible circumstances in which the direction of God's providence has brought the soul. And indeed, the soul abides in Him as she has also received Him. She will also continue to abide in Him by taking refuge in Him. With believing trust and a quiet and calm spiritual disposition, she expects everything from Him. The Word of God will primarily redirect faith in God's Son to these truths, of which we will list the following: Acts 8:37; Romans 1:9; 1 Thessalonians 4:14; 1 John 5:1; John 1:12–13; Matthew 5; and Colossians 3. Blessed is he who believes in the Son, for he has eternal life. He will once be resurrected on a day determined by God. However, "he that believeth not the Son shall not see life; but the wrath of God abideth on him" (John 3:36).

Living by Faith in Christ

Having considered this faith in the Son of God, we must now deal with what Paul did by this faith, for his faith was neither fruitless nor idle. By this faith, he lived his life "in the flesh," for he says, "And the life *which I now live in the flesh* I live by the faith of the Son of God." This subject matter is so profound and has such vast implications that we have often looked up against having to expound it. However, we will, in all simplicity, now pass on to you what we have found through meditation. If someone has different and better things to say about this, then he must do so.

To address you regarding this matter as clearly as possible and without wearying and confusing you with too many details, we will proceed as follows:

1. We will seek to demonstrate what must be presupposed in those who live by faith.

2. Since this living by faith is extraordinarily profound, we will, by way of various remarks, mention a few things so that this may lead to a correct understanding regarding this matter.

3. We will discuss in general terms what this living by faith consists of.

4. Finally, we will specifically point out how believers, in their unique relationships and in the circumstances into which they are led, live by way of fitting acts of faith.

Presuppositions Regarding Living by Faith

As to the first, considering what must be presumed to be the ground upon which this faith is founded, we will only briefly consider a few matters.

True, Saving Faith

It must be presupposed that someone is a true believer. Thus, he will have acknowledged his grievous and wretched state of misery, have turned to Christ in response to the voice of a calling God, and have received Him and fully surrendered to Him to be the property of Christ in life and in death. No one may deny this, for God's Word teaches us emphatically that the just, and they alone, will live by his faith (Hab. 2:4). Therefore, anyone who has not been translated out of himself into Christ by God's almighty power and by the extraordinary and irresistible operation of the Spirit will be entirely unfit for such spiritual life. Paul says that this is "foolishness unto him: neither can he know [it]" (1 Cor. 2:14).

Faith in the Covenant of Grace

If one lives by faith, the soul must be presumed to have genuinely embraced the promise of the covenant of grace with application to himself. Such a person will have received a promise that God has spoken to his soul. Therein he has been privileged to discover Christ as in a mirror, and thereupon he has hoped. No one may lightly deny this, for the essential nature of faith is to acquiesce in a matter upon the testimony of someone whom one esteems to be a person who speaks the truth. Saving faith must therefore rest upon the promise in the most immediate sense of the word. Consider Romans 10:17, where we read, "So then faith cometh by hearing, and hearing by the word of God."

To understand this correctly, we posit that Christ or a specific benefit will only be granted to the soul by the precious promises and affirmations of the blessed gospel. Only therein will the soul behold Jesus and the benefits of the covenant, and she will receive Jesus only in response to them. As frequently as we may have studied God's Word and in whatever way God has dealt with His people, we will always be able to clearly discern this order and these premises. When God appeared to Abraham, He said, "I am thy shield, and thy exceeding great reward" (Gen. 15:1), and He also established His covenant with him (Gen. 17). When God spoke to Jacob, He said, "I am the God of Bethel" (Gen. 31:13). David received a word upon which God caused him to hope. When Paul was encouraged amid his strife and assaults, it was by this word, "My grace is sufficient for thee" (2 Cor. 12:9). This enables the soul to reflect on how she has received Christ and how faith must consequently be exercised by the promises. It will also serve to unmask those who can indeed speak of remarkable stirrings of the heart, visions, and ecstatic moments that were not generated by the Word. If there is any mark of a deceived soul, then this is it! Give heed, therefore, how matters are with you and whether you have been brought to Christ through the Word. Should that not be so, then you may speak of Christ, of ecstatic moments, and stirrings of the heart, but it will be nothing but deceit! Unless you are blind, your actions and disposition should reveal this to you. Such people will be careless, irreverent, and indifferent regarding the means of grace, and they will also neglect to read and meditate on God's Word. The cause of the latter is that they have never experienced its sweetness as experienced by David. Some have thus been prompted to speak disingenuously by maintaining that one can have communion with Jesus apart from the means and that the Word is but a dead letter, etc. No one may object that there are many instances in the Old Testament of encounters with God apart from the means, for before Moses, there was no written Word. Therefore, you will observe that as frequently as the patriarchs had such experiences, such occurrences became subsequently increasingly rare, for God now only works by, in, with, and according to His Word.

Two Ways to Make Use of the Covenant
To make sure that none of God's beloved people be confused regarding this, you need to know that there are two ways by which the soul can be led to exercise communion with the God of the covenant by way of the promises.

1. It will occasionally happen to God's beloved people that the promises of the covenant are not explicitly impressed upon their hearts. Instead, the soul

will be led to God's promise by a quiet, calm, and gentle arousal and exercise of faith. It can be that the soul will be led into a quiet meditation upon God's covenant and of the way in which He will save a sinner according to this covenant. Thus, it can be that the believer's attention will not be directed to a specific promise, but rather that in meditating upon God's glory, he may behold Christ's fullness and the steadfastness of the covenant. In so doing, he can experience such a heartfelt approbation of and delight in the covenant that he will unreservedly subscribe to this covenant, embrace the God of the covenant, and exercise communion with all three persons of the Godhead. And indeed, each person is uniquely involved in the salvation of a sinner. Such a person may thus embrace God apart from as much as one explicit promise. This can occur solely by and according to the Word of God apart from the application of a particular word or promise. David's exercise of faith in 2 Samuel 23:5 may have functioned in this way when he spoke of a well-ordered covenant in which was all his desire. It may also be that the soul is led into a unique situation in which she, to retain her stability, needs a particular promise or word upon which her faith can focus. Though such occurrences are rare, God will see to it that it remains clear to believers that they are comprehended in the covenant. The Holy Spirit will quietly engage them to reason by faith, leading them from the realization that they are partakers of the covenant to the endorsement, believing embrace, and making use of a particular promise that applies to them. Paul does this by his believing interaction with God's Word when he appropriates the promise made to Joshua (Heb. 13:5; cf. Josh. 1:5).

2. A specific promise can also be bound upon the soul. That can be a new promise, such as Abraham experienced in Genesis 15 and Paul in 2 Corinthians 12. It can also be the renewal of a previously given promise. Jacob experienced this when God said to him, "I am the God of Bethel" (Gen. 31:13; cf. Gen. 28:19).

Faith That Produces Evidence
To live by faith, it must also be presupposed that the soul will manifest certain marks that affirm that she, by a divine work, has been led to trust in Christ and God's faithfulness as expressed in His Word. When that is lacking, as is far too often the case with struggling believers, the soul will be unable to live by faith. Such souls will then be tossed to and fro. They will be fearful and discouraged and will all too readily say, "My way is hid from the LORD, and

my judgment is passed over from my God" (Isa. 40:27). However, the irrefutable proofs whereby one can know whether, by divine power, he has been led to rest in Christ as revealed in the promise are, among others, the following:

1. Such a person, being quietly disposed, may note that the Word had an exceptional efficacy to stir up his entire soul, render it sensibly active, and bestow a gentle peacefulness.

2. Such a person will know how his heart has melted so that with inner delight and complete spiritual spontaneity, he could pour out his heart before the Lord. He will know what transpired within him during that spiritual frame of mind, namely, that he had high thoughts and a deep awareness of God. In such a disposition of the soul, one will experience a Bethel and a Peniel, and one will be able to say, "Surely the LORD is in this place" (Gen. 28:16). He will know that never before did he have such a felt and striking insight into his own nothingness and utter guiltiness. Being but a speck of dust and a man of unclean lips will cause him to exclaim frequently, "Should God 'look upon such a dead dog as I am' (2 Sam. 9:8)?" They will therefore ask, "Lord, is this word addressed to me? May I believe it? Is this not too great and wonderful? Could I not be deceiving myself?"

3. When God leads a person to rest upon His Word, he will know that God will so remove all obstacles that one will not meet with any impediment upon the pathway of faith. How bowed down his soul was before he was privileged to do so! Questions will arise, such as, "Would I dare to come? May I appropriate this? Are my utterly provocative sins not too great? Is my heart not too rebellious and too cold? Am I not too leprous and unclean? Granted, others are not cast out, but there is no one as wretched as I am. Therefore, not only am I unable, but also I neither dare nor am willing to come." However, when God thus brings about a resting upon His Word, the soul will be so illuminated by divine light that such a person will be inwardly persuaded of the freeness and full extent of grace as well as the merits of Christ's blood. That blood of Christ is so all-sufficient that it can reconcile sinners with God—even if they had committed all the sins of the entire human race. Consequently, all stumbling blocks will be removed so that they will not be an impediment to sinners.

4. They who by God's power were led to rest in Christ could perceive and ascertain at such moments that they saw more than mere words and letters.

Yes, in the words of the promise, they saw Christ Himself in the glory of His person and the all-sufficiency of His fullness, for the promise is indeed a mirror in which we may with open face behold the glory of the God of the covenant (2 Cor. 3:18). Before these experiences, how the soul went, seeking her way while sowing with tears and with weeping and supplication! Often she attempted to embrace the promise, but she did not at all behold Christ's Person in it. She could not find comfort, resolution, and deliverance, causing her continually to be bowed down and uncomforted. However, now she may behold the King in His beauty (Isa. 33:17), whose beauty is so perfect and so enamors her soul in an unforgettable and all-surpassing way, that she must exclaim, "What I have heard with my ears was but a very faint portrayal of what I may now see with my eyes! Oh, I have never been told even one hundred-thousandth of a part! I am overwhelmed with adoration!" Here we observe a very apparent distinction between God's children and presumptuous Christians. If the latter, in their perplexity, take refuge to a specific word of promise, and if they detect some emotion in their inner exercises, they can readily be satisfied. However, a true Christian must see something of Jesus Himself, or else, he will remain comfortless—just as Mary Magdalene could not be satisfied until Christ revealed himself to her with the word *Mary*.

5. By His own work and based on His promise, God will lead the believer to rest in Christ. He will then be enabled to trace how his soul has been exercised regarding Christ in the most intimate embrace and heartfelt reception of His person. The soul will then lay Him as "a bundle of myrrh…betwixt [her] breasts" (Song 1:13). Figuratively speaking, she will then surrender herself fully in such a heartfelt, unreserved manner to Him and will most intimately unite herself to Him. "He that is joined unto the Lord is one spirit" (1 Cor. 6:17). For faith will behold Him by that divine light that illumines the mind, the will chooses Him and will love Him most intimately, and all the affections are rooted in Him and will cling to Him more surely than a belt encircles the waist of a man. Such is the soul's experience when she is translated into Christ as a branch is grafted and transplanted into a vine. The soul will thus become the property of Another. Oh, I am hopeful that hypocrites who can speak so much about Jesus will examine their souls' exercises in light of these matters and the order in which they transpire. They will come short in the one as well as the other! Let me mention one instance. They will never be acquainted with the extrinsic acts of faith to unite themselves to the Surety by embracing and receiving Him. From their side, they know nothing more

than a cordial demonstration of reverence and indebtedness. However, a true believer must first know of an unveiling and revelation of Christ to his soul before he can come to a surrender that will yield peace to him. Only when Jesus is then subsequently revealed will there be an embracing and reception of Him, and after that, there will be a consecration and surrender to Him.

6. He whom God leads by His mighty hand to a resting in Christ in the word of promise can perceive upon reflection how his heart valued the exercises of faith of which we spoke. He cannot readily forget how his burden of sin that so greatly weighed him down was removed, how he beheld God as Father, Son, and Spirit, and how everything was positively radiant, etc.! He now knows himself to be justified by faith and to have peace with God (Rom. 5:1), experiences a joy in the Holy Spirit that passes all understanding (Phil. 4:7), and a sprinkling of his conscience with the blood of Christ that cleanses from all sin (Heb. 12:24; 1 Peter 1:2; 1 John 1:7). Though someone may possess grace and yet lack a conscious knowledge of it, as long as he lacks this assurance, he will be incapable of living by faith.

7. Finally, when God leads someone to rightly rest in Christ as revealed in the promise, he will observe that in casting himself entirely upon this Surety, his soul will be ignited with an inner inclination and love for sanctification. Oh, if only he could now run without impediment, and if only he could indeed do that for which his heart has been won over! He will pursue it and seek to live and walk, both publicly and in secret, in filial fear before God and men. Based on these and other spiritual experiences, the soul can determine that she has been rightly led to rest in Christ in response to the word of promise. She will thus be able to ascertain the presupposition mentioned above. You may read more about this in *The ABC of Faith* under the rubric "To Hear."

Faith in Particular Promises Suitable for the Present Need
To live by faith, it must also be presupposed that a believer will be acquainted with a particular promise for particular circumstances. The faith he must exercise will be grounded in this promise, and thereupon he will rest. Though every believer does indeed have the right to be exercised by faith with all the promises, the experience of believers teaches nevertheless that they cannot possibly ward off spiritual assaults and strife. The granting of such particular promises will be experienced in the life of faith so that they will be able to keep their heads uplifted in specific circumstances.

Upon having obeyed God's call, how would Abraham have been able to keep his head uplifted if he had not received the promise that God would be his shield (Gen. 15:1)? And indeed, he had been called to traverse a way unknown to him. How else would Paul have been comforted when he suffered shipwreck while at sea and be assured of a good outcome? If he had merely been able to rest in general promises, he would have had nothing more than the knowledge that all would redound to God's glory and his salvation. However, he knew that the waves of the sea would not swallow him up in light of the particular promise that he would bear witness to Jesus in Rome as he had done in Jerusalem.

Likewise, the soul will need a particular promise for particular circumstances which she, as stated earlier, will appropriate and embrace by faith. For example, someone may have been powerfully converted in his youth. For a season, he will then walk in love and be meticulous regarding his godly walk. However, his heart can nevertheless be enticed to sin because of a youthful temptation or some other sin. Upon yielding to such sin, his spiritual light would gradually be extinguished, and he would begin to neglect the duties of his secret walk with God. Spiritually he will then gradually and increasingly become dull and barren. He will become conformed to this world and spiritually insensitive. He will also be little troubled by this and hardly think of repenting.

However, after living in that condition for a season, God will again be mindful of him. His sins will be bound upon his heart, and, so to speak, he will experience a "second conversion." He will then be granted the privilege of becoming reunited with Christ. In the meantime, he can again be greatly assaulted, albeit not regarding his conversion and the exercise of his faith. Certain bosom sins will have come to the fore. They will assault the soul with a strong temptation, and these sins will have lost little of their power despite his being watchful and prayerful regarding them. It will continually be impressed upon the soul, "Things will again turn out as they used to be. Then you were also serious, and it subsided. So it shall be again!"

How much strife and distress this can cause is best known by those who have been enrolled in this "school." However, it now pleases the Lord to make Himself known to them with or by a particular word, saying, "Behold, I send an Angel before thee, to keep thee in the way, and to bring thee into the place which I have prepared" (Ex. 23:20). They will then perceive that God Himself will undertake for them by driving out their sins. They will then experience that God will engage Himself for the mortification of their lusts and their sanctification. This experience will give them liberty and confidence and will in the life of faith always serve as a foundation upon which they can rest and plead during times of spiritual warfare. It may be that they will only be able to say, "Lord, I am fearful. Now is the moment for Thee to 'remember the word unto thy servant, upon which thou hast caused me to hope'" (Ps. 119:49). He who may have spiritual light can expand this to all manner of particular spiritual and temporal circumstances. One will then perceive how essential it is for faith to rest upon a particular promise to remain steadfast amid all assaults. Oh, faith will cast its anchor upon Christ employing a word explicitly applicable to them. That anchor ground is so secure that they will not drift away even when storms and waves arise. Yes, even "though the earth be removed, and though the mountains be carried into the midst of the sea" (Ps. 46:2), they "shall be as mount Zion, which cannot be removed, but abideth for ever" (Ps. 125:1).

Experiential Knowledge of the Gospel

To live by faith, it is required and must be presupposed that the soul, by the powerful instruction of God the Holy Spirit, will be experientially acquainted with the way of the gospel. As beneficial as it may be to know this intellectually, he who wishes to make progress in the way of the gospel shall experience that such intellectual knowledge will be of little help. In fact, he will recognize that he needs the anointing of the Holy Spirit, who will teach him all things. We observe, therefore, that many believers frequently walk in darkness, having but little knowledge of the way of the gospel. Consequently, they will not experience much peace except when they are in a good spiritual frame. Among other things, there are six or seven factors that hinder the life of faith.

1. For the believer, the perception of his sinful nature and the God-dishonoring nature of his life is a hindrance for the exercise of faith. Though he yearns for Jesus, many a believer will thus stand from afar and exclaim, "Oh, what a sinful man I am! Would it not be a manifestation of pride and inexcusable brazenness if I were to embrace Christ upon God's offer and take refuge to Him?" Therefore, many of God's children who are unacquainted with the penetrating light of God's way of grace are almost never, or at least rarely, focused on the exercise of faith. Instead, they will say many times, "If only I could mourn my sins until my death," and many similar exclamations.

This proves their aversion to sin and their love for God. Nevertheless, this is a serious hindrance—both at the outset and later on in their spiritual lives.

2. The life of faith can be hindered by certain manifestations of indwelling corruption that the believer cannot overcome no matter how much he fights against them and prays and supplicates that he may overcome them. As a worm, this gnaws at the root of all his liberty to exercise faith. Since he continues to sin and succumbs to the same sins and then takes refuge to the blood of Christ, it appears to him that he misuses the blood of Christ and makes Jesus out to be a servant of sin. The strongest among believers frequently experience that this will greatly inhibit them in the exercise of faith.

3. The life of faith will be hindered because the soul is so intent on a specific emotional experience that believers dare not come, unless their hearts should first be contrite and humbled. Though no one will embrace Christ to live by faith out of Him without such stirrings of the heart, they are nevertheless not the ground for the soul's liberty.

4. Also, when the believer, reflecting on previous exercises of faith, detects a lack of fruit, he can be significantly hindered in believing, for the genuineness of faith must be affirmed by works.

5. The believer can also fear that even though Christ is willing to receive others, He will not receive him. The soul will often be strengthened in that perception when she perceives much willingness on her part without Jesus, in turn, manifesting His willingness toward her.

6. Another hindrance can be that believers fear that their hearts will not be as tender and sensitive to impressions as when they exercise their faith. They know this by grievous experience, for some of their friends were of a very tender disposition as long as they went their way dependently and hesitatingly. However, when they would come to some liberty, they would go their way with much more freedom.

7. Finally, the magnitude of the matter can be a hindrance. This, and many other factors, can be such a hindrance in the life of faith that the soul will always be and remain despondent—except when the Spirit Himself instructs them regarding the way of the gospel. Thereby the way can be opened, and by divine light the soul will see that God has no other intent upon this way

except to erect eternally abiding memorials of free grace. Then it will become manifest what eternal and pure mercy can bring about. Then it will become very evident that God will manifest His grace to such who, in their own estimation, are the worst of all. Believers will then transcend all the hindrances that have been listed, and they will learn to understand fully the force of the words "that Christ Jesus came into the world to save sinners; of whom I am chief" (1 Tim. 1:15). This will then enable them to live by faith.

Experience Gained by Trials

To live by faith also presupposes that spiritual experiences and trials encountered by the believer have produced a sanctified knowledge, for it is precisely in such ways that God fulfills His promise to the soul. And indeed, believers will often come upon pathways unknown to them and encounter distresses that a believer with but few spiritual exercises would have to exclaim, "All these things are against me. How will this culminate in a way in which the promise will be fulfilled?" The experience of all who fear God does indeed teach how often they seemed to succumb in new situations due to not knowing God's way with them, thinking "my hope is perished from the LORD" (Lam. 3:18; cf. Ps. 77:7–10). As the means whereby such knowledge of faith may be acquired, the believer must note carefully the ways in which God leads him. In so doing, one will observe that "hope maketh not ashamed; because the love of God is shed abroad in our hearts" (Rom. 5:5).

Keeping God's Commandments

Bypassing other matters, to live by faith presupposes a godly walk, for God is a holy God, and He will only dwell with those who love Him and keep His commandments. The spiritual light that is always required for the exercise of faith will be obscured by the slightest neglect of duty or indulgence regarding any given sin. One's freedom in the presence of God will be negatively impacted when a given lust gains the upper hand or when a particular sin oppresses the conscience for which they have not found atonement in the blood of Christ. Such tenderness of soul will manifest itself as follows:

1. One will live in a continuous awareness of the Lord.

2. One will have a deep reverence for God's majesty.

3. One will also fulfill all obligations conscientiously and therefore shun all sin and opportunities to sin.

4. In one's conduct, one must continually speak, think, and undertake everything in the Lord's presence, asking himself continually whether a given word or deed will be to God's honor. Am I called to say or do this or that? Do I perceive it to be founded upon God's Word?

5. A person will carefully consider the various manifestations of Spirit-wrought grace in the heart. As long as one lives with an intimate and heartfelt reverence and tender love for God and His will, a person will see to it that they do not decline. For when the soul begins to decline, and one initially does not recognize it, spiritual poverty and weakness will overtake them "as one that travelleth" (Prov. 6:11).

6. Finally, one will continually make use of and take refuge in Jesus's blood to secure His peace by a continual surrender of himself to the Lord Jesus.

A quiet and calm reflection on these things could be used as a means in God's hand to persuade the natural man how deeply ignorant and estranged he is from a life with God. The little ones in grace could determine what they are lacking and whereby the power of unbelief oppresses them. And those who are more advanced upon the way of faith will receive insight regarding the necessity of a tender and godly walk. May the Lord grant that His Spirit would thus be bestowed on us all in a rich measure.

Clarifications on the Life of Faith

The second matter to be considered regarding living by faith will be addressed through various remarks that will enable us to grasp the life of faith better. We will endeavor to do this as briefly and transparently as possible.

Faith and Feeling

Our first remark is that faith and feeling are two entirely different matters. There can be the first (as we shall yet consider) without the second. However, the second, that is, feeling, can never exist apart from the exercise of faith. Since many weak believers fail to note this, they are constantly focusing on their emotional frame. One moment they will say, "By thy favour thou hast made my mountain to stand strong; I shall never be moved" (Ps. 30:6–7). And the next moment, they can be so troubled by the hiding of God's countenance that many a believing child of God will be inclined to deny all that God has ever done for them. They will then experience comfortless days and miserable nights.

To instruct you regarding this, we must show you the distinction between faith and feeling.

1. They differ as to their *object*. The object of faith is indeed Christ as revealed in the word of promise, whereas the object of feeling is Christ as He manifests Himself to the soul in a very intimate and blessed way. With old Simeon, the soul will then have the Child in her arms, enabling her to praise God.

2. Faith and feeling also differ as to their *activity*. Faith is exercised toward a Jesus in whom is an all-encompassing fullness, and it also rejoices that everything is to be found in Jesus. However, feeling does not focus on who Jesus is for its comfort but rather upon what it receives from Jesus, and it will rejoice in proportion to how much she perceives of this within herself.

3. Faith and feeling differ as to the steadfast *nature of the assurance they produce*. And indeed, assurance of faith will then not be impaired by serious doubts, spiritual darkness, etc., because it rests in God's promises. However, the assurance of sense (feeling) usually lasts no longer than the duration of one's spiritual frame, for it rests in that frame and emotionally stimulating exercises. Since the believer's heart cannot look beyond its doubts, it will readily say that there is no deliverance. Everyone can thus perceive how the one differs from the other. That being the case, for a Christian who desires to live by faith, it is of utmost importance that he does not confuse the two and live partly by faith and partly by sense. A believer may indeed cherish his feelings, but the foundation of his assurance should not be a combination of his feelings and Christ. Else he will continually falter spiritually. He must have Christ *alone*, and then he will remain steadfast.

Faith's Orientation to Past, Present, and Future

Our second remark is that the faith whereby the soul lives will be exercised regarding matters that pertain to the past, the present, and the future. If one neither considers this nor correctly understands how faith is exercised toward these three distinct matters, one cannot understand in some measure what it is to live by faith. Much less shall one be able to make any progress in thus living by faith.

1. One will live by faith regarding matters that have transpired in *the past*, doing so either regarding one's portion in the grace and favor of God in Christ, or the promise that he has embraced by faith and particularly appropriated

for himself. With a joyful awareness, the believer can recall these matters and be convinced upon good grounds that he has truly been ingrafted into Christ and has become His property. This is the life of faith of many Christians who are not privileged to experience that God in Christ by renewal appears to them. Nevertheless, they know that from being dead, they have become alive, and that enables them to keep their head above water. One may by no means view such a life by faith as suspect, for God knows that they long for a new revelation of Himself and also earnestly pray for this. We also know that God is sovereign in the bestowal of His favor. For some, He will only permit the divine light to arise once in their lives when they place their feet upon the pathway of life. The Lord will for some time deal tenderly with others, but afterwards, He may for years not cause them to experience His favor in that measure.

2. As to matters that pertain to *the present*, one lives by faith when he is privileged, to transact with Christ and truly enter into union with Him—to make use of Him unto "wisdom, and righteousness, and sanctification, and [complete] redemption" (1 Cor. 1:30), and to entrust his soul to the Lord. In Christ, he can then exercise communion with God in whom is complete salvation, and his soul can entrust himself fully to Him. This living by faith generates great joy and yields a deep satisfaction to the soul because the soul, in and through faith, will be filled with joy, peace, and comfort. However, we must not speak of this living by faith as if it only consisted of this. That would be a snare for us and others, for faith is very rarely engaged continually regarding present matters.

3. Regarding *the future*, one lives by faith when Christ reveals Himself to the soul in His Word. We observe this when grievous and stubbornly persistent sins are subdued or when the disposition of his heart is enlivened. We observe this also when one receives a particular blessing; when one experiences a deliverance personally, for one's family, for God's church in general and certain of her oppressed members; or in connection with specific truths of the faith. The believer can also live by faith when the things regarding eternal salvation are impressed upon him. I repeat, someone lives by faith regarding these matters when in God's promises he can behold them from afar, when he can rest in God's faithfulness, and when he can know himself to be at ease by the Word of God over against all the assaults that are made upon his faith. Doing so is to believe in God in hope against hope

(Rom. 4:18) and without conferring with flesh and blood (Gal. 1:16). We can learn from this that though this is indeed one and the same faith, one lives thereby in various ways. Furthermore, we observe that all the designations for faith apply to these matters. Finally, we observe that this third way in which this life of faith functions cannot exist without the first. It is equally evident that one can live by faith as to the first and third mode while missing the second. I will leave any further elaboration regarding these truths to the attentive and God-fearing reader.

Weak and Strong Faith

Our third remark is that we must learn to distinguish between weak and strong acts of faith. There exists a misunderstanding that all acts of faith must be equally strong and must have the same effect upon the soul. By subscribing to such a view, one will seriously inhibit his own life of faith and that of others. The slightest whimper or motion of the most insignificant part of the body is in natural life as much a symptom of life as is eating, drinking, and being joyful. This is equally true in spiritual life. Weak acts of faith belong as much to faith as strong acts. One also lives by them. When a person quietly lifts up his heart, may look to Jesus, yearn for Christ, etc.—these are also genuine exercises of faith, even though they do not yield refreshment to the soul. It will yield hidden support, just as strong acts of faith yield strong encouragement. (See the word "Persevere" in *The ABC of Faith*.)

Believers Sometimes Oppressed by Unbelief

Finally, we remark that one can justly be said to live by faith even when, in particular cases, he will be oppressed by the power of unbelief and will in such situations be unable to stir up his heart to trust by faith. This was to be seen by Abraham, Moses, and others. Although they lived by faith, they lived at times in an unbelieving disposition.

To Live by Faith

In our discussion of the life of faith, we have now arrived at our third main heading. We will now, in general terms, identify the essence of this life of faith. We will set before you the fruit of our meditation regarding this matter, recognizing that there is room for improvement.

General Consideration of the Life of Faith

When we consider this life of faith in general terms, we note that it is a life where the believer has a joyous consciousness of his gracious state before God. The believer will discern the evident marks of a child of God within himself and may view the triune God as his God. The apostle expresses it in these words: "Who loved me, and gave himself for me." Elsewhere he says, "I know whom I have believed" (2 Tim. 1:12). And the church of God confesses, "The LORD is my portion, saith my soul; therefore will I hope in him" (Lam. 3:24). As to the essence of this life of faith, we wish to make the following remarks.

1. Many of God's children have stumbled along for quite some time before they are at liberty to say this. Having such liberty will be for them a matter so marvelous and inestimable in their eyes that they cannot express it in words. However, we presently live in a time when most people know of no strife regarding this point. They have never "been emptied from vessel to vessel," and, with Moab, have been at ease from their youth (Jer. 48:11).

2. A believer will not always consider his state of grace with the same measure of light. Frequently, he can only deem his state to be gracious by virtue of his sanctified memory and his awareness of what has transpired between God and his soul. Consequently, he will not always be filled with the same measure of inner amazement and adoration regarding his blessed state. Believers will, therefore, neither always have the same inner enlargement nor have the same liberty by virtue of their filial rights to draw near to God in prayer as their God and Father in Christ.

3. Though the believer lives by faith, this does not mean that he will no longer experience spiritual strife. Sometimes, his assaults will be of short duration and be as arrows that whiz by him. They cannot inflict much harm upon the soul and will be rebuffed by faith. However, sometimes they will last longer and be more persistent and appear to be so intimidating that the believer must do battle against them. When the believer is then privileged to remain steadfast in his righteousness, he will be most blessed indeed. However, many struggling souls think that they would be able to endure all tribulation if they could but believe that they possess grace. But experience teaches that the sharpest arrows and most intense assaults will ambush an exercised saint following such spiritual liberty.

4. A soul can live by faith without having the courage to say so. However,

experience teaches that there can be something on the bottom of his heart that causes him to act like a believer in prayer, even though he will flatly deny it apart from prayer. A hypocrite's words will always exceed what he experiences, whereas an upright soul will always speak below the actual spiritual frame of his heart.

Specific Exercises of the Life of Faith

This life of faith will also consist of the quiet manifestation of the spiritual exercises of believers. Life will always manifest itself in some motion or activity. In this life of faith, the activities of the soul are many and varied. We will only mention a few of them and leave the others to interested readers as food for holy meditation.

1. Believers actively lift their hearts heavenward where Christ is. He hopes that he may soon arrive there, and he exhorts his own soul, saying, "My heart, look heavenward, for you will not find it here below. True living, loving, and lauding will only be experienced where one sees Jesus."[7]

2. They will actively search out the incomparable beauties and excellencies of the Surety as displayed in the glorious luster of His Person. Their high esteem and love for Him will then so stir within them that they will arise from the dust with eagles' wings and lose themselves in Him who is "fairer than the children of men" (Ps. 45:2) and who in every respect is "altogether lovely" (Song 5:16).

3. Their souls will delight themselves in Him as their Shield who protects them; as their Sun who illumes in them; as their Refuge in whom they are secure; as their Head who governs them; as their Lord, only King, and Lawgiver whom they obey; as their Strength who strengthens and emboldens them; as their Guide who leads them; as the One who gathers them in His arms, carries them in His bosom, and cherishes them in every way. How sweet and ravishing are such meditations to the soul, causing her to exclaim, "I will greatly rejoice in the LORD, my soul shall be joyful in my God; for he hath clothed me with the garments of salvation" (Isa. 61:10)!

4. Believers will at times marvel at their blessed portion. They will then say, "God has made me, who by nature is a child of Satan, a son, a daughter of

---

7. This is a translation of the opening lines of the first stanza of a poem by Jodocus Lodensteyn entitled "Heerlyckheyds loff'" ("Worship in Glory").

the Most High! He called me when I was polluted in my blood and there was none to pity me, saying, 'Live; yea, I said unto thee when thou wast in thy blood, Live' (Ezek. 16:6). God has brought me, even me, into a relationship with Himself, so that He says to me, 'I am and shall be to you a God!'" Oh, when the believer may perceive these things—this living by faith and the exercises of this faith—and how sovereign and undeserved they are, he will exclaim, even when he neither has clothing with which to dress himself nor a piece of bread to eat, "The LORD is the portion of mine inheritance and of my cup: thou maintainest my lot. The lines are fallen unto me in pleasant places; yea, I have a goodly heritage" (Ps. 16:5–6).

5. Then again, believers will expose their souls to the warming and heart-melting rays of the Sun of Righteousness, as well as to the rain and dew of the Spirit's grace so that they may be fruitful and manifest growth. One's objective will be that the wilderness may become a fruitful land, and that "instead of the thorn shall come up the fir tree, and instead of the brier shall come up the myrtle tree" (Isa. 55:13), for he who lives by faith desires to grow and increase in grace.

6. Believers will at times look upon Jesus as the brazen serpent who is lifted up in the proclamation of the gospel and as the Lamb of God that takes away the sins of the world. In so doing, the soul will be given to behold by faith that her sins are being forgiven and that she has been made whole.

7. There are also times that believers intensely yearn for Christ to draw near and come into the heart so that they may truly have fellowship with Him. They will pant more after God, after the living God, than "the hart panteth after the water brooks" (Ps. 42:1).

8. Then again, believers may also experience that they are intimately united to Him, thereby being rooted in Him by love, and finding their steadfastness in Him.

9. Believers reflect at times that their walk according to the law is so precious to their souls that they wholeheartedly subscribe to it, for the law has also been written upon their hearts.

Though an attentive reader may add more to this if he so pleases, I will do so with but a few words unto edification.

a. A person must know that he can live by faith when praying and meditating and so doing even when exercising one's daily calling. If our soul were more spiritually minded and our hearts more enflamed in love, we would not be in the least inhibited. We have indeed found it to be so experientially, for it is a true adage that one will rather be where he loves than where he lives.

b. You ought also to know that if we continually stir and stimulate ourselves accordingly, by God's gracious influence, living by faith will increasingly become habitual for us. The Lord will generally not withhold this influence other than when there is a prior offense.

c. Although one will not always perceive the same fruits and experience the same emotions in the godly exercise of this life by faith, one must therefore not in despondency let the hands hang down. Instead, one should endeavor to continue. Afterward, you will perceive that there has always been some secret support. We also observe regarding the saints in Scripture that though they begin with lamenting, they end in worship. You will observe this time and again when perusing the Psalms.

d. Since every believer will indeed perceive his deficiencies, everyone must strive to be humbled by this and stir himself up to live by faith.

Resting in the Lord's Attributes

The life of faith will, generally speaking, also consist in the soul wholly and entirely trusting in the Lord, the God of the covenant. This trusting in the Lord we encounter so frequently when we read the sacred pages of God's Word. This trusting is the committal of ourselves and our way to the Lord—a relying upon the God of the covenant. We will not discuss this any further as we have already done so in *The ABC of Faith* under the rubrics of "Entrusting" and "Reliance." We will only say this: that all who live by faith, and in so doing rest in God, will have three important foundations upon which they rest.

1. They *rest in God's truth* as expressed in His promises. There is no other foundation upon which the soul can ground her expectation. That foundation is solely the Word of that God who cannot lie and who has engaged Himself by oath so that the heirs of salvation can enjoy an abundant comfort. And indeed, the substance of what is being promised is great. The way in

which the promises are fulfilled can be so obscure to the eye of faith. The assaults upon the soul can be so manifold, and the fluctuations of one's frame of heart can be so erratic! Living by faith would be impossible if the soul could not rise above all this and rest in God's truth, for she knows that her unfaithfulness cannot annul God's faithfulness.

2. The soul that lives by faith and finds her rest in God will also *rest in His omnipotent power*. Nothing less than this omnipotence can sustain the soul, for frequently light must arise from darkness, the crooked must be made straight, mountains must be removed, and valleys must be exalted. Furthermore, spiritual wickedness must be opposed and overcome. Abraham believed that God, as the Almighty One, was able to do so.

3. When resting in God, believers must also *rest in His immutability*, for they change continually. When their faith is grounded in their frame of heart, and when that falls away, they will also lose the foundation for their liberty! It is the reality of their spiritual lives that they often, though not consistently, think that, contingent upon their spiritual frames, God loves them one moment more than another. Though that may be true regarding the manifestations of God's love, it is not true regarding His love as such.

The Experience of Resting in the Lord
We need to consider a few more matters.

1. The soul will generally find her rest in God after she has encountered many difficulties. She will thereby learn experientially that only God in Christ, as He has revealed Himself in His covenant, can be the basis and foundation of her hope. We are generally inclined to seek this within ourselves, our fellow creatures, or the means of grace, albeit that they all exclaim, "It is not to be found with me!" Nevertheless, we are neither willing nor able to believe this until the Lord by many and repeated spiritual experiences will show us that all that is not God is no more than an empty vessel that lacks a foundation upon which one can rest and also does not minister a drop of comfort to our weary souls.

2. The soul will only rest in God through Christ and entrust everything to Him when God reveals Himself in glorious light. His glorious all-sufficiency will be revealed to the soul in such a way that everything else will vanish and become invisible. The soul will then see that all that is of value to her is found

in the God of the covenant Himself. Likewise, when a man does not focus on the sun, he will delight himself in all the things that so marvelously appear in the light shining forth from the sun. But when he looks at the sun itself, everything around him will vanish from sight. That being said, one needs to keep in mind that the soul will only in this way draw nearer to God, for experience teaches us how being prodded by a measure of spiritual illumination, someone can behold the blessedness of this state before God. Yet, the soul will at times seek to enter into this in her own strength rather than allowing herself to be illuminated by God's own light. Instead, she will increasingly drift away from this and never arrive at the place where it would be so good for her. Consequently, believers will remain disconsolate and never find rest in the Lord Himself to the complete satisfaction of their souls.

3. We must remark that the utmost care is needed not to be disengaged from this rest by our innate sinful restlessness or to do something whereby this light will be obscured. A curtain will then move before our eyes, preventing the beams of God's light from shining into our souls. Nevertheless, that light is so absolutely essential to remaining in this blessed rest. Experience has indeed taught us that someone acquainted with this rest can readily lose it through sin and neglect of living a godly life as required by the precepts of the gospel. Then it can happen that such a person will never again experience this rest in the same measure and therefore will appear to descend into the grave in bitter sorrow. Brothers and sisters in the Lord, beware, therefore, that you walk circumspectly!

Having Our Eyes Fixed on Christ

Living by faith will generally also consist of the believer seeing himself as he is in Christ and what he is in Christ. I am not saying that he must never view himself as he is. By no means! The saints have done that also, saying, "To me, the chief of sinners and the least of all saints, this grace has been bestowed." This is most necessary for various reasons: on the one hand, to always value grace highly, and on the other hand, that there would be matter for confession in our prayers. After all, we cannot but say that our sins are more in number than the hairs upon our heads. We must also acknowledge that if God were to enter into judgment with us, we would not be able to answer one question in a thousand.

It is also necessary so that we will freely condemn ourselves and come to God with the noose around our necks. Furthermore, it is necessary to prevent us from having a proud heart. We are very much inclined toward this, even when we are proud of borrowed goods! Finally, it is also good when we esteem another higher than ourselves.

In the meantime, however, the believer must frequently lift his head and fix his eyes upon Christ to not be overcome too much by despondency. He who first saw himself in his misery and clothed in filthy garments will now see himself clothed in a change of raiment (Zech. 3:4), and thus with the perfect righteousness of the Surety. In reflecting upon his misery, he who only saw his deficiencies and imperfection, will then see that he is perfect in Christ as his Head. He who had to assess his prayers so negatively due to their deficiencies and a lack of fervency will then see that Christ will render every prayerful sigh so delightful with the incense of His merits that his sighing will be noted as a calling forth. He will then experience that his eyes will overcome Jesus (Song 6:5) and stir up His tender mercy. (You can add additional matters to delight yourself in this holy reflection on the life of faith.) My beloved, much is comprehended in the life of faith. If you may but practice this in a holy manner, your heart will be fully enlarged to practice all the works of gratitude with a joyful heart.

Responding in Faith

To live by faith will generally also consist of responding in faith to all with which the soul is confronted by saying: Christ Jesus! As we have observed, the life of faith is not without strife—and not without many assaults and unflinching demands to pay what we owe. When believers come into such straits, many who have not made progress upon the pathway of faith will be terrified by a sight of their guilt or their enemies. It can also be that they become despondent when they perceive their deficiencies and impotence or that they will work themselves to death to remove these perceived deficiencies. In so doing, they will neglect to practice that which can lead them to rest. However, they who live by faith and whom God Himself has brought in this way will exclaim with a holy, reverent, and humble demeanor, "I am not liable according to the law. If there are any demands, you must speak to my Husband, Christ, to whom I am betrothed." Hereupon the soul will turn to Christ by way of believing transactions that I will not enumerate. I will leave that to your holy meditation upon these matters.

The soul will cry out mournfully, "Oh, my beloved Jesus, I am being confronted and grievously threatened. Oh, Jesus, dost Thou not remember how

Thou didst win over my heart for Thyself and how I acquiesced to enter into a marital union with Thee? Then, as Thy bride, did I not fully surrender myself to Thee to become Thy property? Thou art neither willing nor able to deny that. Here are the staff and signet Thou hast given me. Are they not Thine? And if they are indeed Thine, dost Thou then not know that the condition was that I could not do anything and that Thou saidst to me, 'Be of good courage. Though you have nothing, I have everything. If you are unable, I will bring it to a good end for you.' Therefore, I now desire to come (says the soul), and I beseech Thee to be so gracious and good to be mindful of Thy Word to help me." The soul that will thus have strengthened herself by these believing transactions will respond with the triumphant words of Paul, "O death, where is thy sting? O grave, where is thy victory? The sting of death is sin; and the strength of sin is the law. But thanks be to God, which giveth us the victory through our Lord Jesus Christ" (1 Cor. 15:55–57). By faith, the soul will say this expressly to herself.

Transcending This World

The life of faith is generally a life that will neither be encouraged or discouraged by that which pertains to this present world. With Moses, the soul will see "him who is invisible" (Heb. 11:27) and can rejoice even when there is "no herd in the stalls" (Hab. 3:17) because she is refreshed by that which is to come. This faith enables her to transcend all difficulties.

Taking Hold of Christ

Though there are yet other matters to be addressed in a detailed discussion about this life of faith, we will not discuss them now. Therefore, we will conclude by saying that this life of faith consists of a continued taking hold and making use of Christ by walking in Him as you have received Him (Col. 2:6). As to how the believer lives by faith in various circumstances, we will unfold this in a few sermons in greater detail.

APPLICATION

My beloved, you have seen how someone lives and dies, and that not of himself, but rather through Christ who works in his heart the faith by which he lives.

In light of all that has been said, much can be applied to us. However, having already expounded everything clearly and experientially, we will add but a few words.

1. You who are unconverted, consider all of this attentively so that you may be convicted of your state of death by nature and of the necessity of possessing spiritual life. Every point that we have considered will give you clear direction. May God Himself arrest your attention regarding these matters.

2. Believers, you have been privileged to receive several spiritual benefits, and we have given you many directions to instruct you regarding the exercises of faith. We will leave them with you and recommend them to you. And our prayer is that God will work all the good pleasure of His will and efficaciously work the work of faith in us. Amen.

CHAPTER 12

Faith, a Grace That Yields Daily Justification

For with the heart man believeth unto righteousness.
—ROMANS 10:10

The ceremonial law required that one be cleansed of the least defilement before fulfilling a specific ceremonial (cultic) obligation. Likewise, beloved, it is indispensable during the New Testament dispensation that before drawing near to God, one cleanses his conscience from dead works in the blood of Jesus Christ that cleanses from all sins (1 John 1:7). We wish to draw your attention to this truth, namely, how one lives by faith unto daily justification.

In verse nine, the apostle has set before us that they who confess with the mouth and believe with the heart shall be saved. He proves this in the words of our text, for one believes with the heart "unto righteousness."

These words bring two matters to our attention that we now wish to address:

1. The subject of the activity described in our text: the heart;
2. The activity itself: believing with the heart unto justification.

BELIEVING WITH THE HEART

In the first part of the text, the apostle speaks of the heart. He who reads God's Word attentively will know that the heart must frequently be understood as synonymous with the soul. Thus, the word *heart* encompasses all the faculties of the soul, such as mind, will, discernment, and conscience. Having addressed this subject in-depth in connection with Psalm 45:1, we will not do so now. We merely wish to state that we understand the heart to refer to all that pertains to the soul. Though the mind is indeed the preeminent seat of faith, faith is embedded in all the soul's faculties. He who carefully considers the designations ascribed to faith will observe that they are linked on one occasion to the mind and another time to the will. With emphasis, the apostle speaks here of the heart. He does so partly to distinguish clearly between the believing assent of historical and saving faith. The first only engages the mind, whereas the second the entire soul. Thereby the apostle also reminds us that saving faith must always issue forth from the heart, and that we must examine all our spiritual exercises in that light.

BELIEVING UNTO RIGHTEOUSNESS

Second, having spoken of the heart as being the source from which the exercises of faith must proceed, the apostle teaches us that thereby we believe *unto righteousness*. No one will expect me to explain in detail how, before God's tribunal, the sinner is justified by faith, faith being the mediate cause whereby he takes hold of and appropriates the righteousness of Christ. We have done this extensively when, in expounding Romans 5:1, we have spoken of faith (back in chapter 2) as the grace exercised by the ungodly sinner whereby he is justified. You will also not expect us to discuss some of the various views regarding this matter. This treatise focuses primarily on the experiential life of the believer, and it would be regrettable if our hearts were to be distracted by a semantic dispute. Upon carefully considering all the different views among orthodox theologians regarding initial or secondary (daily) justification, we will perceive them as semantic rather than substantial.

In short, we will consider this righteousness as it pertains either to the person—and thus as referring to his actual acquittal—or to his deeds. As to the second, it refers to the actual acquittal that follows the exercise of faith in connection with the deeds committed by the one who has been justified. In reference to the latter, we will now speak of living by faith "unto righteousness."

To do so with utmost clarity, we will consider various matters of which your hearts will approve, and that will lead us to the actual subject of this treatise.

The Inability of All People to Perfectly Obey God

You know that since the fall of our first parents, no man is able to keep God's commandments. Daily and every moment we transgress them in thoughts, words, and deeds.

The Sinfulness of Mankind

God's Word teaches this extensively: "Every imagination of the thoughts of his heart was only evil continually" (Gen. 6:5), and "the heart is deceitful above all things, and desperately wicked: who can know it?" (Jer. 17:9). No one is so righteous that he does not sin. The most righteous man will sin seven times daily, and we are admonished to forgive our brother seven times. Therefore, we conclude with the apostle John, "If we say that we have no sin, we deceive ourselves, and the truth is not in us" (1 John 1:8). When we are persuaded to believe this, our hearts will be filled with very humble thoughts regarding ourselves, for we will perceive the inexpressible corruption of our nature that continually inclines us toward all evil. Add to this that our growth in grace is to be measured accordingly, for the more we recognize this—with a deep insight that melts the heart and humbles the soul—the more we will grow in the knowledge of the omnipotent God, of Jesus, and of ourselves. However, if a soul is not arrested to be thus exercised with an inner abhorrence and loathing of self, it will unmistakably prove that he is not a true Christian. Or it may prove at best that his spiritual life is in serious decline and near demise. We maintain a thousand to one that this [loathing of self] is lacking in all nominal Christians. They will always speak haughtily and desire to be acknowledged above others. There will not be an inner sense of insignificance, reverence, and humility, nor will this manifest itself outwardly.

The Unconfessed Sins of Believers

2. Furthermore, God's children may have committed sins about which they have not been humbled. They have not taken refuge in the blood of Jesus Christ so that they might expressly experience forgiveness in their souls and the cleansing of their consciences regarding the guilt they have incurred. Consequently, as long as the guilt of these sins weighs down a soul, she will neither be able to have communion with God nor live the holy life to which she is obliged. As a shadow follows the body, the commission of sin will likewise result in spiritual deadness and decline (Rom. 6:23). He who takes note of himself will experience that sin obscures his inner light, and his "moisture [will be] turned into the drought of summer" (Ps. 32:4). This wretched frame will impact the soul until she is humbled and, by renewal, makes use of the blood of Jesus Christ—not only by an intense yearning for it but also by appropriating it.

Someone might have specific questions about this matter that will be of interest to all who are concerned about this.

Question 1

One might ask: If a soul cannot function spiritually as long as there is some sin of which she has not truly and personally repented and concerning which her faith has not been exercised, and if that sin renders a person unfit to have communion with God and live a sanctified life, whereby shall I then know for myself how I can correctly be made aware of the ill disposition of my soul?

We will respond to this highly significant question by considering a few of the many things that experience teaches us. If you may have a measure of spiritual life, pay careful attention so that you may see what your condition is and how matters are between God and your soul.

A believer can know this because:

1. His soul is at such a distance from the Lord. He will be able to detect this by how he performs his prescribed religious duties. Though he may engage in them, he must nevertheless exclaim, "Oh what a grievous distance there is between the Lord and me. The distance is so great that I do not perceive anything of God either in my praying, listening, reading, or meditations." God's children of all ages have complained about this: "Why standest thou afar off, O Lord?" (Ps. 10:1). Though a soul may otherwise know God, she must exclaim, "Oh, it is as if I am calling upon an unknown God!" The soul is responsible for all this, for God is near to them that fear Him.

2. Of a noticeable lack of light when he engages himself to reflect on these matters. When the believer is in his proper place, and an unforgiven sin does not weigh down his soul, his eye will be single (Matt. 6:22). His soul will be full of light so that in God's light, he perceives matters as they truly and essentially are. However, when there is unresolved guilt between God and His child, it will be as if a fog settles upon the soul. Darkness will gradually and persistently increase, doing so for an extended period. Consequently, rather than seeing things as they indeed are, such a person will only view them as he imagines them to be—even though he can simultaneously increase in his understanding of sound doctrine. Therefore, considering that seeing he does not see, and is thus blind and spiritually insensitive, we can safely conclude that many sincere Christians are at bottom spiritually ill, even though they speak much and often about spiritual matters to others.

3. In such circumstances he will deduce this when he lacks freedom to have intimate fellowship with the Lord Jesus. And indeed, when guilt does not oppress the conscience, the soul will interact with Jesus as a bride with her bridegroom. She will then say, "My beloved is mine, and I am his" (Song 2:16). However, when a soul has sinned and has not yet repented and engaged in a genuine and personal exercise of faith, there will be fear, sorrow, reticence, and misgiving. And as much as the soul may reach forth the hand of faith to take hold of Jesus, she cannot behold Him, and she will draw back her hand empty.

4. He will detect this by ascertaining how little inner joy and refreshment he experiences when he thinks upon God. When spiritual life is healthy, and sin does not oppress the heart, the soul's disposition will be as David's when he said, "How precious also are thy thoughts unto me, O God! how great is the sum of them! If I should count them, they are more in number than the sand: when I awake, I am still with thee" (Ps. 139:17–18). However, when any measure of guilt oppresses the soul, such thoughts will at best be as those of a friend whom we have angered. Since there is a corrupt element in the conscience, such thoughts will also not yield inner joy.

5. Of the fickleness and instability of his thoughts, for when his soul is in a peaceful condition, his heart will steadfastly focus upon the Lord in all that he does. However, when sin causes separation and the soul can no longer delight in the Lord, he will engage in thousands of frivolous pursuits—one moment this, and then again something else. He will go from one broken vessel to another, thus wearying himself by seeking some delight in and with a mortal creature, all of whom exclaim to him, "It is not with me" (Job 28:14).

6. Of his disposition when he observes his religious duties. He will look up against them and detect no desire to engage in them. He can be barren, irreverent, and insensitive. He wants to be done quickly; he will not wait upon the Lord, etc. These unmistakable signs indicate that there is some sin within him of which he has not repented. However, the soul that has been cleansed by the blood of Jesus will be "lifted up in the ways of the LORD" (2 Chron. 17:6).

7. Of the bondage he will find himself in, preventing him from giving heed to all that stimulates spiritual life. Although a believer may not yet have repented of particular sins, he may nevertheless experience that the incurred

guilt begins to oppress his heart. He will begin to see the unseemliness of his careless life. His heart will now inwardly be wrought upon, and he will intensely desire to walk in God's light and favor. However, in the meantime, he perceives that regardless of how much he wishes to do so, he cannot stir up his heart when he fervently seeks to engage himself. He will perceive that as much as he may desire to be set free from this prison, he continues to be in bondage. Thus, in all that he experiences, his heart will not transition into the realm of God's light, nor will there be the lively spiritual exercises that he desires and experienced earlier. He will only experience a desire for them. The reason will undoubtedly be that there is a particular sin of which he has not repented.

8. Of how feeble all his efforts are to crucify and subdue his sinful lusts. When a soul does not actively seek pardon regarding a specific sin, she will impede her spiritual strength and invigorate her old man, resulting in the indulgence of its lusts. Initially, this will cause much strife, but gradually this will lessen—evidently because one has not repented of having committed particular sins. Consider only a soul who is at the beginning of the way of life. When the blood of Christ has cleansed her conscience, she can boldly and heroically place her foot on the neck of her most cherished lusts and trample upon them as rubbish. However, when this is interrupted by unrepentant sin, one may exclaim, "Awake, Samson, show forth your strength against the uncircumcised that are now attacking you!" However, she will then discover that she will no longer be able to do so until her locks have grown again—that is, until she repents and makes peace with God by taking hold of Jesus Christ.

9. Either his fruitfulness or fruitlessness when he uses the means of grace. (Many other things recorded in my notes I will not mention since I wish to leave something for you to meditate upon.) When the believer's soul is at peace, he will always benefit from using the means of grace. In Micah 2:7, we read, "Do not my words do good to him that walketh uprightly?" However, when he has not repented of a given sin, the most efficacious means of grace will not benefit him. The Lord will blow upon it (Isa. 40:7). As characteristic as it is of an unhealthy person that the food he ingests will not strengthen him, so infallibly will be the indication that a soul is weighed down by the guilt of sin when the Word bears no fruit for her. Therefore, you will observe that people will begin to say, "If only we had but suitable means and suitable ministers! Then there would be hope!" And should there be such ministers,

such individuals will become increasingly barren under their ministry, for the guilt of sin weighs down their hearts. As long as this continues, all will be in vain until she has been convicted of her sin—even if Paul himself were to come with all the comforts of the gospel. Experience teaches that a soul who may have remained fruitless under the means of grace may yet be led by God's providence to be under spiritually deficient means so that such inferior "means" may, however imperceptibly, be a blessing to her.

Question 2

If this is all true, which I must affirm, how can I discern the specific sin I am guilty of that incapacitates me from having communion with God and living a sanctified life? Though I have long believed that there must be an issue, I do not know how to determine this.

We will respond by focusing on the following matters:

1. It is so indeed, for your divinely sanctified nature can know from all that has been said that matters are neither as they ought to be, nor as you have experienced them to be, nor as you so very much desire them to be. Nevertheless, the actual cause can be long hidden to the soul. There may be unresolved guilt for a long time already. At times, this can occur already at the outset of the new life so that one's first love will largely be extinguished, and the believer never arrives at confessing the sin of which he is guilty. It may also be that though such guilt will somewhat dawn on a person, the soul will nevertheless rationalize that she is either in the right or that there will be grace for her. Any notion of being explicitly guilty will be set aside so that the soul will not be consciously arrested and will thus not be restored.[1]

2. It may also occur that a given incident or circumstance may prompt the believer to rationally acknowledge the corruption of his heart and the spiritual barrenness of his life. He will thereby be somewhat humbled, and experience in some measure a loathing of himself about his altogether barren and condemnable condition. Though he will thus appear before the Lord with the noose around his neck, yet there will be no restoration because he does not acknowledge the particular sin of which he is guilty, but rather his

---

1. Here I have followed Bregman's retranslation. He writes in his footnote, "This re-translation is an attempt to understand Comrie correctly. Several things are unclear in the last part of his complex sentence, and this might be attributed to either a printing error or his attempt to state something very compactly."

generic guiltiness. The weakening of the life of grace not only is caused by such generic guilt but also is primarily due to being guilty of a particular sin. We will therefore observe that God's children will be convicted of this before restoration can occur. It will be easier to acknowledge one's guilt in general than his guilt about a specific sin. We observe far too often that one will not admit the latter!

3. I wish to remark that obviously I cannot know the specifics of everyone's guilt, and yet I wish to say how everyone in his own situation can know this. Everyone should carefully take note of the state of his heart. A person can be either very distressed and oppressed in his soul, or the Lord will lead him in various ways of trial. The Lord can either chastise him or walk contrary to him. If he then considers his soul carefully, he should perceive that his conscience will show him with great clarity the specific cause of all this. Simultaneously, his conscience will rebuke and condemn him. Whether one has committed a sin of either commission or omission, one must view this as his explicit guilt. Here one must pause and consider until the soul will explicitly be contrite and repentant regarding that sin and in a most personal manner make use of the blood of God's Son.

The soul of one who is unwilling to do this will remain sickly and anemic. Although there may be some relief, one will not be spiritually restored, and one will increasingly decline. Whatever such souls may perceive of their sins will be filed in the book of forgetfulness. Though the root of the matter may be in them, they will display "a form of godliness" rather than its power (2 Tim. 3:5).

No Fellowship between the Holy God and Guilty Sinners
We will now proceed to address the truth that God is so holy that He neither can nor shall have communion with a soul weighed down by the guilt of unrepented sin. We are taught this expressly in multiple passages, and all the mandatory purifications during the time of the Old Testament also depict this. God's dealings with His children—and they know this experientially—affirm this abundantly, for God will therefore leave them to fend for themselves in certain circumstances and withhold from them His counsel and guidance. Even though they are oppressed, it will then appear as if their cause is of no concern to Him. He will then neither restrain nor hold back their enemies. They will experience no comfort, and their troubles will become so intense that they go their way bowed down. Whatever they

undertake will not prosper. One rebuke will follow another as one wave follows another one until all God's waves and billows have gone over them (Ps. 42:7). Thorns will then hedge in their way, their tongue will cleave to the roof of their mouth, and they will be isolated as a removed or menstruous woman (Ezek. 18:6; 36:17). Even when God then somewhat draws near, it will but be for a brief moment—just as a stranger who passes by but will not enter to stay. There will be a controversy and an anathema that rests upon the soul, for there is guilt that they have not yet dealt with uprightly. I have addressed all of these matters only in so many words. Meditate upon them and consider how it is with your soul.

The Necessity of Living by Faith unto Righteousness
As a final matter, we will draw this conclusion from the preceding: It is abundantly evident how necessary it is to live by faith "unto righteousness." The saints longed for this; Christ has taught us to pray for this, and no one shall prosper unless they live by faith.

How to Live by Faith unto Righteousness
We will now proceed to set before you how a believer lives "unto righteousness."

Faith Perceives Guilt
Faith will experientially confront the believer with his guilt and transgression against the Lord. Thereby he will not only assess sin verbally and intellectually but rather in its monstrous and God-dishonoring nature. He will also perceive sin's inescapable and dreadful consequences for the soul (cf. Rom. 2:9; 6:23). That perception will remove sin's mask, and he will see Satan's seduction and deceit. The soul will also become aware of her own incomprehensible foolishness in exposing herself to such an indescribably great danger for such short-lived and often imaginary pleasure. The church confesses in Isaiah 59:12, "As for our iniquities, we know them," and in Jeremiah 3:13, "Only acknowledge thine iniquity, that thou hast transgressed against the LORD thy God."

Faith Considers the Full Extent of Guilt
The faith that is exercised "unto righteousness" will cause the soul to stop and consider when she views the extent of her guilt. This will so arrest her

that she will continue to see and think about it. A hypocrite or temporal believer will generally conduct himself as a man who briefly sees himself in a mirror and then immediately forgets what he has seen. With some light, he will now and then perceive his guilt. Such a sight is not pleasant to him, and it will soon begin to trouble him. He will go to his room, confess his sin, be exercised with the knowledge he has of the Surety Jesus (although not yet a suitable object for Him), and thereby his guilt will vanish from sight, and he will be satisfied and happy. Such a person can yield to his lusts all day long, give free rein to his passions, and pollute himself with a thousand and one things. At the end of the day, he may then perceive something of his guilt, be occupied with it a quarter to half an hour, then, so to speak, wipe his mouth, and reassure his soul that all is well. However, a genuine believer's transgressions will confront him in such a way that they are ever before him. Yes, he strives for a continual confrontation with them, and he will fear that he does not fully recognize his guilt. And no wonder, for such awareness of guilt is always and absolutely necessary to stir his soul to be genuinely sorrowful and render him a proper subject of sovereign grace.

Faith Views the Guilt of Particular Sins

The faith that is exercised "unto righteousness" will not only confront the soul with her guilt in general but also with her being guilty of specific sins. Thus, the believer will view his guilt in very explicit terms which will weigh heavily upon his heart. This will powerfully distress his conscience, and this guilt will seriously inhibit his liberty. Darkness and a separation between him and the Lord will be the result. And indeed, it is characteristic of faith that it will never deal merely with generalities but will instead focus on specifics. Only consider David in Psalm 51. That must teach you that someone can spend hours reflecting on his misery in general terms and do so even without emotion. However, that will not bring him to the place where the faith that is exercised "unto righteousness" will bring us. One will only arrive there when one's mind is focused on particular matters in the past.

Faith Brings Contrition and Humility

The faith that is exercised "unto righteousness" will render a soul to be intensely sensitive. Whatever the believer beholds will touch his heart. In secret, there will be a low esteem and loathing of self, a being ashamed, blushing for shame, a weeping, mourning, and groaning of the soul unto the Lord.

"My soul melteth for heaviness" (Ps. 119:28). "I have surely heard Ephraim bemoaning himself thus" (Jer. 31:18), which means that he wept about his condition with an intensely felt sorrow. The soul will thus be contrite and deeply humbled before the Lord. As a worm, she will crawl before God's footstool with a most intense desire, saying, "Oh God, 'that thou shouldest look upon such a dead dog as I am' (2 Sam. 9:8)."

Faith Tastes the Bitterness of Sin

The faith that is exercised "unto righteousness" will cause the soul actually and expressly to experience the bitterness of sin in an intense, spiritual, and profoundly thorough way. That experience causes believers to desire atonement through the blood of Christ. In Jeremiah 2:19, we read, "Thine own wickedness shall correct thee, and thy backslidings shall reprove thee: know therefore and see that it is an evil thing and bitter, that thou hast forsaken the LORD thy God."

Two things in particular make this bitterness so bitter. First, it is *beholding the guilt of having sinned* against such a merciful, benevolent, and compassionate God. The soul will thus frequently address herself, saying, "Is this your beneficence toward your Benefactor who in your misery caused His eye to fall upon you and exclaimed, 'Live; yea…Live' (Ezek. 16:6); who frequently embraced you in grace when you returned to Him; who never denied you His help; and who until this hour has pursued you with His benefits! Is this the way you are rewarding Him for this?" This awareness, and much else, causes the soul to grieve bitterly, especially when the Holy Spirit impresses a particular passage upon the heart. For example, the words of Jeremiah 2:31, "O generation, see ye the word of the LORD. Have I been a wilderness unto Israel? a land of darkness? wherefore say my people, We are lords; we will come no more unto thee?"; or "They have forsaken me the fountain of living waters, and hewed them out cisterns, broken cisterns, that can hold no water" (Jer. 2:13). Those who have experienced it know best how bitter this grief is.

Second, this bitterness is caused by a deeply felt *sense of what the believer is presently missing* compared to what he was accustomed to enjoying. The soul will then remember how time after time she was privileged to behold the incomparable beauty of Christ, to sit under His shadow, to experience His loving embrace, and to have access through Him unto the throne of grace! However, she must now sit down in solitude, in darkness, and be uncomforted. The grief and deeply felt bitterness that this produces cannot readily be expressed in words.

We believe that all temporal believers lack this and will always continue to secretly indulge in some form of sinful corruption. When the believer truly tastes the bitterness of sin as sin, he will part with this sin precisely because it is sin. And although temporal believers may experience the bitterness of sin, it will merely be because they either grieve due to an awakened conscience or due to the punishment that is to follow. They will never consider sin bitter because it is sin.

Faith Produces Hatred for Sin

The faith that is exercised "unto righteousness" will engender in the soul a very thoroughgoing, all-encompassing, and complete hatred for all sin. This hatred pertains to the most cherished bosom sin and all other sins. The proof will be that the believer will lay these sins before the Lord as the Searcher of the heart in his prayers and confession of sin. He will do so with the most intense and sincere desire for the mortification of these sins. The mortification of the secret sins of his heart would be a greater delight to him than if one would give the whole world to him.

Much could be said about this hatred for sin when considering, in general, its cause and consequences. Hatred is generally triggered either by something we consider hostile to our nature or due to a great injustice inflicted upon us or our best friend. This, in turn, will trigger a strong emotion when we think about that issue or friend, resulting in a loathing and abhorrence that will prompt us to carefully avoid all occasions that would lead us to encounter either that issue or that person. All of this applies to that hatred for sin whereby a person is exercised "unto righteousness." Believers will view sin as being incompatible with their sanctified nature. Since their sins are the thorns that crowned Christ, they have become the murderers of their Surety. Consequently, perceiving this will stir their souls, cause them to abhor sin, and cause them to be fearful when opportunities to sin present themselves. They will hate sin as hell itself. The psalmist experienced this when he said, "If I regard iniquity in my heart, the Lord will not hear me" (Ps. 66:18). All who love the Lord are exhorted to do likewise and to hate evil.

Faith Motivates Humble Confession and Pleading

The faith that is exercised "unto righteousness" will enable the soul not only to confess sin in general but also to confess specific sins readily, spontaneously, and wholeheartedly before the Lord without wanting to either hide or minimize anything. And no wonder, for the soul finds intense delight when her heart melts for shame and when she can magnify her sin—if that were even possible—by mentioning all aggravating circumstances. The opposite is true for temporal believers. Their confession of guilt is compulsory rather than voluntary. There will be a legal fear such as is true for an untrustworthy salesman who does not want anyone to examine the record of his debts. However, when one's confession proceeds from faith, the soul will be willing to confess her guilt. We will therefore observe that forgiveness is frequently linked to confession.

Faith Produces Submission

The faith that is exercised "unto righteousness" will engender a humble disposition in the soul so that believers will bow before God and acknowledge all His dealings with them to be entirely just and equitable, acquiescing in His justice if He were to punish them. They will also acknowledge that it must necessarily be so, for they are not on equal terms with the Lord. They will thus freely condemn themselves. It is noteworthy that they will do so in the severest of trials, as is evident in Lamentations 1:18: "The LORD is righteous; for I have rebelled against his commandment."

Faith Causes Mourning over Sin

The faith that is exercised "unto righteousness" will cause the soul—bowed down by her burdens, and "laboring and heavy laden" (Matt. 11:28)—to mourn intensely about herself and to groan and cry out of the depth of her misery, accompanied "with groanings which cannot be uttered" (Rom. 8:26). One moment she will say, "I have sinned; what shall I do unto thee, O thou preserver of men?" (Job 7:20), and then again, "Have mercy on me, O Lord, thou Son of David" (Matt. 15:22). The soul will then proceed to plead the promises, and by a hidden power that enters the soul, this pleading will turn into a spiritual wrestling with the Lord. And indeed, believers must find mercy and hear the word of pardon!

Faith Leads to Grace for Deliverance

The faith that is exercised "unto righteousness" will lead the soul to traverse the way of grace. This way has been conceived by God the Father, opened by the Son and His blood, and will be applied by God the Holy Ghost. By renewed illumination, the soul will see the way of escape solely grounded in sovereign mercy. The soul will simultaneously become conscious of her soul's disposition toward the three divine Persons regarding this work of grace. However, we will presently not address this.

Faith Focuses on Christ Crucified

The faith that is exercised "unto righteousness" will direct the soul's attention to the Surety of the covenant, and then specifically to His suffering whereby He fully satisfied divine justice. Believers will then see Him with illuminated eyes as the slain lamb of God whose blood is of such efficacy that it "cleanseth us from all sin" (1 John 1:7), and "which taketh away the sin of the world" (John 1:29).

Faith Chooses Christ as Sufficient

The faith that is exercised "unto righteousness" will now incline itself toward Christ in a heartfelt choice of Him, thereby acknowledging His all-sufficiency and intensely desiring to draw nearer to Him. The soul will thus be enabled to have spiritual dealings with Him.

Faith Receives Christ for Salvation from Guilt

The faith that is exercised "unto righteousness" experiences that these exercises will strengthen the soul. As she perceives God's free offer and has drawn nearer to Christ, she will solemnly cast all her guilt to Him. With the hand of faith, she will then take hold of Him and exclaim, "I have a debt of ten thousand talents, but since Thou hast been designated by God to be the only atoning sacrifice, I cast my guilt upon Thee. I take hold of Thy perfect blood to be reconciled to God so that I may be righteous."

Faith Draws Near to God

Hereupon, the soul will seek to be justified as she draws near unto God by faith. She will behold Him as being well-pleased with His Son upon whom she has cast her guilt. She will draw near to Him with the greatest reverence and receive her acquittal out of His hand.

Faith Brings Peace

Finally, the faith that is thus exercised "unto righteousness" will turn to the soul by communicating to her the receipt of her acquittal upon embracing

Christ and a taking hold of His blood. Thereupon, the soul will experience peace, enlargement of heart, confidence, and spiritual vigor. This will engage all the soul's faculties, and each faculty will function in conformity to the benefit bestowed upon it. To keep from becoming too detailed, we cannot describe these activities. Instead, we will only make a few remarks.

1. We must note that a soul in dealing with the common weaknesses that cleave to her may indeed maintain her peace with God by looking unto Jesus without having to experience all that we have addressed. The soul primarily experiences them when and after she stumbles.

2. We need to know that when a soul does not perceive herself to be guilty of a particular sin, she must seek to be justified regarding secret departures.

3. Finally, to enjoy spiritual comfort, the soul needs to conduct herself accordingly regarding every sin of which she is convicted.

APPLICATION

Behold, my beloved, we have shown as clearly as we could what a life of faith "unto righteousness" entails regarding the daily guilt that we incur in all of our deeds.

Let us now apply all of this to ourselves so that we would give closer attention to this matter.

Questions for the Unconverted

Unregenerate man, whomever you may be, consider this message to examine your conduct and your religious activity more closely. Hopefully, there will be no one among you who would be so bold and blind to either say or think that he has cleansed his heart and hands to such an extent that he is now free of sin and that his progress is such that he no longer stumbles. Indeed, we offend in very many things (James 3:2). "If we say that we have no sin, we deceive ourselves, and the truth is not in us" (1 John 1:8). As true as it is that we are all sinners, we must realize that this is not an innocent matter, for God cannot have communion with such creatures. On the contrary! He is greatly provoked to wrath by our sins. Therefore, my most urgent question, to which I ask you to respond, is, "How are you dealing with the guilt incurred by your sins?"

A Right View of Sin?

Do you see your sins in their true manifestation and nature? Do you thus perceive that sin is the most hateful and damnable matter to be found upon the face of the earth? Sin makes the earth a second hell and people the bond slaves of Satan. Do you perceive that whatever sin promises and gives, in the end, it amounts to nothing more than gravel in the mouth—that it is nothing more than the gall and wormwood of bitterness—that it is nothing more than grief, trouble, and a nagging in the soul? Do you perceive how abominable it is to sin against such a majestic and benevolent God and His holy and good law? My beloved, probe your heart deeply and see and consider whether you have such a view of sin. And then we are not only talking about very inordinate and grievous sins, and not only about the sins of others, but rather about your sins—even the very least of them. Yes, we are speaking of your bosom sins that are most pleasing to your heart. What do you think? Do you have such knowledge? If you lack such a view of sin, you will never be capable of believing with your heart "unto righteousness," and you will also never be able to bid sin farewell.

Grieving over Sin?

If you claim to have such a view of sin, then I ask you what it is you see. Does it convict and preoccupy you so that you can no longer escape scrutiny? Are your sins thus ever before you? Does this cause them to press down heavily upon your shoulders and, so to speak, choke your neck? Do they touch your heart so that you will withdraw yourself and look for solitude to weep bitterly over them? Wives, do you perceive this in your husbands? Husbands, do you see your wives removing themselves to weep and lament? Parents, do you perceive this in your children? And if it remains hidden, does it prompt you to lay this before the Lord and to say, "I have sinned; I will make supplication to my Judge and fall at His feet"? My friends, if you have no experiential knowledge of this, then your faith has never been appropriately exercised, and you do not have saving faith.

Finding Peace in Christ Alone?

Perhaps you say, "Yes, I appear to be acquainted with these matters." My final question will then be, What, in the end, is it that gives you peace? Does your sorrow resolve itself? Do your own tears wash away your guilt? Do you draw a conclusion based on your own reasoning? Then it is not well with you!

However, perhaps you can say, "Oh no, even though I pray, sigh, and mourn, my sins continue to oppress my soul like a heavy burden and grievous yoke. I cannot get rid of them until God leads me by His light upon the way of salvation and reveals His Son to me as 'the Lamb of God, which taketh away the sin of the world' (John 1:29). I cannot get rid of them until I cast all my guilt upon Him as the only sacrifice for sin. I cannot get rid of them until I again embrace His mediatorial blood, apply it to and sprinkle it upon my conscience. I cannot get rid of them until I avail myself of that blood as the 'fountain opened…for sin and for uncleanness' (Zech. 13:1)." If it is so, you may be at peace.

My beloved, you ought to have perceived that many of you, despite your daily sins, are not so engaged as to have your guilt removed. Oh, that you would truly be convicted of this and would learn to long for it.

Questions That Believers Ask
Children of God, in examining the matters we have discussed, as well as the distinguishing traits of grace, you have been able to perceive that you believe with your heart unto righteousness regarding your daily sins. You will also have observed how one is to be exercised regarding this. I will, therefore, not address any other matters, for you yourself are conscious of the fact that this way describes your life. I only wish to address some issues of the heart by using the question-and-answer format. Take note of whether your condition will also be addressed.

Question 1: Must one always be engaged in that exact order and linger by every phase until the guilt incurred by a specific sin has been removed? That would cause confusion and great perplexity regarding one's experiential life, for God does not immediately grant pardon, and the soul must often struggle with an unrepentant heart before she repents. Furthermore, an innumerable number of sins will be committed between the specific sin that incurs guilt and its forgiveness.

Answer: We are not at all saying that a long period of time is requisite. For the sake of an orderly presentation, we have reduced this matter to several particular components. However, one may frequently experience in a short period what we have discussed here. Jesus needs but to turn around to look upon such a person, and everything we have mentioned happens immediately.

The order we have stipulated must indeed always be thus experienced, for God teaches us no other way in His Word than that we must take refuge in the blood of Jesus with "a broken and a contrite heart" (Ps. 51:17).

Though you may commit many other sins, you need to consider that the unforgiven guilt of which we have spoken will, to a large extent, be the cause of other sins. Let this neither confuse nor perplex you. When that guilt is blotted out, other sins will also be blotted out.

Question 2: I do indeed perceive that I am presently in darkness and feel spiritually barren, yet I cannot think of a specific sin as its cause. I also know that the Lord will not hide His countenance due to common weaknesses. What then must I do?

Answer: You would have to be a very conscientious person to be at liberty to say that there is nothing between you and the Lord other than common weaknesses. We are so blind and dull that much can be happening of which we are not conscious. Give this some careful thought!

Indeed, the Lord does not hide His countenance due to His children's common weaknesses, but rather He remembers that we are dust. Nevertheless, if you have neither mourned over these common weaknesses nor sought immediate pardon by a renewed embracing of Jesus for the wandering of your heart, your coarseness, your lethargy, and your spiritual barrenness, such weaknesses will then become your explicit guilt, and the Lord will hide His countenance.

In such circumstances, even when nothing changes, you are obliged to persevere in prayer and a humbling of yourself until you are permitted again to experience the nearness of the Lord.

Question 3: Regarding our incurred guilt, must we be as continually exercised as you have described? You will then be repeating the same thing. Must we not also perform other religious duties, making use of Jesus as given unto sanctification, wisdom, and complete redemption—and even unto justification? Must we not pray without ceasing?

Answer: As long as we are guilty of sin, we must labor to have it removed. Only if you are free of guilt can you cease to live thus by faith for the removal of your guilt. However, if you are guilty and neglect to deal with it, you will greatly regret this later.

One must do the one and not neglect the other. Thus, you must make use of Jesus in all instances. However, you need to know that we will never correctly pursue sanctification except by way of daily justification. Our guilt will interrupt both spiritual exercises. Therefore, we must strive to repent of this and avail ourselves of the blood of Jesus for the cleansing of our consciences. Upon having done so, we can, relying upon Christ, be exercised regarding our sanctification as described on more than one occasion.

When we consider our exercises of faith, we will always detect many deficiencies. Therefore, as we have described earlier, we must time and again be engaged to have the guilt that cleaves to our holiest exercises removed. And even if you had to repeat the same exercises because you have done so deficiently—even if you had to do so right now—how will that harm you? Are you prospering by remaining inactive?

Question 4: Though I perceive my guilt, I can bring myself neither to repent nor to cast my guilt upon Jesus.

Answer: Perhaps you are seeking to repent in a way that is inconsistent with the way of the gospel. Seek it in the way of the gospel, and you shall find, for the Lord will take away your stony heart and give you a heart of flesh (Ezek. 36:26).

Be not discouraged as you seek in this way. If you presently have been unable to do what you desired, it may perhaps be given you before an hour has passed.

Question 5: Not to add any additional questions, someone might finally ask, "There are sins for which I have sought and found pardon, and yet they will later again come to mind. What am I to think of this?"

Answer: Your experience is not unusual. The saints in Scripture also experienced this (cf. Ps. 25:7; Job 13:26). Rather than being an indication that your sins have not been forgiven, the Lord thereby wishes to keep you humble and from breaking forth into sin.

Therefore, children of God, if you may thus live by faith, your spiritual life will remain viable, and it will, like a regular meal, minister peace to your soul. May God enable you and me accordingly. Amen.

CHAPTER 13

Faith, a Grace That Is Exercised in Darkness

When I sit in darkness, the LORD shall be a light unto me.
—MICAH 7:8

One of the chief obstacles to exercising faith and living accordingly during seasons of darkness is that the believer judges God's favor more by His providential acts than by His Word. If we were more accustomed to interacting with God's Word, we would readily perceive that the Lord withholds the tangible manifestations of His favor so that the glory of their bestowal will shine forth all the more distinctly. We observe a remarkable example of this in Christ's dealings with Lazarus, Martha, and Mary: "Now Jesus loved Martha, and her sister, and Lazarus. When he had heard therefore that he was sick, he abode two days still in the same place where he was" (John 11:5–6).

We have chosen the words of this text (Mic. 7:8) so that we might learn to live by faith even during the darkest of times. The chapter in which our text is found describes the church and her condition amid very troubling times. Ungodliness prevailed everywhere. Hardly a grape or summer fruit of genuine conversion and transparent godliness was to be found. Ungodliness was so pervasive that "the son dishonoureth the father, the daughter riseth up against her mother, the daughter in law against her mother in law" (Mic. 7:6). The prophet, as the mouthpiece of all who fear the Lord, responds in verse 7 by stating what they shall do. Since God's church knows that God will punish by tribulations, she addresses those who rejoice in her grief in the first part of our text and forbids them not to rejoice against her. In the words of our text, the church expresses the lively exercises of her faith: however grievous and dark her circumstances may be, the Lord shall be a light unto her.

We must consider two matters:

1. The circumstances in which the church must live by faith: "When I sit in darkness."

2. Her life of faith in those circumstances: "The LORD shall be a light unto me."

SITTING IN DARKNESS

The church first describes for us the condition in which she lives by faith, namely, that she sits in darkness, for we read, "When I sit in darkness."

The Experience of Darkness

The church here speaks of darkness. Everyone knows so well that darkness is the absence of light so that we need not explain this further. God's Word speaks of darkness in the literal and figurative sense of the word. In its literal sense, it expresses natural darkness. In Genesis 1:2, we read, "And darkness was upon the face of the deep." In its figurative sense, the word *darkness* is at times descriptive of the wretched state into which Adam's descendants have fallen by his transgression of the covenant. They are now void of God's image which consists of knowledge, righteousness, and true holiness. The apostle speaks of this when he says, "For ye were sometimes darkness, but now are ye light in the Lord: walk as children of light" (Eph. 5:8). Elsewhere, he says, "Having the understanding darkened, being alienated from the life of God through the ignorance that is in them" (Eph. 4:18).

The figurative sense of darkness is also used to describe the state of all who are deprived of the preaching and proclamation of the gospel—in contrast to those to whom the gospel is preached. "The people that walked in darkness have seen a great light: they that dwell in the land of the shadow of death, upon them hath the light shined" (Isa. 9:2). Christ is therefore referred to as *the Light of the Gentiles*, for He "hath brought life and immortality to light" (2 Tim. 1:10). Then again, darkness is used in its figurative sense to describe the punishment of the ungodly in hell. "Cast ye the unprofitable servant into outer darkness: there shall be weeping and gnashing of teeth" (Matt. 25:30). This darkness can also be descriptive of the trials and calamities that befall men, robbing them of the enjoyment of good things. Therefore, when the Lord, through Isaiah, announces that calamities will befall the daughters of the Chaldeans, He says, "Get thee into darkness, O daughter of the Chaldeans" (Isa. 47:5). Finally, darkness in its figurative sense also expresses the condition of some of God's children when they are deprived of the LORD God's sweet comfort and when they must mournfully go their way in a state of spiritual desertion.

We must interpret the darkness of our text in light of the last two instances. It refers to calamities in the external sense of the word and the hiding of God's countenance in its spiritual significance. We will briefly address both.

External Calamity and Adversity

Thus, darkness refers, first of all, to calamities and adversities. God's Word expressly testifies that they are many: "Many are the afflictions of the righteous: but the LORD delivereth him out of them all" (Ps. 34:19); "In the world ye shall have tribulation: but be of good cheer; I have overcome the world" (John 16:33). God's people must count on it that they will not enter into their rest except by suffering and cross bearing. The apostle states that "all are partakers" of this (Heb. 12:8).

If you wish to know what some of these dark external providences are (among many), then take note of the following:

1. Sometimes, there will be darkness that afflicts the body externally when the godly are *deprived of all or some means whereby they must sustain their lives in this world*. Job, the godliest of all men on earth, is a remarkable example of all this. In one moment, he was nearly stripped naked and robbed of all his possessions (Job 1). Sovereignly, God will still deal with some of His children in like manner. It can be that He sends a moth or a worm (Isa. 51:8) into all their business endeavors whereby their profits gradually diminish. It will seem as if they put their "wages…into a bag with holes" (Hag. 1:6). It may also be that the Lord crosses them in all that they undertake by either fire, water, theft, or something similar. If God has a controversy with His people, He will indeed have a thousand ways and means to strip them until they are entirely destitute.

2. We can also readily reckon as external darknesses *all that afflicts the body*. In His adorable way, God will deal with some of His children accordingly. The book of Job yields a compelling illustration of this. Not only were his possessions and children taken from him, but God also permitted his body to be grievously afflicted with sores (Job 2). The experience of all ages teaches us abundantly that some of God's children experience such darkness. Some

are burdened because they do not feel well physically, so that their "moisture is turned into the drought of summer" (Ps. 32:4). Some struggle so much with physical ailments that it renders them incapable of not only exerting themselves spiritually, but their souls will also be filled with many despondent, anxious, and terrifying thoughts and imaginations. This will mortify them, and they will be so wholly bereft of spiritual refreshment that these terrors will deprive them of all rest. These terrors will become all the more intense because such persons neither can nor are willing to believe that they issue forth from their body being ill-disposed. Again, others will be tormented by mental illness shortly after their conversion or even after they have already been on the way of life. Thereby they will be deprived of the use of their minds and will often spew forth very inordinate words that we would rather not mention. Given its origin, we would also consider this a bodily affliction.

3. The *assaults of Satan* can also be categorized as darkness that comes from without. By way of a bodily apparition, he can torment and intensely trouble and abuse God's children in ways that we would rather not mention as it would not profit everyone to know of them. We could enumerate many examples from historical documents written by credible authors, as well as the experiences of several saints. Paul provides us with a compelling example, for he writes, "And lest I should be exalted above measure through the abundance of the revelations, there was given to me a thorn in the flesh, the messenger of Satan to buffet me, lest I should be exalted above measure" (2 Cor. 12:7). Commentators have many and diverse opinions regarding the sharp thorn in the flesh given to Paul—also what we are to understand by the messenger of Satan and his buffeting of Paul. It would take me several hours to mention them all. The text itself is not obscure, but the commentators have made it obscure. The difficulty arises from the distinction they make between the thorn and the messenger of Satan and his buffeting of Paul. Instead, the one is but an exposition of the other, for the apostle uses a metaphor to describe what he experienced. To him was "given…a thorn in the flesh," so that he would not exalt himself. And to acquaint us with that thorn in his flesh, he explains it with an expression that we are to interpret literally rather than metaphorically. The thorn in his flesh was the "messenger of Satan" who intensely abused his body by pummeling his face with fists. The translators of the Dutch Bible wish to express this transparently

by inserting the word *namely*.[1] We thus observe that this was a dark way for Paul.

4. Such external darkness can also be imposed on God's children by *all the outward circumstances the world inflicts upon them*. For the Lord's sake, they may have to endure this in reference to their good name, possessions, and family relationships. Such things may also happen because they are being punished and chastised for specific sins. God's church indeed recognizes that God may permit such things to chastise her, for she can be exiled to Babylon for a season and dwell in darkness. When we consider the lot of the righteous, we will discern that they must traverse dark ways. However, they have been appointed in God's eternal counsel to experience all these vicissitudes so that they may be conformed to Jesus, their Head. This yields for them irrefutable proof that they are sons rather than illegitimate children. I believe that if we may view this by faith, our souls will be strengthened to prevail in such dark providences and, in some measure, have Paul's disposition when he said, "And not only so, but we glory in tribulations also" (Rom. 5:3).

Spiritual Darkness in the Soul
Even though our text speaks primarily of external darkness, it does not preclude spiritual darkness. We must, therefore, focus on this also, as many of the Lord's children are led in and along dark ways—and then primarily those who are exercising their faith. To address this clearly, we will consider the following matters as briefly as possible. We will

- explore several synonymous expressions in God's Word;
- identify several aspects of such spiritual darkness;
- identify the essence of this darkness;
- identify what may accompany such darkness; and
- identify the causes of such darkness.

Similar Expressions in the Holy Scriptures
We will consider the synonymous expressions in God's Word. At times, the condition of spiritual darkness is described as spiritual desertion: "My God,

---

1. The Dutch rendition (Statenvertaling): "Zo is mij gegeven een scherpe doorn in het vlees, *namelijk* [namely] een engel des satans."

my God, why hast thou forsaken me?" (Ps. 22:1). (Please consult the excellent treatise of the godly Voetius about such desertion.)[2] At other times, it appears as if God hides Himself (Ps. 10) so that it seems as if one's prayers are not being heard.

In the experience of the godly, they can become so weary of groaning that it will prompt them to cry out, "How long, how long? How long wilt Thou hide Thyself, oh Lord?" This will produce a lamentation as an expression of intense and grievous inner turmoil: "I am bowed down greatly; I go mourning all the day long" (Ps. 38:6); my strength is consumed, and "my moisture is turned into the drought of summer" (Ps. 32:4); "I am become like a bottle in the smoke" (Ps. 119:83). They will thus experience the spiritual darkness of which Isaiah speaks: "Who is among you that feareth the LORD…that walketh in darkness, and hath no light?" (Isa. 50:10).

From these quoted passages, one can readily note that when a believer finds himself in such a situation, he will be miserable and distraught and his soul will be "tossed with tempest, and not comforted" (Isa. 54:11).

The Nature of Spiritual Darkness

We will now consider the nature of such inner darkness. It will consist of,

1. *A withdrawal of the Holy Spirit's blessed and illuminating influences* upon the soul. This will bring God's children into a situation that will prompt them to cry out, "We grope for the wall like the blind" (Isa. 59:10). In His adoring lovingkindness, the Lord will illuminate His people for a shorter or longer duration. How this will rejoice, refresh, and enlarge the heart! However, for wise and just reasons, the beams of that light will begin to diminish. The soul will no longer be able to see the hand of the Lord in the way that she must go. The heart will miss its inner stirrings and its warm expressions of love. The soul becomes confused and unbelieving. She can no longer see things in their true proportions. At best, there remains a faint recollection of spiritual matters—similar to the recollection one may have of a friend whom one has not seen for an extended period. The soul will then lament her spiritual

---

2. Comrie here refers to *Spiritual Desertion*, trans. John Vriend and Harry Boonstra, ed. M. Eugene Osterhaven (Grand Rapids: Reformation Heritage Books, 2010), authored by Gisbertus Voetius and Johannes Hoornbeeck, professors of theology in Utrecht. This treatise was published in 1646. Though Voetius's treatise is theologically oriented, strands of a practical and experiential nature are not lacking. However, Hoornbeeck's treatise is much more oriented toward the experiential life of the Christian.

blindness and ignorance regarding God. Therefore, she will frequently exclaim, "Oh, if only it would be with me as in former days! Oh, that God would send forth His light and His truth to lead me (Ps. 43:3), and that He would shed light upon my path (Ps. 119:105)."

2. *A withdrawal of the Lord's sanctifying influences.* The soul has experiential knowledge of such times when, with liberty and the witness of a good conscience before the Lord, she may say unreservedly, "Get thee hence!" (Isa. 30:22). Such believers had the courage to cut off their right hand and to pluck out their right eye. They were then able fully and unconditionally to lay bare their entire souls before Jesus so that He could unreservedly reign in them and shatter all enemies (none excepted) as a potter's vessel. Yes, they could declare this without there being even the slightest desire that a single lust would be exempt for even a brief moment. During such times, the soul appeared to be capable of valiant deeds, and she seemed to make so much progress that she was often hopeful that she could almost prevail over sin. However, such impressions began to decline. Her old lusts would stealthily regain control of her affections. The soul's tenderness will decline; the enemy will entice, seduce, and distract her. The soul, lacking the strength to resist, will then be swept along, resulting in a darkness that will cause the soul to exclaim, "Iniquities prevail against me" (Ps. 65:3); I "do fade as a leaf" that is carried away by the wind (Isa. 64:6), and I "have no might against this great company that cometh against us" (2 Chron. 20:12). As you know, "the beasts of the forest do creep forth" when it is dark (Ps. 104:20).

3. *A lack of comfort.* Darkness is a metaphor for despair and despondency. God's children need joy for their help and support. The joy of the Lord must be, and give them, their strength (Neh. 8:10). However, in this condition, He who customarily comforted their soul is far from them. As a result, her eyes will pour out tears unto God (Job 16:20), and the harps will hang upon the willows (Ps. 137:2), for she will go mourning and be in the dark while she seeks Him whom she cannot find. If someone were to say, "Mary, why weepest thou?" she would readily respond, "because they have taken away my LORD, and I know not where they have laid him" (John 20:13). And while her ears hear the question and her mouth answers, her heart will frequently be so overcome with grief, and there will be so many groans out of the depth of her heart for a token of communion with God, that she will only be able to express herself in broken sentences.

4. *Being in bondage.* The soul will notice this when she engages in her religious duties. After all, darkness is symbolic of captivity and bondage. How often the soul must exclaim, "Why hast thou…hardened our heart?" (Isa. 63:17). The soul will experience that at times she cannot even sigh. And even when she can bring herself to utter groans due to certain impressions made upon her heart, she will perceive them to be so faint and of such short duration. The soul cannot persevere in importunate prayer, and even if she may earnestly persevere, the way to the Mediator will remain closed to her. She will not find any relief as far as the frame of her heart is concerned. Thus, there will be no inner relief, for the bondage remains, and her soul continues to be oppressed. As much as such a soul may endeavor to surrender her heart, she will experience that her condition prevails and that she remains in bondage.

These will be the most essential aspects expressed in the metaphor of darkness.

All-Encompassing Darkness

If someone were now to ask what this darkness pertains to, we would say that it pertains to all aspects of spiritual life. However, we will only mention a few.

1. This darkness will *cause the Lord to be hidden to the soul,* and a heavy cloud will come between the Lord and the souls of believers. Therefore, they will lose sight of the Lord, and they will misjudge Him regarding the way in which He is leading them. Consequently, they cannot take hold of His attributes as multiple supports to lift them up. Instead, they will have anxious, distorted, unsettling, and hard thoughts about the Lord. When Asaph thought upon the Lord in his darkness, he was troubled and complained (Ps. 77:3). They who are acquainted with this trial will understand this.

2. This darkness will *hide Christ from the soul* so that the soul will be incapable of seeing Him in His all-sufficient mediatorial satisfaction. Even if they see a glimpse of it, His willingness will remain hidden. And even if they perceive it in some measure, it will be so faint and from such a distance that it will not incline the affections to make Him their wholehearted choice.

3. There can also be *darkness regarding the covenant of grace* when believers have distorted and erroneous views regarding it—as if it implies such conditions that no one may take hold of it unless he meets these conditions.

It may also be that one is in the dark regarding the steadfast, well-ordered, and immutable nature of this covenant. The soul will be greatly confused by this.

4. There can be *darkness regarding a believer's state of grace and the work of the Spirit within their hearts*. Consequently, they will detect nothing but common convictions within themselves, causing them to be fearful that they will have deceived themselves in the end. It cannot be expressed in words how frightening that can be!

5. There can be *darkness regarding the circumstances in which believers find themselves*. They will then fear that the Lord will leave them to fend for themselves and give them no light to perceive what they must either do or refrain from doing. As much as they may pray or supplicate, the Lord appears not to hear them.

6. Such darkness can pertain to *the outcome of various matters* since God will frequently hide it from them—as imminent as that outcome may be. Yes, precisely when deliverance is imminent, God will cause everything to become even darker. Such was the experience of Joseph, David, and others. Everyone will be able to add personal instances and thereby enlarge this point.

Weakness in Spiritual Exercises
We need to be acquainted with various matters that will accompany this state of darkness so that, being in darkness, we will not be all too surprised and troubled.

1. When a believer finds himself in such a condition of darkness, he will perceive how completely incapable he is of functioning spiritually. The Savior says, "Walk while ye have the light, lest darkness come upon you: for he that walketh in darkness knoweth not whither he goeth" (John 12:35). A God-fearing person will then perceive how *impossible it will be for him to engage in any spiritual activity with a measure of delight*. His prayer will be obstructed by a lethargic heart that lacks earnestness and is spiritually slothful. It will remain unmoved and unyielding. As much as he attempts to surrender everything into Jesus's hands, it is of no avail. His bondage continues, and he lacks all liberty. I admit that there may be strong stirrings to engage in spiritual exercises that will exceed one's strength. Since, however, the believer cannot follow through regarding such stirrings, his heart will be subjected

to intense accusations—accusations that originate with the Evil One rather than God's Spirit. This will especially be so when the soul is stirred to do something she can presently not perform. God's Spirit will not require a child to do the work of a man, and much less that a spiritual struggler would arise to shoulder a heavy burden. Instead, one must engage himself in a manner suitable to him and according to the situation in which he presently finds himself. A child must act like a child and a weak person as a weak person. If fright and apprehension accompany such stirrings, they do not originate with the Spirit, and the heart will be increasingly oppressed and begin to resemble a stone. Rather, the Spirit of adoption works in the soul in a gentle and benevolent way. He will tenderly incline the will and the affections, causing the soul to yearn in love for God and sweet communion with Him. Even if light does not dawn for the soul, the soul's intense desire for it—that inner witness of what the heart's desire is—will give her some rest. Thus, such inner stirrings do not proceed from the Spirit if the soul does not perceive any strength to follow through on them. After all, the Spirit is a Spirit of power who "giveth power to the faint; and to them that have no might he increaseth strength" (Isa. 40:29). Therefore, it would be best if the believer would quietly respond to such stirrings, saying, "I will run the way of thy commandments, when thou shalt enlarge my heart" (Ps. 119:32). He should engage himself consistent with his frame, eagerly yearning and groaning for light, waiting "for the LORD more than they that watch for the morning: I say, more than they that watch for the morning" (Ps. 130:6).

2. Believers will occasionally find that *much fear and distress* can accompany such a season of darkness. I read of the sixty valiant men who stood around Solomon's bed that they all held their swords upon their thighs "because of fear in the night" (Song 3:7–8). Asaph also experienced this when he cried out, "I remembered God, and was troubled: I complained, and my spirit was overwhelmed" (Ps. 77:3). Heman was thereby "afflicted and ready to die from [his] youth up" (Ps. 88:15). The soul will then reside in "the lions' dens" and upon "the mountains of the leopards" (Song 4:8). I neither may nor dare say what one may then experience. If you are exercised in the ways in which God is leading you, consider your soul and reflect upon the way you are traversing. You may understand to a greater or lesser degree these words: "The sorrows of death compassed me, and the floods of ungodly men made me afraid. The sorrows of hell compassed me about: the snares of death prevented me" (Ps. 18:4–5). For your instruction, let me merely note that such

distress can arise as suddenly as an intense wind when certain thoughts are injected into the soul.

The soul will thereby be so intensely assaulted that everything will shake and tremble as did Job's house due to the wind. The believer will then utterly lose his presence of mind and will be cast to and fro as one "tossed with tempest, and not comforted" (Isa. 54:11). At times, such distress can be triggered when the soul, so to speak, perceives that a given calamity is about to descend upon her, suspecting that it will inescapably strike her. It robbed Job of much of the inner delight he enjoyed when he prospered. He was fearful of the evil that had now come upon him! Such distress can also be caused by a given lust or sinful thoughts, or by sudden injected thoughts regarding one's spiritual state before God, causing the believer to experience inner distress. Such a believer could have never imagined that such thoughts would ruminate in his heart! That causes him to exclaim, "My name is Legion" (Mark 5:9).

3. Believers will observe that their *indwelling corruption will suddenly flare up* with unusual fortitude in such circumstances. "Thou makest darkness, and it is night: wherein all the beasts of the forest do creep forth" (Ps. 104:20; cf. Isa. 13:20–22). Paul was undoubtedly in such a situation when the law that was in his members brought him "into captivity to the law of sin" and caused him to cry out, "O wretched man that I am! who shall deliver me?" The believer will experience that not only will new sinful desires emerge, but also old lusts—and that more forcefully and violently than ever before. All the while, the believer thought that these lusts had been mortified and nailed to Christ's cross. Thus, the soul will exclaim, "Iniquities prevail against me" (Ps. 65:3); "We have no might against this great company" (2 Chron. 20:12).

4. Finally, believers will also discern that during such spiritual darkness it may frequently happen that *they will be led astray as inexperienced travelers* are led astray during dark nights by will-o'-the-wisps. They will then, if God does not hold their hand, be in danger of going astray either to the right or the left and be exposed to great danger. We could say more of this were it not that the situation forbids us where one and the other in our land exclaims, "Lo, here is Christ, or there" (Matt. 24:23). Instead, remain faithful to God's Word and "let that therefore abide in you, which ye have heard from the beginning" (1 John 2:24).

I must remark, however, that not all believers become ensnared in the dark ways of which we have spoken so extensively. Many believers resemble captains who always remain focused on the shore and therefore experience but few spiritual fluctuations. God sweetly sustains and deals tenderly with them, whereas others are driven forth by towering and tumultuous waves and know of little relief during their lifetime.

Causes of Darkness
Since nothing happens uncaused, someone might ask, What are the reasons why God permits this? I will mention a few, for I cannot possibly name them all, which would also lead us too far astray.

1. In the free and sovereign way in which God leads His own, He will lead some of His children into darkness *without any preceding guilt* being the cause why He is pleased to chastise and discipline them. How God dealt with Job from the outset to the conclusion of his trial is a clear example of this. The Lord will do so to manifest the uprightness and steadfastness of His children. Oh, how remarkable it is when one will kiss the rod and will nevertheless wholeheartedly love a God who smites and hides Himself—when one clings to Him with intense spiritual affection, more than a "girdle cleaveth to the loins of a man" (Jer. 13:11).

At times, God will be pleased to show something of His wondrous power, goodness, mercy, etc. The man born blind had not been born as such due to personal guilt or the preceding guilt of his parents, but rather "that the works of God should be made manifest in him" (John 9:3). One can recognize this to be so when one's conscience does not accuse him of being guilty of a specific sin as the cause of such darkness. One will then observe that his love for the Lord does not decline and that he will not be inhibited in addressing the Lord in prayer. Job is a clear example of this, for he adhered to his righteousness until the end.

2. We can also identify as a cause the ease with which *a soul believes what Satan says to her* regarding either the Lord or her spiritual state. Satan's intent is always subtly to stir up unbelief in the soul, for when one yields to this, unbelief will be cunning and very powerful. As true as it may be that fear for self-deception fuels the believer's reaction, it is never a good thing to give the enemy too much of a hearing.

3. Darkness will occur *when one looks too much within*, focusing upon the wretchedness of one's heart and disposition, without a yearning for and active taking hold of Jesus. It is indeed good to have an inner sense of one's misery and to examine the recesses of one's heart. However, if this causes one's heart to be inhibited and anxious, it would be better to shift his attention from himself by looking unto Jesus and the offer of His grace. And indeed, if one continually and too often focuses on his misery, the heart will increasingly lose its liberty.

4. Darkness can also be caused whe*n a soul all too readily concludes that she is void of saving grace* because she fails to experience any evidence of it. Believers will then continue to be in the dark until God Himself sheds light upon this for them. What matters is that the soul be of a humble disposition, for a feeble groaning and yearning for Jesus are as truly exercises of faith as its most vigorous acts.

5. Darkness can also be caused *when a soul always insists on finding something within herself before she dares to exercise faith*, and that she would do so if the experience of her radical poverty and misery were such and such. However, when the soul is enabled to transcend this in response to the offer of Jesus to the chief of sinners, light would dawn upon her, and by this exercise of faith, she would remain in the light.

6. Furthermore, darkness can be caused *when the soul does not sufficiently acknowledge the slenderest manifestation of the Lord's favor toward her* by not honoring Him accordingly. Therefore, the disciples found themselves and their ship in a storm, for we read in Mark 6:52, "For they considered not the miracle of the loaves: for their heart was hardened." How great a sin it is when one assesses God's special grace as common grace, or even as the work of Satan! Are there possibly some among us with whom God, therefore, has a controversy?

7. Darkness can be caused by *infrequent use of the Word of the living God*. Oh, that Word describes the work of grace so genuinely, plainly, and simply that it would be as a shining light if we would find all our delight in God's Word! One would thus be able to transcend such darkness.

8. Darkness can also be caused *when heartfelt and upright expressions of love and tenderness toward the Lord begin to diminish*. When one follows the Lord

in ways of prosperity and adversity, His light will shine within our dwellings. However, when one forsakes his first love, the candlestick will be removed out of its place (Rev. 2:5).

9. Finally, there will be darkness *when one cherishes some sinful lust* while simultaneously seeking to serve the Lord—like all who arrived in Canaan and served the Lord as well as the idols of the land. Oh, God is a jealous God who insists on being the sole Possessor of our soul.

When all of the things above occur, we should not be surprised that the soul will come into darkness.

The Meaning of "Sitting" in Darkness

However, in our text, the church does not speak of darkness in general, but rather of a sitting in darkness: "When I sit in darkness." Regarding this sitting in darkness, we wish to note the following:

Occasional Walking in Darkness

We read of an occasional walking in darkness when there is no light (Isa. 50:10). We must understand this to refer to the exercise of the soul in which she, as troubling and dark as her circumstances may be, makes some progress in the way. One could compare this to a sea captain who, having some acquaintance with the course to be traveled, lets the ship sail in the dark. He will thus gradually approach the desired harbor. Such will be the experience of a soul exercised in ways of trial and tribulation and therefore "knows the way." The believer knows what pathways he must pursue and thus proceeds, hoping that the blessed light of the morning will arise following a dark night of spiritual desertion.

Prolonged Sitting in Darkness

However, our text speaks of sitting in darkness rather than walking in darkness. Upon consulting the Word of the Lord, we will note that such sitting expresses a longer duration and a measure of permanency. Thus, the sitting of Christ at God's right hand clearly communicates the permanency of His glorification. However, when we proceed with our investigation, we will perceive that this sitting refers to a traveler overcome by darkness on his journey. This sitting, therefore, graphically depicts the traveler's fatigue, sorrow, despair, and soul's distress. The scriptural passages and examples are too well-known to mention here. We will reference them as we proceed with our exposition. When, therefore, the church here speaks of a sitting in darkness, she wishes to indicate that this pertains to a long season during which God hides Himself. In this condition, she will sit down as one who, weary, powerless, helpless, and despairing, weeps over herself, laments, and yearns for light.

My beloved, you will thus see that this brief explanation yields so much subject matter that we cannot possibly address it all. Let us, therefore, only consider the following:

Abiding in Darkness

Sitting is indicative of the long duration of this condition. It is as if the church says, "Even though it must take a bit longer before I shall be delivered, my hope continues to be in the Lord and He shall be my light." As we explore this further, we need to know that there is a difference between *being* in darkness and *abiding* in darkness.

As to the measure of darkness, we wish to note that all darkness is not descriptive of pitch-black darkness. Indeed, there are dark nights in which the stars are shining even though neither the sun nor moon are visible. Such is the spiritual meaning of our text. There can be darkness when the sweet countenance of the Lord and the friendly heart of the Lord Jesus remain hidden and invisible, whereas the soul may discern the marks of grace as shining stars. This will enliven the heart to some extent. However, when nothing can be detected, and thus there being no light whatsoever, it can be challenging to maintain one's integrity and to trust in the name of the Lord.

As to the duration, we observe that though some of God's children are acquainted with both light and dark ways, yet they are in darkness for only a very short season. To the glory of sovereign grace, they can say, "For his anger endureth but a moment [and it is but for a moment!]; in his favour is life" (Ps. 30:5). However, this is very rare and is the portion of very tender and exercised children of God. Experience teaches that, like Queen Esther, one may not see the king's countenance for thirty days. One can use the means of grace for two years without any light arising and having one's heart being swallowed up in God. What am I saying? Many have dwelt in darkness for twenty or even thirty years. Heman was such a person, for he was "ready to die from [his] youth up" (Ps. 88:15). Others remain in bondage their entire lives. In our text, the church speaks of "sitting" and thus of a lengthy period of darkness.

Weariness and Exhaustion

Sitting is the position of a weary person. When Christ was tired after His journey, He sat down near Jacob's well (John 4). When believers are overcome by darkness, they will fret and toil and make vain efforts in their own strength before they sit down. When at last they have exhausted themselves and are short of breath, they will, as weary ones, cease from all their heavy toil. They will then surrender into the Lord's hands and sit down as powerless men until help arrives.

Helplessness

Sitting is also the position of one who is at his wit's end. Hagar was at her wit's end before she laid down her child in the wilderness and sat down over against him. Such is the case with a soul that sits in darkness. When she goes "forward…he is not there," and when she goes backward, she "cannot perceive him" (Job 23:8). When she turns either to the right or the left, she cannot perceive His presence, prompting her to say, "We are at our wit's end, 'neither know we what to do: but our eyes are upon thee' (2 Chron. 20:12)."

Grieving and Groaning

Sitting is the position of one who grieves deeply. "By the rivers of Babylon, there we sat down, yea, we wept" (Ps. 137:1). Oh, when a soul must sit in darkness for a season, how she will melt "for heaviness" (Ps. 119:28)! How many intense groans arise from the depths of misery (Ps. 130:1)! How frequently such a soul lifts a grieving eye heavenward, saying,

> How long, O Lord, wilt Thou disdain our prayer?
> For Thou hast fed us with the bread of tears,
> And bitter sorrow Thou hast made us share.
>   (Psalter 218:2—Psalm 80)

As you will perceive, with this the church wishes to say, "Even if I must dwell in darkness for a season as one whose heart is weary, despairing, and bitterly grieving, do not rejoice, oh my enemy!"

> Why, O my soul, art thou cast down within me,
> Why art thou troubled and oppressed with grief?
> Hope thou in God, the God of thy salvation,
> Hope, and thy God will surely send relief.
>   (Psalter 115:4—Psalm 42).[3]

---

3. In the Dutch version, Comrie quotes two stanzas of a Dutch poem. Rather than translating them, I have selected two stanzas from the Psalter that express the same truth.

LIVING BY FAITH IN THE DARKNESSS

We will now address a second matter, namely, how a soul lives by faith even in darkness. The second part of the text expressed that emphatically. To expound this clearly for you, we will focus on two particulars.

Believing in Seasons of Darkness

First, we will consider the exercise of faith itself, for the church says, "The LORD shall be a light unto me" (Mic. 7:8).

The Name of the Lord

The church speaks of the Lord God, who is the Creator and Sustainer of everything that lives and exists. She calls Him by His covenant name, His incommunicable name Jehovah, so that she may be strengthened in the exercise of her faith. Indeed, He is Jehovah, the I AM THAT I AM. He is the God whose love is immutable; the God who "will rest in his love" (Zeph. 3:17); the God whose faithfulness cannot be annulled by her unfaithfulness, for the girdle of his loins is righteousness and faithfulness (Isa. 11:5). And all His promises are in Christ "not yea and nay," but "in him are yea, and in him Amen" (2 Cor. 1:19–20) to the glory of His incomparable name and the salvation of His beloved. Oh, that we would learn from the church that we first must also lay such a foundation when we begin to exercise faith and live by faith! That will yield support at the outset, continuance, and culmination of our exercise of faith. If we proceed differently, we will experience that we will quickly lose courage, and we will no longer be able to persevere in faith and do battle with unbelief.

The Lord Our Light

The church says and believes that God shall be a light unto her. Light is among the most marvelous things God has created. Without light, the world would be no more than a gloomy cave. Therefore, the Preacher says, "Truly the light is sweet, and a pleasant thing it is for the eyes to behold the sun" (Eccl. 11:7). Since light is such a magnificent creation—we will not distract you with a philosophical description of it, lest we generate darkness—God's Spirit speaks of light metaphorically. The word *light* is expressive of all manner of peace, joy, prosperity, and invigoration—physically as well as spiritually. Since the nature of light is so superb, God is frequently denominated as Light in whom there is not a trace of darkness. Christ is denominated as the Light of the world "which lighteth every man that cometh into the world" (John 1:9), and as the cloudless Sun of Righteousness "with healing in his wings." Since light will reveal what is hidden and lay bare what is unjust, the Word of the Living God is compared to a light and a lamp. Thus, the Holy Spirit uses it to convict and enlighten in the knowledge of Christ—and also to comfort and sanctify the saints who are sanctified because the Word is truth (John 17:17). As to the matter itself, we will only set before you what is subservient to our objective.

God Is Light in Physical Blessings

God is a light, so to speak, in the physical sense when He keeps a man from adversity and grants him outward prosperity, positive opportunities, and delight. When Job wanted to indicate and describe his state of prosperity—when he washed his steps with butter, and the rock poured out to him rivers of oil—he said that God's candle shone upon his head and that by His light he walked through darkness (Job 23:6, 3). Thus, it is as if the church is saying in our text, "The Lord shall set me free from my bondage and exile and restore my former prosperity and status." God did so when the seventy years that Jeremiah had prophesied came to an end. The books of Ezra and Nehemiah abundantly affirm this.

God Is Light in Spiritual Blessings

However, our primary focus here is upon the spiritual dimension of the matter. If someone were to ask me, When does the Lord become a light spiritually? then I shall explain it to you, my beloved!

Generally speaking, we may say that the Lord becomes a Light when He causes spiritual darkness to yield and depart so that the soul becomes light in the Lord. "For ye were sometimes darkness, but now are ye light in the Lord" (Eph. 5:8), and "The people that walked in darkness have seen a great light" (Isa. 9:2).

However, the Lord is also a Light unto the soul in a very special sense.

1. The Lord does so *when He causes some beams of light of His divine gospel to enter in upon the soul.* When the believer is in the dark, the veil of Moses will cover his eyes. The nature of this will be such that, because of the veil of the law, the soul can neither behold Jesus nor embrace Him upon His own warrant, even if Christ is preached and offered. The soul will reason and argue herself further and further from Christ, changing grace into work and work

into grace. However, when the Lord comes as a Light to deliver her from this darkness, several gospel thoughts will enter in upon the soul—either in the way of quiet meditation or by certain gospel truths. This will make the soul receptive, and with some inner stirring, she will begin to see that Christ has been commissioned "to seek and to save that which was lost" (Luke 19:10). She will start to perceive that He calls and invites the chief of sinners and that no matter in what the condition of the soul may be, if she but comes, she will in no wise be cast out. (Other illustrations could be added.)

The soul can now no longer deal so harshly and pitilessly with herself. On the contrary, the soul's affections will begin to burn within her, and she will be encouraged to draw near as an ungodly one. And even if the believer does not receive additional light at that moment, he is driven to his knees based on what might be. He will experience some stirring and liberty in his soul to recommend and offer himself to an all-sufficient Jesus. With a bleeding heart, he will exclaim, "Lord Jesus, art Thou willing to save sinners? Here is the chief of sinners! 'If thou wilt, thou canst make me clean' (Matt. 8:2). Considering my sins and hell-worthiness, I would not have dared to come of my own accord, but I come in response to Thy calling voice. Behold, here I am with all my stripes, festering sores, and wounds—as one unwashed, unbandaged, and bleeding!" Love and esteem are now stirring, and desires arise from the depth of the soul: "God be merciful to me a sinner" (Luke 18:13). These are the initial exercises of faith, and they prove that the LORD is becoming a Light unto this soul.

2. The Lord becomes a light unto the soul when, by His Word and Spirit, *He reveals Himself more familiarly to the heart*, proclaiming to a poor soul, "Behold me, behold me" (Isa. 65:1).[4] The Lord will then begin to speak, "I have surely heard Ephraim bemoaning himself (Jer. 31:18); I do earnestly remember him still (Jer. 31:20); How shall I give thee up, Ephraim? (Hos. 11:8); My bowels are troubled; mine heart is turned within me (Lam. 1:20)." The Lord will say, "Mine heart is turned within me, my repentings are kindled together" (Hos. 11:8); "I will surely be merciful to you" (Heb. 8:12). He then bares His heart to the soul and says, "When I hid my countenance, and when in some measure I showed my displeasure, you thought this to be a reflection of my heart. However, consider that as the heart of a father is compassionate toward his children, so I am merciful toward you. Yes, more! A woman

---

4. The Dutch rendition reads, "Behold, here I am, here I am."

may forget her sucking child, but I will never forget you. 'For the mountains shall depart, and the hills be removed; but my kindness shall not depart from thee, neither shall the covenant of my peace be removed' (Isa. 54:10)." He will then unveil His ear and His arm, saying, "My ear is not heavy that it cannot hear, and My arm has not been shortened so that I neither can nor will help you. I do all of this because I love you. 'I will; be thou clean' (Matt. 8:3)." Oh, what blessed light this sheds upon the knowledge of the Lord Jesus Christ! This is a Peniel!

3. The Lord is a Light unto the soul *when He breaks all her bonds* and leads her to experience the blessed liberty, peace, and freedom of God's children in Christ Jesus. Both elements coalesce in a lovely way in Isaiah 42:7: "To open the blind eyes, to bring out the prisoners from the prison, and them that sit in darkness out of the prison house." They also coalesce when the Lord becomes a Light unto them. The believer who previously had offered and committed his heart and yet could not fully surrender it, now senses the translation of his heart into Christ, that He accepts it, and that it now belongs to Another. Oh, what a blessed translation this is! Who would not value this more than a thousand worlds?

4. When the Lord becomes a light unto the soul, *He will pour balm into her wounds*. He will give joy to those who mourn and "the garment of praise for the spirit of heaviness" (Isa. 61:3). This is beautifully expressed in the rhymed version of Psalm 97 (Psalter 423:7):

> Jehovah's kindly face
> Gives happiness and grace
> To all that are pure-hearted;
> To them is life imparted.
> Rejoice in God, ye just,
> He raised you from the dust;
> Give thanks, ye people all,
> His holy name recall,
> Repose in Him your trust.

That joy will be so pure, so heavenly, so soothing for the heart, so exhilarating, and so incomprehensible that it will pass all understanding. Come, see, taste, and relish—and it shall give you some knowledge and experience of these matters.

5. The Lord is a light unto the soul *when He in some measure sanctifies her and transforms her into His image*, for "we all, with open face beholding as in a glass the glory of the Lord, are changed into the same image from glory to glory, even as by the Spirit of the Lord" (2 Cor. 3:18). After Moses had ascended and descended the mountain, his countenance shone. Likewise here, for such a person shall be a "seed which the LORD hath blessed" (Isa. 61:9). He who sees these blessed ones will know them, for the Lord will cause them to be perfect in beauty by putting His comeliness upon them (Ezek. 16:14).

6. When the Lord becomes a light unto the soul, the believer will experience that he is so *satisfied and delighted to have God Himself as his blessed and all-sufficient portion* that it would be well with him even if he had neither bread to eat nor clothes to put on. Oh, when God became a light unto Asaph in the sanctuary, he sang precious words that are expressive of a delightful spiritual frame: "Whom have I in heaven but thee? and there is none upon earth that I desire beside thee. My flesh and my heart faileth: but God is the strength of my heart, and my portion for ever" (Ps. 73:25–26). He unto whom the Lord becomes a Light may indeed say at such moments, "The LORD is the portion of mine inheritance…. The lines are fallen unto me in pleasant places; yea, I have a goodly heritage" (Ps. 16:5–6).

7. Finally, when the Lord becomes a Light unto the soul, she will find *a resolution for all that befalls her, for His eye is upon her* (Ps. 32:8). The believer will then prosper in all that he undertakes. How delightful then it will be to do the works of God, for the light of the Lord will be shining upon his tent. Yes, believers will then proceed from virtue to virtue and from strength to strength until they will enter where God Himself shall be their Sun that will never set. There "the Lamb [shall be] the light thereof" (Rev. 21:23), who "shall lead them unto living fountains of waters" (Rev. 7:17).

A Few Propositions and Remarks
We are yet to consider the following two propositions.

1. We must bring to every believer's attention that we do not wish to stipulate what the degree or measure of one's experience must be. You also must not interpret what I have said to mean that every believer experiences each situation I have described. That is not so, for the grace and illumination wrought by God's Spirit can be minimal and yet genuine and proper.

2. Unregenerate men who hear this, for lack of understanding, will gravitate toward two extremes. They may possibly label these matters as fanaticism and thereby malign the work of God—an abominable sin. They may also be swept away by fanaticism themselves. Since they do not comprehend the matters wrought by the Word and the Spirit and espouse carnal notions regarding spiritual matters, they will speak of voices, visions, dreams, and other things. Thereby they will be grievously deceived, and they will attempt to deceive others.

The Believer's Reasons to Walk by Faith

Someone might say, "If the church can thus live by faith during seasons of darkness, how glorious that is! How blessed are they indeed who can then trust in the Lord! However, what are the reasons why the church and every believer are thus enabled to live by faith?

Preliminary Matters

Let me speak briefly of this by addressing two matters.

First, believers are not only exhorted to do so (Isa. 50:10), but they have also done so. This must stimulate, encourage, and motivate us to do likewise. In Job 13:15, we read, "Though he slay me, yet will I trust in him." And Habakkuk writes, "Although the fig tree shall not blossom, neither shall fruit be in the vines; the labour of the olive shall fail, and the fields shall yield no meat; the flock shall be cut off from the fold, and there shall be no herd in the stalls: Yet I will rejoice in the LORD, I will joy in the God of my salvation" (Hab. 3:17–18).

Second, that faith whereby the soul lives during seasons of darkness is not a faith that liberates and enlarges and gives the soul the matter she desires. Rather, it is the longing, anticipating, and yearning disposition of the soul for this matter. We have addressed this extensively in *The ABC of Faith* under the rubric "Waiting Upon."

The Root Cause of the Life of Faith

We will now briefly indicate from whence this life of faith originates.

The primary and preeminent cause is the divine pledge and promise in which the Lord promises profusely that He will refresh and comfort His children. However, since we will speak more extensively of living by faith in reliance upon the promises, we will presently forego this.

The relationship with the Lord bestowed upon the soul yields abundant reason to expect all good things from Him. Prior experience also gives reason to say, "Who delivered us…in whom we trust that he will yet deliver us" (2 Cor. 1:10).

APPLICATION

You will now have noted how the Lord becomes a light unto the soul when she sits in darkness, and also the reasons why believers believe this. Since we are now only addressing God's people, we will discuss only two matters by way of application.

For Young Christians

Young believer, you who have entered upon the pathway to heaven for a period of only one to four years, we will first address what awaits you.

Matters will not always be as you presently experience them. Your sun may possibly be obscured at midday. You can count on it, and you should anticipate it, for it will surely come. Should you not do so, it will overwhelm you when it happens. Just as there can be light upon one's pathway, there can also be darkness. How trying it will be if one is not acquainted with this!

Since darkness will come, you must now, during your summer season, make provision for seasons of darkness. Take note of your spiritual experiences and, if at all possible, commit them to writing or to your memory. There will come a time that you will need them when you will be compelled to resort to earlier experiences. If you do not clearly write down how matters are currently with you, your perception of them will be distorted.

Keep your sails low! Perhaps you are now looking down upon old and seasoned Christians, who are spiritually so barren and dwell in darkness, though they have a lengthy tenure upon the pathway of life. However, during the initial season of their new life, they were as lively as you are, and perhaps even more so as you are now. There shall possibly come a time—and it may be nearer than you think—that Jesus will say to you, "Nevertheless I have somewhat against thee, because thou hast left thy first love" (Rev. 2:4). How you will then regret that you have looked down upon experienced Christians—you who have only recently entered upon the pathway of life! After all, the best captains generally stand on land and think they can say, "Such and such is the way it must be done!" However, when their turn comes, they will be fearful and not know what they should do. Older and experienced Christians, on the contrary, will have learned a thing or two experientially.

For Believers in Darkness
And you, believers who are in darkness, we have already said several things to you, and therefore we will only say the following:

1. In your condition, do not search too much for many proofs and marks of spiritual life. For though they are present, you cannot see them because it is dark. Wait until light arises.

2. Endeavor to focus much upon the foundations of your hope, and in quietness wait upon the Lord. Be assured that He will be a light unto you! And may God strengthen you to remain steadfast in this way. Amen.

CHAPTER 14

Faith, a Grace That Feeds upon the Promises

These all died in faith, not having received the promises, but having seen them afar off, and were persuaded of them, and embraced them, and confessed that they were strangers and pilgrims on the earth.

—HEBREWS 11:13

David says, "Unless thy law had been my delights, I should then have perished in mine affliction" (Ps. 119:92). Thereby he wishes to express that in all that befell him, the Word of the Lord lifted him up, and in that Word, he found counsel and direction in all the vicissitudes of his life. And indeed, he meditated in it day and night, and thereby he remained steadfast.

This is the subject matter we now wish to consider, namely, how believers live by leaning upon the promises, for therein they find their delight so that they will not succumb to their trial.

Having spoken of the life of faith of various believers before and after the flood, the apostle shows in our text how they exercised their faith and what effect it had upon their walk. We will proceed by

1. expounding the text itself; and
2. extracting various lessons from it.

LIVING BY FAITH IN GOD'S PROMISES

We will first briefly expound the words we have selected as the basis for our discourse regarding a life that leans upon the promises by faith.

The Persons in View: Old Testament Believers

We must take note of the persons of whom the apostle is speaking: "These all"—namely, all believers of whom the apostle had spoken and whose exercises of faith he had described. As to death, Enoch is the only exception, for he did not see death. The Lord took him away after he had so faithfully walked with God for many years. And even though the apostle mentions but few believers between Abel and Abraham, we can readily surmise that there must have been more. Thus, the word *all* includes them as well.

One could also consider that the apostle, in verse 8, is referring to Abraham and his descendants, having first spoken of Abraham's calling to depart from his own land to sojourn in the land that the Lord would give to him and his posterity. They would have to wait until the Lord would fulfill the promise regarding Canaan (an earnest of heaven) by giving them full possession of it as He had promised.

Patient and Persevering Faith

The apostle says many things regarding these believers.

Dying in Faith

He says that they have all died in faith, implying that they all died trusting in God's promise. While they were alive, they embraced God's promise by faith, and with complete confidence they lived by the fact that He would do what He had said. Upon their deathbeds their hope was not cut off as that of hypocrites. Instead, they proved to be true and upright believers who even in death continued to hope and trust that of all the sublime words God had spoken, not one would fail to come true. At the Lord's appointed time, they would all be fulfilled. Thus, they departed with peace in their souls, saying with Jacob, "I have waited for thy salvation, O LORD" (Gen. 49:18).

Oh, my beloved, a conscientious godly life will generally be crowned with a dying in faith. The Lord will give all who have walked uprightly before Him a distant glimpse of Immanuel's land before they enter Canaan by crossing the Jordan of death. When the moment of death came for Paul, a tender Christian, he died courageously and exclaimed jubilantly, "I have fought a good fight, I have finished my course, I have kept the faith: henceforth there is laid up for me a crown of righteousness, which the Lord, the righteous judge, shall give me at that day: and not to me only, but unto all them also that love his appearing" (2 Tim. 4:7–8). However, a spiritually loose life will usually culminate in a troubled deathbed, for God will then arm the conscience and let it speak without restraint so that such souls will be saved as by fire.

We have frequently observed, therefore, that those who, following their conversion, have always or often exercised their faith boldly have departed in a dark cloud. However, struggling believers who were rarely assured of their state before God and anticipated death with a great measure of anxiety, have departed full of peace and joy in the Holy Ghost. Assured believers must therefore be on guard and see to it that they walk circumspectly. Furthermore, let it be an encouragement to struggling believers, for "they that [always] sow in tears shall [at last] reap in joy" (Ps. 126:5)!

Not Having Received the Promises
We then read that they had not received the promises. Promises are here synonymous with the matter being promised, for, as is evident from that which follows, they had seen them from afar and believed and embraced them. As to the promised matter that they had not received, I dare not exclude the land of Canaan. However, the preeminent focus is upon the coming of Christ in the flesh to satisfy the claims of God's justice as Surety on their behalf. Though He had been promised to them, they did not receive the fulfillment of the promise. For wise reasons, God postponed this until the fullness of time would come.

This should be instructive for believers to whom God has promised that their children will be converted. Though they do not see its fulfillment during their lifetime, they must learn to die in faith, being confident that God at His time will grant them that which He has promised. I have heard of a godly mother who was very exercised regarding her daughter and received many promises from the Lord regarding this child. However, she died in faith without having received the substance of the promise. Nevertheless, she said to all who surrounded her that they should keep an eye on this fatherless and motherless child, for, she said, the Lord has given her to me. Long after her death, it proved to be so—as was testified by many, including the daughter. Oh, believers, trust forever in the Lord regarding this matter!

Beholding the Promise from Afar
They saw the promises from afar; they believed and embraced them. The exercise of their faith regarding the promised matters is described very pointedly and in a threefold manner. Do not expect me to enlarge upon this here, for we will naturally arrive at this as we subsequently address the life of faith upon the promises.

1. *They beheld the promised matter in the promise.* The essential nature of faith is that it causes things to be a spiritual reality for the soul. Faith ascribes to

matters in the soul a *hypostasis* or unique identity, as is evident in Hebrews 11:1. Faith will not permit the soul to cling to vain notions but rather enables her to behold matters as they are. Although Abraham died long before Christ came, he truly rejoiced to see His day (John 8:56). Let this be a touchstone whereby we examine our faith. If our faith does not make Christ, and all that has been promised, a reality for our soul, but instead, lets us cling merely to notions and perceptions of these matters, then our faith is not the faith of God's elect as described by the apostle in verse 1. They saw them, albeit from afar.

This seeing from "afar off" of the matter or matters promised can be addressed in a threefold manner.

a. First, this can refer to a *location* that we designate as far removed—and thus far removed from our present location. If we would view the land of Canaan as the promised matter—for the holy patriarchs a pledge of heaven—then they saw the promise (or rather the promised matter) "afar off," for Immanuel's land is the distant land of heaven above. If, according to the calculation of astronomers, it would take a bullet, traveling at its highest speed, thirty years to reach the sun, how much longer would it take to reach the fixed stars, each of which may be a sun for planets that are constantly in motion as they revolve around them. How many untold millions of years would be required to arrive in the third heaven, the paradise of God, the "Jerusalem which is above [and] is free" (Gal. 4:26), a city "not made with hands" (Heb. 9:11), "whose builder and maker is God" (Heb. 11:10). There will be neither sun, moon, nor stars, and there will be no more weeping, for God Himself will be their light and the Lamb their candle. All sorrow and sighing will vanish forever, for "God shall wipe away all tears from their eyes" (Rev. 7:17; 21:4), and "the Lamb…shall lead them unto living fountains of waters" (Rev. 7:17). Every inhabitant of that "afar off" country will eternally be satisfied from these fountains with magnificent joy—joy unspeakable and unquenchable.

b. Second, this seeing "afar off" can pertain to the *spiritual discernment* of believers regarding the promised matters. These believers had a limited and minimal perception of these matters that were still wrapped within the womb of the promise. This is very evident regarding older believers who only saw things from "afar off" and obscurely by means of but a few promises. These promises would have to be clarified by the more explicit promise regarding the glorious coming of the Messiah. Abraham looked forward to this in his day but did so obscurely and from "afar off," for light was only beginning to arise. As far as that is concerned, even the New Testament believers died in faith without having obtained the many promised matters regarding the fall of the Antichrist, the glorious state of the church on earth, the glory of heaven, and other matters. They saw them as "through a glass, darkly" (1 Cor. 13:12).

   c. Third, we can consider this viewing "afar off" in reference to *time*. Believers saw the promises "afar off" in reference to *time*, that is, the period between the announcement of the Messiah and His actual coming. That period encompassed hundreds of years and extended even to the time of the patriarchs, for it was not until the promise of Haggai 2:6–7 that it is stated that they would only have to wait a short time until the Lord would "suddenly come to his temple" (Mal. 3:1).

2. "These all" *believed* the promises. The Greek word used here is very forceful. It expresses that they were fully persuaded in their hearts of God's truth and faithfulness as embedded in the promise. Therefore, their souls could rest with a blessed confidence that He who had said it would also do that which would redound most to the glory of His eternal purpose at His time and in His manner. What a glorious and necessary exercise of faith this is for all who desire to live by the promises!

3. Finally, they *embraced* the promises. The word means that one with both hands takes hold of something with such inner emotions that it is as if one wishes to absorb it in his heart. This expression is derived from the custom of friends or loving parents who wrap their arms around the friend or children they love with intense tenderness, kiss them, and enwrap them in their innermost soul. They will do so when those friends or children have been absent for some time and then return to them. As to the promised matter, such embracing expresses that the believers of antiquity looked forward to that day with a most intense joy. They embraced the promises with utmost reverence, and their soul was so moved by them that they melted away in love and with intense longing. In the promises, they so took hold of Jesus, the promised Messiah, that they desired to enclose them in their hearts to lie as "a bundle of myrrh…all night betwixt [their] breasts" (Song 1:13).

We will give you a further unfolding of these matters as we proceed with our exposition. We are now merely laying the foundation.

Strangers and Pilgrims

Fourth, the apostle testifies regarding "these all" that they "confessed that they were strangers and pilgrims on the earth." Such was the effect upon their heart of this blessed life of faith upon the promises. It left them neither empty nor unfruitful, but rather, it caused them to live as "strangers and pilgrims on the earth"—so much so that they confessed it publicly.

The apostle uses two words: *strangers* and *pilgrims*, words that are nearly identical in meaning. They are descriptive of a person who resides in a foreign country and is traveling to his native country, affirming the adage that there is no place like home.[1] One can also understand the first word to refer to a stranger who does not continually travel abroad but rather for only one night (Jer. 14:8). The other word (*pilgrim*) would then describe a stranger who periodically resides in various places as required by his business ventures. If we consider the literal sense of these words, then all the patriarchs were strangers and pilgrims in the absolute sense of the words. Therefore, the godly and aged Patriarch Jacob said to Pharaoh, "The days of the years of my pilgrimage are an hundred and thirty years" (Gen. 47:9). However, besides being strangers and pilgrims, this also describes the condition of their hearts and the exercises of their souls regarding their being here on earth. And indeed, they sought to arrive at their heavenly home—the city not made with hands "whose builder and maker is God" (Heb. 11:10), "wherefore God is not ashamed to be called their God" (v. 16). We will not detain you by considering the similarities between literal and spiritual strangers and pilgrims, for we have already done so on an earlier occasion.

"These all" confessed this. The word *confessed* is a powerful word that expresses that these believers publicly professed their faith to be grounded in the promises. That was the foundation of their sanctified meditation.

Observations

The words we have briefly expounded for you contain a great measure of instruction. For our purposes, we will only mention the following:

---

1. The Dutch adage reads as follows: "Oost, west, thuis best," that is, "East, west, home is best."

1. God's way with His children is in the sanctuary (Ps. 73:17), shepherding them here on earth by the promises regarding His gracious benefits, rather than by granting them the promised matter itself. We read, "These all died in faith, not having received the promises."

2. The Lord's children live a life of faith resting in these promises, which they see "afar off" and yet believe and embrace.

3. Such a life of faith in the promises always affects the soul and one's walk of life, manifesting itself in heavenly-mindedness and being a stranger and pilgrim.

APPLICATORY LESSONS ABOUT LIVING BY FAITH IN GOD'S PROMISES

We have thus expounded the words of the text as transparently and briefly as possible and have selected for our purpose the elements that are embedded in the text for further instruction. With the Lord's help, we will now enlarge upon these elements.

The Father's Way with His Children

The first point of instruction pertains to God's way with His children in the sanctuary. Here on earth, He leads them by promising them His gracious benefits rather than by granting them the promised matter itself.

God Leads His Children by Promises

We will enlarge upon this in an orderly fashion by affirming for you that the Lord indeed does not bestow upon His children in this life all that which He promises them, but rather leads them by the promises. Granted, though the apostle speaks in our text of the patriarchs, we will clarify that from the beginning to the end of the world the Lord frequently deals with all His children as He dealt with them.

How God Leads the Church

This fact will be evident when we focus our attention on how God generally leads His church. We will then find sufficient and clear proof to convince us of this truth.

From Adam to Abraham, the Lord God led His church as far as we know by but one promise regarding the seed of the woman (Gen. 3:15). There evidently was no further elucidation of this promise throughout this entire period. From Adam to Abraham, all believers had to believe that such a seed would come! However, they did not know how or when He would come to satisfy God's justice on their behalf. Nevertheless, God's Word obliged them to anticipate the coming of this seed, their doing so with such confidence as if it had already occurred. All who expected this with an upright faith were justified before the bar of God's justice—as can be ascertained from Abel and others.

From Abraham to Moses, in addition to the mother promise,[2] believers were led by other promises that served as an exposition and affirmation of the first promise. The words of the Lord to Moses affirm this when He addresses him in Exodus 6:2–3, saying, "I am the LORD: and I appeared unto Abraham, unto Isaac, and unto Jacob, by the name of God Almighty, but by my name JEHOVAH was I not known to them." As some have insisted, that does not mean that the fathers did not know the name Jehovah before Moses. The contrary is evident from their history as truthfully recorded by Moses. However, it was as if the Lord said, "I gave my trustworthy promise to the patriarchs, and as their El Shaddai I have shown them the inexhaustible treasures of My omnipotence to fulfill that promise at the time appointed by Me. They have thus believed the promise without having witnessed its fulfillment. However, I will now make Myself known to you and your children as the Lord [Jehovah] who will truly fulfill the Word in which the fathers have trusted." And yet, this promise was not actually fulfilled until the days of Joshua.

From Joshua, as the foreshadowing of the true Joshua (that is, Jesus), the Lord continued to lead His church by promises. The law and the prophets were until John the Baptist (Luke 16:16), the forerunner of Christ. Granted, though the promises became increasingly transparent and specific, the church did not have the promised matter itself for nearly four thousand years.

From Christ's exaltation till His return when He will establish His kingdom, three prominent periods are designated as seals, trumpets, and vials (Rev. 5:1ff; 6:1ff; 8:2ff; 15:7ff; 16:1ff). Seven time frames within each of them contain specific promises by which the church is led. Should you desire to study Revelation and the prophetic Word carefully, you will readily find it to be so. Regarding all believers who die before the fulfillment of that which

---

2. In Dutch theological literature, the original gospel promise of Genesis 3:15 is referred to as the "mother promise"—the promise that gives birth to all other promises.

has been promised, it must be said that they have been led by the promises without having witnessed their fulfillment during their lives.

I need not now speak of the promise of heaven, for God obviously leads His church by this promise that will only be fulfilled when believers enter into the joy of their Lord. The soul will experience this upon the moment of death and after that in soul and body on the last day. Believers will then be resurrected in glory. They will be publicly acknowledged and justified, and with Christ they will enter into the full enjoyment of God to all eternity.

How God Leads Each Believer

When we consider God's way with each saint, we will observe the same. God led Abraham for a long time by the promise of a child. While Moses dwelt in the house of Pharaoh, it was revealed to him before he manifested himself to his brethren that God would use him to lead Israel out of Egypt. And yet, how long did he not have to wait till God actually used him! According to God's promise, David would become king, but its fulfillment did not occur until long after it had been given.

Every believer will have experiences that will affirm this. Many have received word when they were anxious and grieving, such as: "I will direct their work in truth" (Isa. 61:8); or, "I, the LORD, will stablish you" (cf. Rom. 16:25). And yet, they will go their way struggling and bowed down, fearing that all their work is nothing but deceit and imagination. Others who groan because of their barren and insensitive hearts, crying out to the Lord that their hearts are harder than a diamond, have received this word, "I will take away the stony heart out of your flesh, and I will give you an heart of flesh" (Ezek. 36:26). In the meantime, they will weep before God until their death—and frequently in the presence of His children—about the unyielding and indescribable hardness and insensitivity of their souls. Again others, by divine illumination, perceive the eminent beauty of a holy walk. They mourn and weep from the bottom of their hearts about their lack of conformity to Christ. They cry out to God in Christ, beseeching Him to sanctify them and conform them to His image. And though these people have received the promise, "And I will put my spirit within you, and cause you to walk in my statutes" (Ezek. 36:27), they can perceive very little of it.

Many, when looking back, have not seen the matters that were promised. I have observed that many thereby either almost despaired or concluded that it was not well with them regarding their state before God, or that at least they failed in applying the promise. However, the instruction we have extracted from the words of our text can be a means whereby the Lord can keep His children from losing their footing. It is indeed God's way to lead His people by way of the promises. They often die in that faith without having received the promised matter on this side of eternity.

God's Reasons for Making His Children Wait

Someone might ask why the Lord thus deals with His children. Since they are so focused on what has been promised, why then does He not grant them the fulfillment of His promise (or at least in a greater measure) but rather leads them by what He has promised? Though this question could be answered in many ways, only consider the following reasons. If other or better reasons come to mind, then please add them to these.

God's Sovereign Freedom

We could silence everyone with this argument: "Even so, Father: for so it seemed good in thy sight" (Matt. 11:26). What is now left for us to say? The Father can indeed do with His own as pleases Him. And who then either can, dares, or may say to Him, "What doest Thou?" or "Why art Thou dealing thus?" Oh, if we may have high thoughts of God's adorable sovereignty, we will be silent and cease with all our carnal reasoning. The soul filled with a deep sense of this will fully and unconditionally surrender to the Lord and His will. Such persons will experience that they will arrive in the haven of true and steadfast rest when their mouths are silenced and their will is submissive. By reducing the reasons for God's actions to His will, we are not dodging the issue, for there will not be a different or better explanation for very many circumstances. As long as we are here on earth, we "see through a glass, darkly" (1 Cor. 13:12); "For we know in part, and we prophesy in part" (1 Cor. 13:9). However, when we arrive in heaven and consider how God has led us, we will see the reasons for His ways and eternally worship God with hallelujahs.

God's Revealed Reasons

However, in advancing some reasons, we say:

1. God in His wisdom leads His church at large and every believer individually in such ways *that they may see and observe all the providential ways of the Lord attentively*. When the believer may observe these ways and keep them in his heart, he will in some measure ascertain the profundity of the Lord's

incomprehensible ways and be incited to engage in worship and adoration. Consider, for example, a businessman who knows there to be a richly laden ship at sea representing his entire wealth. Once he has been notified of this, he will daily pay careful attention to the wind, weather, and other circumstances because so much is at stake. He will continually assess the daily state of affairs; that is, how far his treasure has advanced toward him, when he will joyfully behold it, etc. What motivates him to do this? His treasure has not yet arrived in his home but rather is still on the ship and on its way. Once it has arrived safely at his home, many days and weeks will pass that he will not even think about the wind and the weather!

Such is also true here: the Christian has the promise, but not yet the promised matter, and that prompts him to carefully and painstakingly observe every way in which God leads him. Thus, when he consults his diary, he will find a treasure trove of experiences that will enable him to speak of God's wondrous ways. He does not find it necessary to speak continually of his initial spiritual experiences, for a day will not pass, or his journey will either have been peaceful with the wind in his back, or the current and the wind will have been contrary.

I find this to be explicitly true for Moses, for we read in Exodus 12:41, "And it came to pass at the end of the four hundred and thirty years, even the selfsame day it came to pass, that all the hosts of the Lord went out from the land of Egypt." Here we observe that the church maintained a diary for four hundred and thirty years. What prompted her to do so? They had Genesis 15:13 in view: "And he [the Lord] said unto Abram, Know of a surety that thy seed shall be a stranger in a land that is not theirs, and shall serve them; and they shall afflict them four hundred years." Such was the promise, and therefore believers were able to recount to Moses every detail of God's providential way so that they could say, "It happened precisely on that day!"

There is another example that affirms this. The Lord had said to Moses that He would lead Israel to Canaan and do wonders before Pharaoh. That was the promise. Moses, therefore, carefully noted each day and each event in light of God's providence. When his father-in-law, Jethro, visited him, and they engaged in godly conversation, Moses told him everything the Lord had done to Pharaoh and the Egyptians on behalf of Israel. He told Jethro of all the difficulties they had encountered on the way and how the Lord had delivered them.

Since God intends to lead His people by the promises, let everyone, therefore, carefully note God's providential government and maintain a diary to know what happens daily on the way in which God leads you.

2. God also leads by way of His promises because He wants to *continually maintain in His children a prayerful and wrestling disposition of soul.* There is no means more efficacious than that, for if one does not have the promised matter and yet see its necessity, there will be a yearning for it. It will also prompt the believer to lay before the Lord many a supplication to fulfill His Word. The soul will then come to God, lay His Word before Him, and cry out to Him, "Lord, is this not Thy promise to Thy servant?" I so much desire it. I must have something of what has been promised, even if it were but a crumb. Oh, give me something, for I neither may nor can desist until Thou dost bless me according to Thy Word. Lord, though Thou wilt not do so for my sake—I confess that I am unworthy—do it for the sake of Thy Word and Thy truth, etc.

For an honest person, there is nothing that means more to him than his word. Since this is particularly true for the Lord, David spoke accordingly when he brought his petition before Him. He most humbly said, "Remember the word unto thy servant" (Ps. 119:49). Consider how the godly Jacob drew near to God when he was afraid of his brother. Jacob said, "O God of my father Abraham, and God of my father Isaac, the LORD which saidst unto me, Return unto thy country, and to thy kindred, and I will deal well with thee" (Gen. 32:9). He continues with even greater urgency by pointing to the promise: "And thou saidst, I will surely do thee good" (v. 12). In Genesis 31:13, we find the promise upon which he so fervently pleads, and we should learn from this how we are to conduct ourselves when we have not yet received that which has been promised.

3. God leads His children by promises so that *they may have a more firm and assured foundation than can be derived from what they see and feel.* We are naturally very prone to spiritual fanaticism. Due to our innate darkness, we will be particularly prone to this when we begin to think seriously about His salvation and divine realities. Because of that darkness, we do not understand the things of the Spirit. We will then be inclined to form vagarious notions regarding matters such as conviction of sin, beholding the Person of Jesus, the exercise of faith in Him, communion with God, etc. This will prompt people to tell all sorts of stories. There will be those who claim to

have been greatly convicted of sin to have seen the elements burning, to have seen hellish fire, or that they have been in such darkness that they could not distinguish anything. Others will claim that they have seen either an angel or a vision at home or by the way, and then again, others will say that they have heard an audible voice that spoke to them, "Your sins are forgiven." They may even claim to have seen Christ before their eyes with outstretched arms and His blood dripping upon them. Then some speak of peculiar ecstatic experiences of being spiritually drawn up into heaven, or of dreams and too many other things to be mentioned. The devil is peculiarly involved here to deceive them. We cannot indeed consider all that is told in a given story to be accurate. However, we do believe that Satan has a remarkable influence on people, and he so deceives and misleads them that they have carnal thoughts regarding the nature of the work of grace.

I have known a person who was viewed favorably by all who spoke with him, and there were sufficient reasons for this. This man heard God's children speak about the seeing of Jesus (meant in a spiritual sense), and he read the excellent and unforgettable work of Thomas Shepard[3] about this matter. However, somehow it was impressed upon this man that God's children see a physical or glorious appearance of Jesus when they embrace Him by faith. Since this man did not understand this very well and was very fearful of deceiving himself, he became spiritually perplexed and ensnared in great unbelief. This situation lasted approximately six weeks, and he never told anyone why he was so troubled and grieved. During this period, he uttered many heartfelt prayers to God that he might have such an appearance. These prayers were lifted up to the Lord with intense supplications and wrestlings without him perceiving that any of them were heard or that there was such an appearance. This man was very despondent, and for six weeks he wrestled day and night. Finally, there came a change. In his sequential reading of the Bible, he read 2 Corinthians 5 that evening and arrived at verse 16. There the apostle writes, "Wherefore henceforth know we no man after the flesh: yea, though we have known Christ after the flesh, yet now henceforth know we him no more." By these words, it pleased the Lord to illumine his soul so that

---

3. Comrie is probably referring to *The Sincere Convert—Discovering the Paucity of True Believers, and the Great Difficulty of Saving Conversion*. Thomas Shepard (1605–1649) was a Puritan preacher who departed for America in 1635 and was very influential there. In addition to this book, he also wrote an extensive exposition of the parable of the ten virgins, a work published by Comrie. Comrie may also have had this book in mind.

he saw clearly how the devil had ensnared him under a pious pretext. The Lord showed him that there is no true embracing of Jesus by faith other than by the Word of promise. The words of Peter immediately affirmed this: "And this voice which came from heaven we heard, when we were with him in the holy mount. We have also a more sure word of prophecy; whereunto ye do well that ye take heed" (2 Peter 1:18–19). Thus this person was set free, and he melted away in deep shame before God, having tempted the Lord. His mouth and heart were filled with thanksgiving because the Lord had delivered him from Satan's deceptions. He was determined steadfastly to guard against this and warn others that they should learn that here we are to live by faith rather than by beholding.

4. God thus leads believers in His wisdom so that *their hearts may continually end in Him and desire Him more than any gracious gift He may bestow.* We can hardly grasp how to do this in our imperfect state, and we are nearly incapable of doing so. When we may greatly rejoice in the promises and their fulfillment, how difficult it then will be to be steadfast in our reliance upon the Lord, and thus look away from what has been given as if we did not have it. How difficult it will then be to believe that our salvation does not consist of what we possess but rather that the Lord Himself is our salvation! I believe this to be an important reason why the promised matter is not given. Therefore, Paul did not receive the token of God's favor, for which he prayed three times. Instead, he only received this promise, "My grace is sufficient for thee: for my strength is made perfect in weakness" (2 Cor. 12:9).

We will now consider how to make use of this instruction.

Introduction to God's Promises

We will now deal with our second main point: Since God's way is to lead His people by the promises, they must also live upon the promises by faith. This truth is embedded in the words of our text: "Having seen them afar off, and were persuaded of them, and embraced them." Thus, we have arrived at treating a most essential component of Christian experience: to live by faith upon the promises.

To explain this well for you, we will prove that believers whom God leads by His promises have already lived upon them and also must continue to do so. We can be all the more brief here in light of what has been said already and because the text clearly states this. Of Abraham, it is said that he "believed God, and it was accounted to him for righteousness" (Gal. 3:6). Thus, as he lived upon God's Word by faith, "he staggered not at the promise of God through unbelief; but was strong in faith, giving glory to God" (Rom. 4:20). The apostle then writes, "Now it was not written for his sake alone… but for us also" (vv. 23–24).

Living upon the promises by faith encouraged David in all the circumstances in which he found himself, and, therefore, he says, "Unless thy law had been my delights, I should then have perished in mine affliction" (Ps. 119:92). To detain you no longer with affirming what is already apparent, Paul says more than once in general terms that we live by faith; that is, we live upon the promises. And indeed, the distinguishing act of faith consists in setting to one's seal that God's testimonies are true.

We will now speak of the promises themselves upon which the believer lives by faith. To do this carefully and accurately, we will describe what a promise is. A promise is the actual revelation of God's will in His written Word regarding all things for which His children need His help and assistance. According to His sovereign good pleasure and out of pure mercy, the Lord reveals this because He has purposed to grant them this in conformity to their needs and circumstances. As a warrant that His promises will be fulfilled, He pledges to His people His faithfulness, truthfulness, and power.

There are many elements in this description that we could readily enlarge upon—and probably to your edification. I will address some of the main points and leave the rest for you to consider and meditate upon in your closet.

First, the fountain from which all promises proceed is God's eternal, sovereign, and unmerited goodness and mercy toward poor and wretched creatures. Nothing in us could have initiated this, for we are all in a loathsome, guilty, and mortally impotent state before the Lord. Therefore, I can never either read or reflect upon these words without being inwardly stirred, "I, even I, am he that blotteth out thy transgressions for mine own sake" (Isa. 43:25); "Not for your sakes do I this…O house of Israel" (Ezek. 36:32). Yes, Lord, so it is indeed!

Second, it is essential to note that God's promises encompass what He has eternally decreed. They are not unintentional utterances of the moment, but rather that which He has purposed in His eternal and carefully considered divine wisdom. God will, therefore, never repent of having granted these matters to His children in the Word of His promise. Consequently, the sure mercies of David are more immutable and steadfast than the mountains and the hills which upon earth the most immovable objects. However, though even they may depart and be removed, God's promises shall neither depart nor be removed to all eternity. If one were to reflect on this carefully, it would remove many serious concerns of an upright soul. Many will indeed say, "My conversion and experience cannot possibly be genuine, for I am shamefully unfaithful to God. If He were to have anticipated that, He would have never bestowed anything upon me in His promise." But, my beloved soul, God knew from eternity and in the smallest detail how you would fare. However, that could not prevent Him from abandoning His loving decree. Oh, let this not, therefore, cause you to suspect His love in unbelief, but rather may it cause you to prevail in worshiping and adoring Him that He has thus purposed it. I do not say this to give someone license to abuse this and continue in sin. Far be it!

Third, let it be emphasized that the promises are even as many proclamations of God's will in which He clearly reveals what He desires to do for His people. Every promise is the same as a public declaration, made in the presence of men and angels, to all who hear it. Therein the Lord declares, "I desire to do such and such to a poor and needy people to the glory of My own name." Therefore, every promise must be read, heard, and embraced as a word that comes to the believing soul as a clear proclamation and declaration regarding what the Lord will do for them for His name's sake. We refer to it as a proclamation of the divine will because no one knows the secret will of God. It would have never entered into the heart of either angels or men that God desires to do such things for wretched creatures if God Himself had not made it known.

Fourth, it must be said that all these promises have been recorded in God's Word, and believers should, therefore, not expect any other. We must view the Bible as a magnificent treasure chest in which all these jewels are carefully kept.

Fifth, and lastly, we declare that the Lord voluntarily obligates Himself toward His children to whom He makes all these promises that He will validate and fulfill them. Therefore, they may not only pray for and long for their fulfillment, but they may also most humbly demand their fulfillment. I will leave any further enlargement to you.

Conditional and Unconditional Promises
The promises of which we are speaking are twofold as to their character

and content. They are either conditional or unconditional (absolute). Proportionate to the light we have received we will say something regarding both categories.

Conditional Promises

Thus, we will first address conditional promises, and to speak clearly of this for your instruction and to your benefit, we will reflect upon the following matters.

A Description of a Conditional Promise

We must know what the essence of a conditional promise is. We will articulate this by way of a brief description: A conditional promise is the actual declaration of the will of God in which He clearly reveals that it is His divine good pleasure to bestow His temporal, spiritual, and eternal blessings upon everyone in whom certain dispositions, spiritual frames, and spiritual exercises are genuinely and sincerely found, doing so purely as an act of His unmerited grace and mercy.

We wish to address several matters embedded in this description, and therefore take note of the following:

First, we observe that in all conditional promises, a particular disposition, spiritual frame, or exercise is presupposed as genuinely extant in a person who is upright before the Lord who searches the heart and the reins (Jer. 17:10). Presumption can indeed not please God. He who would be inclined to examine all conditional promises shall always find this element at their core (cf. Ex. 19:5; Pss. 106:3; 112:1; 119:2; Matt. 5:3–11; Rom. 2:7; James 1:25).

Second, we observe that the blessings connected with such dispositions and exercises are temporal, spiritual, or eternal blessings.

Temporal blessings are frequently mentioned. In Isaiah 1:19, we read, "If ye be willing and obedient, ye shall eat the good of the land." Aside from God's sovereign good pleasure, we can deduct from this text why many struggle with poverty: they lack the tender exercise of godliness. And indeed, godliness has the "promise of the life that now is, and of that which is to come" (1 Tim. 4:8).

Spiritual promises are abundant: "Ask, and it shall be given you; seek, and ye shall find; knock, and it shall be opened unto you" (Matt. 7:7). We can hereby deduce why many receive so little and live such barren and spiritually anemic lives. They are remiss in earnest supplication, wrestling, and spiritually persevering with God. Indeed, the Lord has never said, and never shall say, to the house of Jacob, "Seek ye me in vain" (Isa. 45:19).

Eternal promises can be found aplenty (cf. Matt. 5:3, etc.). All who have the spiritual disposition that is spelled out in various places shall eternally be blessed in the enjoyment of God. As much as this may be true, one should note that the Lord has so ordained it according to His sovereign good pleasure that in proportion to the perfection of the spiritual disposition and exercises of believers, so shall be the degree of their glorification. Reflecting on this carefully should powerfully motivate us to seek the highest degree possible so that, by sovereign grace, we may also attain a high degree of glory.

Third, these promises give us the solid assurance that all who know of such presupposed spiritual frames are the objects of God's favor and shall receive His blessings. Indeed, the Lord pledges His faithfulness and power to those in whom such spiritual frames are found, for He has connected the warrant of the bestowal of His benefits to these spiritual frames. That applies to temporal, spiritual, and eternal blessings.[4]

God's Purposes in Conditional Promises

We could proceed to ask, What is God's objective in giving conditional promises? We could say that this is solely the glory of His name—a name never adequately praised. However, to answer more explicitly, we will say,

First, God does not intend to impress upon us that such characteristics, dispositions, or exercises—whatever you wish to call them—are the actual and meriting cause of the promised matter. Far from it! All these matters are wrought in us by the Spirit. They are not rewarded as the work that we perform in our own strength but rather as the outworking of the Spirit's irresistible grace within us.

Second, it is actually so that with this the Lord wishes to show us what the relationship is between these matters when sinners are saved. In the order God has established in His wisdom, hungering, thirsting, and mourning necessarily precede eating, drinking, and being comforted. Similarly, striving, persevering, and overcoming precede the blessed rest above.

Third, we must very consciously and clearly see the true distinction between nature and grace and between temporal and true grace. In conformity to these conditional promises, we can thus arrive at a valid assessment

---

4. This sentence is added for clarity and is implied by the context.

of our own state before God. Indeed, each of these promises makes mention of true and infallible marks of grace.

Fourth, the Holy Spirit aims to give God's children a solid foundation upon which He assures them of and seals their state of grace in the way of means. For such sealing in the way of means, the Holy Spirit will use a syllogism. The major premise is found in the Word, that is, in the conditional promise, and the minor premise issues forth from our heart and our spiritual exercises. The conclusion drawn forth is a powerful application of the promise to us personally, for, according to the touchstone of His Word, before God we have the spiritual disposition that is linked to the promised matter.

Fifth, its purpose is that believers who lack immediate assurance and are led to a lesser degree by the unconditional promises would nevertheless take refuge to these conditional promises in times of trial. They will then be able to perceive that based on the promises, the work of God is present in their souls so that they may be delivered of many doubts.

As to the use of the conditional promises, we can deduce from all that has been said that, on the one hand, they are subservient to self-examination, and, on the other hand, they will assure us of God's favor when we may know of such spiritual frames.

Overcoming the Fear of Self-Deception in Applying
Conditional Promises

Finally, we need to resolve a difficulty. A sincere child of God will always be suspicious toward himself. He fears that he will come short and deceive himself regarding the assurance he may have based on his inner experiences—experiences that are manifestations of grace based on the conditional promises. He will therefore say, "Oh, I dare not deny that I mourn, etc. But how do I know whether this is of a true origin? Or whether it is deep enough? Or whether my heart—though I shed tears—melts, is broken, and is humbled? Therefore, I neither can nor dare apply the conditional promises to myself."

Though much could be said in response to this, we will address the essence of the matter in a few words.

First, if this fear of yours is genuine and proceeds from concern, you possess one of the most genuine evidences of faith. That which you may genuinely receive will not make you proud, and it will not permit you to rest in and think something of yourself. Instead, it will make you even poorer and all the more destitute and needy so that you will intensely long for more, and you will condemn yourself because you do not become what you desire to be. Fear not, for there is hope in Israel regarding your condition! I have never observed that the experiences of temporal believers make them poorer in hindsight, but rather that they become prouder and live quietly and carelessly.

Second, no specific degree or established measure must be attained experientially, but it must only be in truth. All of this can be as feeble as a mustard seed and be accompanied by a great deal to the contrary. For example, there can be sorrow, and yet there can be much hardness and insensitivity.

Third, be assured that you have the requisite degree and measure when the measure you may have does not satisfy you and that you desire a deeper and more steadfast measure instead.

Fourth, endeavor to apply the conditional promise in proportion to what lives within you. If you fear that what you have is deficient, attempt to flee from the conditional to the unconditional promises. You will experience that the same gracious gifts are promised unconditionally. Plead on them, and your faith will be strengthened to embrace the conditional promises. After all, whatever the requisite condition may be, it is promised without any conditions in the unconditional promise.

For example, let us consider, "Blessed are they that mourn" (Matt. 5:4). This mourning, declared to be blessed in the conditional promise, is expressed in the unconditional promises: "They shall come with weeping" (Jer. 31:9); "And they shall lothe themselves" (Ezek. 6:9); "I will take away the stony heart out of your flesh, and I will give you an heart of flesh" (Ezek. 36:26). This applies to all other promises.

Upon considering the conditional promises, one thus takes refuge to the unconditional promises, doing so to negate the accusations resulting from the soul being affronted regarding the measure, degree, or sincerity of the spiritual exercise addressed in the conditional promise. If one may thus take refuge in the unconditional promises, one need not become so embroiled in such spiritual strife but rather take hold of the unconditional promise. And even if the soul cannot appropriate that promise by faith, let her then plead upon that promise by crying out to the Lord, "Lord, I am afraid to appropriate the promise made to those that mourn, for I fear that I do not mourn enough and that my heart does not melt like wax before the sun. And yet, Thou art my witness in heaven that I yearn for the grace that breaks the heart and humbles the soul. Therefore, Lord, since I perceive my absolute impotence to soften a diamond, I take my refuge to Thee. Hast Thou not promised to take away the stony heart? Oh God, I surrender my heart unconditionally to Thee as clay into the hand of the great Potter. Oh Lord, Lord, do with me according to Thy Word, etc." You will perceive an enlargement of soul, and your faith will be strengthened to apply to yourself and appropriate the conditional promise.

Unconditional Promises

We will now proceed to speak briefly and plainly about unconditional promises. We will do so by giving you the following description: An unconditional promise is a proclamation of the divine will in which the Lord reveals that He will grant to His people, consistent with their deficiencies and circumstances, all temporal, spiritual, and eternal blessings without in any way taking into consideration as a prerequisite the condition of their hearts, their spiritual frames or exercises, doing so solely to the glory of His sovereign grace.

I will also expound in greater detail the matters comprehended in this description upon which hinges so much so that everyone may clearly perceive the content of these promises and exercise their faith accordingly.

To do so, we will consider the matters promised in the unconditional promises, which we have reduced to three categories.

Unconditional Promises Regarding Temporal Needs
There are unconditional promises that declare to believers that all their temporal needs will be met insofar as they are subservient to God's glory and their genuine benefit. Though there are many such promises, we will categorize them by mentioning a few of them, leaving the addition of others to you.

1. There are many unconditional promises in which God promises His people that He will *provide for their bodily needs*, promising them nourishment and clothing in such a measure as their heavenly Father deems to be in their best interest according to His eternal wisdom and love. "Bread shall be given him; his waters shall be sure" (Isa. 33:16); "And why take ye thought for raiment? Consider the lilies of the field, how they grow; they toil not, neither do they spin: and yet I say unto you, That even Solomon in all his glory was not arrayed like one of these. Wherefore, if God so clothe the grass of the field, which to day is, and to morrow is cast into the oven, shall he not much more clothe you, O ye of little faith?" (Matt. 6:28–30). David could, therefore, say, "I have been young, and now am old; yet have I not seen the righteous forsaken, nor his seed begging bread" (Ps. 37:25). When one attempted to get the

holy martyr, Haring, to change his mind by pointing to his seven small children to whom he could leave nothing, he said, "The God who cares for the ravens shall not permit the small Harings to perish in want." Consequently, wealthy believers have abundance, and day by day they who are poor will have their daily bread.

Oh, how this ought to make the soul grateful and reflect in holy meditation that all that they possess flows to them through the channel of the promises! Such reflection would be as a delightful sauce upon tasteless food, and will cause the least little thing—as if something could be called little for someone who has forfeited everything—to be viewed as a great matter, causing one to say, "This is my covenant bread, my covenant water, and my covenant clothing." These promises are indispensable for living by faith as to our daily needs, for we have truly forfeited everything. God knows how deficient our faith is and how inattentive we are. If God were only to provide for us in proportion to the exercise of our faith in these promises, we would have perished long ago!

2. There are unconditional promises in which the Lord promises believers absolute *safety and protection in all of life's circumstances*, whether significant or insignificant. "The angel of the LORD encampeth round about them that fear him, and delivereth them" (Ps. 34:7). "[They] shall dwell on high: [their] place of defence shall be the munitions of rocks" (Isa. 33:16). "The LORD will be unto her a wall of fire round about" (Zech. 2:5), and God shall be with them when they pass through fire and water. The water may come to the lips, but they shall not overflow them, and the fire shall not burn them (Isa. 43:2). The angels "shall bear [them] up in their hands, lest [they] dash [their] foot against a stone" (Ps. 91:12). Without the will of their heavenly Father, not even a hair (which according to the promise have all been counted!) can fall from their head (HC 1; see Matt. 10:30; Luke 21:18; Acts 27:34).

3. There are also unconditional promises regarding *tangible support in all the vicissitudes of life* they encounter. "I will heal all your diseases and be with you" (Ps. 103:3; Isa. 53:4). Consequently, no "tribulation, or distress, or persecution, or famine, or nakedness, or peril, or sword" (Rom. 8:35) can separate God from them and them from God. As we have done here, seek out these promises and take note of them for your spiritual use.

Having addressed the unconditional promises regarding temporal blessings, I wish to conclude by making one more remark. Experience teaches that it is more challenging to live by faith regarding temporal matters than to live by faith regarding spiritual matters. The reasons for this are the following:

First, it is more challenging to believe that Christ has purchased temporal blessings with His blood than to believe that He has done so regarding spiritual benefits.

Second, when it comes to believing and trusting in the promises regarding spiritual life, the soul may detect even a slight stirring of affections, which will significantly undergird faith. On the contrary, when it comes to trusting in the promises regarding this temporal life, it may seem so improbable that the soul cannot see a way out.

Third, any assaults upon the soul to get her to doubt the promises that pertain to temporal matters may strongly influence her. Believers are most vulnerable regarding issues that pertain to the body.

Fourth, though there is the promise that that which is needful will be provided, the measure of that provision is not stipulated, nor is there the guarantee that we will securely retain it. Furthermore, such promises are more general in nature, so that it is difficult to apply them to every specific circumstance of our lives. Therefore, it will be very challenging for a Christian in need of these things and who must cope with want or poverty to live by faith upon the promises that pertain to this life.

Unconditional Promises That Pertain to Spiritual Life
Just as there are unconditional promises that pertain to this temporal life, there are also a large number of promises that pertain to spiritual life in which spiritual benefits are unconditionally promised. They are all as so many foundations for faith so that upon perceiving her deficiency, the soul will most assuredly trust that God will grant the promised matter to the glory of His grace. There are:

1. Promises regarding *the forgiveness of sins* for a believer who labors and is heavy-laden by a grievous sense of his sins. Among these promises, the following should particularly be noted: "I, even I, am he that blotteth out thy transgressions for mine own sake, and will not remember thy sins" (Isa. 43:25); "In those days, and in that time, saith the LORD, the iniquity of Israel shall be sought for, and there shall be none; and the sins of Judah, and they shall not be found: for I will pardon them whom I reserve" (Jer. 50:20); "Son, be of good cheer; thy sins be forgiven thee" (Matt. 9:2); and "Daughter, be of good comfort; thy faith hath made thee whole" (Matt. 9:22).

2. Promises and pledges that *the power of sin causing a true believer to be bowed down shall be subdued*. When a believer cries out, "Iniquities prevail against me" (Ps. 65:3), there are the promises, "He will subdue our iniquities" (Mic. 7:19); "For sin shall not have dominion over you: for ye are not under the law, but under grace" (Rom. 6:14); and "My grace is sufficient for thee: for my strength is made perfect in weakness" (2 Cor. 12:9).

3. Promises that *the soul shall return and be graciously received when she has backslidden*: "They shall come with weeping" (Jer. 31:9); "I will heal their backsliding, I will love them freely" (Hos. 14:4).

4. Promises regarding *sanctification* that include all the ways and means to foster and perfect it. There can be rebukes and admonitions when believers yield either to the right or the left. They will then hear a voice behind them, saying, "This is the way, walk ye in it, when ye turn to the right hand, and when ye turn to the left" (Isa. 30:21). Oh, if one were to believe this, every admonition and rebuke would be viewed as the fulfillment of a covenant promise. We would then welcome such rebukes with the greatest joy and open our hearts for them so that they would penetrate our souls powerfully and deeply. All the words regarding trials and cross providences pertain to this as well as those that speak of the purging of all that is excessive, barren, and corrupt. "Then will I visit their transgression with the rod, and their iniquity with stripes" (Ps. 89:32); "Therefore, behold, I will hedge up thy way with thorns, and make a wall, that she shall not find her paths. And she shall follow after her lovers, but she shall not overtake them; and she shall seek them, but shall not find them" (Hos. 2:6–7). Also, "every branch in me [Christ] that beareth not fruit he taketh away" (John 15:2); that is, all excess growth will be removed, and all that is dead or corrupt will be cut away. Promises regarding the means of grace are also applicable here: "I the LORD do keep it; I will water it every moment" (Isa. 27:3); "For I will pour water upon him that is thirsty, and floods upon the dry ground" (Isa. 44:3); "I will give them teachers according to their heart, and thereby the desert will be changed into a fruitful land";[5] and "instead of the thorn shall come up the fir tree, and instead of the brier shall come up the myrtle tree" (Isa. 55:13). Many other words of Scripture could be applicable here, and you should make this application when you read God's Word. We can also include the

---

5. Here Comrie combines elements from various texts.

promises regarding the indwelling of the Holy Spirit. He initiates sanctification, advances it incrementally, and ultimately brings it to perfection. "And I will put my spirit within you, and cause you to walk in my statutes, and ye shall keep my judgments, and do them" (Ezek. 36:27).

5. Promises regarding *preservation*. The soul that frequently says, "I shall now perish one day by the hand of Saul" (1 Sam. 27:1), will perceive that her perseverance is so sure that she cannot possibly fall from grace. The following promises will often come to the fore: "For the mountains shall depart, and the hills be removed; but my kindness shall not depart from thee, neither shall the covenant of my peace be removed, saith the LORD that hath mercy on thee" (Isa. 54:10); "Neither shall any man pluck them out of my hand" (John 10:28); and "Though he [the righteous; v. 21] fall, he shall not be utterly cast down: for the LORD upholdeth him with his hand" (Ps. 37:24).

The promises about preservation also include the promises that speak of continuing upon the way. "But the path of the just is as the shining light, that shineth more and more unto the perfect day" (Prov. 4:18). These promises also speak of strength when believers are weak. "[They] shall renew their strength; they shall mount up with wings as eagles" (Isa. 40:31), so that even in old age, they shall be as green trees of righteousness. "Hearken unto me, O house of Jacob, and all the remnant of the house of Israel, which are borne by me from the belly, which are carried from the womb. And even to your old age I am he; and even to hoar hairs will I carry you: I have made, and I will bear; even I will carry, and will deliver you" (Isa. 46:3–4). These promises also speak of the subduing of all enemies because the Lord will soon crush Satan under His feet.

6. Finally, promises of *comfort* for all the mourners in Zion. These promises are comprehended in all the promises that have already been referenced, for they all contain comfort. Beloved, I cannot mention all the situations to which the unconditional promises are applicable. However, I am confident that there is not a single situation in which a God-fearing person has ever found himself or can find himself, or there will be a promise in the Bible that pertains to it and upon which he may live by faith in that situation. Oh, what a rich supply there is in the Word of God! Search this Word day and night, and only then will it become sweet to you.

How great are the promises that pertain to eternal life! "Eye hath not seen, nor ear heard, neither have entered into the heart of man, the things which God hath prepared for them that love him" (1 Cor. 2:9). One day in the Jerusalem above will reveal more than a thousand books can contain. This we know: We have been promised that we shall see Him as He is!

No Conditions in These Promises for Believers
Another truth encompassed in the description of the unconditional promises is that all these promises are made to believers without any presupposed condition having to be fulfilled by them. The notion of any condition having to be fulfilled is so far removed that whatever is required as a condition or a duty is plainly and explicitly promised. We read, "Happy is the man that feareth always" (Prov. 28:14). That is the condition. We also read, "Let him be your fear, and let him be your dread" (Isa. 8:13). That is a command. However, both are expressed in the unconditional promise: "And I will give them one heart, and one way, that they may fear me for ever" (Jer. 32:39).

Additional Promises
Having explored the promises, we need to recognize that in addition to all those passages in which the unconditional promises are explicitly articulated, we must also view as promises the following two matters:

Promises Implied in Biblical Prayers
Such is true for prayers recorded in the Word of God that pertain to a specific matter, for all the prayers of the men of God were sustained by God's promises. And indeed, it is a requisite for a good and appropriate prayer that all supplications and petitions must pertain to that which is promised in the covenant. That being the case, the number of divine promises embedded in the Psalms and other passages will become exceptionally large! We are thus taught not only to unite our hearts with the supplications of those saints but also to trust firmly that the matter is promised and shall be granted to us for the sake of Christ's merits.

Promises Made to Specific Saints
Then there are the particular promises that God has made specifically to some of His people, along with all the circumstances in which they have experienced God's help and deliverance. The first will be evident when we compare Hebrews 13:5–6 and Joshua 1:5. There we find a promise that was explicitly made to Joshua and pertained to the work he was called to do:

"I will not fail thee, nor forsake thee" (Josh. 1:5). Though this promise was addressed to Joshua, the apostle transfers this promise for common use by all believers. He desired that everyone would have the liberty to draw the following conclusion: "The Lord is my helper, and I will not fear" (Heb. 13:6). If the first is true, the second must also be true.

However, I wish to add two remarks. First, we need to know that we must experience a very powerful operation of the Holy Spirit to appropriate for ourselves the special promises and unique circumstances of the saints as recorded in the Word. We need this to illuminate us and to stimulate and strengthen our faith so that we can apply the promises to ourselves consistent with God's will. We will thus be enabled to anticipate a specific situation with believing expectation, patience, and quiet longing of the soul. Experience teaches indeed that the soul will be wrought upon by the Spirit in a twofold manner regarding promises made to others as well as their unique circumstances. It is very well possible that one may perceive a broader or wider application as one reads or meditates about them. In their prayers, such souls may plead and wrestle with the Lord to appropriate the matter they so very much wish to claim as their own. Though this has a sanctifying effect upon the soul and yields a sense of calm, it is not a sufficient basis for believing, "The Lord will also grant this to me." Many have stumbled here, having drawn a conclusion about the matter itself by the broader and wider application of the promise. They will often, and not without much turmoil, be disappointed in the outcome.

However, as to these promises and unique circumstances of God's people, there is a second way the Holy Spirit works in the experience of the genuinely godly. Not only will He give them enlargement of soul in their spiritual exercises regarding a specific matter, but He will also very powerfully and convincingly assure the soul that precisely what is being affirmed in such a promise or what may have happened to a believer in such a situation, shall also be done for them. Thus, He will strengthen their faith—which cannot make a personal application without special appropriating grace—in such a measure that it will banish all fear. Such souls will thereby be enabled to rely upon that word of promise and anticipate its fulfillment with such assurance that it will be as if they already possessed it. A most tender and intimate communion with the Lord and a careful walk are absolutely requisite for such an experience. Though I know that an example would clarify this, they who are experientially acquainted with this will not be offended if I forego this. Others will not be able to understand it at all.

Prophetic Applications of Promises

Second, there will be some very tender children of God who still have the Spirit of prophecy in connection with these special promises or situations. However, we firmly believe that the Spirit of prophecy is neither present in the church to reveal new doctrines following the completion of the canon nor does it obligate others to submit to this as a prescriptive rule of obedience, for the written Word is our only rule. However, with most godly ministers in Scotland and Wilhelmus (Father) Brakel among the Dutch, we believe fervently that the Spirit of prophecy is still in the church for various beneficial purposes.

If such be the case—which we will demonstrate by way of several examples—then it must proceed from, through, and according to the inscripturated Word of God. However, as excellent and precious as the general promises may be, they do not lend themselves too well for this. Therefore, such prophecies must issue forth from these special promises and particular circumstances regarding which the soul is exercised—as we have already described. However, should we examine such experiences in retrospect, we will find incontrovertible proof that this Spirit of prophecy is still in the church.

I will not gather examples from Mr. Fleming's book *The Fulfillment of Scripture*—a book that is very precious to me. He was one of the most esteemed ministers that ever served the Scottish church in Rotterdam. Rather, to buttress my argument, I will extract two examples from the biographies of two eminent Scottish ministers. The credibility of these examples cannot be challenged, for these biographies were published when thousands were still alive who have heard with their ears and witnessed with their eyes all that is described.

Alexander Peden (1626–1686) was a very worthy man during the persecution of the Presbyterians by Charles II.[6] In addition to many noteworthy incidents from his life, it is told of him that he was preaching with great zeal in an open field during a "stealth gathering" as these gatherings of the godly were then called. The outposts issued a warning that the royal cavalry was approaching them with full speed. His hearers who had gathered at the risk

---

6. Peden was one of the leading Covenanter divines in Scotland.

of their lives were greatly frightened by this news, and it began to cause great disarray. The godly man paused for a moment and turned to God in prayer, crying out silently to God. Though danger was imminent, the people stayed where they were to receive a blessing from him or some direction before everyone would seek to escape safely. The man of God began to address those who were so greatly troubled and said, "Stand still, and see the salvation of the Lord. Let no one leave his place, for God will cover you all under the shadow of His hand so that the hostile troops will not be able to come near any of us but instead they will be ensnared in their own destruction." He then continued with his sermon, and his hearers became so calm that no one—even though many thousands were present—gave any indication that they would depart. Shortly after he had said that he would not leave, God caused such a heavy fog to settle that his hearers could yet hear his voice, but those who sat a bit farther away could not see the minister. The royal troops were so unnerved that they had no idea how to retreat since most of the horses sank so deeply into the swamp that they could not be extracted. You can imagine that these people sang the praises of the Lord, and their hearts were strength-ened—just like the Israelites were when they had been delivered out of the hands of the Egyptians.

Then there is the following incident regarding the venerable Mr. Peden. He and many other hundreds were subsequently imprisoned on account of their religious convictions. The bloodthirstiness of the royal court had somewhat lessened, or else they were at a loss to execute so many people simultaneously and so tyrannically. It was, therefore, determined that the punishment would be that Mr. Peden and his following would be banished to a settlement in America. They were all placed on a ship, and because there were so many of them, the captain had strict orders to shackle them. Upon the lifting of the anchors, the ship departed with a favorable wind. However, the first order of business was that these pious people would be "cared for," which meant that they would be securely shackled! Some of the prisoners were very fearful, and the heart of Mr. Peden became very shaken when he heard the rattle of the iron chains. After he had spent some time in prayer, he said, "Be of good cheer, for no one's hands or feet will be placed in chains. And we will also not be taken to this settlement." This gave the people much confidence in their hearts because they knew he was such an eminent man. As the sailors were preparing the shackles, a strong wind arose, and they had to lower the sails. As the storm continued, the ship was driven along the

English coast. When they had passed Yarmouth, the wind turned from the east to the southeast, and the seriously damaged ship was driven into the Thames. Mr. Peden and his entire entourage were set free. After having been treated well by the English, they each returned home, richer than they had ever been.

I also promised that I would give an example from the biography of Mr. Welsh, a man who belonged to a family of Scottish nobility. In his youth, he lived a very licentious life. However, upon having been powerfully converted, he became one of the most eminent and exemplary ministers the Scottish church has ever known. The story is told of him that during his life his knees became as calloused as the soles of his feet due to continued prayer. This Mr. Welsh fled to France along with a young nobleman for whom he had many promises that he would be converted. This young man became ill in France, and he died—so it seemed. Mr. Welsh replied, "He is not dead, but he sleeps." He insisted that there be no preparations for his funeral. After Mr. Welsh prayed and fasted for several days, the young man became conscious again. God then used him as a useful instrument in His hand in the revolution that occurred under the Prince of Orange[7] whom we remember with much esteem. As is recorded in this biography, the nobleman himself testified of this. Moreover, Bishop Burnet[8] (to whom our family is related with blood ties) writes in his overview of his contemporary history that many of these ministers foretold things that also truly happened. His testimony is all the more convincing because he belonged to the opposing party that oppressed these people, even though he himself disapproved of such actions.

Even a casual reader of the Word of God can easily determine that promises and situations of this nature are mentioned. And we believe, as we have stated, that these tender and godly persons experienced the working of the Holy Spirit.

---

7. Comrie here refers to the Glorious Revolution in 1688, known in the Netherlands as the "glorious crossing." It was the assumption of power by the Dutch William III and his spouse as king and queen of England, Scotland, and Ireland at the invitation of several Protestant leaders in London. Consequently, the Roman Catholic king, James II, the cousin and father-in-law of William III, fled to France.

8. Alexander Burnet (1615–1684) was a clergyman who fervently promoted the interests of the Anglican Church of England. He concluded his ecclesiastical career as the archbishop of St. Andrews.

Living by Faith in the Promises

When speaking of the promises, we must take note of their characteristics. They are very lovely and have as their specific purpose to strengthen faith. However, since one can deduce these distinctive marks from the description of the promises, we will not address this any further.

We will now proceed to say a few words about living by faith in the promises. To do this as succinctly and plainly as possible, we will consider four matters according to the measure of light we have received.

The Persons Who May Appropriate the Promises

Who are they that may legitimately appropriate the promises and live by them? This is a matter of the utmost importance, for many upright souls will exclaim when they consider the promises more closely, "Oh, how great and excellent are the promises! But how can I know whether they are addressed to me?" Therefore, consider the following matters, and that should give you some insight.

General Observations on the Warrant to Believe

Generally, we may say that whoever hears the gospel and to whom the promise comes as the proclamation of the divine will has a legitimate right to respond by appropriating the promise for himself. He may do so by virtue of the revelation of God's will, and he may plead upon his warrant to do so before God's judgment seat. Nevertheless, one needs to make a significant distinction regarding having a legitimate claim upon something. One can have a legal claim *de jure* [by law] (emphasizing the claim's legitimacy) and *de facto* [by fact] (emphasizing actual possession). As soon as he is born, a son has a legal claim *de jure* to take ownership of his father's possessions and inheritance. However, he will only have a legal claim *de facto* when all these possessions actually become his. Believers have a legal claim upon the promises only in the second sense, and thus *de facto*, for based on their union with Christ, they have truly been made partakers of all the promises. Nevertheless, everyone that hears the gospel has a warrant *de jure* to the promises. They have this warrant by virtue of the proclamation of God's will by His prophets, apostles, and heralds, and by virtue of the free offer of grace. Based on that warrant, they may come and take refuge to God's grace. They may take hold of that grace with a faith that is inherently saving. They may also insist upon and lay claim to that warrant so that they may indeed become partakers of God's grace to which they may lay claim solely based on the offer of grace.

Imagine that a general pardon is proclaimed for all deserters. Every deserter will then have a legal claim upon the pardon that has been promised in that proclamation. However, it is true that no one will actually secure the pardon of his crime except he who responds to this proclamation within the stipulated time frame. He who responds relies upon the good faith of the authorities that they will be faithful to what has been expressed in the letter of pardon causing the guilty one indeed to experience the fruits of the promised pardon. Such is also the case here. He who believes and is conscious that he is a sinner has a warrant to embrace this pardon, and based on that pardon, to take refuge to the God who proclaimed that pardon. He that comes in this manner shall in no wise be cast out (John 6:37). My beloved, everyone can thus perceive his warrant to make use of the promises. He who will make use of this warrant will enjoy its fruits. And although many objections will arise in a troubled heart, I am assured that the content of the promises is such that these objections will all be resolved.

The Persons Who May Claim the Promises as Theirs
Specifically, the following persons have a warrant to apply the promises to themselves and consider themselves the persons to whom they are addressed.

1. He who is *inwardly convinced of the necessity of obtaining what is promised* and has a deep and abiding impression of this in his heart can and may conclude that he has a warrant to apply the promise to himself. We do not intend to say that having some intellectual convictions gives one the right to appropriate the promises, for such convictions can arise apart from the Holy Spirit's saving operation and be sustained by meditating upon divine truths while the soul is nevertheless inactive. Having a view of and being impressed with the urgency that we have in mind here is of such a nature that it will deeply penetrate the soul. It will cause the soul to cry out and lament before God's throne of grace, and the soul will be so filled with a desire for the promise and for Christ as its fulfillment that they will be unable to rest until they may have Him. If such a soul had a thousand worlds, she would happily part with them in exchange for one promise upon which she may lean and upon which she can trust. The soul that has such impressions of this urgency has the warrant to apply to himself the promises of which we have spoken. The soul that plainly perceives

the danger to which she is exposed knows herself, so to speak, to be at the edge of the abyss of eternal perdition and that she will descend in it if she cannot take hold of the promises. She will view the promises as ropes and cords descending from heaven to be taken hold of. She will be convinced that she will not sink into perdition if she can take hold of one of these ropes. Consequently, she will perceive the necessity of taking hold of the promises. That perception will cause her to cry out, wrestle, groan, and supplicate for the promise and give her the warrant to apply it to herself. This is consistent with these passages: "Ho, every one that thirsteth, come ye to the waters" (Isa. 55:1), and "Come unto me, all ye that labour and are heavy laden, and I will give you rest" (Matt. 11:28).

2. He whose heart is governed by *esteem for the promise and its content* has the warrant to apply the promise specifically to himself. Such esteem does not merely consist of assenting that Jesus and the promise are to be valued above all else, but rather, it is generated by considering Christ's excellency and suitability. This will have such an impact upon the heart that the soul will count all things to be "but dung…for the excellency of the knowledge of Christ Jesus" (Phil. 3:8). She will be able to testify that all that she may find in Jesus is altogether lovely to her so that she will view Him as "the chiefest among ten thousand" (Song 5:10). The soul will view herself as exceedingly blessed and satisfied with Him—even if she would possibly have to miss all that pertains to this life. Yes, she would rather hang on a cross on Golgotha with Him than be seated for thousands of years upon a throne of joyful prosperity. Proverbs 8:17 and 21 appear to state this clearly: "I love them that love me…that I may cause those that love me to inherit substance."

3. You have the warrant to apply the promise to yourself if you are so disposed that *nothing can comfort you in your sorrow, anxiety, afflictions, and whatever else may befall you except for God's promise.* Thus, he will view everything, except for that one promise, as merely poor comforters and cheap and tasteless food such as the white of an egg. He will also continue to be weighed down by his burdens until he receives a new promise from the Lord or his faith is again exercised with this or that former promise so that she can lean upon that word of promise and that the Lord will "remember the word unto [His] servant" (Ps. 119:49). We will presently not add additional points since we believe that the three points we have addressed sufficiently enable us to perceive whether we are indeed the object of God's promises.

Guidelines for Applying the Promises

By way of some remarks, we wish to give some directives that one ought to keep in mind when applying the promises to himself. This will be subservient in answering an important question posed by a troubled soul who may say, "Do those whom you have described have the warrant to appropriate the promises? I cannot deny that I do experience these things. However, I dare not engage myself to apply these promises to myself, for I do not know how to go about this. And if I were to go about this in the wrong way, I would only spoil matters and deceive myself. Oh, tell me, therefore, what it is that I must focus on!" I will tell you.

1. When it comes to applying the promise to ourselves, the first guideline we are to follow is to note the condition in which we find ourselves. The question is indeed whether our circumstances—being bowed down, fearful, despondent, oppressed, and other vicissitudes—are such that a promise is needed to encourage our heart that is overwhelmed, and to make us quiet, patient, confident, and submissive regarding God's way with us. The promises are the delicacies of heaven, the grapes of Canaan, and strong cordials for the heart that will only have their effect in distressing circumstances when we succumb and languish spiritually. Therefore, you will never find an instance in God's Word that one of the saints of the Bible received promises in any other way! To Abraham was said, "Fear not" (Gen. 15:1), when he was in danger. This was also said to Paul when he was in danger. In light of that, we can determine the cause why many believers never or seldom receive a promise after their initial conversion. Apparently, their circumstances no longer make this necessary.

2. When we wish to apply a promise to ourselves, we must certainly keep in mind whether this promise matches precisely our circumstances. That means that there must be something in the promise that we are missing at that moment and yet absolutely need. Else the promise will not resolve our difficulty and fail entirely to encourage our hearts. The Spirit never intends to use a promise to divert us from present circumstances that cause us grief and make us spiritually ill. Rather, He will first thoroughly heal us from the malady at hand before focusing our attention on other matters.

3. Another guideline we are to follow when applying a promise to ourselves is to focus explicitly on the condition of our soul. We must pay careful attention

whether our faith is somewhat strengthened and whether we are led to consider the promises so that we may trust in them. Without this, the promises will not affect us in such a way that we can trust in them. When the promises do not stir us up to believe, they can at best only serve as pleading grounds to come to faith.

4. The next guideline we are to consider carefully when applying a promise to ourselves is to focus continually on what God has given as a pledge for the fulfillment of every promise, namely, His faithfulness, truthfulness, and power. They alone can enable the soul to overcome all difficulties and provide faith with a solid foundation so that she may expect that her hope will not be put to shame (Rom. 4:21; Heb. 11:18; 6:17–18).

5. Another guideline is that we must see to it that in applying the promise, we must particularly focus on Jesus in whom all promises are yea and amen "unto the glory of God" (2 Cor. 1:20). We need to do this so that we who have forfeited everything may have the liberty to remind ourselves how all promises come to us through Him as the Head of the covenant. He has merited their fulfillment by the blood He has shed as God's Son. We may thus receive out of His fullness grace for grace so that we may be sustained in applying the promises in such a measure that we will neither desist nor come short. Oh, how blessed it is when also in this way we may look unto the Author and Finisher of our faith (Heb. 12:1).

6. We must carefully avoid drawing certain conclusions regarding ourselves or insisting that we would experience a measure of sweet enlargement immediately upon applying the promise if only our exercise of faith were genuine. Many will thereby rob themselves of all that they could have consequently enjoyed upon applying the promises, and they will be troubled by an endless sequence of doubts. Instead, we can frequently apply the promises appropriately without experiencing any tender joy or spiritual enlargement during or immediately following our exercise of faith. We observe this clearly with the psalmist. He had taken hold of God's promise and nevertheless had to testify that however much he applied the promises to himself, his soul melted for heaviness and cleaved unto the dust (Ps. 119:28, 25) and that his spirit was failing (Ps. 143:7).

7. Another guideline in applying the promises to ourselves is that we are by no means to put our faith and trust in any contingencies. Thus, we are

not to think that the promise shall be fulfilled immediately simply because many things are occurring that make its fulfillment probable. No less are we to believe that its fulfillment shall be delayed simply because all that should lead to it appears to be so obscure and impossible. We shall then be either encouraged or discouraged in proportion to the probability of the promise being fulfilled. Instead, we are to submit ourselves to the Lord, follow Him in His way, and cleave to Him with good courage and confidence.

8. A Christian who has taken hold of the promise must not relinquish his embrace due to doubt that he experiences following such application. Rather, he must altogether disregard it and enter into a debate with unbelief. Instead, he must plug both ears and follow Abraham's example, who did not confer with flesh and blood, but rather "against hope believed in hope" (Rom. 4:18).

9. The soul who has applied the promises to herself must diligently strive to persevere in prayer for their fulfillment and to note all the ways in which God brings this about so that she may have reason to say, "*He* has said it, and *He* has accomplished it."

The Manner of Applying the Promises to Oneself
In considering the life of faith upon the promises, we also wish to focus your attention on some particulars regarding the manner in which the soul applies the promise to herself. One must know this to live upon the promises. How shall the soul know how to apply the promises if she does not know how to go about it? We will explain it, and therefore pay careful attention.

The Work of the Holy Spirit in Applying the Promises
When the soul correctly applies the promises to herself, there must absolutely be a preceding operation of God the Holy Spirit to enable the soul to engage in this weighty task, for every believer shall experience that the inner principle of the life of grace cannot do so in and of itself. Someone might ask, "What is the Holy Spirit's role in this?" We will explain this by way of the following particulars.

The Holy Spirit's involvement appears to be irrefutable, for God's Word clearly ascribes a twofold operation to the Spirit regarding the elect: the one by which He convicts and the other by which He comforts. John 16 addresses both operations. But how does the Spirit carry out this work? Most certainly not apart from the Word, but rather by means of and according to the Word. He uses the law to convict and the gospel to comfort. Since God is the original cause of all things, one can readily and safely conclude that the work of the Spirit precedes the application of the promise and that the exercise of the believer will follow.

Having thus laid the foundation, we believe the work of the Spirit to consist primarily of the following:

1. The Holy Spirit will so strip and empty the soul that she will be weaned from everything and remain utterly destitute in herself. In the condition in which she will then find herself, she will have nothing on which she can base her hope for deliverance, nothing to which she can cling and of which she can take hold. "The poor committeth himself unto thee" (Ps. 10:14). By His operation, the Spirit most likely brought Abraham into such a situation when God said to him, "Fear not, Abram: I am thy shield, and thy exceeding great reward" (Gen. 15:1). When we meditate upon this, how it should render our soul patient and submissive to all the ways the Spirit leads us, however bitter such ways may be physically or spiritually! They have no other purpose but to empty us and make us receptive to the promise.

2. The Holy Spirit will not only somewhat quiet the great turmoil of the soul, but He will so inwardly engage the will and the affections that her yearning for the promises will be very intense. Thus, the soul will yearn for this with a strong desire, intensely longing that the Lord would speak a word to her soul in conformity to her physical or spiritual condition so that she may cast the anchor of her hope upon it (Ps. 85:9).

3. The Holy Spirit will take a given promise that occurs here and there in the Word and which fits the condition in which the soul finds herself. He will, with some efficacy, impress it upon her heart as if it were explicitly addressed to the soul so that she may personally make use of it. Thus, as the Spirit convicts the soul, He will make the general pronouncements of the law very personal and say to the soul, "It is written that 'the soul that sinneth, it shall die.'" He will say this to you because *you* are a sinner. In like fashion, the Spirit will minister comfort by making the general promise very personal for the soul. He will impress it upon the heart as if these words were addressed exclusively to such a soul.

4. The Holy Spirit will irradiate and illuminate the soul which will now apply the promise to herself with spiritual, divine, and saving light. As in a mirror, she will thus be enabled to perceive with spiritual perception the promised matter itself in the promise as to its preciousness, necessity, and delightfulness. Such a revelation will impact and incline the will most powerfully and irresistibly. It will also move the affections by tenderly inclining them toward the promise. Thus, the soul will be entirely filled with a most intense love and heartfelt desire for the promised matter. Though the soul must be resolute in her response due to the suitability of what is being promised, all of this will mean that she will acquiesce with the utmost willingness in the day of God's power (Ps. 110:3). The apostle has this in mind in his prayer for the Ephesians (Eph. 1:17–19) and applies this to believers in 2 Corinthians 3:18, saying, "But we all, with open face beholding as in a glass the glory of the Lord, are changed into the same image from glory to glory, even as by the Spirit of the Lord." By this operation of the Spirit, Abraham saw the days of the Messiah in the promise and rejoiced in it (John 8:56).

5. The Holy Spirit will clarify for the soul the immovable foundation of the divine promises and her warrant to apply them to herself so that all obstacles that encompassed her will have been removed. A smooth pathway will have been made for the soul so that she may confidently take refuge in the promise and rely upon it.

6. Finally, the Holy Spirit will strengthen faith by engaging it, stimulating it, and powerfully working it so that faith is exercised regarding the promise. The soul will then not stand from afar, but having been fully prepared to do so, she will embrace the promises with both arms.

We could enlarge and clarify this by addressing other matters, but by what has been said, we have addressed the main features of the Spirit's work.

The Exercises of Faith in Applying the Promises
We will now consider what the exercises of faith are when believers apply the promises to themselves. We believe that the apostle limits them to three exercises: they saw them from afar, believed them, and embraced them. Let me say a word regarding each of these exercises.

1. Though the soul does not yet possess the promise and that which is promised, she *anticipates* them with steadfast confidence. For she will perceive that

God's faithfulness and truthfulness are so intertwined with that promise so as to be the warranty of its fulfillment. The soul will be so assured of the matter that it appears as if she already possesses it.

2. When the soul applies the promise to herself, she *believes* it. That implies that she is fully convinced that the promise is the Word of God and that He is speaking to her in her personal circumstances. She will stamp it with the seal of her approval, and her soul will acquiesce in the promise. She will respond, "Amen, Lord! 'Be it unto me [Thy servant] according to thy word'" (Luke 1:38).

3. The soul will *appropriate* the promise with the utmost stirring of the heart. She will take hold of the promise and will apply it very personally to herself. She will thereby fully surrender herself to the Word of an immutable God who cannot lie—the God who will be faithful to His Word and will see to it that His Word will be fulfilled in the minutest detail. We will not venture to consider specific incidents. He who expounds the meaning of these words will perceive which specific aspects belong to the stated components of the text. Anyone who would peruse the verb "To Hear" in *The ABC of Faith* will encounter the distinctive marks by which a soul may examine herself whether she correctly applies the promise to herself.

How the Believer Lives upon the Promises
Fourth, we wish to point out how the believer lives upon the promise she has applied to herself. We will deal with this even more briefly since many of the matters enumerated under the rubric of "Expecting" in *The ABC of Faith* are applicable here.

1. The believer will live his life in the conscious knowledge that the Lord has made a specific promise personally to his own soul. Therefore, the believer must often examine his experience, and he must also seek to be persuaded of that truth so that he can consciously conclude that the Lord has spoken peace to his soul.

2. Such a life will also consist of bringing these promises before the Lord when the soul finds herself in circumstances in which she needs that which has been promised. "Remember the word unto thy servant, upon which thou hast caused me to hope" (Ps. 119:49).

3. It also consists of being confident that the promise will be fulfilled at a time appointed by the Lord, for He is not a God of "yea and nay." Not one iota of His Word shall remain unfulfilled.

4. Such a life also means that one will encourage and hearten himself in dark times by God's promise—just as someone will encourage himself by reading the legal documents pertaining to a given matter, even though he does not yet possess it.

5. There will be a quiet and patient waiting upon the Lord for the fulfillment of the promise by a diligent use of the appointed means. "My soul, wait thou only upon God; for my expectation is from him" (Ps. 62:5).

6. Such a life means that the soul will consider the promise before she undertakes anything spiritually so that she may experience that by faith in the promises, she will be strengthened to engage in that to which the Lord is calling her. When believers may thus live and by renewal take hold of the promises, they will perceive that they will be strengthened according to the inner man.

7. Living upon the promises also implies that one will carefully avoid whatever might delay the fulfillment of the promises. And indeed, the Lord will sometimes delay their fulfillment to punish sin—as is evident from His dealings with Israel. The soul must therefore see to it that she walks circumspectly.

8. Finally, in living upon the promises, it will be beneficial that the soul will not only take note of God's providential leadings but also of all that God has already fulfilled, albeit only to a certain degree. The soul will then be thankful for all that she has already experienced in conformity to the promises, and she will cheerfully anticipate their further fulfillment.

If you would add this to what has already been written, you should be able to perceive in some measure what living upon the promises consists of. May God give you and me both light and grace to do so.

Those Who Live on the Promises Are Pilgrims on Earth

A final lesson to be extracted is that such a life upon the promises will cause one to be truly a stranger here below—something we have already addressed on an earlier occasion. We then also pointed out that faith is a grace that overcomes the world (cf. chapter 6).

CONCLUSION

Therefore, we will conclude this treatise with the wish that the Lord, by His Spirit, may bless all that has been written.

In each chapter, we have addressed these important matters according to the measure of light we have received. Thus, we will hereby conclude our exposition of the distinctive marks of saving faith. If you have found anything to be to the edification and advancement of your spiritual life, give God the honor, and pray for us. Amen.

Scripture Index

Subject Index

Aaron, 121, 263
ABC of Faith (Comrie), xxiv, xxvi, xxviii,
    146, 283, 346, 358, 406
Abel, 410
Abraham, 35, 49, 177, 219–22, 254, 342,
    343, 347, 354, 410, 412, 422–23,
    442, 444, 445
acceptance, 283–84
accusing conscience, 19, 20, 117, 255, 292
acquittal, 34, 43, 44, 368, 378
active obedience, of Christ, 14, 43, 45,
    85–86
actual sin, 44
Adam, 61, 84–85, 178, 201, 339
ad hominem arguments, 277–78
adoption, 123, 138, 153
adoration, 424
adultery, 11
adversity, 233, 242, 252, 387
advocate, 43–44, 54
"afar off," 412
affections, 69, 165, 189–92, 334, 445
affliction, 226, 327, 387–88, 441
Agabus, 133
Agur, 325
Ahab, 190
alive, with Christ, 331–38
allegorical interpretations, 322
America, 437
angels, 49, 54n5, 141, 317, 424, 430
anger, 245–46
animals, 49
"Anointed One," 323
anticipation, 446

antinomians, 11, 75, 280
anxiety, 21, 39, 103, 106–7, 109, 117, 125,
    209, 397, 411, 441
Apollonius of Tyanna, 191n13
apostasy, 316
appropriation, 447
Aristotle, xxix
Arminians, xxvii, xxix, 9, 51
arrogance, 189, 253, 258
Asaph, 81, 113, 196
assurance, 72, 184, 204, 259–60, 270–79,
    288–89, 298, 299, 310, 352, 411,
    420, 426, 427
atheism, 76
atonement, 350, 375
attributum essentiale, 278
Augustine, 143, 167, 190
aversion, 138

backsliding, 108, 111, 432
Balaam, 231
Balak, 231
baptism, 44, 281n6
Barnabas, 59
Barzillai, 183
Bavinck, Herman, xxxi
Baxter, Richard, 194n14
beauty, 95, 326
behavior, 166
being, 152
Belgic Confession, 284n7
believers
    in Christ, 82–83
    in darkness, 408